THE MILWAUKEE ROAD
HIAWATHA

THE COMPLETE BOOK OF MODEL RAILROADING

by DAVID SUTTON

All photographs and illustrations by the author
unless otherwise credited.

Library of Congress Catalog Card Number: 64-21745

Printed in the United States of America

Arrangement has been made to publish this edition by Castle Books,
a division of Book Sales Inc. of Secaucus, New Jersey

ISBN No.: 0-89009-445-4

JULY-1981

To my wife Ruth—for her patience.
To our children Stephanie and Suzanne—for their patient curiosity.
And to the young in heart—everywhere.

Acknowledgments

During the course of preparing, writing and illustrating this book I had the pleasure and benefit of drawing upon the opinions and experiences of many friends and fellow enthusiasts. While a book such as this is essentially an individual effort, it is not entirely a solitary project. I therefore wish to express my sincere thanks to those whom I often plagued with questions and probing cameras and upon occasion entered into opposing—albeit friendly—points of view:

John Allen, Alan Stensvold, Harry Dardis, Morton H. Gould, Don Thompson, Freeman Crutchfield, Jim Foell, Dick Seydell, David Rose, Ward Kimball, Leighton Keeling, Bob Brinkman, Whit Towers, Dick Laugharn, Bob Smith, Bob Steele, Jerome C. Biederman, Jerry Collinson, Harry Gohl, Eric Bracher, Jim Webb, Bob Semichy, Ken Bayless, William Ferrigno.

In addition I would like to thank Linn Westcott of Kalmbach Publishing; Hal Carstens of Penn Publications; National Model Railroad Association; Association of American Railroads; Levon Kemalyan–Kemtron; Dale and Keith Edwards–Kadee Quality Products; M. B. Austin; Nat Polk–Aristo-Craft; Tyco; Joel Rubinstein–Revell, Inc.; Walt Disney Studios; Henry Blankfort–The Blankfort Group.

Milt Grey; Bill Ryan, Pacific Fast Mail; Augie Kniff and Sheldon Ostrowe–Tru-Scale; Ed Suydam & Co.; Model Die Casting; Sol Kramer; Akane; Varney; General Electric; Sylvania; Atlas Tool Co.; Athearn; Tom Ayres; Harry Weiss–Cliff Line; George Hook–Central Valley; Charles Ulrich–Ulrich Models; Mike Ciccarelli–Polaroid Corp.; Members of the Burbank, Encino, and So. Tarzana Model RR Club; Venice Short Line Model RR Club; Glendale Model RR Club; Sierra Southern RR Club; California Central Model Railroad Club; Union Pacific; and Southern Pacific.

With apologies but heartfelt thanks to those whom I may have overlooked.

DAVID SUTTON

Foreword

Ever since that long ago day when man discovered the wheel, all forms of transportation fascinated him. It meant he had found the means not only to move to far-off places, but even to dream beyond the horizon, and then move to those distant vistas.

Perhaps no form of transportation has held more attraction for him, and in fact still does, than the "iron horse." There is good reason for this, for even the most primitive locomotive was a symbol of man using other than his own muscles or animal power to move him from place to place. Psychologically, the very act, in those early days, of converting wood into steam power was actually one of the first major steps in the conquering of nature by man; of converting a stout tree, perhaps even a dead one at that, into live steam.

Today it is electric power and diesel engines, with fuel-carrying tenders now museum pieces. But in retrospect the steam locomotive has been locked deep in our hearts.

Each of these, the Moguls and the Mallets—the wood burners, the coke and coal burners, followed by the diesel hogs and electrically powered monsters of the rails—all were major milestones in the exciting historical road of transportation, with perhaps nuclear power soon to come. Although the prototypes of the ancient engines, and some not so ancient, have gone to rust and have been long dismembered, literally thousands upon thousands of them still run the rails in miniature and authentic form.

These are the steam locomotives and the rolling stock they pull, and sometimes push, that Dave Sutton writes about so well. He has captured the romance and spirit of this intriguing hobby of Model Railroading and miniature steam locomotion. He has brought his skill as a noted photographer, his uncanny sense of reportage, his powers of observation, and his dedicated interest in model railroading to every chapter of this important work; a book that will not only provide hours of enjoyment to the advanced modeler and veteran model railroad tycoon—opening new vistas and perhaps new roads to them—but will also serve the novice in good stead by guiding him along the right track toward scale modeling and prototype operation.

Writing with the flair of a photo-journalist and the daring of a Casey Jones, Dave brings to even the most technical aspects of model railroading the pleasure that is so well recognized and appreciated by every engineer who operates scale model locomotives in the traditions of steam's finest hours.

Although many articles have been written on this century-old hobby, it is propitious that this work comes out at a time when many new technical aspects of model railroading have brought about a renaissance to this most enduring hobby. Dave brings an acute sense of railroading history to every phase of this activity, which has intrigued so many, in this book, the first definitive work on the subject.

But I must sound a warning bell! Anyone who reads it will forever be caught up in the fascinating web of rails, the symphony of engine and locomotive music, and the thrill of building and operating a model railroad empire of his very own. It happened to me!

DAVID ROSE

Contents

Introduction
The Birth of a Hobby

From the first moment that railroads became a means of travel and freight transportation the dawn of a new era was ushered in—hence, the birth of a hobby. For no sooner did the most primitive of locomotives set their wheels to rail than enterprising toymakers both here and abroad began producing miniature trains. And despite the fact that early models were rather crude attempts to duplicate their prototypes, a pastime destined to capture the hearts and imagination of young and old was born.

In the early days of live railroading there were no set standards, and both gauge and style were created to suit the terrain of each particular rail line, providing much confusion and making it virtually impossible to connect one service to another. Couplers, rolling stock, signal devices, and track gauge, among other things, still had a long way to go before approaching any degree of conformity. Such was also the case with model trains, and early attempts to duplicate in true scale proportion would today send even the rankest scale modeler or scratch builder into a padded cell. But as the saying goes, "there had to be a beginning."

In their infancy miniature trains consisted of wooden block affairs (commonly called "floor trains") which our great, great grandfathers pushed or pulled along the floor, at the same time, no doubt, emitting some form of "choo choo" or "whoo whoo" sound, or reasonable facsimile. Today, well over a hundred years later, the world's infant generation continues to be addicted to the pleasures of the push or pull technique of toy trains. On the other hand, scale modeling and prototype model railroading has developed into a many-faceted hobby, due in part to the wide variety of equipment available, spanning better than a hundred years of railroading, in which, more often than not, models ranging from early American types to articulated Mallets and the sleekest of diesels have been faithfully reproduced.

With each new year more models and types are offered as manufacturers try to keep pace with the interests and demands of model rail enthusiasts, for no matter how many new and/or different items are produced, you can always find a prototype for them. *For this reason I have deliberately included the names of manufacturers and/or sources of supply, and in some cases have also listed parts' numbers and catalogue references for the express*

Measuring only 8 inches in length this toy train set, made of tin and fashioned after a very early steamer, was shipped around the Horn by the boatload in 1850 during the California Gold Rush days. Pioneer children, whose families had braved the Western frontiers, were hungry for toys from the East and snatched at this model as a perfect plaything. In time, these small trains became souvenirs of the Gold Rush Days. (Ward Kimball Collection.)

Very rare German porcelain china locomotive, circa 1840. That trains held great fascination for many from the very beginning is borne out by this charming antique, which no doubt graced Milady's vanity table. Silver spoon in foreground is a souvenir of the 1890's and features fine engraving of smoke-puffing locomotive and passenger cars on the handle. (Ward Kimball Collection.)

A push or pull train made of wood, and popular with children in 1870. This model was commonly referred to as a "floor train." Legend on side of passenger car reads, "This Is The Car In Which Good Little Boys And Girls May Ride." (Ward Kimball Collection)

Close-up of pull-type wooden toy train locomotive and tender. Note lithographed reproductions of valve gear assembly and drivers which were glued to side of train. Note also that this early antique model carried the design of an early American 4-4-0, yet bore the imprint "Pacific," which actually has a 4-6-2 wheel arrangement. Firemen feeding lumber to firebox completed the scene for children who happily played with this toy despite its inaccurate title. (Ward Kimball collection)

This is how a model of a Pacific should and does look today. This HO-scale locomotive embraces all the refinements that have taken place in the last 100 years of model manufacturing. Not a toy or a plaything, but a real honest-to-goodness scale and authentic-looking miniature counterpart of its prototype. A detailed, superdetailed, fully working and operating scale-model locomotive.

purpose of making it easier for you, the reader, to be able to track down a particular item or piece of equipment which either strikes your fancy or is important to your model railroading operation. While this may possibly appear commercial in one respect or another, you will find it a definite aid when you visit a hobby shop and attempt to describe a particular item you wish to purchase.

As rail transportation progressed, so did their miniature counterparts, and although railroading was a product of American and English know-how, the world's leading toymakers (primarily found in Germany at that time) rose to the occasion by developing stamped metal units, a number of which employed the friction-drive principle. Action was simple, and when pushed, the large friction wheel contained within the metal cars would develop enough momentum to run a few yards under its own power. This was followed by the ingenuity of a few jewelers and clockmakers who fashioned mechanisms small enough to fit the locomotives (miniature) of their day and thus the wind-up train came into being—increasing the number of enthusiasts in a new avocation which was starting to show signs of growing pains not only among youngsters, but oldsters as well. Needless to say, wind-up and battery-operated trains continue to enjoy widespread use among today's toddlers.

With the advent of model locos being driven under their own power by clockwork devices, flanged wheels and wooden rails soon became a popular accessory, and lucky were the participants who were able to sit back for the nonce and watch their trains follow a specific direction about an oval of track, even though the run was short-lived.

Since steam engines were the very power behind the first commercial forms of rail locomotion, it was only logical that miniature live steamers would find their way onto the toy train market, which by now was beginning to show some semblance of becoming an industry in itself. This form of miniaturization, however, was pretty much confined to those in the upper classes.

The majority of these small live steamers featured alcohol lamps which provided enough heat to generate steam within a small water boiler, and progress moved up a few more inches. Soon, brass-crafted alcohol-burning versions of real locomotives became quite popular, both here and abroad, and, though produced in fairly large quantities in and around the middle of the nineteenth century, their scarcity today makes them very valuable collectors' items.

Within the pages of this introduction you will find a number of fascinating examples of early model trains from the David Rose and Ward Kimball collections some of which are more than one hundred years old. While some of these early miniatures are neither scale nor prototype in appearance, they offer an insight into the enthusiasm that developed concerning miniatures of the real thing. For contrast, some present-day models are also shown.

A number of the miniature live steamers were not as small as the word implies and were well in the neighborhood of one-fourth the size of the original. Many of them found their way into fairs and carnivals in America and England; you might call them the prototypes or forerunners of today's passenger-carrying train attractions at amusement parks the land over. (The trains at Disneyland are classic examples.) Both the amusement-park variety and those which could be held in the hand did much to stimulate continued interest in model railroading, and early rail fans started to develop different camps of interest. Probably the best salesmen to further the cause for model rails were the inventors and pioneers of steam locomotives. Which leads me to mention that many of these men were the world's first scratch builders, i.e. in the train category. No crude mock-ups or makeshift devices were shown to prospective investors and financiers, but, rather, truly scratch-built, well-detailed working models of

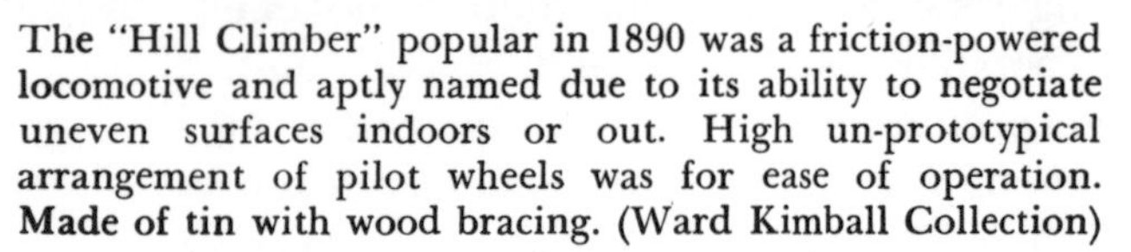

The "Hill Climber" popular in 1890 was a friction-powered locomotive and aptly named due to its ability to negotiate uneven surfaces indoors or out. High un-prototypical arrangement of pilot wheels was for ease of operation. Made of tin with wood bracing. (Ward Kimball Collection)

Ives "Vulcan," popular in the early 1870's, was made of tin, featured a colorful paint job, and was powered by a clockwork mechanism. (Ward Kimball Collection)

Better than one hundred years later this 4-8-4 Northern type in S scale, while often referred to as "tin plate," does nevertheless present a startling contrast in refinement and detailing to its predecessors.

An early "tin plate" of 1860. Production of toy trains was not limited to toymakers alone, as evidenced by this rare and striking antique offered in 1860 by a New England kitchen utensil manufacturer, and now part of the Ward Kimball Collection. A number of these early models were made from re-claimed tin cans and bore the stamped markings, "beans," "broth," "maple syrup," etc., which was usually found on the underside. Though seemingly crude, their appearance was enhanced by hammered embossed designs and gay colors.

Very rare wood and cast iron transition pull (floor) train, part of the extensive antique toy train collection belonging to Ward Kimball. Boiler, domes, and flooring were made of wood, and the balance of cast iron. Circa 1880.

A present-day scale model locomotive. This HO beauty is "articulated" in more ways than one.

The ultimate in wind-ups is seen in this Ives version of an American type 4-4-0, circa 1908. Scaled to reasonably proper proportion, it featured forward and reverse levers and was called Ives No. 40, 2-inch gauge. Constructed of iron and steel, with nickel-plated superstructure details. Note brake shoe between leading truck and driver. (Ward Kimball Collection)

Another "tin plate" live steamer, circa 1870, from the David Rose Collection.

An Ives train set presented in 1902 marked the first O gauge wind-up ready-to-run on put-together track. (Ward Kimball Collection)

Popular in France during the middle of the last century this Tom Thumb type was an early attempt to miniaturize live steamers. Powered by an alcohol burner, it worked quite well, and still does. This prize antique is one of many in the famous collection of noted composer and conductor David Rose.

The "Weeden" Dart, popular in 1887, was also a live steamer powered by an alcohol burner. Funnel and measuring cup were also supplied. (Ward Kimball Collection)

the prototypes. In some cases, the model was also the original, which, when funds were secured, would be built in live size.

While salesmen today carry about samples of their wares to entice consumers, in similar fashion representatives of railroads, engineers, inventors, manufacturers of locomotive equipment, *et al,* in those days carried about gleaming working models authentic down to the last detail and capable of performing in like manner to that of the prototype or principle they were trying to sell or cause to be commissioned for use on a particular railway. Some of these early scratch-built scale models were used for the purpose of extensive experimentation, and with the aid of these models many problems confronting design engineers and builders were solved for their immediate benefit and to the satisfaction of skeptical opposition. In making patent applications, a full set of plans had to be accompanied by detailed working models, and for a long period of time the U. S. Patent Office contained a most formidable collection of early railroadiana. In time, the models were given to the Smithsonian Institute, while some found their way into the hands of private collections. Today they are priceless and if you search hard enough, you might still find examples of these authentic miniatures kicking about some railroad V.P.'s office.

Things were rough for rail fans, including the inventors, since there were no hobby shops as we know them today where an enthusiast could pick up a part here or there to round things out. In those days everything had to be individually fabricated, and you couldn't order super detailing parts A, B, and C from Kemtron or the like. As a result, scratch builders were far and few between.

Soon the advantages of rail transportation brought inquiries from distant lands intent upon advancing their forms of travel, and, so, engineers and railroad representatives armed with plans and scale models traveled the globe from here to Timbuktu extolling the virtues of railroading, particularly among small countries whose revenue came solely from natural resources deep in the interior. Bringing such raw materials to cities and coastal towns for shipment elsewhere had always been a painstaking, time-consuming, and expensive proposition, and this new means of transportation was welcomed with open arms. In agricultural areas many a crop of perishable food never saw a grocer's shelves, let alone reached the dinner table, and even the earliest and slowest forms of freight transportation helped bring about new changes in eating habits.

Working models were looked upon with great interest in the days before the western frontiers were opened to the "iron horse," and though there was skepticism from some die-hard cattlemen, the time was drawing near when a thousand or more head of cattle would be shipped weekly by rail to cities in the East. Heretofore, cattle and livestock, plump and hearty before a drive, were straggling into cattle towns looking the worse for wear. Rail lines soon to come would spread out in many directions, reducing the length of cattle drives by hundreds of miles; thus herds of beef could be shipped in the prime condition they enjoyed before roundup.

Countries abroad such as Russia were fair game for railroad potential, and then, as now, the Russians were quick to avail themselves of Yankee know-how. Czar Nicholas became so enamored of the small steam models that he ordered a complete miniature railroad for his children, and the royal palace was agog when the Czar could often be seen manipulating one of the miniature locomotives.

However, the engineers were not in the business of selling model trains for pastime consumption, but rather to use their samples to encourage the growth and use of railroad locomotion, and shortly afterward, American engineers were commissioned to begin a vast network of rail lines throughout Russia.

Strangely enough, the interest in model trains was both in evidence and use in a number of countries even before real rail-

Union Pacific Rail Road Company

United States of America

Shares 6

No 344

Be it known, that James Fisk Jr. of New York is entitled to Six Shares of One Hundred Dollars each, in the Capital Stock of the

Union Pacific Rail Road Company

which Shares are transferable on the books of the Company at its Office in the City of New York by the holder in person, or by his Attorney on the surrender of this Certificate. New York June 23rd 1868

Transfer Agent. Oliver Ames President.

Registrar of Transfers. Treasurer.

SHARES $100 EACH

The money had to come from somewhere, and it did in the form of shares of stock such as this.

The "Royal Mail," a gleaming study in brass, was a British steamer duplicated in exacting detail of 3⅛-inch gauge and powered by alcohol. Fashioned after an early prototype, this model was popular and widely used in the 1870–1890 period. Though already obsolete at the time, the prototype continued to see service on British railways as a mail carrier between small towns despite the fact that motive power and designs had by then undergone radical changes and improvements. This operating model featured a clutch with forward and reverse drive and speed control, and became a collectors' item almost immediately after it was offered the train-conscious public. Quite valuable today as a representative of an early model live steamer patterned after a prototype symbolic of equally early days of railroad locomotion. This model is not far removed from the types of models that early engineers and inventors built to aid the cause of railroad transportation. A real prize in the David Rose Collection.

Early Union Pacific poster lithographed in gay colors. Below is a very rare children's toy train sold in Omaha and Sacramento called "Reed's Toy Palace Car." This was put together with wooden pegs and square nails, and gave the youngsters something to do during stopovers or while traveling. You might call this a do-it-your-self kit assembly, circa 1875. (Ward Kimball Collection)

The most famous scene in American railroading was in 1869 when Central Pacific and Union Pacific rails were joined at Promontory Point, Utah, with the driving of the Golden Spike. Leland Standford and Thomas C. Durant, officials of the two companies, sent the following message to President Grant: "The last rail is laid! The last spike is driven! The Pacific Railroad is completed! The point of junction is 1,086 miles west of the Missouri River, and 690 east of Sacramento City." And thus the nation was linked together. A historic photograph of a historic moment in American transportation.

10.

Union Pacific Railroad Company
20 NASSAU ST.
New York Jany 14th 1869

Union Pacific Rail Road Company. Complimentary pass Revd A. Catter— over road until December 31st 1869— unless otherwise ordered
Oliver Ames President

The word "complimentary" appearing on the left, Union Pacific memo on January 14, 1869, is sufficient to indicate that free passes were available. This one was good for the entire year of '69.

THE

UNION PACIFIC RAILROAD COMPANY

Proclaims to

FARMERS

Who have spent years grubbing stumps or picking stones, or who pay annually as much rent as will purchase a farm in Nebraska; to

Mechanics

Who find it hard work to make both ends meet at the end of a year's toil, and to EVERYBODY wishing a comfortable home in a healthy, fertile State:

NEBRASKA!

Is destined to be one of the leading Agricultural States in the Union, and greatest beyond the Mississippi; Because,

1st. The land does not have to be cleared of stumps and stones, but is ready for the plow, and yields a crop the first year.
2d. The soil is a deep loam of inexhausible fertility.
3d. Water is abundant, clear and pure.
4th. The productions are those common to the Eastern and Middle States.
5th. Fruits, both wild and cultivated, do remarkably well.
6th, Stock Raising is extensively carried on and is very profitable.
7th Market facilities are the best in the West. The great mining regions of Wyoming, Colorado, Utah and Nevada are supplied by farmers of Nebraska.
8th. Coal of excellent quality is found in vast quantities on the line of the road in Wyoming, and is furnished to settlers at cheap rates.
9th. Timber is found on all streams and grows rapidly.
10th. No fencing is required by law.
11th. The climate is mild and healthful; malarial diseases are unknown.
12th. Education is Free.

TICKETS By way of Columbus and Chicago and St. Louis will be furnished at reduced rates for persons desiring to prospect and select lands in Nebraska.

☞To those who purchase 160 Acres of the Company on Cash or Five Years' Terms, a rebate not to exceed Twenty Dollars, will be allwoed on price paid for Ticket.

FREIGHT: Reduced Rates given on Household Goods, Live Stock, Farming Tools, Trees and Shrubbery, in Car Loads, for Settlers' use.

LEAVITT BURNHAM, Land Commissioner U. P. R. R.

The Union Pacific Railroad and Branches.

Best Equipped, Most Direct and Popular Route to the Rich Mineral Districts, Grazing and Farming Regions and to the Famous Pleasure Resorts and Hunting Grounds of the Rocky Mountain Country.

THE COLORADO CITIES AND RESORTS are best reached via the UNION PACIFIC RAILROAD, Colorado Division. By far the most direct, pleasant and popular route to Ft. Collins, Estes Park, Boulder, Golden, Denver, Central, Georgetown, Idaho Springs and Leadville. Best Hunting, Fishing and Pleasure Resorts in sight of the Union Pacific.

THE BLACK HILLS.—The Sidney Stage Line, in connection with the Union Pacific Railroad, affords the shortest, quickest, and the only safe and pleasant stage journey to Rapid City, Custer, Rochford, Deadwood, Crook City, and other prominent points in the Hills, being the only line passing along the entire length of the Hills.

UTAH, IDAHO AND MONTANA.—The UNION PACIFIC, connecting with the UTAH CENTRAL at Ogden, for Salt Lake City, Frisco, Leeds, and all points in Utah, and with the UTAH & NORTHERN, for the Snake and Salmon River Mines, as well as Helena, Deer Lodge, Virginia, Butte City, Glendale, Bozeman, and all the best mining and Agricultural regions in Montana.

CALIFORNIA, ARIZONA, OREGON AND WASHINGTON.—The UNION and CENTRAL PACIFIC RAILROADS form the only line across the continent, to all points in Nevada, California, Oregon, Washington; and in connection with the Southern Pacific, affords a through rail route to the heart of Arizona; or in connection with the finest Steamship lines, to China, Japan and India.

For information concerning the Resources, Climate, and other attractions of the Great West, address THOS. L. KIMBALL, General Passenger and Ticket Agent U. P. R. R., Omaha, Neb.

Reproduced full page advertisement (printed in 1879) appearing in booklet

The Commerce of Two Cities, the Present and Future of Council Bluffs and Omaha

New and fruitful lands were opened up by the railroads, and grandfather, and even great-grandfather, left his stony New England farm or dismal factory to move to the blossoming West, where this advertisement in 1879 proclaimed, "No Fencing Required By Law . . . And Malarial Diseases Are Unknown." Railroads such as the Union Pacific helped to open new frontiers which not only changed the face of our nation's sprawling wilderness, but vastly added to its growth as well.

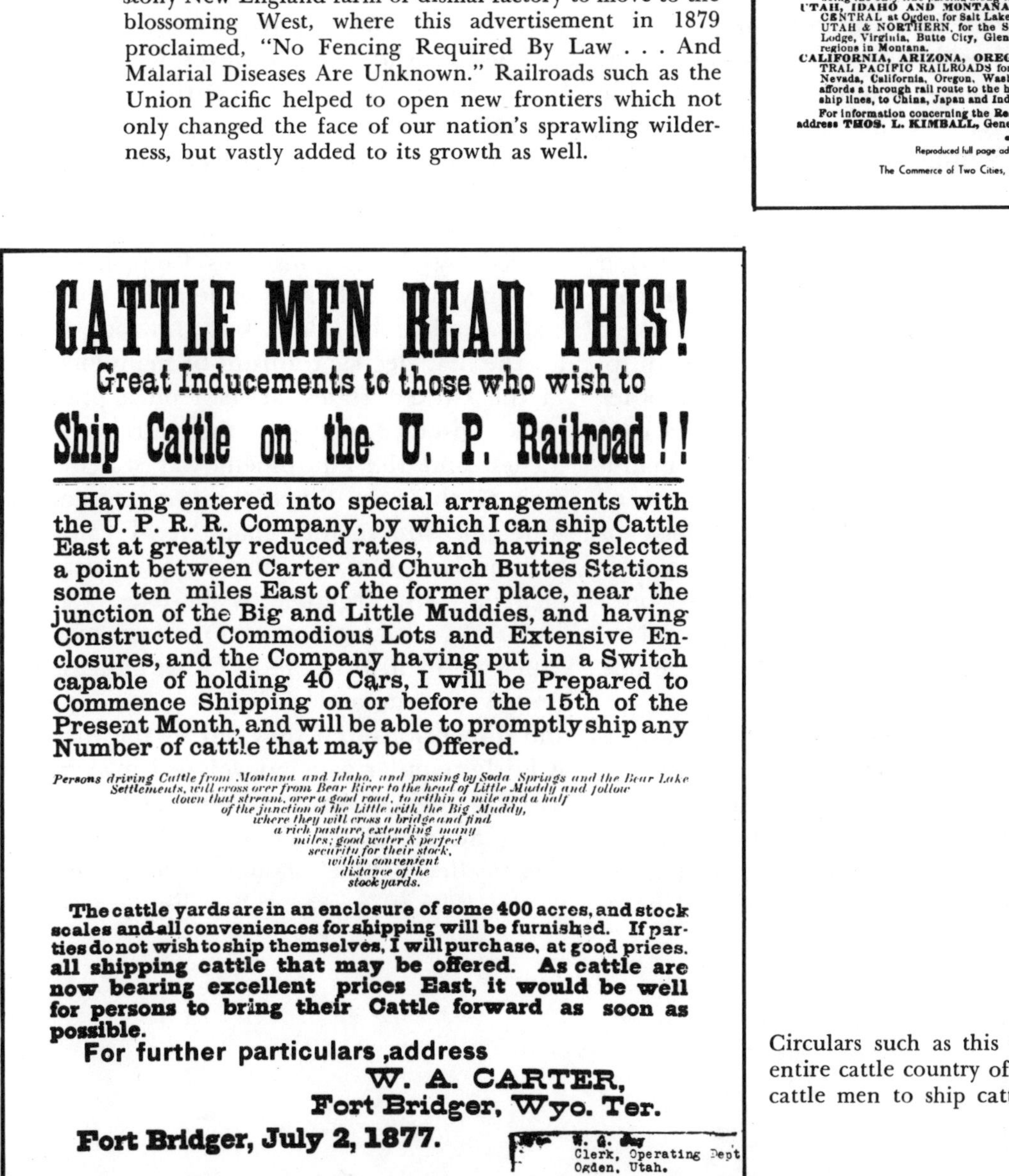

CATTLE MEN READ THIS!

Great Inducements to those who wish to

Ship Cattle on the U. P. Railroad!!

Having entered into special arrangements with the U. P. R. R. Company, by which I can ship Cattle East at greatly reduced rates, and having selected a point between Carter and Church Buttes Stations some ten miles East of the former place, near the junction of the Big and Little Muddies, and having Constructed Commodious Lots and Extensive Enclosures, and the Company having put in a Switch capable of holding 40 Cars, I will be Prepared to Commence Shipping on or before the 15th of the Present Month, and will be able to promptly ship any Number of cattle that may be Offered.

Persons driving Cattle from Montana and Idaho, and passing by Soda Springs and the Bear Lake Settlements, will cross over from Bear River to the head of Little Muddy and follow down that stream, over a good road, to within a mile and a half of the junction of the Little with the Big Muddy, where they will cross a bridge and find a rich pasture, extending many miles; good water & perfect security for their stock, within convenient distance of the stock yards.

The cattle yards are in an enclosure of some 400 acres, and stock scales and all conveniences for shipping will be furnished. If parties do not wish to ship themselves, I will purchase, at good priees. all shipping cattle that may be offered. As cattle are now bearing excellent prices East, it would be well for persons to bring their Cattle forward as soon as possible.

For further particulars ,address

W. A. CARTER,
Fort Bridger, Wyo. Ter.

Fort Bridger, July 2, 1877.

W. G. Gay
Clerk, Operating Dept
Ogden, Utah.

Circulars such as this were distributed throughout the entire cattle country of the nation as an inducement for cattle men to ship cattle on the Union Pacific.

roads were employed, and it has been noted by a few historians that the overwhelming response to the miniatures which preceded their prototypes had a lot to do with the successful acceptance of the latter's arrival.

By 1886, U. S. railroad growth saw the completion and standardization of gauge (4 feet 8½ inches) on all railroads in existence, thus enabling the interchange of cars throughout the country for the first time since 1830, when the English-built locomotive "John Bull" arrived on our shores.

Meanwhile, in the last twenty years before the turn of the century the popularity of toy trains continued on the rise; however, no steps had been taken as yet to standardize either gauge or scale. This resulted in considerable confusion among enthusiasts, whether content with the situation or otherwise. At this time each manufacturer was producing trains and track in a different size, and you either stayed with one source of supply or wasted your money on non-interchangeable equipment. As a result, enthusiasts were as hungry for realism in detail and proper dimension in scale as Russia has been of beating us to the moon. However, fine engraved tooling, die casting, and modern mass-production methods were still a long way off, and hobbyists found out sooner than later that their only alternative was to build their own equipment. And build they did, sparking off another avenue of what has become a many-faceted hobby. By the turn of the century toy manufacturers were turning out train equipment by the carloads; nevertheless, the lack of standards, authenticity, and detailing in relation to prototype design continued to be a source of harassment to potential modelers, and it was still impossible to interchange one line of equipment with another.

As I said earlier, there had to be a starting point; and, while the year 1900 represented better than a seventy-five-year span from the time miniature trains were first introduced to the world, this was still the beginning.

Up to this point few companies had bothered to assign any particular gauge designations to their rail or rolling stock, let alone make any attempt at co-operative standardization. One of the first companies to produce a given rail size was European-based, and the track designation was No. 1 gauge, roughly 1¾ inches between the rails, or, to be exact according to the metric system of measurement used abroad, 45 millimeters. Another company decided to try a slightly larger size, calling their gauge No. 2, and this was approximately 2 inches, or 54 millimeters, between the rails. This was followed by No. 3 gauge (2½ inches between the rails), then No. 4 gauge, 3 inches between the rails. So the battle of the gauges was on, and, while the distance between the rails continued to increase, no real attempts were made to scale the trains to correct prototype proportions; as a result, they certainly suffered by comparison with the prototype.

The time did come, however, when a gauge would be introduced and continue in use up to the present time. Thus, in the year 1910 one of the greatest single advancements in the cause of model railroading was given the scale-conscious rail buffs with the O gauge offered by the famous Ives Company. Ives not only heralded the smallest size commercially produced to date, but also took credit for the first electric trains to be manufactured in the United States, at least on a practical basis. Distance between the rails was 1¼ inches, and the equipment was scaled 17/64 inch to the foot. Since these measurements were one size smaller than No. 1 gauge, it became known as O gauge. These measurements are still regarded as the true O gauge and scale, although most O gauge today is scaled ¼ inch to the foot. Other gauges continued to come and go, bearing various sizes and dimensions, but they fell by the wayside. A fairly popular gauge developed in America was 2⅛ inches, which Lionel referred to as their "Standard" gauge and which American Flyer called "Wide" gauge. Though popular in the 1925-1935 era, it has disappeared en-

1904 version of a 4-2-0 by Howard (surprisingly enough there was a prototype for it; see page 96 of Westcott *Cyclopedia)* featured electric drive powered by battery connected to two rails of 2-inch gauge. (Ward Kimball Collection)

The "Hercules," an American type offered by the Milton Bradley Co. in 1880, was made of wood featuring lithographed detailing glued to the cab and drivers. This push or pull floor train is one of the early and better examples of the attempts that were made to add realism and similarity to prototype design and scale. (Ward Kimball Collection)

Today, HO scale models such as this 2-6-0 Mogul offer startling contrast to the toy train antiques of yesteryear.

tirely from the scene except as a collector's item.

While the Ives Company has been credited with producing the first electric trains in O gauge, it may come as a shocking surprise to learn that electrified miniatures were not entirely new to model railroading. As early as 1835 a Vermont blacksmith, Thomas Davenport, devised a small electric motor fitted to an equally small locomotive, and amazed friends and neighbors by running it about a circular track. With proper financing and support Davenport might have been hailed as a genius with a fortune awaiting him, but his ideas and skills were too advanced for his time, and so the process and technique lay dormant for the next few decades.

In 1851 the Davenport idea, by now modified and improved, was again offered the modeling world, and, while attracting considerable interest, was still considered to be far ahead of its time, so it was shelved again. With the passing of a few more decades, and the ever-growing interest in model railroading, the Novelty Company in the year 1883 produced what is often referred to as the first commercially marketed electric trains in this country. However, it still remained for someone to produce electric-powered miniatures of a widely accepted gauge, bearing reasonably authentic detailing and scale proportion to prototypes. To reiterate, the Ives Company in 1910 finally accomplished this purpose, and electric trains were at last on the way.

In the eighty-odd years since Davenport had run an electric train about an oval of track, many forms of electrification in model trains had been attempted, ranging from wet-cell power to hand-cranked generators, batteries, and the like, but it was simply a question of time for the commercial application of electricity to be so developed as to make it feasible for miniature rail locomotion. The fact that the railroads of the day made no attempts to electrify their own lines surely had a psychological effect on the progress of electricity in connection with their miniature counterparts. For in those days steam was the giant among power sources, and toymakers were not disposed toward producing replicas of steam locomotives powered by volts and amps.

By the mid-1930s there were rumbles within the hobby world of brass hats as talk spread concerning a new and fascinating concept in scale detailing which would be in direct proportion to gauge and, as important, would take up less room in actual operation. To enthusiasts from Maine to California this could mean only one thing: *a smaller gauge.* If reports were accurate, they would not only enjoy the obvious advantages of requiring less space, but would benefit from a reduction in price compared with O gauge. Those fortunate enough to attend the world's fair in Chicago in 1933-1934 were able to see the first introduction of HO gauge put on display in this country. While both the scale and gauge were in direct proportion to each other in relation to prototype design, the details were at best a bit on the crude side, but, nevertheless, it was a sign of things to come.

Following considerable research into the possibilities of HO, and based on developments in England, Eric La Nal, Dr. Alfonse Bacon, and George Stock took a giant step in 1936 by introducing HO to the rumor-washed American hobbyist, and model railroading not only started to change direction again, but soared to greater heights as well.

While until then O gauge had been far and away the most popular size, there now crept into the picture a most formidable competitor which in time would account for no less than 75 per cent of the entire model rail population.

Tracing the actual steps in the development of HO gauge is too involved to go into here, so I will simplify it by stating that it was, roughly a matter of cutting O gauge in half and designating it HO. The "Depressive Thirties," as they are now referred to, was certainly excellent timing for the presentation of HO to the American public, since the

Widely used in England during the twenties, this gauge 1 cast-iron steam locomotive had the wheel arrangement of an American type 4-4-0, but that is where the resemblance ended. Came equipped with a tender and featured forward/reverse levers, a throttle control, and safety valve. Although powered by an alcohol burner, Prohibition did not affect its use. It is still operational today, as attested to by David Rose, one of the world's leading and most knowledgeable enthusiasts and authorities of the many phases of steam locomotion.

Side and rear view of English gauge 1 live steamer. Note direction and pressure controls inside the cab. (David Rose Collection)

Floor train version of a "Mother Hubbard" made of cast iron and in use from 1890–1900. A collectors item today, it is considered very rare. (Ward Kimball Collection)

A present day "Mother Hubbard" in HO gauge.

For additional contrast, compare this HO scale "Camelback" to its antique forerunner.

United States was still suffering the throes of a depression. Money was extremely tight (particularly for hobbies) and space was not to be spared by the majority of families throughout the land. In the latter case the timing was perfect, and one of the most important factors in the widespread acceptance of HO lay not only in the comparatively good-looking appearance of the scale and gauge, but, more importantly, in the fact that a track plan requiring a dimension of 8 feet in O gauge would afford the same action and scenic possibilities in 4 feet for HO. It is no wonder that HO developed an early stronghold in becoming the most widely used gauge and scale since the inception of model railroading. With the popular acceptance of HO, the brass hats settled down for awhile content with two uniform gauges, O and HO. There were a number of abortive attempts to produce other gauges, but they never quite cut the mustard, and disappeared from the scene almost as quickly as they were presented. To be completely accurate, mention should be made of OO gauge, but, again, I have oversimplified to avoid a detailed account of the "battle of the gauges."

Model train production continued at a brisk pace until 1942, when most hobby manufacturing was curtailed because of war production and restrictions. Following the end of World War II, production again resumed, and the American Flyer trains, now a part of the A. C. Gilbert Company, popularized an in-between gauge—that is to say, bigger than HO but smaller than O—which was designated as S gauge. Now there were three gauges in popular use, O, S, and HO, with the latter fast becoming king of the gauges. However, there were still a few dissenters here and there, for model railroaders are a curious breed of hobbyists and are always looking for new techniques and improvements. Therefore, it came as no surprise when TT gauge, invented by Hal P. Joyce, was presented. TT, standing for "table top," was even smaller than HO and featured a scale of 1⁄10 inch to the foot and .470 inch between the rails. Thus, progress continued, and following the war years a hobby whose birth dated back to the early 1800s underwent a revolution of changes and operation, as modern tooling techniques and mass merchandising made it possible for people in all walks of life, regardless of income or bank account, to enjoy a spare-time hobby which at the least helped them forget their problems for awhile.

Development and improvement of detailed parts in kit assemblies, ready-to-run equip-

Another fine example of the advanced techniques in tooling, design and authentic appearance is this HO model of an early Mallet steam locomotive. In fact, it is a miniature of the first Mallet-type locomotive introduced to American railroading.

ment, snap track, self-gauging track bed, efficient power packs, structures either ready-built or in interlocking kit form, custom- and brass-crafted locomotives produced both here and imported from abroad, the introduction of plastics, availability of any number of models ranging back through the last hundred or more years of railroading, and last, but not least, the infinite variety of super-detailing parts and possible conversions that go a long way toward dressing up and authenticating one's equipment are just some of the highlights responsible for making model railroading a universally accepted hobby.

There have been many other contributions to the growth of model railroading, notably the National Model Railroad Association (NMRA), which we shall cover in greater detail in chapters that follow. Of no less importance are the monthly hobby magazines such as the *Model Railroader* and *Railroad Model Craftsman,* which made their entrance on the hobby scene in the 1930s and are still going strong.

The last three decades have seen the hobby of miniature trains emerge not only as a fascinating pastime, but a booming business as well, as evidenced by the fact that thousands of hobby shops from coast to coast have their shelves chock-full of almost every conceivable item that a model railroader can imagine or want. Not uncommon are the shops that deal solely in model railroading; in other words, no airplanes, leathercrafts, sewing kits, games, etc. These are the real meccas for modelers.

Adults no longer have to use the lame excuse, "I'm buying it for my son," and salesmen in hobby shops and department stores no longer slyly wink, for they recognize that the pursuit of model trains as a hobby knows no barriers when it comes to age or, for that matter, sex.

This hobby, avocation, pastime, leisurely pursuit—call it what you will—has indeed come a long way from its inception a score of decades in the past. Scale modeling and the

Announcements such as this heralded great events in American railroading. For example, passenger trains leaving Omaha following the arrival of trains from the East could reach San Francisco, "In less than Four Days, avoiding the Dangers of the Sea!"—quite a saving of time in those days.

operation of model railroads in prototype fashion has now reached a very high plateau; however, the means by which this has come about, as you can see, has been the result of a slow and often awkward form of metamorphosis. For this reason I felt it would be fitting to travel back through the years and acquaint you with perhaps some hithertofore little-known facts concerning the magic spell it has woven from the very beginning to the present time—a present time which now includes exquisitely detailed locomotives, transistorized throttles, radio-frequency control, and many other refinements which are covered in great detail within the pages which follow.

It is not only these latest refinements, and those to come, which will be discussed, but also the basic concepts and rudiments of model railroading itself. For this book has been written and illustrated with a number of purposes in mind: to acquaint or reacquaint you with the different types of equipment that are available; how to build your own models if you are of a mind to do-it-yourself; how to further authenticate the appearance of your locomotive through the addition of extra details; the why's and wherefore's of maintenance which will keep them in top running condition, and the painting and aging techniques which will do much to remedy the "store-bought" look, which in turn will offer a more prototype appearance.

We shall cover the planning of a model railroad—the layout design and track plans with respect to the type of operation your pike will embrace, and the equipment you will employ. In addition, a substantial amount of text and illustration will be devoted to the manner in which scenery is created, mountains are built, and special effects are achieved. Considerable space will also be allotted to rolling stock and the great variety of cars which can be put into use on your model empire; that is, the types and services they perform. And while this book primarily embraces the golden age of steam locomotion, we shall also cover diesels and, for a change of pace, interurbans, which were, and in some areas still are, an important part of American railroading, and modeling, too.

For history buffs, Civil War oldtimers and historic locomotives get their due respect and mention, too, for in this area we have one of the most popular applications of the hobby where modeling and operation is concerned—especially when space is at a premium. Basic wiring techniques are shown and discussed, with an emphasis toward helping you eliminate unnecessary complication and avoiding a rat's nest of wires beneath your layout. Considerable space is devoted to the application and availability of radio-frequency control, which is probably the greatest single breakthrough since the advent of electrically operated miniature trains.

Finally, we shall come to the subject of realistic operation—the moment of truth for each and every would-be or already-established model railroader. We shall draw the line between running trains aimlessly and endlessly, and the pleasures and advantages of operating trains in prototype fashion. These and many more items of interest are on the agenda and await your modeling and, I hope, your reading pleasure.

For the beginner new to the ways and means of model railroading, I most strongly urge that you read this book from beginning to end in order to get a full grasp and picture of a hobby that has more facets than the Hope Diamond. For you will soon discover that while this hobby is a multi-faceted one, each face is directly related to another in more ways than one. Specific chapters can serve as guides to where your own individual interests may lie. For the more advanced model rail, or veteran brass hat, for that matter, while many areas of this book may be quite familiar to you, I am certain that there will be an equal number of areas in the book that you will find stimulating—or re-stimulating, as it were—and in any event I am sure that I will have opened a hornet's nest or two for the edification of all concerned.

The road and journey ahead is filled with many a side trip designed not to sidetrack you, but instead to lead you along various avenues that are most decidely worth pursuing, and whose pursuit will open new vistas to your model railroading pleasure. The ultimate goal, of course, is a well-scenicked miniature railroad using realistic-looking and smooth-functioning equipment which will be operated in a purposeful and prototypical manner.

The golden age of steam is now behind us and the smoke-puffing locomotive as we have known it down through the years is also a thing of the past. While steam-powered locomotion still has some infrequent and scattered use throughout the country, it is isolated and an exception to the rule of the diesels. The day will come, no doubt, when diesels will be led out to pasture as new and more advanced forms of motive power are harnessed for railroad use. Even now there is talk of rocket- or atomic-powered trains, which is enough to make steam lovers cringe, for gone are those smoke belchers and whistle shriekers, gone are those high drivers and flashing rods. Mighty articulateds which once pulled mile-long consists of freight no longer perform their arduous chores, and the air is no longer filled with cinder and smoke. But weep no more, for the memories of what was once our nation's most productive form of transportation has been emblazoned in the hearts of man, never to be forgotten. Our national archives and agencies, such as the American Association of Railroads, have comprehensive records of all forms of railroading from the very beginning. Documents, photographs, blueprints, and every conceivable form of identification have been preserved so that generations to come will be completely familiar with railroading's proudest hours and heritage.

While live railroads may someday see only a minimum of service, their memory in the form of miniature counterparts will live on in the hearts of youngsters and oldsters alike. No other hobby can boast of so early a planting ground in the mind of man as trains. Such an early beginning is bound to sow a good harvest, and may be one of the reasons why model rail aficionados increase in countless numbers day in and day out, making it one of the most popular, fruitful, and magical hobbies of all time.

In all the world no single hobby has been more responsible for the fascinating hours, days, weeks, and even years than that spent in the pursuit of model railroading. Far-reaching and everlasting effects have helped make this pastime both exciting and pleasurable for young and old, making men out of boys and boys out of men. Notwithstanding

A Union Pacific streaking eastward. One of steam's finest hours and the end of an era.

A breathtaking example of a Norfolk and Western 2-6-6-4 Class "A" articulated steam locomotive. No, this is not a "builder's" photograph of the prototype, but actually a photograph of an exactingly scaled and exquisitely detailed HO scale model of its bigger brother. This beautiful and, of course, fully operational miniature is a United model from Pacific Fast Mail and typical of the advances, refinements, and true prototype design with which many scale-model locomotives are today endowed.

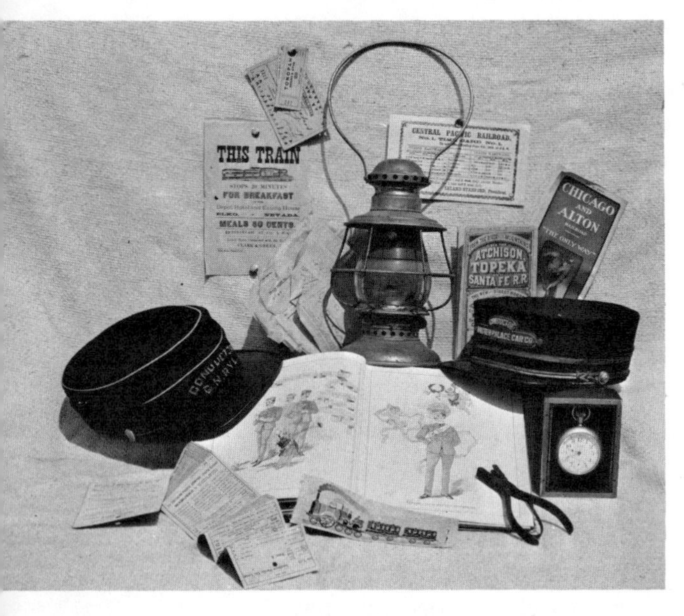

Conductor's paraphernalia from the Ward Kimball Collection includes a cap at left from the Great Northern R.R. Cap at right is from the Wagner Palace Car Service. Small colored embroidered ribbon at bottom is from the 1830's. Book in center is a rare volume of a musical comedy treatment on the dapper and debonair C & A conductor. Plus other nostalgic memorablia.

the fact that new areas of companionship have been fostered between father and son, entire families have been able to enjoy togetherness in one of today's leading avocations. They are no longer looked upon as "toy trains." The old bromide about Dad buying trains for Junior so he himself can play with them no longer applies, and in effect the adult has crowded the youngster out of the role by becoming the top participant.

Toddler or centenarian; youngster, teenager, or adult; scratch builder, kit assembler, ready-to-runner, and even armchair doodler —all have a basic starting point and the common bond of sharing the enthusiasm of spending untold fun-filled hours enjoying the romance of railroading.

No matter the manner, shape, or form. Be it a simple oval on a bare piece of plywood or a maze of track within a well-scenicked pike, the thrill is everywhere, and each in his own way feels it as pounding drivers sing and thunder along the rails. Yes, the golden age of steam locomotion is now behind us, and so is the end of an era that greatly contributed to the exciting growth of our nation, and many another nation at that. But while a steaming behemoth may no longer come "round the bend" puffing clouds of smoke toward the heavens above, each day, in countless homes throughout the nation and lands across the seas, miniature counterparts recreate many a traditional railroad activity and scene within the confines of model railroad empires. And so, the once-glorious era of steam locomotion lives on in a pleasure-filled hobby almost as old as railroading itself.

I

Getting Started

There comes a time in the life of a hobbyist when an inner voice starts whispering, "Where do I go from here?" This applies not only to the rankest beginner, but to the advanced model rail as well. For the veteran hobbyist it isn't too great a transition to advance from kit assembly to scratch building, or from conversions to free-lance building. But to the beginner who has the enthusiasm but may be lacking in knowledge or experience, it is a far more difficult gap to bridge. The result (not uncommon by any means) is an "in-between" stage whereby the novice who wishes to venture beyond the usual ready-to-run techniques gets bogged down in an effort to get into the more challenging phases of the hobby. This can include the desire to graduate from RTR to kit assembly, to replace sectional track with hand-laid ties and rail, to add some details to an otherwise naked locomotive, to place or re-install turnout switches completely out of view, to toss an out-of-scale tunnel in the ashcan (and build one yourself), and, among many other things, to realize that a layout is for model railroading and not intended for Indianapolis speed trials.

When the beginner starts thinking along these lines, he has it bad, he has the fever, he is finally bitten by the bug—in short he is hooked! Happily enough, he is now on the way to becoming a member of one of the world's greatest hobby fraternities, in which scale and its application make the difference between playing with toy trains or authentically operating realistic miniatures.

Nevertheless, many a neophyte, armed with a sincere desire to take the plunge, finds himself hard put for aid and direction. It is, therefore, our hope that this book will help to ease all would-be model railroaders over the hump and into the many facets of model railroading—*on a scale basis.*

First, as indicated in the introduction, the contents of this book will primarily embrace the HO gauge. Nevertheless, aside from the specific HO equipment shown, illustrated, and discussed, most of the techniques and procedures described can be easily applied to that of other gauges.

Within this chapter and many chapters to follow the words "scale," "gauge," and "prototype" will become very familiar to you and at the same time completely understandable

That model railroads are not intended for Indianapolis Speed Trials can be attested to by a detailed study of this photograph of an equally detailed layout built by Dick Seydell. The rural view features a sweeping panoramic curve of over and under trackwork heading away from the "Summit Station." As a caboose disappears through the tunnel portal, a Southern Pacific "Daylight" gracefully rolls by. Entering the station is a Berkshire which was assembled from a Bowser kit. Other effects include a bell ringing, wigwagging signal, a Texaco gas tank made from the top half of a quart beer can and a scratch-built oil well and refinery. Ulrich trucks, Alexander kits, Revell roadside structures, etc, are just some of the ingredients that will add to your railroading pleasure once you are off to a proper start.

in relation to one another. So, to digress for a moment, let's go back to the days when "HO" was a breakfast food devoured by millions of Americans daily and a "brass hat" was a cuspidor found in the local tavern. Model railroading enthusiasts were arguing the pros and cons of clockwork mechanisms versus electrified motive power and the battle of the gauges reigned supreme in conversation whenever model railroaders got together.

Scale and model railroading has come a long way since those early days, but the battle of the gauges rages on. Conversations continue to get heated among the various advocates; nevertheless, the fact remains that HO has been firmly established as the most popular and most widely used among the gauges today. The novice, new to the ways of miniature railroading, then as now looked upon the different gauge designations as so much alphabetical chop suey, and if that didn't frustrate him, the wheel arrangements did. Gauges were listed by numbers, letters, and fractions, while in some cases a gauge here and there combined all three ingredients into a hieroglyphic potpourri further confusing the beginner. Letters to the editors of early issues of model railroad magazines were no less vitriolic in expounding the writers' views than those which are published today. Surprisingly enough, the arguments were startlingly identical to current letters-to-the-editor oratory and just as controversial. I think we can safely assume that as long as model railroading continues to flourish, the battle of the gauges will remain a most provocative conversation piece.

By the same token that the word "prototype" has virtually become synonomous with any item of live railroading equipment, original or otherwise, so has the word "gauge" in like fashion become all-embracing to mean size of track, motive equipment, rolling stock, structures, and the like. Actually there is a distinct dividing line, with "gauge" representing "the distance between rails," while "scale" is the ratio of the model in direct relationship to its prototype. The following table gives the basic differences between the popular gauges in use today:

	O	S	HO	TT
Proportion to Prototype	1/48	1/64	1/87.1	1/120
Scale to Prototype Feet, in Decimals of an Inch	0.25	0.188	0.138	0.1
Scale to Prototype Feet, in Fractions of an Inch	¼	3/16	1/7.3	1/10
Distance Between Rails, in Inches	1.25	.875	.65	.471

From a technical standpoint, this is all good and well, and helps your conversation sound all the more intelligent (if you memorize it) when you get into a discussion concerning gauge and scale—and you surely will. But aside from the use of a slide rule and conjuring up a mental image of how one gauge stacks up against another as to size, your best bet is to visit your local hobby shop and compare firsthand the actual differences in detailing appearance and physical aspects—in other words, how comparatively big or small they really are. The information and observation gleaned will enable you more fully to appreciate and understand the choice you have made.

Now let's get to essentials on the subject of how to get started along the more serious avenues of scale modeling and operation.

One of the first things to do is to find out what the other fellows are doing. Visits to your local hobby shop will not only give you the opportunity to view equipment on display, but also to talk with other enthusiasts. Once you start making friends within your own hobby you will find new ideas flowing toward you at a rapid pace. Visiting local model railroad clubs is also an excellent way not only of hearing what is going on, but seeing as well. In clubs across the nation the interchange of ideas, information, techniques, and operation will help guide you in the di-

"Scale" is the relationship of the model to its prototype. A visit to a railroad, freight yard, etc., will help you appreciate the basic authenticity your models may and should possess. Take along a camera, a notebook, sketch pad and pencil. Make a full record of what you see, particularly to compare your miniature and its live counterpart. Later, when you are at your workbench, you will find this reference material invaluable.

Comparison of gauge, scale and basic size relationships between three Pacific locomotives. From top to bottom are O, HO and TT. Note how the O gauge locomotive, even without the tender, dwarfs the other units.

Two observation cars in HO and TT placed side by side offer another indication of gauge and scale on a direct comparison basis.

Visits to local model railroading clubs will afford would-be scale modelers with a gold mine of information. A firsthand view of a finished layout, or of one in the making, will be of enormous aid for your own undertakings. The good fellowship and discussions you will enjoy are alone worth the trip. The practical information you absorb will not only make you more knowledgeable about the hobby, but will probably spur you on toward the more fascinating horizons and fun of model railroading.

rection of more fruitful model railroading. The warmth and camaraderie of model rail fellowship is alone worth the trip.

Another important move is to subscribe to such monthly magazines as *Model Railroader* and *Railroad Model Craftsman.* These magazines are devoted exclusively to the hobby and are chock-full of informative articles, how-to-do-it picture stories, reviews and tests of equipment, and, among other things, are loaded with advertisements which feature the latest in equipment, materials, and gadgets to stimulate your thinking and fancies. Of particular importance are the addresses of manufacturers, mail-order houses, and hobby shops, the latter of vital importance to those of you who may not live within walking or driving distance of stores catering to the hobby.

Above all, and a must to my way of thinking, is joining the National Model Railroading Association, hereafter referred to as NMRA. This is a national organization which has done much to stimulate model railroading as we know and enjoy it today. Pursuing this a bit further, let me explain that the NMRA was responsible in the development of standardization among model rail manufacturers, and this standardization has been one of the main driving forces behind the successful and popular acceptance of HO scale.

The NMRA, which has celebrated its silver anniversary, now has approximately 15,000 members. In view of what this organization has done to advance the hobby, I feel it only fitting to make more than passing mention concerning the comparatively few who have dedicated themselves to the interests of so many.

Prior to the mid-1930s, scale modeling at best was far from widely known, and, to be more accurate about it, was little known at all. Model trains—scale, tinplate, or otherwise—were all lumped under one heading—*toys*—and an uninformed, uninspired public looked upon the pioneering scale railroader as a guy who "played with electric trains." It was as simple as that—at least to the public. To the modeler, however, it was much more complex and chaotic, considering the fact that standardization, what little there existed, was at an extremely low ebb and interchangeability of equipment from one layout to another was far from the taken-for-granted situation we know and enjoy today. Thus, if one model fan were to attempt to run some of his equipment on a layout other than his own, more often than not he would find that his wheel flanges fitted too tightly in the flangeways of another fan's turnouts, or the third rail shoes wouldn't reach the other chap's third rail. This problem was particularly acute among model clubs whose practice included visiting other clubs for the purpose of operating and displaying newly developed equipment and the like.

Things finally reached such a point that in the late summer of 1935, under the auspices of the Model Railroad Club of Milwaukee, clubs from surrounding areas and states were invited to attend a meeting at the "summit," at which the constitution and code of ethics of the NMRA was framed. In the years that have followed this national organization has been responsible for not only helping to create standards for model railroad equipment, but has increased the camaraderie between fellow railroaders, gathered new converts to the fold, and, lastly, established a new and respected social standing for the hobby in the eyes of the world. The following creed, stated in the original constitution, has weathered many a storm since it was first introduced and, incidentally, has helped keep HO from going the way of the many other gauges that fell by the wayside:

> To assemble, define and set up model railroad standards . . . promote closer understanding and cooperation between model railroad manufacturers, consumers and publishers . . . promote the greater fellowship of model railroading between model railroaders . . . promote better understanding in general of railroad problems.

This model is so exquisitely detailed that it wouldn't be fair to play guessing games and ask you whether it is a prototype or miniature. It is shown at this point with one purpose in mind: to stimulate your interest and whet your appetite for things to come. Just to let you know of the possibilities that lay before you, I mention that this O gauge replica of a Virginia and Truckee early American was entirely scratch-built.

Like the brakeman on the caboose, climb aboard for a ride through many a fun-filled hour of model railroading—where your locomotives will begin to resemble their prototypes, where rolling stock will age and weather as they traverse and roll through many a mile of trackwork, where bare sheets of plywood will become adorned with a criss-cross of rails, where buildings will spring up overnight and scenic effects will blend into the overall surroundings to give your layout a magnificence all its own.

But for the indefatigable efforts of these pioneering scale railroaders in their unflinching climb toward standardization and solidarity among the fellowship of model railroading, our hobby as we indulge in it today might still be devoid of any relation to conformity and prototype standards, and would no doubt still be classed as a "plaything."

If you are interested in a more detailed accounting of the NMRA, how it came into being, and a greater insight into its accomplishments, I heartily suggest you join the NMRA. Simply place a check or money order for $5 in an envelope; include your name, age, and address; and shoot it off to the NMRA, c/o Bob Bast, P.O. Box 1328, Station C, Canton 8, Ohio—you'll never regret it. For $5 a year you will receive the clever and informatively edited monthly NMRA *Bulletin* (this alone is worth the price of admission), periodical issues of *Data Sheets,* an annual *Periodical Index,* and a *Yearbook* listing all members of the NMRA (both here and abroad), their whereabouts and pike details. Clubs boasting 100 per cent membership are also listed. A special gift in the form of a metal gage check is also included upon joining. This gage check is invaluable and you will wonder how you ever got along without it. Descriptions of the many uses of this gage check will be covered in greater detail further along, as in Chapter V.

There are many other benefits of NMRA membership too numerous to mention, and for considerably less money than it takes to buy a tank of petrol, you can find out and reap many rewards. So why wait? Join now. You will be joining the company of the top "brass hats" in the nation, which include the maestro himself, John Allen. The longer you wait, the longer you miss out. *Join now!*

Thus far we have traced the origin of model railroading in relation to live railroading. We have discussed the history and metamorphosis of a hobby which has captured the hearts and imaginations of millions. And we have endeavored to lead you along the paths which will offer you the greatest sources of information and know-how. This has been done with a particular purpose in mind—to give you some of the background and why's and wherefore's as you climb the various plateaus of scale hobbyship.

It has been my observation (and that of other model railroading writers) that many beginners rush headlong into the hobby in such an uninformed manner that afterward they wonder what hit them. I have received hundreds of letters from beginners from coast to coast, and invariably they ask the same questions: "Where can I buy such and such a locomotive?" "Who manufactures the locomotive shown on page so-and-so?" "I would like catalogues and literature from the following—" (this is accompanied by a mile-long list of manufacturers). Queries such as these, however innocent they may be, have made me come to the conclusion that many beginners become so smitten with the hobby that they don't take the time to find out what it is all about. That's why I stress the advantages of subscribing to model railroading magazines, visiting clubs, and joining the NMRA. These things are part of getting started and help you lay the foundation for the sweet smell of successful scale modeling and operation.

But enough of such talk. I'm sure I've made my point. Now climb aboard for a pleasure-filled ride through many fun-filled hours of scale-model railroading—where locomotives look like their prototypes, layouts become more than a bare sheet of plywood, scenery becomes a miniature replica of mother nature, and your own model railroad empire looks like the real McCoy.

II
Selecting Motive Power

"What type of locomotive should I buy?" is a question often asked by new model railroaders. The answer is just as broad as the question, and is determined by such important considerations as *era, size of layout, and curves and operation*. For the benefit of those who don't know what to look for, and considering the fact that the opening query is on the lips of many beginners, let's get to the fundamentals concerning the selection and purchase of motive power, regardless of whether it is your first loco or an addition to the roster.

Locomotives are divided into a number of categories, the basic ones being: switching, freight, and passenger service. Within these listings are more defined groupings which briefly break down as follows: light or heavy switching, light or heavy freight, and high-speed or heavy passenger service. The following charts are modifications of the Whyte Locomotive Classification System. These listings identify wheel arrangements in relation to loco types, and, also, they define the manner of services performed. They will also indicate the proper selection of motive power in direct relation to the size and manner of operation within your layout.

Needless to say, any locomotive that can negotiate sharp curves will be able to handle conventional and broad curves—but not vice versa! Diesels were not included in the above listings since practically all diesels can handle the minimum radius of sharp curves and up. As for articulateds, they were not listed for the opposite reason—namely, the fact that for smooth performance and realistic appearance they require a minimum radius of no less than 24 inches and up (despite the claims in certain advertisements). Pursuing the latter one step further, let me explain that while a few articulateds might be able to traverse a layout consisting of sharp curves, the overhang effect of the smoke box and pilot, as they snake 'round the bend, will be most toylike in appearance. The same thing will occur when rolling through turnouts, for the chances are that a small layout or one in which sharp curves are involved would of necessity feature No. 4 turnouts. This in itself is bound to create a constant source of derailments where even the smallest articulated is involved. In other words, even the smallest articulated needs no less than a conventional curve and a No. 6 turnout. For the benefit of those of you who are new to the

SMALL LAYOUTS—SHARP CURVES (18-inch Minimum Radius)

Wheel Arrangement	Type	Service
0-4-0	Four-Wheel Switcher	Light switching on curves
0-6-0	Six-Wheel Switcher	Freight and passenger switching
0-8-0	Eight-Wheel Switcher	Freight switching in classification yards
2-6-0	Mogul	Originally used for freight, later used mostly on branch lines
2-6-2	Prairie	Light freight
2-8-0	Consolidation	Freight and heavy switching
2-8-2	Mikado	Freight
4-4-0	American	Branch line, freight, and passenger
4-4-2	Atlantic	Fast passenger in early twentieth century
4-6-0	Ten-Wheeler	Passenger and freight
4-6-2	Pacific	Passenger

(Most freight and shorty passenger cars up to 60 scale feet are suitable)

MEDIUM LAYOUTS—CONVENTIONAL CURVES (24-inch Minimum Radius)

Wheel Arrangement	Type	Service
2-8-4	Berkshire	Freight
4-6-4	Hudson	High-speed passenger
4-8-2	Mountain	Fast freight and heavy passenger

(Some articulateds—almost all freight and passenger cars up to 70 scale feet)

LARGE LAYOUTS—BROAD CURVES (30-inch Minimum Radius)

Wheel Arrangement	Type	Service
4-8-4	Northern	Freight and passenger

(Most articulateds—all cars, including standard-length 80-scale-feet passenger cars)

ways of railroading lingo—at least in the model rail vein—let me explain that certain expressions (and definitions thereof) often and commonly used within the fraternity of model railroading may at times be at slight variance with definitions given in prototype railroading, or everyday English for that matter. Therefore, as we go from one chapter to another, various terms and expressions will become more familiar and meaningful to you. For the moment the following explanations in relation to curves and turnouts should help you get the point quickly:

A "turnout" is a device which permits the routing of a train from one track to another, such as passing from a mainline to a stub or siding. A "turnout" is also a fancy word for a switch. Under the heading "Terms Often Confused," in the NMRA *Yearbook,* both words are defined thusly:

Turnout: "the separation of one set of rails into two or more tracks."

Switch: "an electrical control device for closing or opening circuits, *or the movable portion of the turnout; the movable points and rails.*"

Next on the agenda are turnout numbers and what they mean. A No. 4 will branch off into a sharper curve, thus making it most suitable where small layouts are concerned. On the other hand, a No. 6 branches off more gradually and into a more gentle curve, thus requiring more space, but by the same token providing a smoother movement. Therefore, the larger the number, the more slowly the

0-6-0 Switcher: An authentic and exciting-looking model (United), this replica of CStPM&O No. 23 will more than dress up your pike and provide many hours of switching fun. Note detailing and sloped-back tender. RTR in unpainted brass, this loco can hustle through 15-inch minimum radius.

2-8-0 Consolidation (freight): Primarily designed for freight and heavy switching, this type was one of the most truly universal American locomotives ever built. It is also one of the most popular types used in model railroading. For the benefit of those who are sticklers for information, the designation "Consolidation" was originally derived from the engines operating on the "consolidated" roads which merged into the Lehigh Valley System. A fine replica of the Santa Fe Class 1950, it is loaded with prototypical details. This model (United) is well suited to small layouts and larger ones as well. RTR, unpainted.

4-4-2 Atlantic (passenger): This brass beauty is a must if you like fast passenger mainline runs. Modeled after a C&NW prototype, a crack locomotive which saw considerable service starting in the early twentieth century, this model (Tenshodo) will look great hauling a string of passenger cars and will be at home on layouts big or small. RTR unpainted.

In the following selection of photographs you will find five locomotives whose primary function involved switching freight and passenger cars. Two types of switchers are shown: (1) those equipped with a tender that contained the fuel and water supply, permitting longer work periods without refueling and water stops—these locos were real workhorses; (2) then there were the tenderless kind, which featured a water tank draped over the boiler (saddle tank) or alongside the boiler (side tank); these tank engines were designated by a "T" following their classification, such as, 0-4-0T, 0-6-0T, etc.; a large bin or bunker mounted behind the cab contained the fuel. The short length of these tank types made them especially useful around industrial and waterfront areas where the track radius was very sharp. They were also widely used for switching on curves and herding "dead" locomotives onto turntables and riding around with them (roundhouse goats). Needless to say, both types of switchers can be put to a variety of uses on a model railroad, regardless of its size, and they are popular with beginner and veteran alike. In addition, tank-type locomotives lend themselves to various customizings, superdetailing, conversions, etc.

0-6-0 Switcher USRA: During World War I, the United States Railway Administration undertook to provide railroads with the most efficient standard designs of more common types of locomotives. A great number of these 0-6-0 Switchers were built at that time and in the 1920s, seeing considerable service in the decades which followed. This RTR model (Aristo-Craft) has a smooth-working valve gear assembly and features a coal pusher in the tender.

0-8-0 Switcher USRA-Type: Exactingly scaled after a Rock Island Class S-57, the popularity of this workhorse can be attested to by the fact that some 1,400 locomotives of this and varied design were built and saw service on no less than fifty-two railroads. A larger boiler and increased tonnage permitted heavier switching chores than the 0-6-0. Working the larger yards, it was especially useful for hump yard operation, in addition to transfer service between yards. This brass beauty (a Tenshodo model) is RTR, unpainted, and includes a wealth of sharply defined details and "lost wax" castings. For heavy switching chores in steam's finest tradition this model is certainly at home on pikes big or small.

0-4-0T Side Tank Switcher: Inexpensive and small, but don't let the price or size deceive you. A real hustler for moving cars in and out of industrial areas, narrow passageways and scooting through sharp curves and turnouts. A few of these RTR jobs (Aristo-Craft) will certainly liven things up in the yards and on the spurs.

0-6-0T Saddle Tank Switcher: A smooth-working replica of a Union Pacific prototype which worked the yards at Omaha, this model (Revell) will appeal to those who like something a bit different, since it features a smoke-producing heat unit and a sound-producing "clackety-clacker." RTR.

0-6-0T Side Tank Switcher: Modeled after a Baldwin-type design, and bearing an Erie R.R. herald, this yard hog obviously carries more fuel and weight, and can therefore be assigned heavier service than its 0-4-0T brother. RTR (Aristo-Craft).

rails diverge, the longer the turnout, and the gentler its curve—all of which adds up to a more realistic movement through the turnout and onto the siding or wherever you are headed. It also goes without saying that the more gentle the curve of the turnout, the less likelihood of derailments. And since we have been talking about articulateds (whose wheel arrangements include two sets of hinged drivers), you can readily see that a smooth transition will go a long way toward keeping the locomotive on the track.

If I have started to sound like a pitchman trying to sell you a set of technical books, don't be alarmed. I'm not. I'm merely warning you not to make the costly mistake of buying a locomotive that your layout can't possibly handle safely or realistically. So if you entertain the thought of pulling long lines of cars behind an articulated behemoth on a small layout—forget it! You will not only be wasting your hard-earned cash, but you can get two or three smaller-sized locomotives for the cost of one long one and, more important, they will be able to perform more satisfactorily on your pike.

I might also point out that, within the foregoing listings, certain locomotives in the sharp-curve category will operate on as minimum a radius as 6, 8, 10, 12 inches, etc., up to the accepted sharp-curve standard of 18 inches. It all depends on the particular make and manufacture. For example, some 0-4-0 switchers, such as Varney's or Revell's, can scoot trouble-free through a narrow trackage radius such as 6 inches. The Tyco Shifter (0-4-0 and tender) will manage 10 inches. Tyco's General, a 4-4-0 American type, can get through a 12-inch minimum radius and, for that matter, many interurbans can handle the sharpest of curves. As I said, it depends on the make and manufacture—and while two Mikados may have the same wheel arrangements, the actual spacing and diameter of their drivers will have a lot to do with whether they can both handle the same minimum radius respectively. The same applies to those locomotives listed in the conventional curves category whereby, despite the fact that the listing shows the standard 24 inches, certain locomotives listed therein (depending on make) can negotiate a minimum radius of 19 or 20 inches also.

Make a thorough study of these various classifications, for they will inform you of the considerations that must be made in purchasing locomotives. Remember that for smooth performance and realistic operation you should select a locomotive that will be compatible with your trackwork.

To repeat, steam locomotives are divided into various classifications, referred to by type, wheel arrangement, and function, in addition to a few other characteristics. A Pacific, therefore, features two pairs of small wheels (4) up front (leading or pilot truck), followed by three pairs of larger wheels (6) called "Drivers," in turn followed by a single pair of small wheels (2) under the cab usually called "trailing trucks." Thus, the engine is known as a 4-6-2 or Pacific type. The early American type had a four-wheel pilot truck, two sets of coupled drivers, and no trailing truck, hence the designation 4-4-0. Considering the fact that both early and later forms of motive power contained thousands of moving parts (the last Union Pacific 4-12-2 had over 25,000 parts not counting the tender) the wheel-arrangement system for classifying locomotives big or small seems to underestimate their overall ability, plus sounding like a bit of garbled arithmetic to the beginner. However, this system of wheel arrangement and locomotive classification is one of the more important "basics" in railroading and was devised by Frederic M. Whyte, who served for many years as general mechanical engineer for the New York Central. Although the following listing might appear to be an oversimplification, an understanding of the Whyte system will not only acquaint you with type and wheel arrangements at a glance but will also add to your general knowledge.

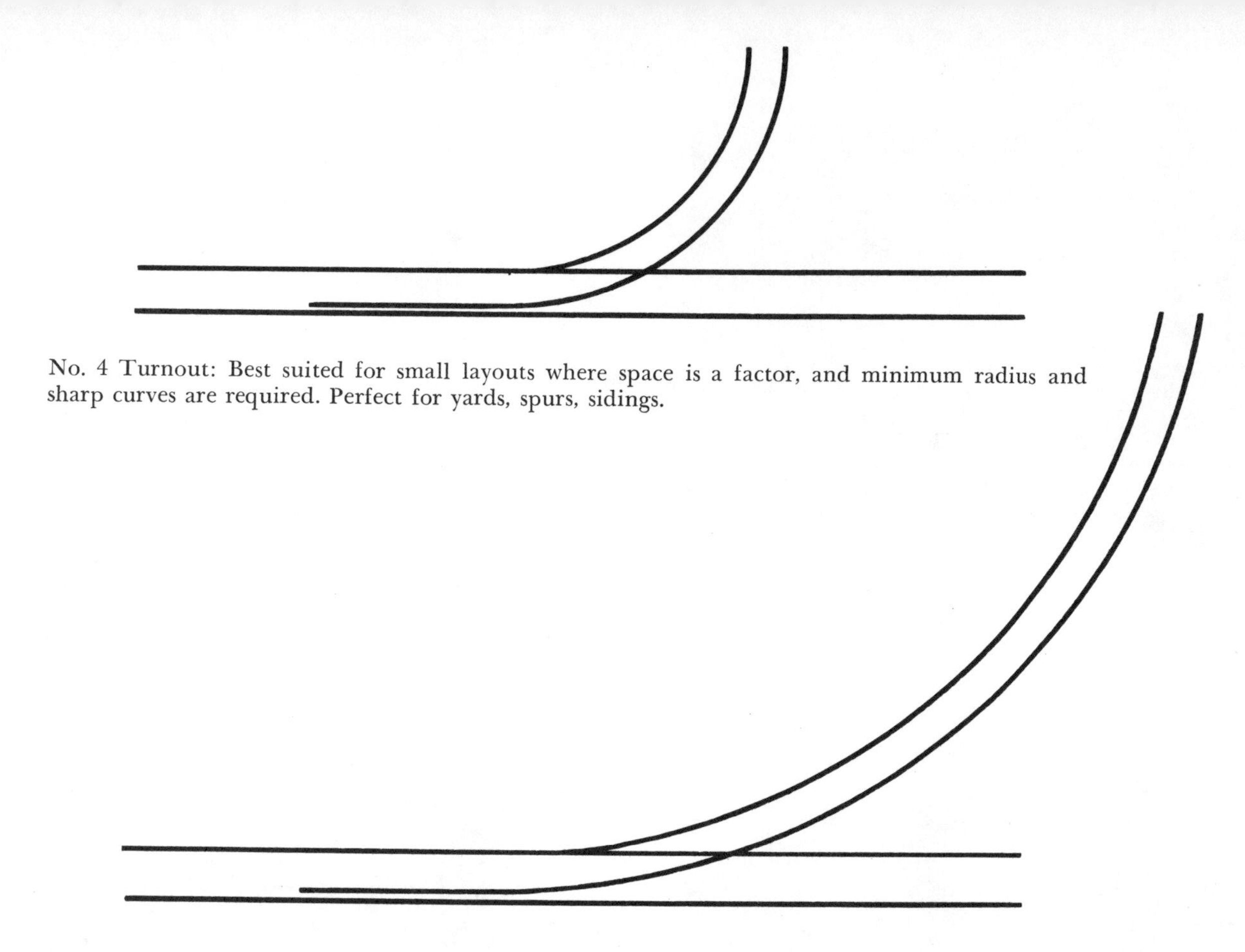

No. 4 Turnout: Best suited for small layouts where space is a factor, and minimum radius and sharp curves are required. Perfect for yards, spurs, sidings.

No. 6 Turnout: Use wherever possible. Gentler curve lessens possibility of derailments and adds to prototypical appearance.

(Note: Above diagrams are for purpose of illustration and are not drawn to scale or true proportion to each other)

2-6-6-2 Articulated: One of the smallest articulated locomotives ever built, this gleaming pulse-raiser is a well-scaled and detailed duplicate of its bigger brother, No. 38 of the Sierra R.R. A classic, the Baldwin prototype is one of the foremost examples of the early small articulated Mallet-type engines that were developed in Europe and re-designed to accomodate American railroading shortly after the turn of the century. Articulated locomotives, including the Mallets, consisted of two locomotives engines (two separate sets of cylinders and drivers) hinged together, but bearing a single boiler. A larger boiler could thus be carried around curves. The swivel action of the front drivers made fairly sharp curves more manageable. This double-jointed wheel arrangement was also devised to produce more power in a given locomotive, thereby saving the added cost and crews needed for double-heading smaller engines. Place this beautiful model (United) on a medium-sized layout, hauling a long line of ore cars, lumber or other heavy freight, and you will operate for hours without let-up. RTR, unpainted.

0-4-0T Saddle Tank: The popular "Dock-sider" can manage the sharpest curves and most extreme minimum radius, and is popular in prototype and model railroading. This RTR model (Revell) can also be fitted with working valve gear.

0-4-0 Switcher: This loco and coal-carrying slope-back tender is popularly known as "The Shifter" (Tyco) and can negotiate a 10-inch minimum radius. RTR.

4-4-0 American: This is the famous "General" of which much has been said. An all-purpose locomotive of the Civil War era, this RTR model (Tyco) can negotiate a minimum radius as small as 12 inches while pulling oldtime shorty freight and passenger cars.

4-6-2 Pacific: A well-detailed and accurately scaled rendition of a Southern Pacific Class P-5, this RTR model (M.B. Austin) is a fine example of the custom brass-crafted locomotives being imported from Japan. Note Vanderbilt tender, awnings on cab windows, safety tread running boards and other prototypical apparatus. Designed for passenger service, this locomotive, though operable on some smaller layouts, will look better on a medium-sized pike that affords more space for mainline runs.

4-4-0 American: The "Texas," an early American type has all the color and authentic trappings of a Civil War woodburner. Spoked pilot wheels, ornately mounted headlight, oldtimer smokestack and motor mounted in the tender, this RTR model (Aristo-Craft) is perfect for small, sharply curved layouts. Like the "General," this locomotive, though less famous, also has quite a history behind her.

Also to be considered is the ERA. For example, if your pike is wild, wooly, and representative of the early frontier days of American railroading, you certainly wouldn't be prototype operating a type of motive power such as a USRA 0-8-0 switcher, which was developed and put into use during World War I. Nor, for that matter, would you be authentic operating an oldtimer of the Civil War period such as "The General" in a layout depicting railroading of the 1930s. Therefore, the scene and background you set as atmosphere for your railroad operation is also a deciding factor in making your selection.

To elaborate a bit further, it is interesting to point out that in the majority of cases where small layouts are required, railroading, from the Civil War through the turn of the century, is very much in evidence. True, the greatest single motivation behind the recreation of this period is the romance, glamour, and history making events of the time. Aside from this, such a choice is quite practical considering the fact that motive power during this early period of steam locomotion employed simple wheel arrangements such as 4-4-0, 2-6-0, and 2-8-0, which enabled the respective locomotive types to safely negotiate circuitously laid track which featured many minimum-radius curves. Reduced and scaled down to HO, the same thing applies. Thus, even the smallest of layouts can easily handle an American type such as "The General," plus the Moguls and Light Consols of the 1880s, while hauling a mixed consist of freight and passenger cars. Hobbyists can also revel in the fact that there is a great abundance and variety of locomotives and rolling stock representative of this era, a period which not only gave rebirth to our nation, but also witnessed the exciting development of American railroad transportation.

For these reasons and many more you will find many aficionados of oldtimers, and for the benefit of those who seek more information concerning the "iron horses" of yesteryear, the photographs and topics of information that follow in later chapters will, I expect, more than whet your appetite regarding the fascinating history and glory of these diamond-stacked, wood-burning, smoke-belching puffer bellies. Suffice to say for the moment that where minimum space and small size of layouts are concerned, oldtimers are the best bet.

Along these same lines is the question of operation—main line or branch line, freight or passenger, lots of switching or continuous laps about the oval. There is no law that says you cannot use a Mikado (freight) to haul passenger equipment, for upon occasion various types of motive power were pressed into duty, performing services they were not otherwise intended for. Actually, during the later years of steam power "general purpose" locomotives were frequently used interchangeably for both passenger and freight service, the "GS" series of Southern Pacific 4-8-4 engines being an example. Chances are you could do the same without creating any consternation from visiting brass hats, but if you were to use a 4- or 6-wheel switcher to haul a line of passenger equipment, then you would really be stretching things. Nevertheless, you could get by with a "bobtail haul"—it's as short as it is long (no pun intended).

The important point to remember is that, among other things, you are model railroading for the sake of authenticity, at least within reason, and you alone are the final judge of how you combine your equipment and operation thereof into the overall scheme of things.

Thus far we have covered the various aspects which must be taken into consideration when selecting locomotives. On paper it sounds good, and if you combine the aforementioned facts with an equal measure of common sense, your purchases will pay off in the long run. Once you have established the type of locomotive which will best serve your railroad, the next thing is to determine whether to buy it in kit form or ready-to-run. Let's start with the latter, since the following chapter covers the kits in detail.

WHYTE SYMBOL	FRONT TO BACK	TYPE
0-4-0	OO	4-wheel switcher
0-6-0	OOO	6-wheel switcher
0-8-0	OOOO	8-wheel switcher
0-8-8-0	OOOO OOOO	Mallet (Articulated)
0-10-0	OOOOO	10-wheel switcher
2-6-0	oOOO	Mogul
2-6-2	oOOOo	Prarie
0-6-6-0	OOO OOO	Mallet (Compound)
2-6-6-2	oOOO OOOo	Mallet (Articulated)
2-6-6-4	oOOO OOOoo	Mallet (Articulated)
2-6-6-6	oOOO OOOooo	Allegheny
2-8-0	oOOOO	Consolidation
2-8-2	oOOOOo	Mikado
2-8-4	oOOOOoo	Berkshire
2-8-8-0	oOOOO OOOO	Mallet (Articulated)
2-8-8-2	oOOOO OOOOo	Mallet (Articulated)
2-8-8-4	oOOOO OOOOoo	Yellowstone
2-8-8-8-2	oOOOO OOOO OOOOo	Triple Articulated
2-10-0	oOOOOO	Decapod
2-10-2	oOOOOOo	Santa Fe
2-10-4	oOOOOOoo	Texas
2-10-10-2	oOOOOO OOOOOo	Mallet (Articulated)
4-4-0	ooOO	American
4-4-2	ooOOo	Atlantic
4-4-4	ooOOoo	Reading
4-4-4-4	ooOO OOoo	4-Cyl Non-Articulated
4-4-6-4	ooOO OOOoo	4-Cyl Non-Articulated
4-6-0	ooOOO	10-wheel
4-6-2	ooOOOo	Pacific
4-6-4	ooOOOoo	Hudson
4-6-4-4	ooOOO OOoo	4-Cyl Non-Articulated
4-6-6	ooOOOooo	Tank
4-6-6-4	ooOOO OOOoo	4-Cyl Articulated
4-8-0	ooOOOO	12-wheel
4-8-2	ooOOOOo	Mountain
4-8-4	ooOOOOoo	Northern
4-8-8-2	ooOOOO OOOOo	Mallet (Articulated)
4-8-8-4	ooOOOO OOOOoo	Mallet (Articulated)
4-10-0	ooOOOOO	Mastadon
4-10-2	ooOOOOOo	Southern Pacific
4-12-2	ooOOOOOOo	Union Pacific

2-6-0 "Mogul": An all-purpose locomotive, though primarily used for freight. This type, first built in 1850, looked so big in contrast with the 4-4-0, that people called it a "Mogul." Maturing in design by the mid–1860s, additional development and great railroading popularity were achieved before the turn of the century. The "Mogul," thereafter, was used mostly for light freight hauls on branch lines and continued in service up to the 1930s. Equally popular among model railroaders, this RTR model (Aristo-Craft) can be found on layouts from coast to coast and is available from a number of different manufacturers. Boasting details characteristic of oldtimers, yet similar in some respects to 2-6-0s built as late as the 1920s, this loco is definitely a good buy, particularly where small layouts and minimum radius are concerned.

"MA & PA" 2-8-0 Consolidation: Although 2-8-0 types were built many years before the turn of the century, this comparatively light consol built by Baldwin for small roads was one of four locomotives purchased between 1902 and 1912 for service on the Maryland & Pennsylvania R.R. Soon becoming a proven favorite, this 2-8-0 became affectionately known as a "MA & PA" and continued to operate for many years. An authentic brass replica of its prototype, this model (Akane) features a wealth of details, such as brake cylinders, cab awnings, marker lights, working headlights, etc. Tender details include a rerail, poling rod, back-up light, grab irons, etc. Primarily regarded as a freight engine, it was often used for switching and upon occasion was pressed into duty for passenger service. A universally used locomotive in both prototype and scale form. RTR, unpainted brass. This model is at home on an oldtime layout, short line, or even a more contemporary pike.

USRA 2-8-2 "Mikado": Miniaturized after a Baltimore & Ohio Q-4b, the prototype, a light "Mikado," was among the first and most successful 2-8-2 designs developed by the United States Railway Administration during World War I. Too numerous to mention are the many originals and modified copies which were delivered to more than fifty different railroads, including the B&O. As a point of information, it is interesting to note that the name "Mikado" was derived from the fact that in 1897 the first small 2-8-2s were built by Baldwin for Japan. Despite our war with them during the 1940s, the locomotives of this type continue to bear the designation "Mikado." The RTR, unpainted brass model (Akane) has a smooth-running valve gear, other well-detailed working apparatus and hauls the popular Vanderbilt tender. Also called a "Mike," this universally accepted freight loco features blind center drivers that help it negotiate many a sharp curve.

Denver & Rio Grande Western, Narrow-Gauge 2-8-2: For a change of pace, and for the benefit of narrow-gauge buffs, this RTR model (United), a fascinating brass replica of its prototype, is shown in all its glittering beauty. Bearing the class number K-27, and referred to as a "Mud Hen," this locomotive produced a breathtaking picture as it chugged its way through challenging canyons and over barren passes of the Old West. For mining and logging operations which would normally be inaccessible for standard railroad service, the narrow-gauge line not only offers a charming diminutive touch, but an authentic one as well. In scale modeling this size is known as "HOn3," which means HO narrow-gauge. The scale is the same; the difference lies in the gauge, or distance between the rails.

In the following photographs three models are shown in RTR form. This means that the model is completely assembled, fully operative, painted, lettered and with couplers attached at the time of purchase.

2-8-0 Consolidation: This light consol RTR model is very smooth in operation and includes a full working valve gear assembly. A ball-bearing motor is located in the tender, with power transmitted to the locomotive drivers by means of a drive shaft. This model (Aristo-Craft) will lend itself to additional detailing if the purchaser is so inclined.

4-4-2 Atlantic: Modeled after a Southern Pacific Class A5, and bearing a striking and accurate resemblance to its prototype, this RTR model (Aristo-Craft) can creep along at a snail's pace without stalling, or really highball it. The smooth action of the Walshaert valve gear will keep you watching for hours. The smoke box has been painted a silver gray, a practice employed by certain roads.

4-6-2 Pacific: In wide use among many model railroaders, this RTR model (Athearn) includes a working headlight, smooth-running valve gear and piping. Details easily visible are a good example of what can be obtained in materials other than brass. Note riveting on tender.

In the factory-assembled area of things, we find considerable equipment lumped under one heading—ready-to-run. Hereafter referred to as RTR, this type of model railroading item has become a popular byword among hobbyists from coast to coast. For example, an RTR loco is exactly what the name implies—a locomotive that is completely assembled, painted, lettered, and with couplers attached. You have but to remove it from the carton, wrappings, etc., place it on the rails, and give her the juice. All that remains is reasonable care and occasional maintenance from then on. (Some RTR locos come bone dry and seriously in need of lubrication. Almost all locos need a break-in period if smooth performance is to be obtained—see Chapter V.) Popular as the expression "RTR" has become, it is also rather broadly used to include not only factory-assembled, mass-produced equipment, but custom-built, hand-crafted, and specialized superdetailed locomotives both of domestic and foreign origin. In fact, in recent years many a piece of locomotive equipment has been given the designation "RTR" solely on the basis of its being operable at the time of sale—despite the fact that it may not be painted and will need breaking in. Therefore, when you consider the fact that motive power ranging in price from $7.95 to $150, and covered by the all-embracing "RTR" connotation can mean anything from a molded plastic shell to a gleaming brass beauty, then you should also consider that there is certainly more to it than meets the eye. Thus, it is quite unfair to compare an inexpensive locomotive of sometimes doubtful origin with that of a well-defined and well-detailed miniature of a prototype; that is to say, unfair to the latter when both locos are classified under the same "RTR" heading.

Needless to say, within the "RTR" category you will find some equipment that is junk and some that is par excellence, and in the following we will try to guide you in its determination. Generally speaking, most RTR locomotives come pre-painted—at least those which are produced in the United States. On the other hand, much of the equipment being imported from abroad, notably from Japan, is offered completely rigged out and ready to roll—but in unpainted brass form. The modeler is therefore required to finish things himself (see Chapter VI) . This, however, is no longer the problem it used to be, as will be shown and discussed later.

At this point a brief mention of couplers seems appropriate. And in most cases you will find that the average RTR locomotive is already equipped with couplers that are commonly referred to as "NMRA couplers." This style coupler is also referred to as "horn type" or "X2F." Actually, the NMRA discourages the use of the term "NMRA" in connection with these couplers in order to avoid any implication of endorsement or official sanction, despite the fact that the design was developed by an NMRA committee. Its simplicity, however, has resulted in the widespread use of "NMRA" by manufacturers of HO ready-to-run equipment. The more discriminating rail buffs use Kadee Magne-Matic couplers, which by virtue of more prototypical appearance and smoother operation have become widespread in their use. In view of the popularity of the Kadee couplers, quite a few manufacturers are now equipping their locomotives in that manner. You will find this more prevalent among the medium- and higher-priced equipment. At the same time, you will find some locomotives that are devoid of couplers, in which the final choice is left to the modeler.

So don't be to alarmed if the locomotive you purchase does not include couplers—or, for that matter, includes couplers that are not compatible with your other equipment. Change-overs and re-installation of a coupler of your own choice is a minor chore, as described later.

Much of the equipment being imported from Japan is referred to as "custom built," and justifiably so, for it it handcrafted in

Known for its brute strength and smooth pulling power as a freight, passenger and dual service locomotive, the Northern type had many virtues. One in particular was its ability to maintain steady fast speeds while hauling long heavy loads. First built by the American Locomotive Company (Alco) in 1926, this locomotive type was quickly accepted by many major roads and saw service well into the 1950s. A popular locomotive among model rails, the Northern is best suited to layouts large enough to permit the use of broad sweeping curves and lengths of trackwork that enable the use of a twenty-or-more-car payload. While some models featuring the 4-8-4 wheel arrangement can negotiate the conventional curve radius of approximately 24 inches, the fact remains that, from the standpoint of appearance and prototypical operation, this type of locomotive will look its best rolling through broader curves and pulling a long line of cars—all of which a larger-sized layout will allow.

CB&Q "0-5" 4-8-4 Northern: If you are a stickler for realism, this polished brass, eye-catching rendition of a Chicago, Burlington & Quincy prototype will certainly quicken your pulse beat. Typical of a series of limited production models called "Crown" types, you can easily see why this Japanese import has that "custom" look. This model (United) is RTR, unpainted.

gleaming brass and fully ornamented with all the necessary detailing and styling to conform to true prototypical design. By and large, these particular track-tested items require no additions in the way of detailing or improvement, since they have been exactingly produced (some in limited quantity) to the ultimate degree in scale miniaturization and workmanship, certainly on a much higher level than mass production and factory assembly will allow. In our own area of native manufacture, we also find customized equipment that has reached the highest plateau in workmanship and scale reproduction. Custom-built, hand-assembled, mass-produced, or what have you—each offers a constructive contribution to the field, the merits of which are evenly divided.

First off, look for the following prior to making your purchase: be sure that the locomotive you have in mind completely conforms to NMRA standards. There is no particular problem to speak of where U.S.-made equipment is concerned. However, some of the lesser-quality equipment produced here and abroad will sometimes fall short of the tolerances required for smooth and trouble-free operation. For example, look at the wheels and drivers. If the flanges are too deep or do not conform to NMRA specifications, they will not roll through the flangeways or turnouts smoothly, resulting in derailments, stalling, shorts, and other miseries. These problems will also crop up if the wheels and drivers are out of gauge (see Chapter V for gauge and flange check). If the wheels and drivers are not properly insulated, more troubles will occur. From the standpoint of common practice, you will find that the drivers on the right side of your

4-8-4 "Great Northern": Another great refinement of steam power was the "Great Northern," a popular favorite among rail buffs. Baldwin first delivered these Class S-1 oil burners in 1929. This model (Tenshodo) is about as RTR as it will ever be. Custom built, painted, lettered and bearing the GN herald, this fine scale counterpart has all the original detailing and authentic appearance of its prototype. In actual operation this model is real smooth and can easily handle a long string of cars.

4-4-2 "Hiawatha": Steam lovers and diesel fans take note—this striking locomotive enables you to eat your cake and have it. This streamlined, shrouded Atlantic, built by Alco in 1935, was the first of a line of Class A "Hiawathas" which were to highball for the Milwaukee R.R. between Chicago and the Twin Cities. A fast passenger locomotive, she easily hauled 500 tons while taking 1- and 2-degree turns at 80 to 90 miles per hour. This model (Aristo-Craft) is RTR, and finished in the true color and trappings of the prototype. It can handle twenty cars or more without the slightest strain.

locomotive are not insulated, whereas the drivers on the left side are insulated—this in turn prevents short circuits occurring through the axles. The opposite can be said of the tender. Insulated truck wheels are on the right side, non-insulated on the left. In locomotive drivers you will generally find the insulation between the outer circumference of the wheel center and the tire. Wheels, on the other hand, are usually insulated at the axles, and, as an aid for easier identification, most manufacturers leave some form of mark or color at the insulated areas.

Mechanical coupling between tender and locomotive is accomplished through the aid of an insulated drawbar, and electrical connection is made by a wire running from the motor to the frame of the tender. For the sake of appearance, however, quite often a "wireless" metal drawbar is employed; in this case, the drawbar itself permits the flow of electricity between tender and motor to complete the circuit, thus eliminating the need for a conspicuous-looking connecting wire. At the same time, the wireless drawbar serves to couple the units together. In either event, proper insulation is necessary.

Another thing to consider when purchasing a locomotive is the amount of detailing on or about the superstructure, boiler, cab, tender, etc. The clarity of details, such as sand domes, steam fittings, water lines, piping, whistles, bells, water pumps, brake shoes, and other functional apparatus will add much to the realistic appearance, and should be weighed carefully when you are viewing a locomotive you would like to buy. In some cases you will find these parts to be of molded design and an integral part of the locomotive, although, depending on the resourcefulness of the manufacturer, the overall appearance is sometimes three-dimensional. On the other, hand locomotives whose boilers and superstructures boast accessories which have been separately attached are more desirable not only from the standpoint of duplicating the prototype, but also where damage and subsequent repairs are concerned; in short, a particular damaged part can be more easily removed for repair or replacement. It becomes a matter of whether you prefer details that are separate parts and have been individually attached or whether you will settle for those which are part of the overall mold—and in some cases look that way.

Pursuing things one step further, and with an eye to the future, do you want a locomotive loaded with gingerbread or do you want to do some or all of the detailing yourself? Do you want a working headlight or will you settle for a sparkling jewel? Do you want a simple slide gear or do you prefer the flashing action and monkey motion of valve gears? Will the locomotive you have in mind lend itself to "oldtimer-izing"—if you decide to—or modernizing, whichever the case?

And what about authenticity? Do you want your model to be fashioned after the prototype of a particular railroad such as Pennsylvania, Boston and Maine, Southern Pacific, New York Central, etc., and to be as exact as possible? If so, you are following a solid direction, for by embracing the operations and motive power of one of the bigger railroads you will benefit in many ways. For example, Santa Fe, one of the largest and most colorful railroads in the country, has been duplicated in miniature by a number of model train manufacturers. This has resulted in a wide variety and availability of Santa Fe locomotive types. At the same time, an equal variety of assorted parts and details are also available. This is a boon to the modeler when it comes to repair, replacement of parts, and, last but not least, superdetailing.

To familiarize yourself with the various characteristics of size, shape, and design, a fair amount of research is in order—the public libraries are a good source of information. Magazines such as *Model Railroader* and *Railroad Model Craftsman* are excellent points of reference and your direct link to what is going on in the model railroading world. In addition, the *Steam Locomotives Cyclopedia,* edited by Linn Wescott, offers a wealth of information and photographs of the more popular locomotives from the simplest wheel arrangements up to the heavier tonnage articulateds. You can also write to the railroads (address your query to the Public Relations Department) asking for photographs. They will reply as per your request. Try to be specific, however, when writing them.

A discriminating model railroader studies every photograph, drawing, and description he can lay his hands on of the prototype he has in mind. When his mind is made up, he purchases the particular model which in his estimation most closely resembles the real thing. For this reason hobby manufacturers, with an eye toward increasing the demand and sales of their line of equipment, have over the years been more exact in the making of their end product—namely miniature locomotives that really look like their prototypes. Some manufacturers work from blueprints (drawn to scale) of particular prototypes. This results in a pretty accurate scale rendition. On the other hand, some companies combine the best and most popular ingredients of various locomotives. In cases such as this, the model has no actual prototype, but is nonetheless legitimate-looking in appearance. By the same token, you will upon occasion come across locomotives of somewhat doubtful origin—doubtful not only where the general appearance is concerned, but also questionable from the standpoint of wheel arrangement, over- or undersized scale, in-

4-6-6-4 Articulated UP "Challenger": If a picture is worth ten thousand words, then this exquisitely detailed model of a Union Pacific "Challenger" should certainly do the trick. A limited production model (Tenshodo), this exciting replica is the ultimate in custom craftmanship. As Japanese imports go, this one is in a class by itself. The detailing is almost unbelievable. RTR, unpainted brass.

0-4-0 Baltimore & Ohio "Docksider": Referred to as "Little Joe," this popular tank switcher is reportedly the most widely sold and copied locomotive in HO. Produced by many manufacturers this particular RTR model (Sakura) is all metal and features many details, including a full working Walshaerts valve gear. A perfect loco for the beginner, it is also a favorite with the veteran. It is natural for the smallest of pikes and at home on any size layout representing railroading from early 1900 to the present. Used extensively for all light switching chores, the 0-4-0 also herded larger locomotives onto turntables. Many hours of exciting pleasure can be obtaining using an 0-4-0 to spot cars on spurs and sidings, making up trains in yards and otherwise performing innumerable tasks in the same tradition as its prototype.

0-6-0 Southern Pacific: Sophistication in detailing and authenticity is more than evident in this scale model of an SP Class S-12 switcher. An exciting model (M.B. Austin) to operate, this loco will add considerable class to your layout. It includes a modified version of the Vanderbilt tender, which enabled the engineer and fireman to get a clearer view to the rear—an unusual tender rarely found on six-wheel switchers. Detailing includes operating headlight, boiler steps, washout plugs and a wireless drawbar pick-up. A flashy valve gear adds to operating pleasure. RTR, unpainted brass, it can easily handle minimum radius curves.

2-6-6-2 "Mallet" Articulated Compound Freight Locomotive: This polished brass jewel presents a startling contrast to its toy predecessors of one hundred years ago, pointing up the high quality available in model railroading today. This model (Akane) is at its best on medium- to large-sized layouts, and comes equipped with a tender (not shown). RTR, unpainted.

4-6-4 "Hudson": For the discriminating brass hat this model (Tenshodo) of a Sante Fe "Hudson" Class 3460 is a delight to behold. A high-speed passenger locomotive with a top of 90 miles per hour, this model is better suited to medium- and large-sized layouts which have sufficient room for long mainline runs, where you can "let her out." RTR.

4-8-4 Northern: The Santa Fe Northern Class 3776 built in 1941 by Baldwin represented the most modern developments in steam at that time. Designed for speed and power, they performed admirably on the system's toughest and steepest mainline grades. Not al miniatures can boast a wealth of exterior detail such as the pantograph stack-lifter with actuating cylinde, Worthington feed-water system, injector system, power reverse, etc. The Buckeye trucks on the tender are fully sprung. This model (United) is an exciting powerhouse and should be given the benefit of a reasonable space to operate in. RTR, unpainted.

GEARED LOCOMOTIVES

Few locomotives have ever captured the fancy of the populace as did the Shay, Heisler and Climax types. The application and use of geared locomotives within the framework of model railroading will permit one's imagination to soar to great heights, opening new vistas for realistic operation against a background embracing scenic effects galore. The Shay, first introduced in the 1890s, was invented by Ephriam Shay, whose basic design consisted of a flat car with a donkey engine hung over the side and geared to the wheels. Following this principle, Shay locomotives, built by Lima, became the most popular form of motive power for drone operations in logging industries and mining, and quite often were used on scenic railways. Since the Shay could easily negotiate rough track and sharp curves, and climb steep grades it became almost a prerequisite for certain forms of operation, particularly in mountainous areas where circuitous routes were par for the course. All three geared locomotive types were essentially the same where service and performance were concerned. The only major difference worth noting was in the actual placement and location of the cylinders, rods and other working apparatus that employed the geared locomotive principle. At a quick glance, however, they were quite similar to the eye. A fascinating bit of engineering, these locomotives remained in use even after the diesel came of age. If logging camps, mountainous terrain, and sharp and winding grades are your cup of tea, then any one of these geared locomotive types will provide you with a form of operating and viewing pleasure which almost defies description.

The Heisler: One of the most highly detailed models ever offered the scale enthusiast, this geared locomotive features over 400 parts. All movements of this powerful puller are clearly visible and it is a thrill to watch the cranks and valves in motion. Different from the Shay in one respect, the Heisler was powered by a V-type engine. If you enjoy switching around the yards of industrial plants, hauling logs through the woods over rough spur track and up steep switchbacks, then the Heisler (United) will make a welcome addition to your other areas of operation. RTR unpainted brass.

The Shay: One of the most striking and detailed models ever offered the model rail fan is this brass replica of the prototype. Used extensively in the open pit mines of Utah, it also achieved broad use in railroading areas from coast to coast where a bit of the impossible was required. Featuring a three-cylinder vertical engine with a shaft geared to its four-wheel trucks, this unusual locomotive really set up a chatter in operation. In fact the Shays, while sounding like they were going a mile a minute, actually moved at little more than a walking speed. This was due to the unique gear reduction principle they employed, the gearing being 4:1 to 6:1. When it came to "creeping" the Shay couldn't be beat. This model (United) in RTR, unpainted form, a Class B-2, is cause enough to stimulate any modeler to build his model railroad solely around the operating possibilities of a Shay locomotive—a form of motive power that will certainly enlarge one's horizons and points of view.

The Climax: Another stunning example of a geared locomotive in miniature form which embraces all the unique styling and details of the prototype, the Climax was a special type of geared locomotive designed to meet certain requirements beyond the ability of the conventional side-rod type. Primarily used in logging from one end of the nation to the other, this locomotive was also employed in all manner of industrial service. Drives through geared mid-shafts; operates exactly as on the original. This model (United) in RTR, unpainted brass form is certainly a fitting climax to all that can be desired in unusual motive power.

accuracies in selection and positioning of details, and other considerations which definitely detract from rather than enhance the overall situation. To wit, I can only repeat, *Caveat Emptor!* Aside from your own knowledge and experience, one way of helping insure the wisdom and quality of your purchase is by patronizing a bona fide hobby or model train store, a place where the people on the selling end of things are more than conversant with the hobby itself and can serve you accordingly.

These are just some of the factors to be considered, along with that of layout size, wheel arrangement, radius, era, and type of service performed. So walk—do not run—to your nearest hobby shop. And while on the way, bear in mind what has been explained thus far. Model railroading is as much an affair of the heart as it is of the mind, and when you hold that Atlantic, Pacific, or whatever loco in your hand for the first time and your heart skips a beat—that's the loco for you.

However, affairs of the heart can sometimes be costly, and that first tug of your heartstrings might later prove to be puppy love and knock the pins out from under your pursestrings. Consider the patience and sophistication with which a veteran model railroader selects and purchases a new locomotive. Among other things, he will whip out his NMRA gage and waste no time checking the flange depth of drivers, wheels, and other tolerances that are important to smooth performance. And since most hobby shops usually have a small layout or section of track for demonstration and bench testing, the wise purchaser will use these services before he takes his purchase home. In the case of a mail-order purchase, you can't test the item before you buy it. However, if you do business with a reliable firm, you need have no fear in the event your locomotive is defective or inoperable.

While at first there may appear to be a lot of effort and thinking concerned with the mere purchase of a locomotive, bear in mind that you are laying the groundwork for future operation and enjoyment. And the more understanding and know-how you develop as a rail buff, the more you will enjoy it as you put things into actual practice. In the chapters which follow the comments and illustrations should more than answer the question, "Which locomotive should I buy?" And within these and accompanying pages you will see a selection of locomotive equipment that will not only make your heart beat faster, but will stimulate your thinking along the lines we have been discussing. One thing is certain—before we reach the end of the line you will know exactly what types of motive power will best serve your needs and those of your model railroad.

III

Primer for Kit Assemblers

The art of modeling railroads can truthfully be thought of as a lifetime avocation—at least from that moment when an enthusiast gets caught up in the complete fascination of the hobby. Considering the wide range of ready-to-run locomotive equipment, and its availability, coupled with the fact that the average model rail has one notion in mind—"to get operating as quickly as possible"—it is easy to see why "already assembled motive power" has become so widespread in its use. The fact that in more recent years the availability of locomotives of varied and detailed description has made it possible for the modeler to do nothing more than place a loco on the rails and give her some juice has been instrumental in furthering this ready-to-run trend. Nor can it be denied that a good portion of this pre-assembled equipment is absolutely breathtaking to behold. However, if during the lifetime of your hobby you have never attempted to build a locomotive from a kit, then you are certainly missing a good bet. Not only do you lose out on the pride of seeing your own hand-assembled Atlantic or Pacific hauling a string of cars with top performance but you also miss out on the knowledge and experience gained from such endeavors. This knowledge will go a long way toward acquainting you with not only the working parts of locomotive equipment, but the trouble spots that are likely to develop as well. It will help you understand many characteristics of the locomotive you have just assembled and also those of your other equipment, RTR notwithstanding.

It has been the opinion of this writer that quite often the beginner knows little about the working parts of his locomotives, whether his roster includes one engine or several. Among other things, the two basic reasons for building a locomotive from kit form are: (1) the pride of doing it yourself; and (2) the knowledge gained. The latter is without doubt the most important factor to be considered. To repeat, notwithstanding economy, pride of accomplishment, changes that can be effected as you go along, and numerous other advantages, the greatest benefit that accrues is the knowledge and actual experience gained. This comes in handy when valve gears bind up, motors stall, wheels operate in out-of-quarter fashion, and other assorted pitfalls develop which spell troublesome operation. This same information, gleaned through study and the building of at least one kit, simple or

This diagram, taken from a page of the instructions which accompany a Varney ten-wheeler kit, is a typical example of the wealth of information you will absorb during the course of assembly. This exploded overall view not only shows you at a glance the manner in which the locomotive is put together, but also lists the full nomenclature and part numbers of the items you will be working with. The numbered descriptions make it easy to follow the instructions and to order new or additional parts in the event of loss or damage. Before you have completed assembling the locomotive, you will not only be more familiar with the names of the parts involved, but the functions they perform as well. An education in themselves, the instruction sheets will become invaluable at some later date when repairs, maintenance and other reasons for disassembly become necessary. When your project is complete, be sure to file away the instruction sheets for future reference.

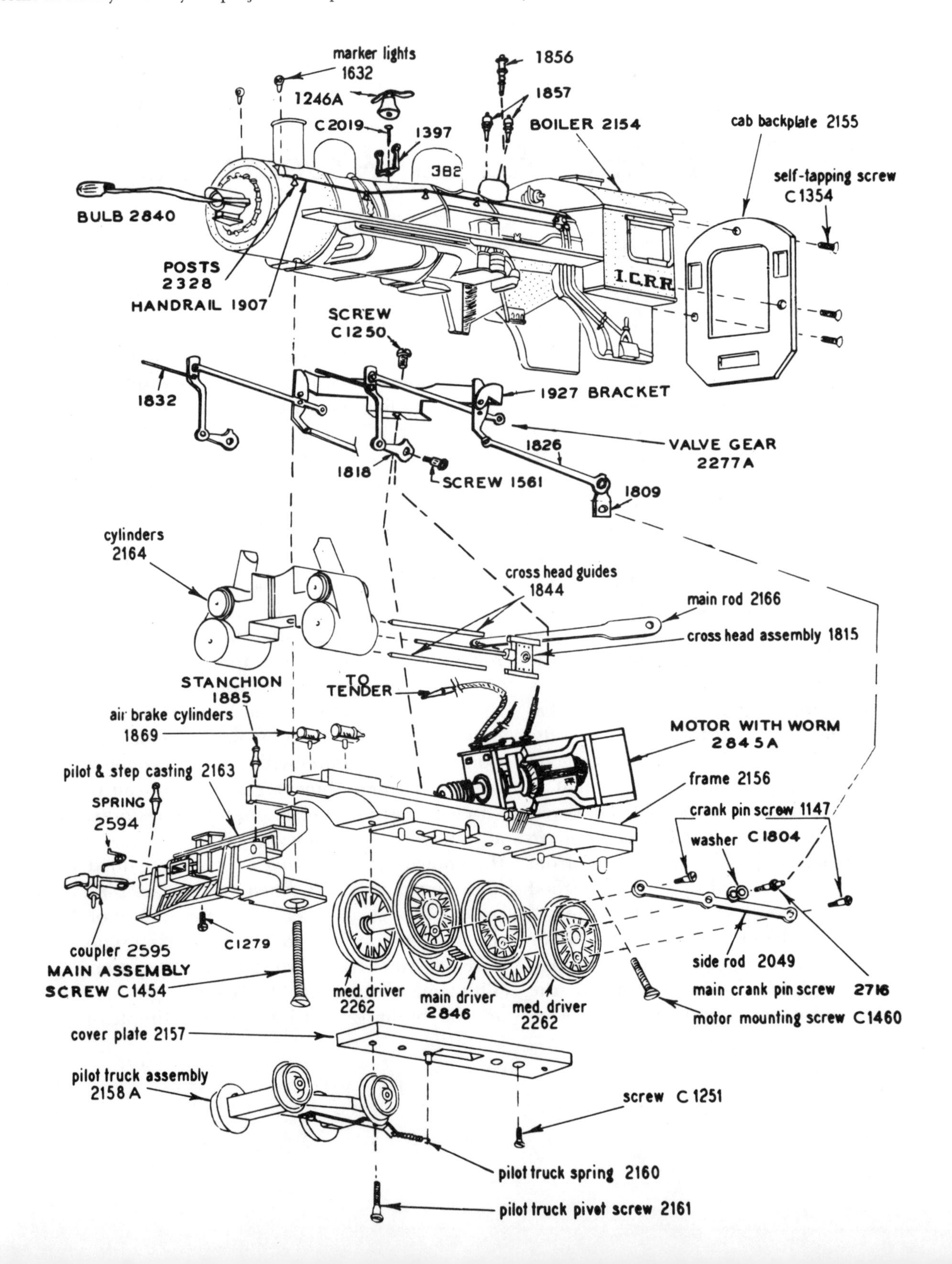

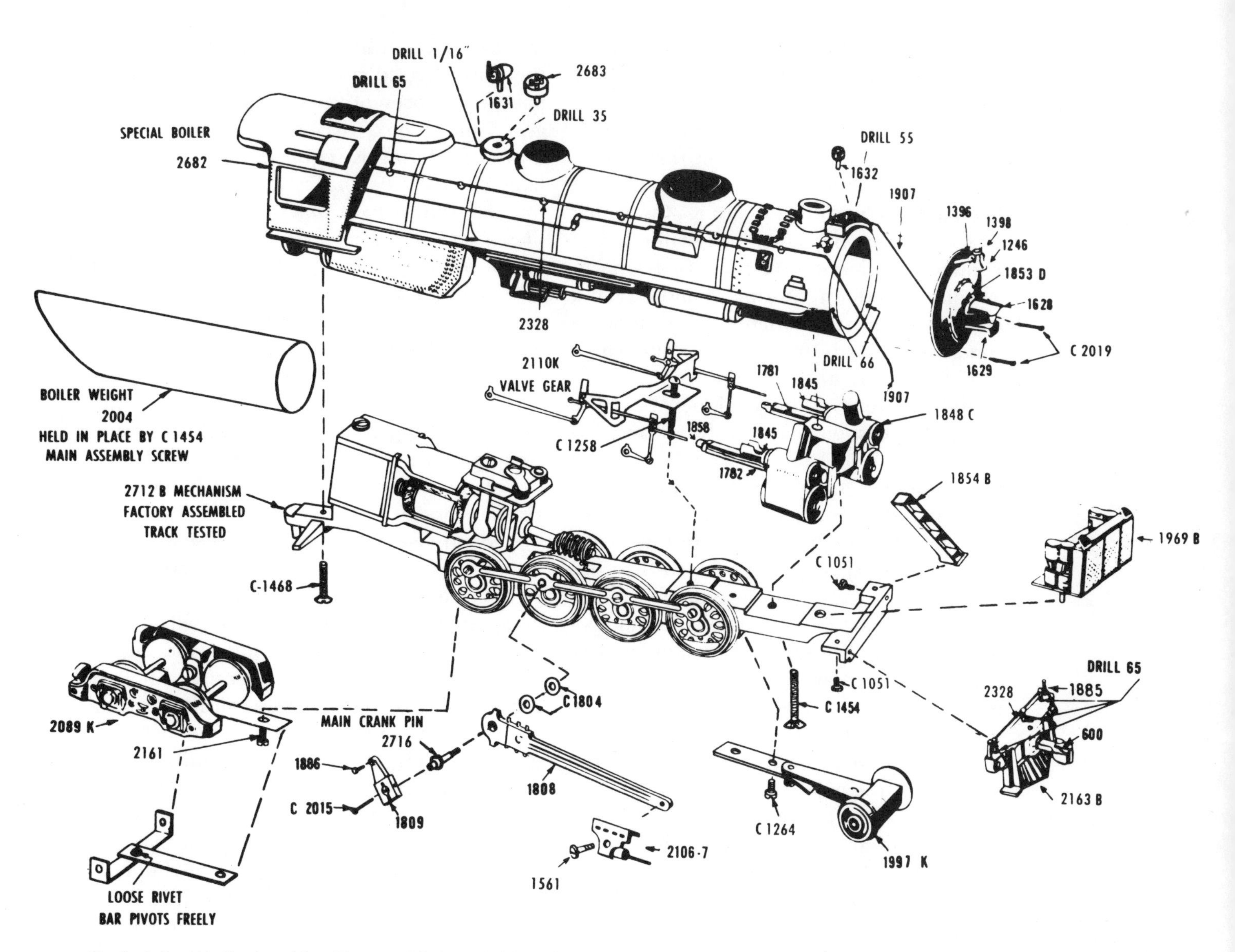

Exploded overall view of a Varney 2-8-4 Berkshire kit is clear and to the point. Most instruction sheets start with an overall view such as this so that the kit builder can immediately familiarize himself with the general scheme of assembly with respect to the parts that are to be employed during the building up of the particular locomotive. Before undertaking a project of this scope, it would be best to tackle one of the more simple "screwdriver" assemblies. For the advanced modeler and builder, this 2-8-4 Berkshire is a kit to really sink your tools into.

Enlarged and detailed views of cylinder and valve gear assembly from the instruction sheets of the Berkshire kit. A fair amount of soldering and riveting is needed, as indicated.

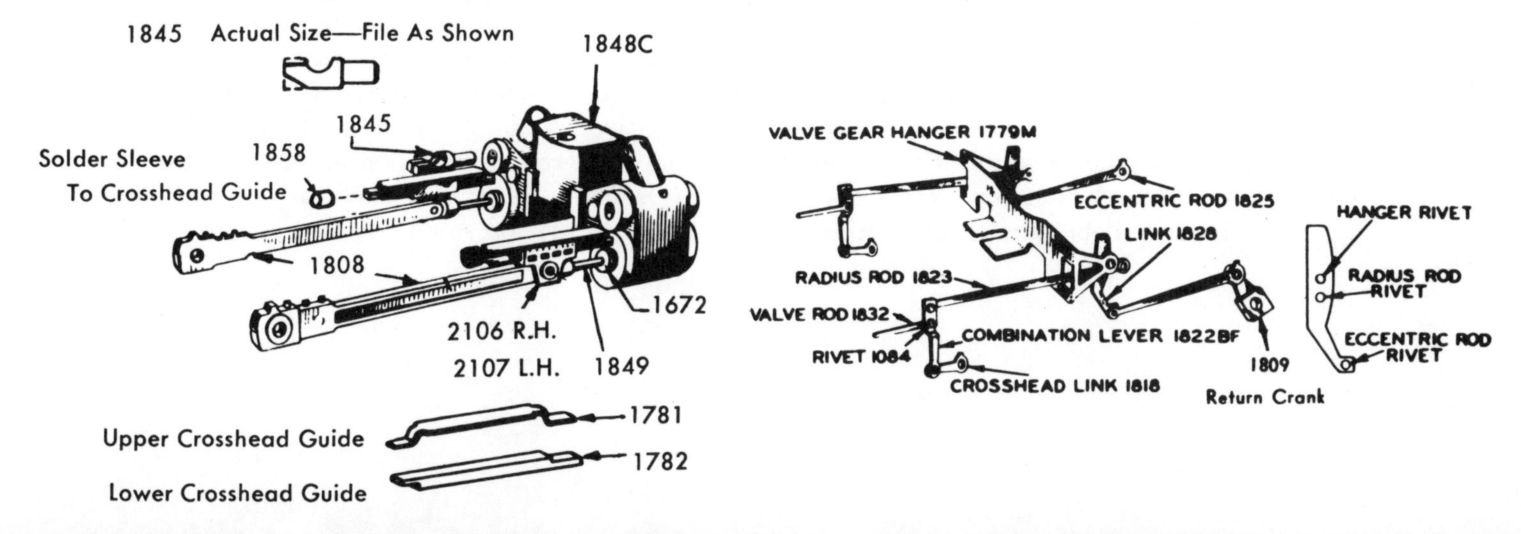

otherwise, will aid you in quickly finding the trouble spot and restoring things to working order.

Nevertheless, many modelers shy away from kit assembly for the same reason they shrink from soldering, wiring, scenic effects, and other facets of model railroading—for which they feel they are not suited or qualified. And yet, building a locomotive from kit form can be a simple matter, requiring no more than a few tools, time, and patience. In fact, some locomotive kits require less time and effort to complete than the assembling of certain cars and structures. Many beginners have the mistaken impression that a factory-assembled locomotive will look better, run better, and hold up longer than the same locomotive done on a do-it-yourself basis. This is not necessarily the case by any means, for I have seen some pretty sloppy workmanship and poor performance on factory-assembled equipment. In the case of a particular locomotive that is available from the same manufacturer in either form, bear in mind that the only basic difference between RTR and kit assembly is the fact that someone else has put it together for you; another difference is the cost, the kit costing less. In the latter case, the savings can be poured right back into the locomotive in the form of parts for superdetailing and the like. More often than not, this will result in a more authentic-looking locomotive than the RTR counterpart.

Today kits come in a wide variety of wrappings and headings suitable for the serious modeler and the rankest beginner. They range from the superdetailed building assemblies to the "quickie" kits, both of which will more than satisfy one's particular needs, time, and capabilities. Let's take a look at some of them.

Starting with the model rail who likes to do all the assembly himself, we have the giant-sized jigsaw puzzle type of kit. This requires more than a fair amount of skill and experience to complete the project from start to finish, and definitely is not recommended for the novice. This type of kit consists of all the basic ingredients required to fit out a particular locomotive—superstructure, valve gear, smoke box, drivers, cab, etc. A good deal of soldering is required plus removal of flash. *"Flash," by the way, is the term used for the thin ridges and webs of metal or plastic which remain between the two halves of the forming die or mold, characteristic of the "die casting" process. In "lost wax casting" the parts are attached to "sprues," which are also easily removed. Care must, of course, be taken to be sure that adjacent areas are not nicked or marred.* Once assembled, the addition or affixing of numerous detailing parts completes the project, and, aside from breaking in and painting, it will be ready for many years of operation, depending, of course, on the adeptness of the builder in assembly and fit. Some of these kits are also referred to as "scratch builder assemblies," the difference being that instructions are minimal and/or not as specific on a step-by-step basis. Superstructures and boilers often consist of hollow tubing with only the barest outline design. And it is not uncommon for the modeler, upon occasion, to have to do additional research concerning design and placement of prototypical details. He might also have to fabricate certain parts which are not included in the kit for reasons of economy or simply to stimulate the builder and leave a little to his imagination and "enginuity." While these kits are complicated and time-consuming, they are a challenge and an education in themselves.

An extreme contrast to these kits are the "screwdriver assemblies," so designated because they require no tools other than a screwdriver. No drilling, tapping, soldering, or riveting is required, having already been taken care of at the factory. In addition to this, the valve gear is pre-assembled. Some of these kits come pre-painted also. Assembly is relatively simple, for in most cases all flash has been removed; if not, an X-acto knife or reasonable facsimile, such as a penknife, razor blade, or small file, will do the trick

A preview of things to come and techniques to be applied is apparent in this final view of the Berkshire, shown completely built up and raring to go. Painted a dull flat black, the piping and other details now take on a new prominence. The appearance of this smooth-running powerful locomotive is further enhanced by the addition of a Vanderbilt tender. Replacing the X2F couplers with Kadee Magne-Matics would also be a good step in the direction of prototype realims.

Another fine kit for the beginner and advanced modeler is this 2-8-0 Heavy Consol, also available from Varney Scale Models. In the same category as the Berkshire kit, the assembly of this locomotive requires a bit of soldering, drilling, shaping of wire, riveting of valve gear and a few other chores to keep you busy for several evenings—but the final results are well worth the effort.

Available from Varney Scale Models, this locomotive features considerable details and piping, some of which are an integral part of the superstructure in three dimensional form. Shown here in assembled form, all that remains is the addition of handrails, breaking in and painting. Kit includes a long-distance coal tender.

Overall view taken from the "Old Lady" instruction sheet clearly indicates the simplicity of assembly. Nothing hit or miss about building up this locomotive. Just follow the instructions.

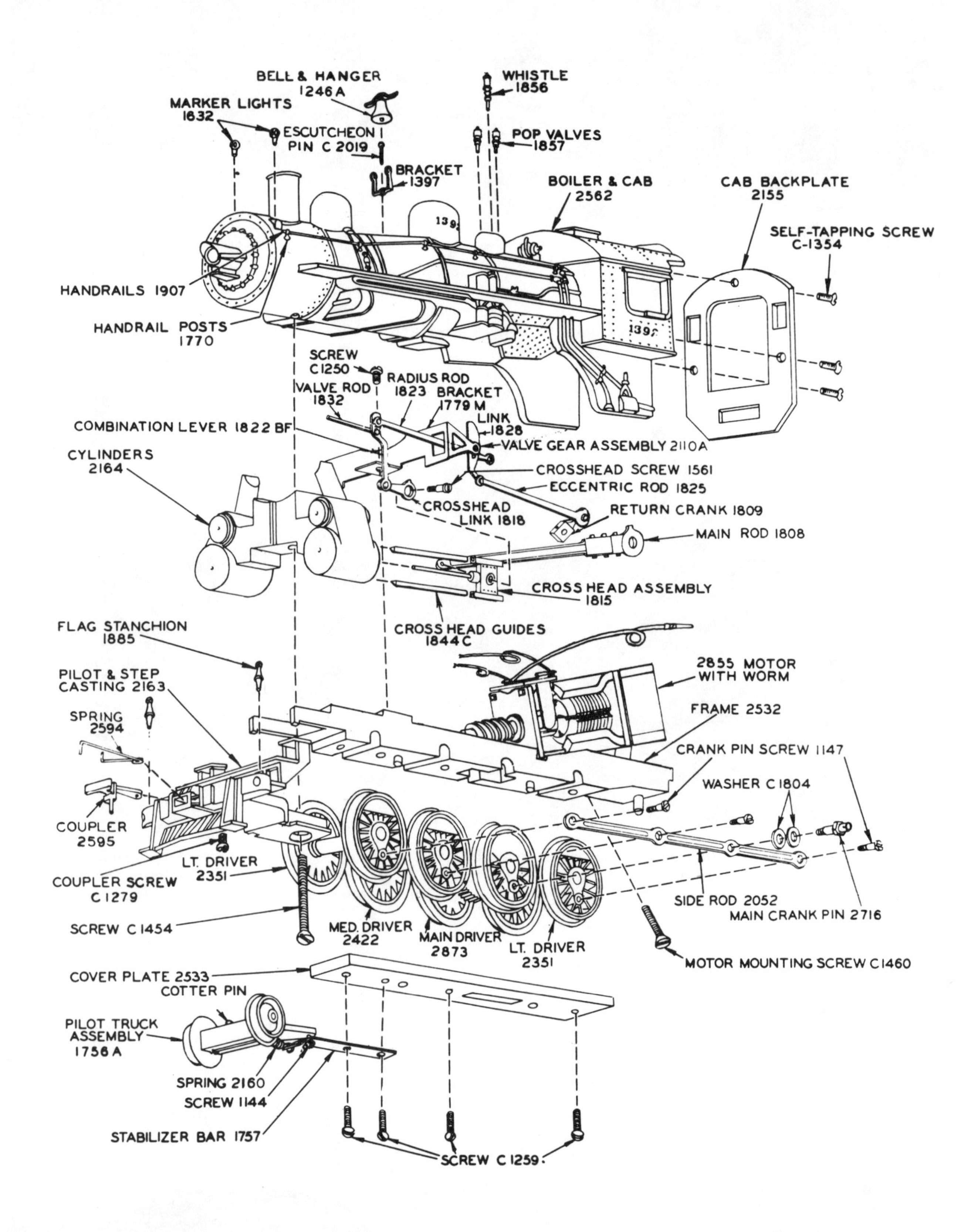

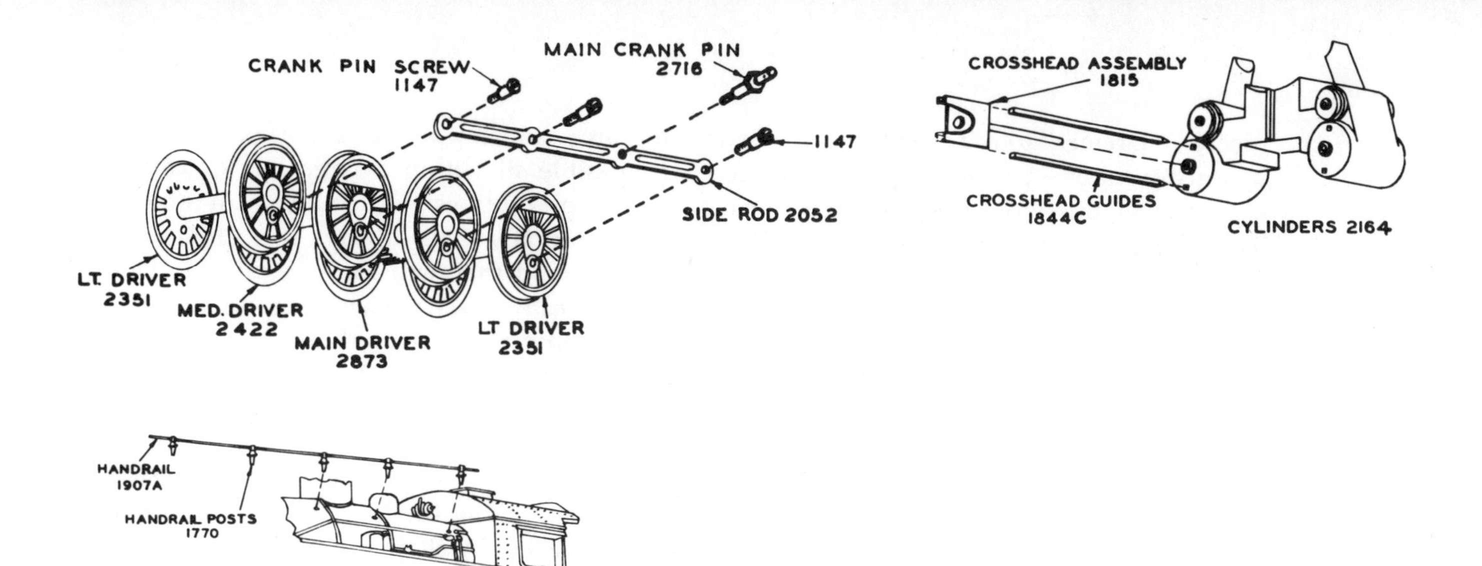

Additional diagrams are evidence of the ease with which this locomotive is assembled. Side rods are attached to drivers by means of screws. Crosshead and Crosshead guides are attached to Cylinders by means of press fit insertion and the posts which hold the handrails are fitted into pre-drilled holes in the superstructure.

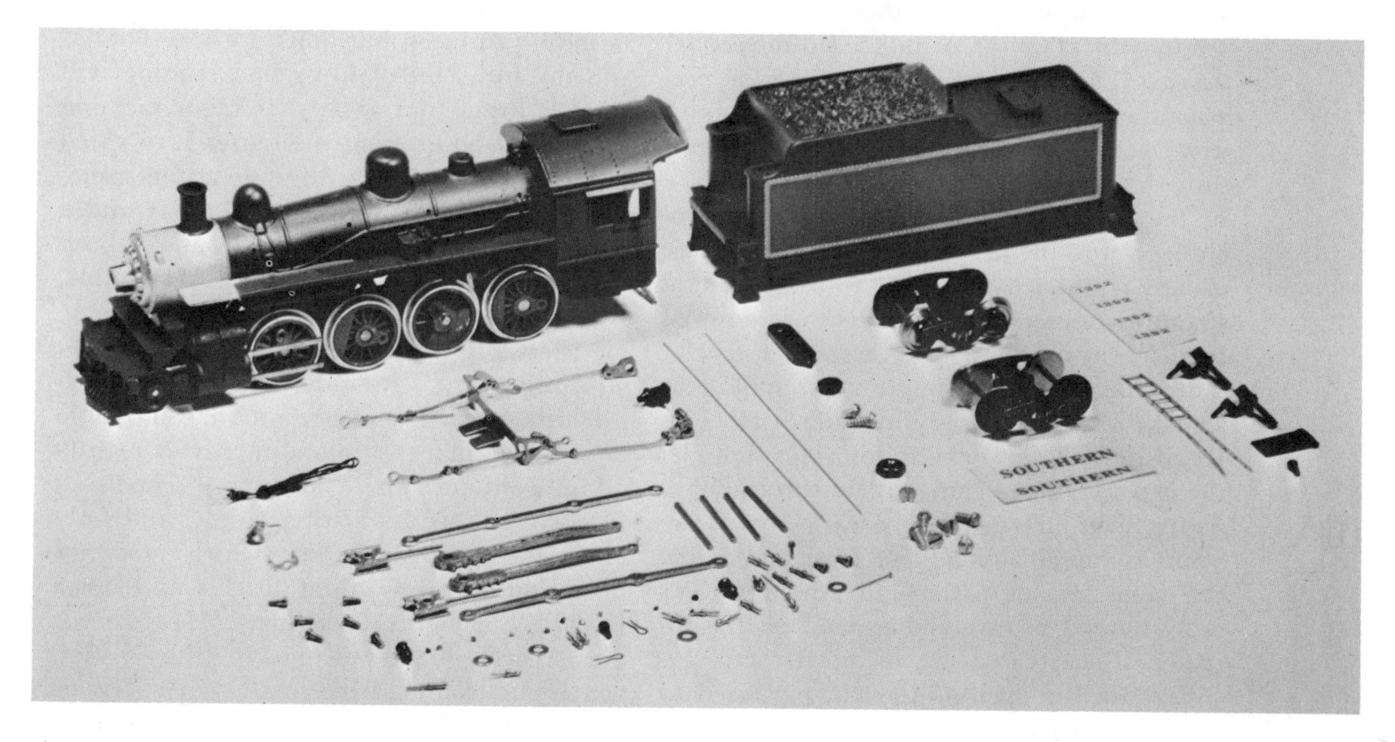

A popular kit among beginners is Varney's "Old Lady," a 2-8-0 Consolidation. Screwdriver assembly features pre-assembled valve gear, and pre-painted loco and tender. Don't let the number of parts and details deceive you—the entire unit goes together quite easily and is ready to run after an evening's work.

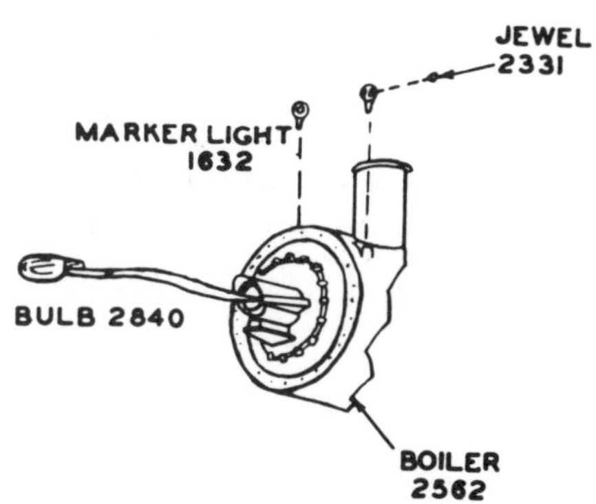

Connecting working headlight is a snap, too. Simply fasten wire ends to motor leads by twirling them together, after which wrap with electrical tape. Typical of the screwdriver kits, no soldering is required. However, at your own option you may do so if you wish.

nicely. A Dremel Moto Tool will also aid you in getting rid of superfluous material. Perfect examples of this type of kit are the Varney Ten Wheeler and Consolidation screwdriver kits pictured within these pages. The screwdriver type of kit has become increasingly popular in line with the demand by most modelers who want to get running in a hurry and yet have a bit to do with the building of their motive power.

Next are the "quickie" kits, and I hasten to explain that this particular designation is absolutely no reflection on the quality or performance of the item involved, but merely denotes the virtual ease of assembly. Parts are few, with most of the assembly already taken care of by the manufacturer. Superstructure detailing is either soldered on, screwed in place, or of molded dimensional design. The underframe, consisting of preassembled valve gear, drivers, pilot, motor, drive gear, etc., are all part of one integral unit that is easily slipped up and into place in the bowels of the boiler. If the loco includes a working headlight, the wire ends are usually connected; if not, it will only take a second. Lead and trailing trucks are screwed in place in a jiffy, as are the tender trucks. This type of kit is so simple to assemble that a shake of the box will almost do it for you. Regardless of the type of kit you assemble, the experience you gain will aid you in eliminating such bugs or kinks as exist or will develop as you go along. Since most kits follow the same sort of pattern in assembly, let's draw a word picture and expand on the instruction sheets that are included.

Even before opening the kit, pay heed to your working area. It should be clean, uncluttered, and level, well illuminated and with plenty of elbow room. Another point to bear in mind is the possibility of dropping one of the parts on the floor. (Did you ever try to find an optical screw on a rug or heavily patterned linoleum? The same thing goes for a sawdust-covered floor, rubbish, or what have you.) Spread paper below your working area—and, by way of slight exaggeration, if possible sit within a large box or carton. These precautions will aid you in quickly retrieving any small objects that elude your fingers (and they will for a certainty). Now we are ready to start assembling the kit.

The first thing is to thoroughly read the instructions, familiarizing yourself with the various individual components involved in the step-by-step assembly. Be sure there are no missing or damaged parts, otherwise somewhere along the line (such as midnight, when the hobby shop is closed) you will be at a stalemate for lack of a screw, washer, or other detail. The next thing is to carefully remove all flash and/or surplus material from the parts involved in the assembly and final fit. Try to avoid nicking or marring the surrounding surfaces, but don't go into shock if you do, for a bit of filing and sanding will smooth things out. The reason for tackling the flash deposits from the outset is to speed things up as you get further along the assembly line. In other words, it is a delay and a pain in the neck when, just as you are about to pick up an item and attach or assemble, you have to stop and remove the flash. Some modelers prefer to remove the flash as they go along on the assumption that a bit of flash might be needed to insure a more compatible fit in the event a corresponding part is slightly off in contour. There are many schools of thought in this fascinating hobby, and only experience will determine which mode of operation you will adopt in this and other facets of model railroading. (Many parts, particularly details such as bells, whistles, water pumps, etc., have small projections or nubs which aid in the final connection or fitting. Do not confuse them with flash, for they are not to be removed.)

Don't let the number of parts deceive you into thinking that you are going to become bogged down in confusion and inability to put them together. The bark is worse than the bite, and when you are finished you will be quite pleased and surprised, not only with

An easy kit to assemble, Varney's popular "Old Lady" 2-8-0 Consol is now shown in final built-up form, and ready to run the rails. The application of the decals (road names, lettering, marker numbers, etc.) that come with the kit can be used or replaced with lettering, marking and insignia of your own choice.

Another locomotive you can quick-build is Varney's 4-6-0 Ten-Wheeler. While tagged the "Casey Jones," it bears a startling resemblance to and has been patterned after a Southern Pacific 4-6-0. Pictured here in built-up form, it is also available in the form of a screwdriver kit. Pre-painted, pre-drilled, pre-assembled valve gear are some of the innovations which make this one of the most popular locomotive kits among model railroaders.

One of the easiest kits to assemble is the famous "999," a 4-4-0 American type. This locomotive goes together as quickly as the prototype broke all records when it established a speed of 112.5 miles per hour in 1893. All brass, it features authentic details, working headlight and bell. As you can see in the photograph, little remains to be done but attach the trucks, pilot and headlight wire leads, after which slip the superstructure in place, and you are ready to highball.

Shown in built-up form, this locomotive contains all the authentic flavor of its prototype—a locomotive that was once referred to as "the fastest thing on wheels." A bit of research, some additional superdetailing and this model can be made to look like an exact duplicate of its bigger brother. A perfect choice for turn-of-the-century railroading, this locomotive will be in place on layouts big or small, and can easily negotiate the most minimum radius trackage. If you lean toward historic locomotives, this one is a must—and just look at those high-stepping 86-inch drivers.

Because of its simplicity and ease of assembly, no instructions are included with this particular locomotive kit. A diagram similar to that included with the "999" locomotive kit is all that is needed to aid you in putting things together. The quality of this loco is obvious. A quickie kit in name only, 75 per cent of this handcrafted brass model has already been built-up at the factory. Electrical hookup between tender and motor employs use of simple dress snaps. Female end attached to motor lead snaps onto male end soldered to floor of tender. Originally imported by Aristo-Craft, the manufacturer was even thoughtful enough to include a bag of scale-sized coal.

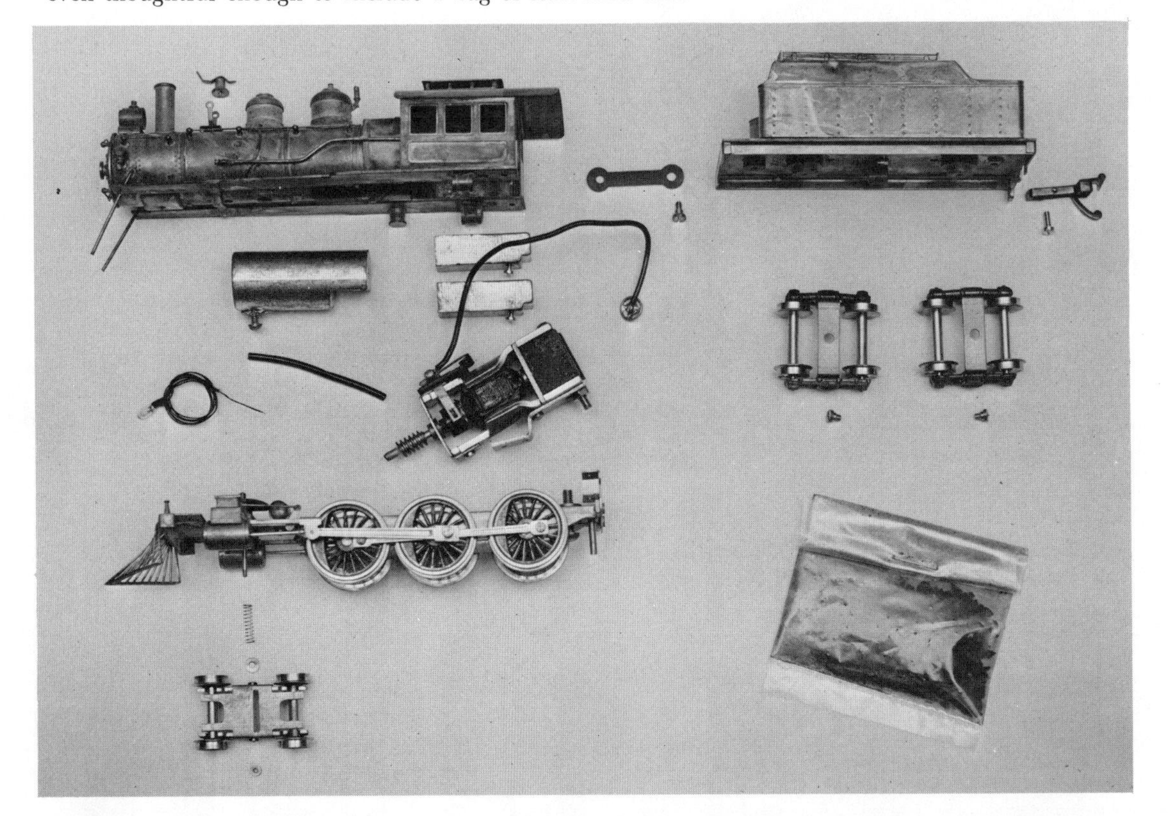

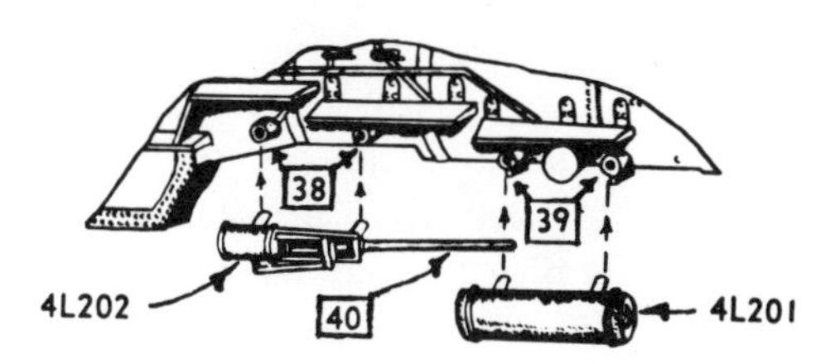

Details from Model Die Casting kit are easily attached by means of a press fit. Note projecting nubs on reverse gear (4L202) and air tank (4L201), which when inserted in respective holes (38 and 39) on superstructure, make for a flush fit and connection without the need for soldering.

Flash (tiny ridges of metal) is easily removed with the aid of an X-acto knife, small files and the ever-useful Dremel Moto Tool. In cutting or filing away the flash, care must be taken not to nick or mar details or surfaces of areas you are working on or about.

Here is the fully assembled ten-wheeler, and a mighty famous one at that. In case you haven't recognized it, you are viewing the one and only "Casey Jones." This model has been patterned after the Illinois Central "Cannonball," a locomotive immortalized in saga and song. This kit easily lends itself to exact duplication of its prototype down to the last detail. The first change can be seen in the form of a Kadee coupler in place of the one that came with the kit.

the results, but with the ease of assembly as well. Sure, you will drop a screw here and there, drill a hole too big or too small, do a bit of swearing and get downright frustrated. You will modify, rearrange, add a few of your own tricks and "imagineering" not covered in the instructions, and otherwise have a thoroughly enjoyable time.

Instructions vary from one manufacturer to the other, and in the step-by-step vein certain kits will have you start with the valve gear assembly, whereas others leave it for the halfway mark. Most modelers will tackle this right away for, once assembled and installed on the drivers and fitted to the cylinder, you can do a bit of breaking in by running the motor in opposite directions for brief periods of time while you are working on other assemblies of the kit. More on this later.

Handle the valve gear parts with care and caution. Follow the directions explicitly. You will find that there are right and left sides that simply cannot be ignored or overlooked, even though at a quick glance all things look equal. Some kits provide for valve gear assembly by means of optical screws, and this will call for jeweler-type screwdrivers. Other kits provide for valve gear assembly by means of riveting. If the latter is the case, then a small anvil, a center punch, or similar flaring tool will be invaluable. Hobby Line has a small rod with a hollowed end that will do the trick nicely. It sells for about 35¢. A small hobby hammer, such as the type made by X-acto, is also needed to flatten things out. Tweezers and needle-nose pliers will be of great benefit, too. Following the instructions, rivet the parts together as indicated. A few light taps with the hammer will flare the shoulders of the rivet, after which you can give it the final flattening treatment—not too vigorously though, otherwise the parts will not move freely. If you overdo it, try working things back and forth by hand. Don't rely on the working motion during breaking in, or actual operation, to wear things down to a looser fit, since such tightness and binding of parts will only add to the load your motor has to overcome. If you made too tight a rivet and can't loosen it sufficiently, don't feel ashamed—we have all done it at one point or another. Just remove the rivet by filing or drilling it out, and start all over again.

Many kits provide the underframe with drivers and motor already mounted. If not, it is a simple matter to take care of. Just be sure that the driver axles fit snugly in their slots in the underframe. If they do not, check for burrs, which are easily removed with a round file. Some modelers enlarge the slots and insert half-round bearings for the axles to rest against—a practice not recommended for beginners. Once the drivers and valve gear are assembled, and have become an integral working unit, the time will have come to check for binds, kinks, and other impediments to smooth operation.

Now, most manufacturers advise against removing the motor, which has been factory set. They further state that the worm and gear are in perfect alignment and need not be adjusted. However, that being the case, the only way you can check the action and motion of the drivers and valve gear is through the use of alligator leads attached to both motor and power pack —in short, electrically. It is much more advisable to remove the screw which secures the motor to the underframe and to put both of them aside for the moment. Now the geared driver and other drivers are unrestricted. Place the entire unit on a 24- or 36-inch length of track, give it a gentle push and your reward, if you have done things correctly, will be a smooth-rolling forward motion. Now, at eye level you can move the unit back and forth while observing every action that takes place. Any binding or fouling up that occurs will be immediately transmitted against the pressure of your fingers, and should things freeze up, you can locate the trouble area and make on-the-spot corrections or repairs. Another test would be to raise one end of the track an inch or so above the table level and

The Dremel Moto Tool is one of the most widely used hobby tools and a must for the hobbyist. Removes flash, drills and reams holes, plus a thousand other uses.

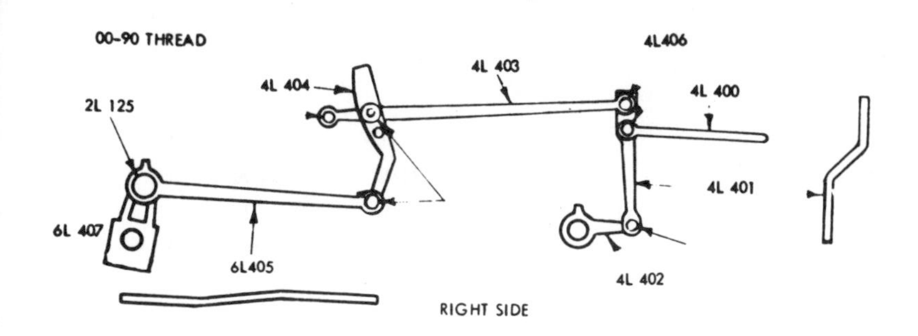

A small modeler's anvil or a bar of steel is the most suitable surface upon which to do your riveting when assembling the valve gear. A few light taps with a hobby hammer should produce the flared edges necessary to hold the parts together. If you are too heavy of hand, try using a small center punch as indicated in the diagram. Push downward and twirl in either direction. The fitting should be loose enough to provide a free motion of the parts. If you overdo it, and the rivet is too tight, simply file it off or drill it out, and start all over again.

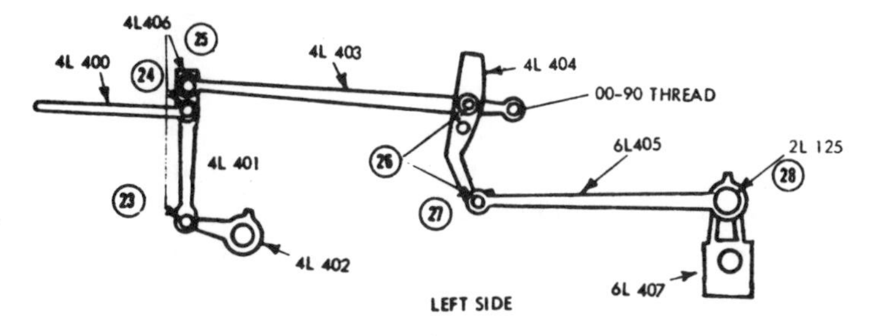

Carefully study all the parts involved in the assembly of the valve gear. As this diagram from a Model Die Casting instruction sheet indicates, there are two sides to everything—in this case, a right and left side. It is very easy to get the parts mixed up (it happens to all of us). To avoid this, place all parts from right and left sides in separate areas, and follow the instructions to the letter!

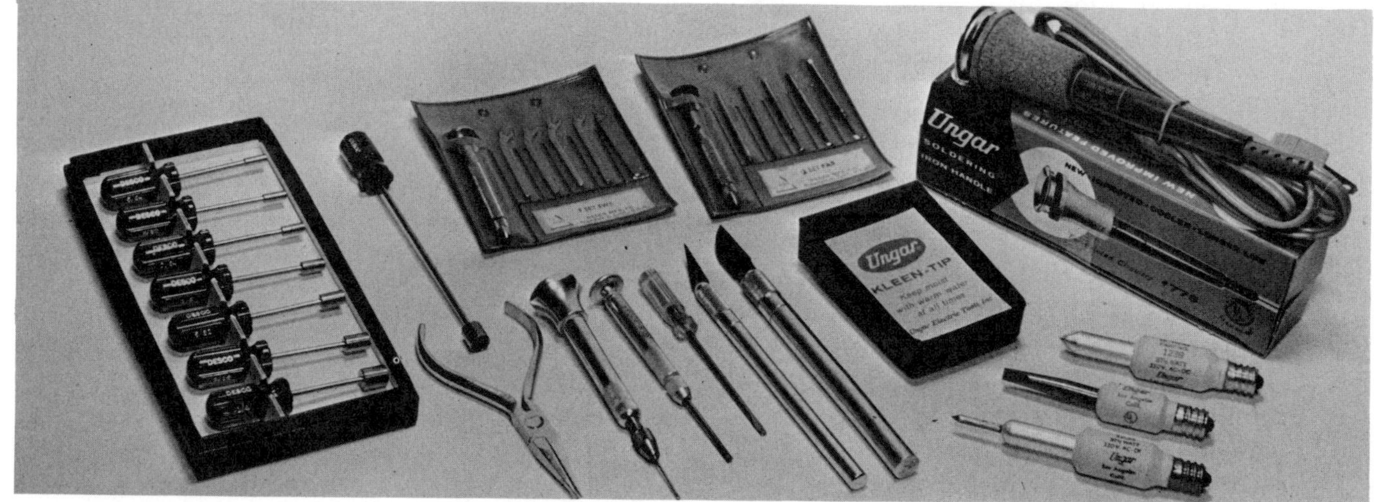

Desco Allen and socket wrenches for those tiny nuts and bolts, some of the famous X-acto tools for the model railroader, and Ungar accessories for easy soldering.

Check the axle slots for burrs or flash. A few light and careful strokes with a round file will smooth rough areas (if they exist), providing better running during operation. Care must be employed in the use of the file to avoid nicking the surface of the slots, otherwise the drivers may develop wobbles.

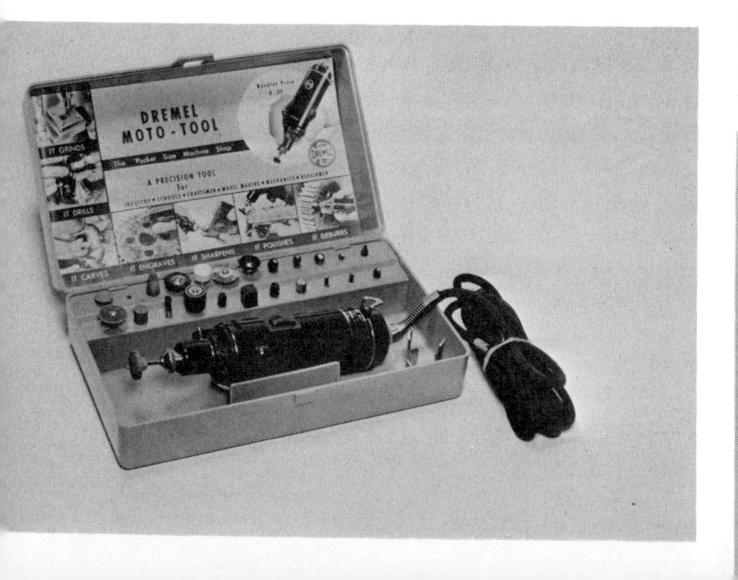

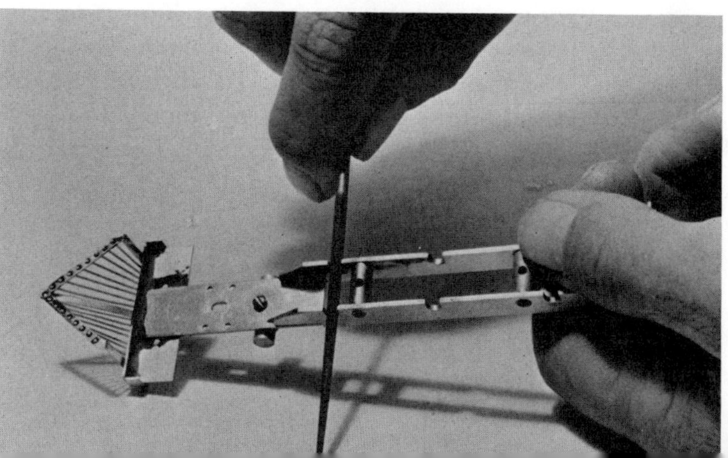

place the unit at the top of the incline; it should roll down smoothly under its own weight. If not, check the entire working mechanism. Side rods and valve gear may not be completely free of each other; the piston rod may be too short or too long; cylinder holes may not be deep enough; crankpin screws may be loose; eccentric cranks on drivers may not be loose enough. In other words, one or more parts may be too loose, too tight, or bumping into each other. If so, then now is the perfect opportunity to smooth things out before remounting the motor. If you are a stickler for perfection, you might try a technique employed by master builders. This consists of placing your partially assembled unit on a sheet of glass rather than a section of track and performing the test described above. If the drivers turn without slipping, then you have really accomplished something. Don't be too disappointed though if you don't quite succeed, for this is an acid test. Suffice to say that if your unit rolls smoothly along a length of track, you have still passed inspection with flying colors even though you may have encountered skidding during the glass test, which, to repeat, is employed only by veterans and master builders.

Assuming that you have accomplished everything thus far to your satisfaction, remount the motor with the screw provided, being certain that the worm does not ride too deep or too shallow in the gear. If so, a thin shim, placed fore or aft, beneath the motor will assure a more compatible mesh. There should now be a slight bit of play, or backward and forward motion. You can check this by moving the drivers in both directions.

It goes without saying that there must be some lubrication, and I assume that no one would either bench test or operate without attending to it. Use fine oil sparingly on the working parts of your valve gear, axles, and other parts of the mechanism subject to friction or leverage. As for the worm and gear, the application of a bit of Lubriplate (Kemtron) will last you for many hours of operation. During the breaking-in period—and, by the way, this on the average is about three hours of running time—the mechanism will improve in performance. Before final assembly you can check to see if any screws have worked loose or popped out.

(Don't construe the three-hour break-in time to mean that it must be done before the final assembly. For whatever operating time you log during assembly can be added to the overall break-in period.)

At this point you can now give the partially assembled locomotive some juice for purposes of breaking in. This can be done in the form of a bench test or by running the unit about an oval of track. The latter is actually better from a breaking-in standpoint, since the free-running bench type of test produces no tractive effort on the part of the motor drivers and valve gear assembly, although you can keep a closer tab on things should trouble develop. For such bench testing you can support the underframe at either end, being sure that the drivers and gear assembly are free of any obstructions. Two lengths of wire, with alligator clips at both ends, will serve as the power line from pack to motor. Connect the leads to the pack, and on the other end of the leads attach a clip to one of the motor terminals and the other lead to the underframe. Slowly turn the throttle from zero to one-quarter position and let it run for about ten minutes, after which reverse the direction and let it run for the same length of time. You can do this periodically during the course of the next few sessions in the completion of your locomotive, and when you are ready to make the final assembly, your motor, drivers, and valve gear will be partially broken in. If you prefer to use an oval of track for breaking in during assembly, you will have to use the tender. If your kit includes a wireless drawbar, fine; if not, don't rely on the wire from motor to tender to act as the connecting link between same, but rather hook up the insulated drawbar that comes with that type of kit. In this way you will be less likely to pull the wire out of position.

Once the valve gear is completely assembled and installed, the preliminary test is in order. This pre-check will possibly save you considerable grief later on and is the quickest method of determining whether you have done things according to Hoyle. As described in the text, the slightest resistance and binding of parts will be transmitted to your touch as you move the unit back and forth along the rails. Should you encounter any flaws in your assembly, now is the time to make the corrections.

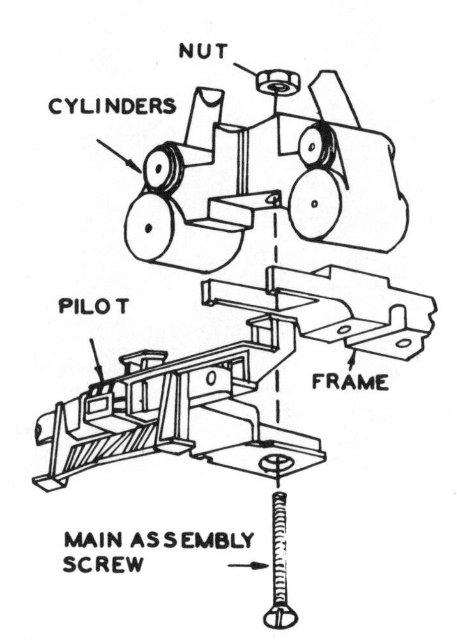

Temporary attachment of pilot, frame and cylinders will hold things in place and keep valve gear from flopping about during preliminary check described in the text.

With respect to the foregoing, bear in mind that the application of the procedure I have outlined may in some cases require a bit of modification on your own part in relation to the particular kit you may be building. I do feel it wise, however, to be sure that drivers, motor, and valve gear are in proper and compatible working order before track testing them. For when you do reach that point, you will not only have partially broken in the mechanism, but also will have helped work out any bugs and kinks, which is one of the most important factors and advantages of kit assembly over RTR, namely, the opportunity to work things in as you go along.

One other item included in the kit is that of a lead weight. Shaped somewhat like a cigar, it is placed within the boiler and held secure by a screw. You will note that for the most part the lead weight is evenly distributed over the drivers—a great aid where traction is concerned. Further along we will discuss in greater detail the "weighting down" of locomotives and how such applications will not only improve traction and performance, but also enable you to haul longer trains over steeper grades without stalling the motor or slipping the drivers. For the moment, however, follow the instructions concerning the lead weight and its installation. Later on you may replace it with a larger weight, or stuff additional weights into the boiler.

Last but not least, save the instruction sheet. File it away for future reference. It will be handy to have for that time in the future when you have to take things apart for maintenance, repair, painting, etc. You will note that no mention has been made concerning any finishing such as painting, lettering, superdetailing, and the like. These subjects are dealt with in greater detail in later chapters. Suffice to say at the moment that during the break-in period you will be handling your locomotive often. At the same time you might correct or modify certain items of assembly here and there. Final finishing is therefore left in abeyance until you are satisfied that your locomotive is functioning smoothly and efficiently. The latter is pretty much standard operating procedure where kit assembly or unpainted pre-assembled equipment is concerned.

This 0-6-0T Yard Hog, a saddle tank-type switcher from Model Die Casting, is a popular kit for beginners, and lends itself to additional detailing and conversion. Kit included X2F couplers, but Kadee couplers were substituted in the final assembly. Valve gear kit is available from Kemtron when you get ready for dressing things up a bit.

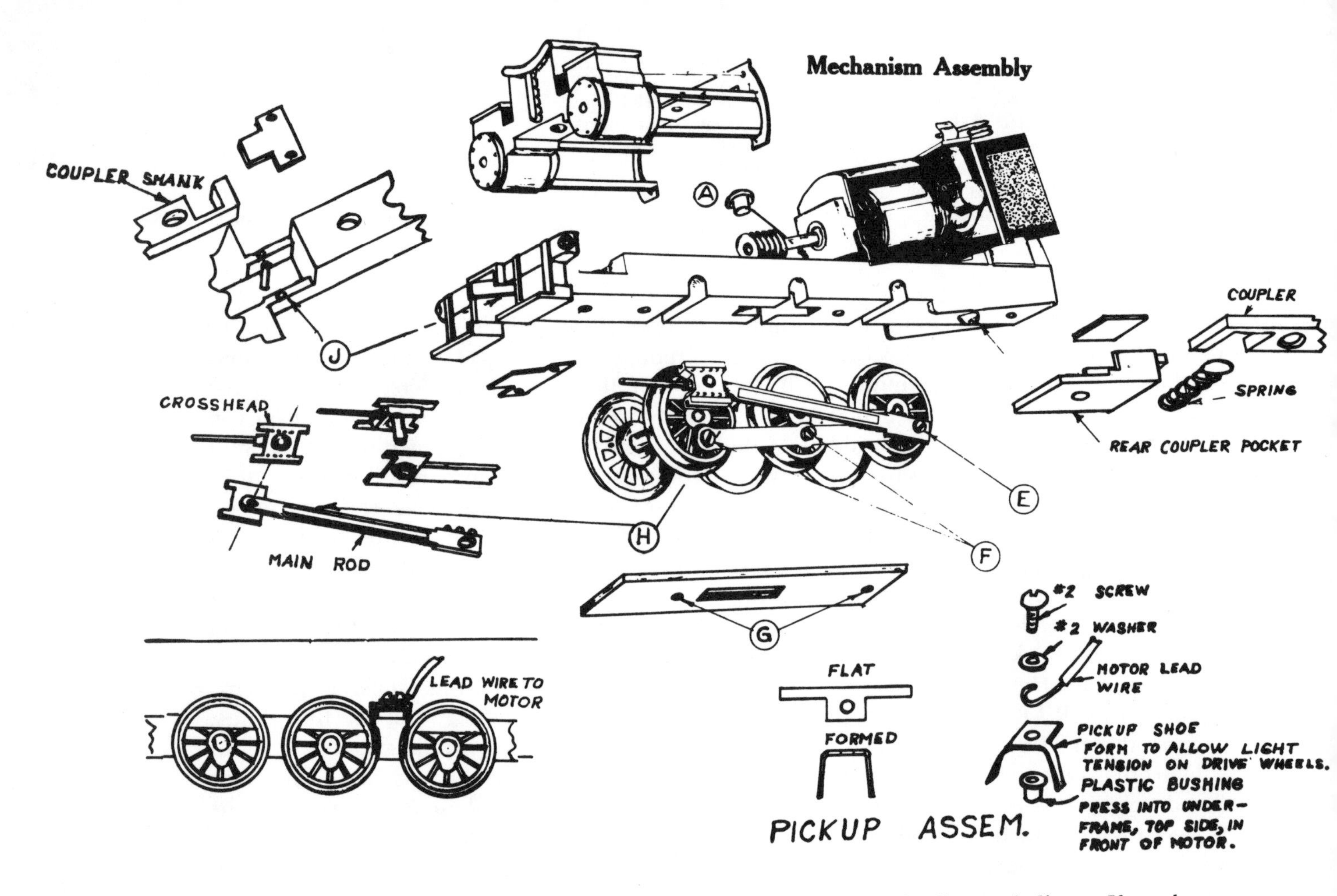

Mechanism assembly of the Model Die Casting 0-6-0T Yard Hog is quite simple, as the diagram indicates. If you have never built up your own locomotive, this kit would be a good one to start with.

Another all-metal kit from Model Die Casting is this 0-6-0 Switcher and tender.

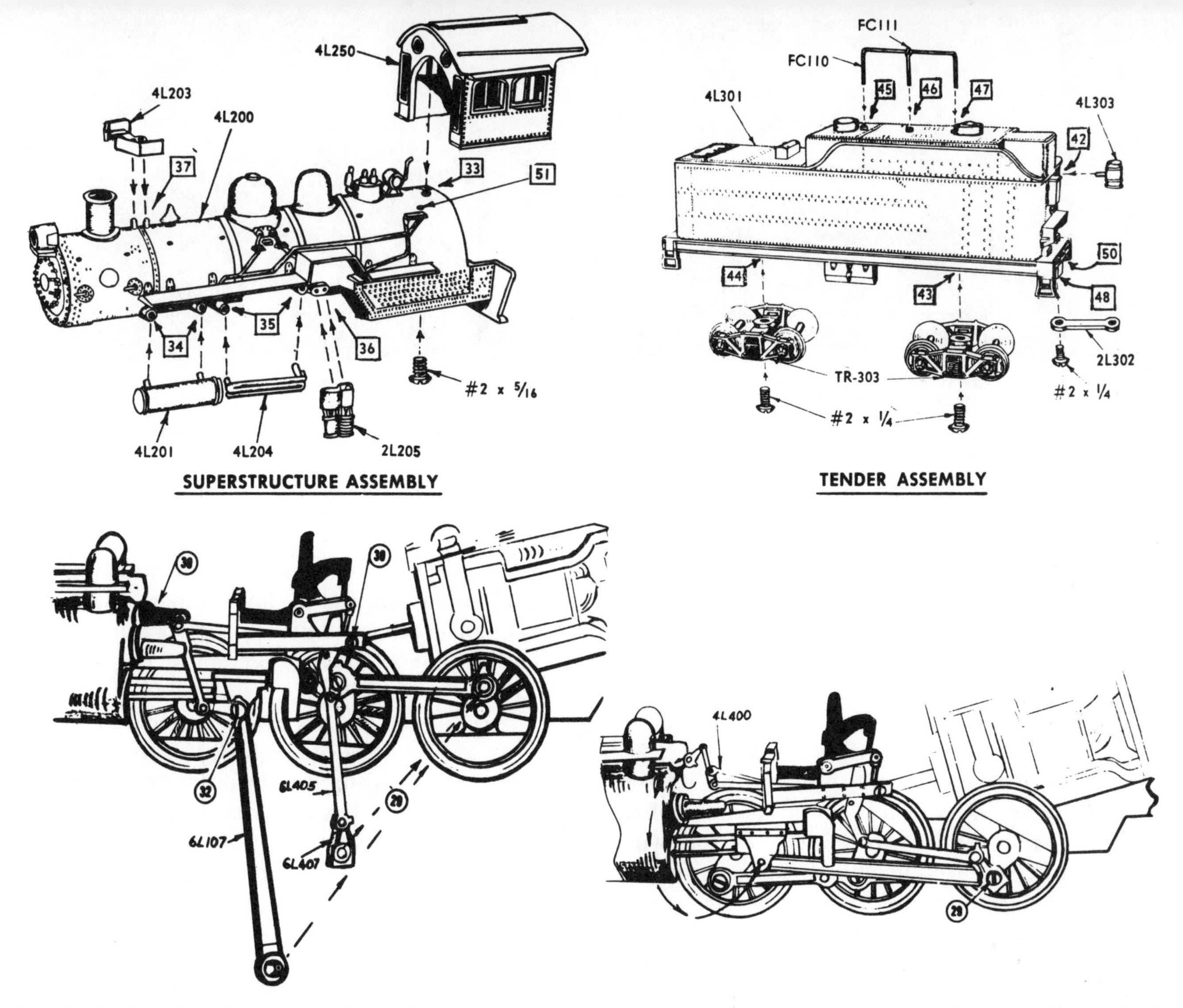

Despite the fact that kits such as this require removal of flash, soldering, drilling, perhaps some tapping, threading and other forms of assembly, the bark is usually worse than the bite. Some of the diagrams from the instruction pages of the Model Die Casting locomotive kit are shown here to allay any fears about tackling kits other than simple screwdriver assemblies.

Another all-metal kit from Model Die Casting, this 4-4-2 Atlantic follows the prototype in both design and authenticity. Kit contains numerous parts for superdetailing. Note tool box and rivet detail on tender.

Completely built up and painted, the 2-6-2 takes on added realism with some extra details such as the engineer in the cab (A) and the marker lights (B). Replacing the molded rigid bell with a working bell will also enhance the railroading appeal.

One of the more popular American-made locomotives is this well-detailed, power-packed model of a Prairie 2-6-2. Available from Model Die Casting in kit form, it is a perfect project for the beginner who has already put together a switcher or two. Well-molded piping, riveting and other details add to the overall appearance and realism.

As far as couplers are concerned, bear in mind that not all kits contain them, since some manufacturers realize that the choice of couplers is better left with the modeler. Of course, should your kit contain a pair of couplers, you are not compelled to use them unless they conform to what you have been using or plan to use on all your equipment. With respect to the balance of the assembly, it is merely a case of following the instructions, attaching the detailing, pilot, lead, and trailing trucks, if any, etc. There was a time when the hobbyist had to indulge in kit building to a far greater extent than he does today.

The popularity of RTR, custom-assembled, and custom-built equipment, plus the average desire to get operating in a hurry, have, as I mentioned earlier, been somewhat instrumental in a slight decrease in the building up and production of locomotive kits. However, there still remains more than enough kits to go around for those new and old to the hobby who wish to do things for themselves. Companies such as Model Die Casting continue to manufacture no less than four different locomotive types in kit form. Tyco continues to produce locomotive kits which are identical to their RTR equipment. Browse through your local hobby shop and you will uncover kits of varied make and description. You will, no doubt, also come across kits which are no longer in production, but which nonetheless will make for a fine project and addition to your roster. Mail-order firms and hobby magazines are also an excellent source of information, and can guide you in the direction of the type of kit you are seeking.

Needless to say, you should select a kit not only on the basis of the final use to which it will be put within your layout, but, more important, on the basis of what you are capable of successfully completing. If you have never built a kit before, you would be best advised to start with a four- or six-wheel switcher featuring a simple slide gear, or the more simple type of screwdriver assemblies. As you progress, and your skill increases, you can go on to the more complicated valve gear mechanisms and wheel arrangements. Through the use of a set of taps and drills, you will be able to enjoy new vistas in the way of modification and improvement of the very locomotive you are working on. The monotony of removing flash, the painstaking care required in riveting valve gear parts, the frustration of having tiny screws escape your grasp and fly off into dark corners—these and other challenges to your skill, patience, and sanity will pleasantly vanish when you give it the throttle and it responds faultlessly. And if you never look another kit in the face again, you will have had the satisfaction of including in your roundhouse at least one locomotive that you built yourself—a locomotive that should give you many hours and years of pleasure-filled operation.

IV

Superdetailing and Conversions

The art of superdetailing locomotive equipment was developed for a number of reasons, primarily the fact that modelers wanted to add to and give their locos a more prototypical appearance. The need for detailing also arose from such conditions as the following: said equipment was basically bare of expected appointments, details were rough in design and/or in the wrong position, and upon many occasions did not belong at all. Thus the art of superdetailing was broadened to include not only a more positive eyeful of authenticity, but also to improve, reposition, and replace, or add to the overall scheme of things. By and large, the results have always spoken for themselves, namely, a locomotive more representative of its bigger brethren.

Whether you are undertaking superdetailing for the first time or not, the following basic creed is one that is followed by many modelers: "What can I add that I can see?" In other words, will the detail you add get lost in the shuffle, requiring a magnifying glass to observe, or can you see it with the naked eye without having to get right up to it? Modelers employing this credo do so on the basis of a 3-foot distance. If they can see the detail at 3 feet, they will add it to their loco. On the other hand, there are modelers who don't care if the detail they add gets lost or hidden by other details, for they are sufficiently satisfied to know that the detail is there, whether they can see it or not. Which is right and which is wrong is easily debatable, for they both have their merits. For example, in photography the proper way to view a print is at arm's length, yet many photographs are looked at much more closely. The same can be said of art; many a viewer will back off before a painting to appraise it, whereas an equal number will stand directly before it to drink in every brush stroke. Similarly, in superdetailing, as in every other facet of model railroading, it is entirely up to the modeler's own preference, and he will get out of it that which he puts into it.

There is another byword attached to superdetailing which is well advised—namely, the fact that you should start with the heavy items first, leaving the lighter ones for the last. Considering the fact that most of your detailing will be attached by means of soldering, the reason is quite logical. In adding details, the heavier the item, the more heat required; the lighter the item, the less heat. If you left

Plans, drawings, research, imagination: these are some of the ingredients that go into super-detailing, the further authentication of a locomotive with respect to its prototype.

Diagrams such as these, which appear in the Kemtron catalogue, can be of enormous help in determining the proper placement of parts and extra details. Part numbers make it easy for you to select a given item at the time of purchase.

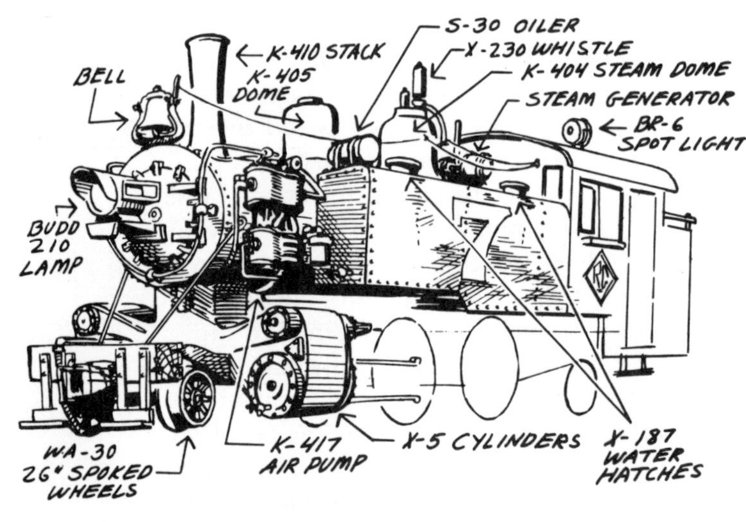

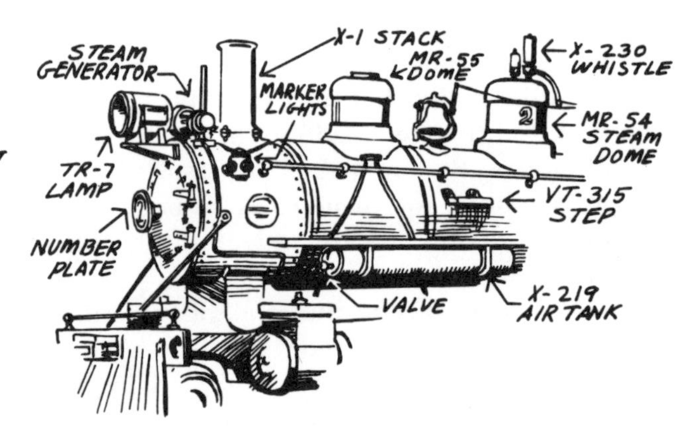

On a standard kit engine just changing the stack and domes gives it an altogether new look. A few more small parts and no one will recognize the engine.

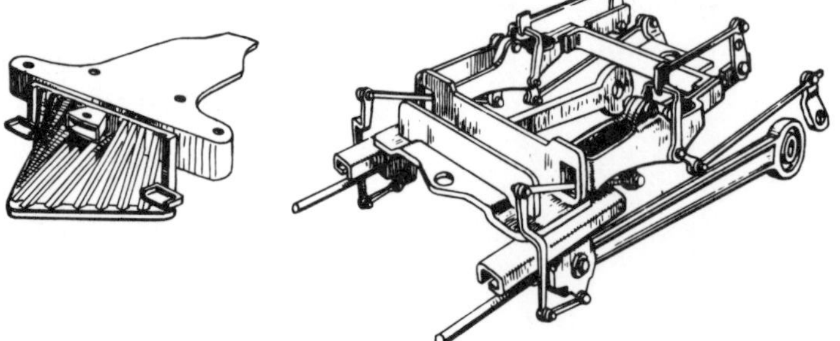

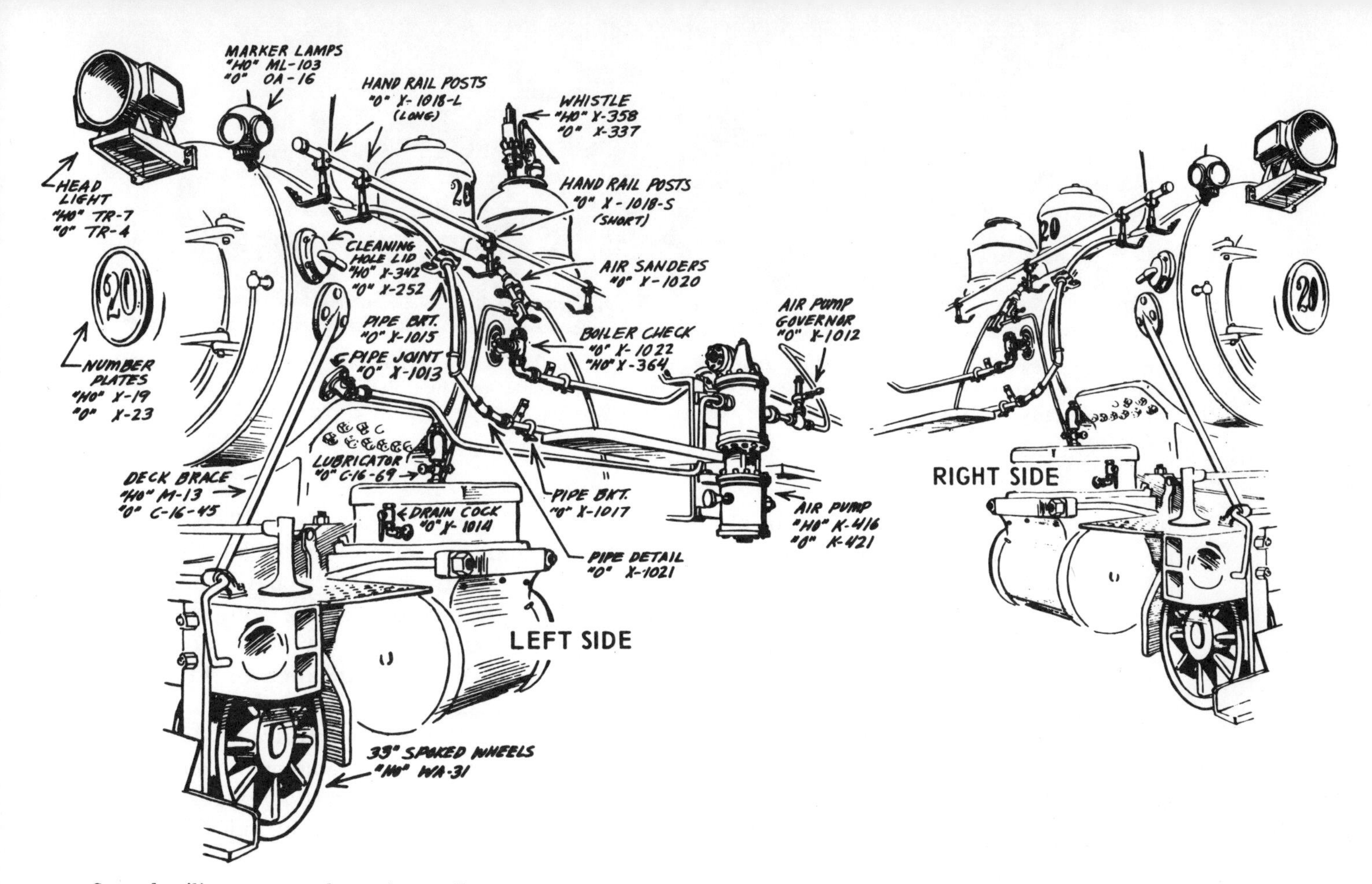

Superdetailing parts such as these pilots, pumps, sand domes, smokestacks, generators, etc., will go a long way toward helping you dress things up a bit. Parts available from Kemtron and other sources are well-detailed castings whereby the simple addition or changeover to a more realistic-looking pilot or other detail will make the difference in railroad-like appearance.

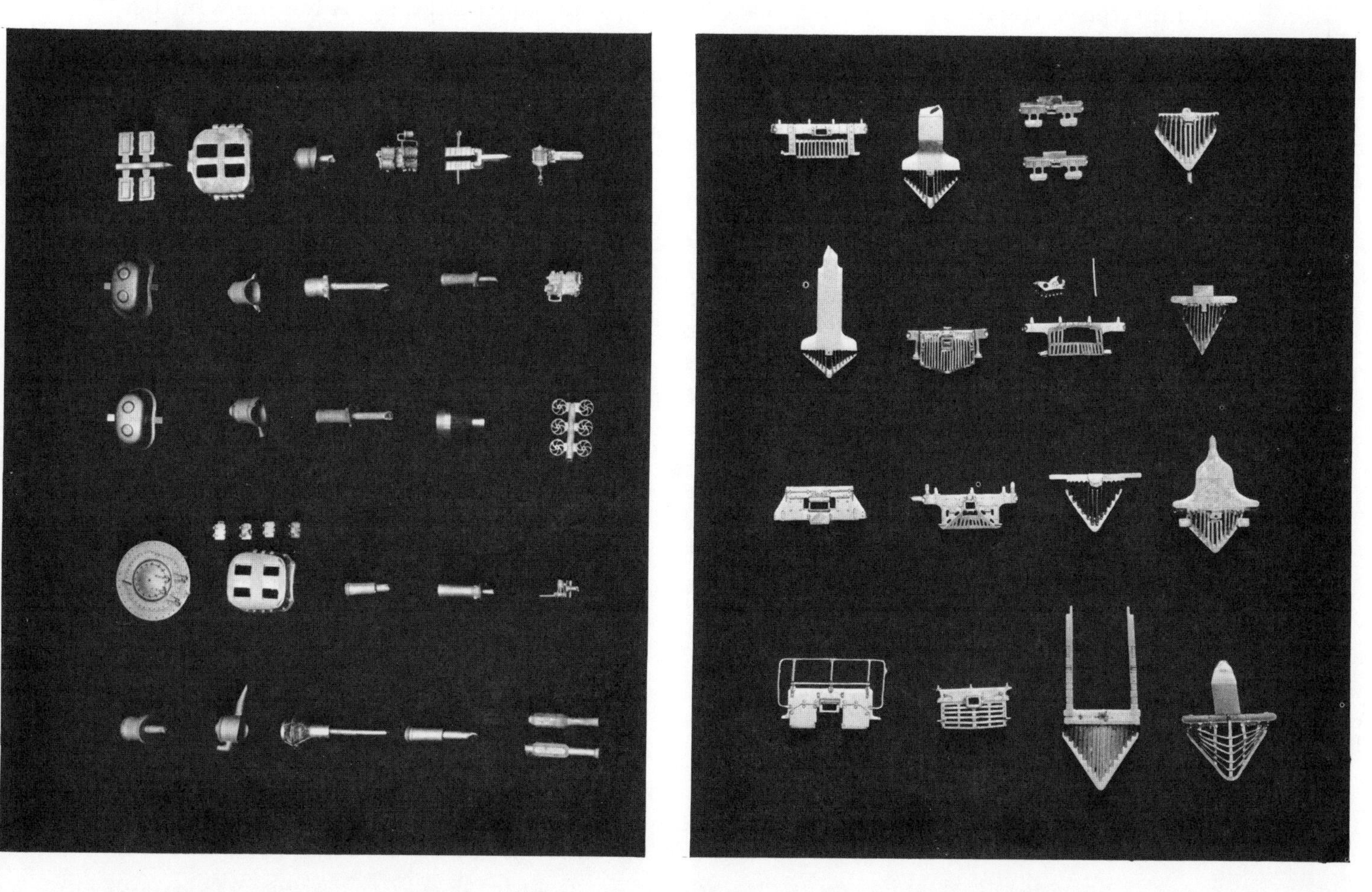

Sometimes a few simple changes are all that are needed to make a locomotive different looking from thousands of others of similar manufacture. This modified "Belle of the '80's" is a good example. Introduced early in HO's history, it has proved popular among modelers for detailing and freelancing of design.

the heavy items until last, the amount of heat needed in proportion to the item being added might be enough to loosen or de-solder the lighter items you put on previously.

Before doing any superdetailing to a particular locomotive, the first thing is to check your loco against pictures and/or plans of the prototype. This will tell you immediately whether or not the manufacturer has incorporated an authentic degree of design, detailing, and proper placement. Westcott's *Cyclopedia* is without doubt one of the best sources of reference, and practically a must if you plan to dress up your equipment in prototype fashion. In checking your loco against the original you may find that the headlight is the wrong shape or style, is supposed to project from the top of the smokebox front rather than sit atop the boiler or rest just above the pilot, as is the case with certain articulateds. The same applies to other details, such as smokestacks, sand domes, water lines, etc. Also bear in mind that much of the equipment underwent changes from the moment it was born and rarely looked the same after it left the shops. For example, some Moguls had balloon stacks and others plain straight stacks, yet both are prototype. In locomotives of the same identical manufacture and class, one might have the bell hung on the side of the boiler and another atop the boiler. Therefore, the modeler has much leeway in effecting the changes or improvements he wishes to make to his equipment.

Once the model rail has established what has to be done to a given loco, he has to consider the details themselves. Today, modelers can revel in the fact that an enormous amount of detailed castings are available—certainly enough so that a superdetailer could purchase all the ingredients from axles on up to not only build the locomotive itself, but detail it as well. Notable among the various companies who offer locomotive gingerbread is Kemtron, whose catalogue includes detailing items of broad and varied description. For example, on one page of their catalogue you will find pictured and listed no less than eighteen smokestacks, a dozen smoke box fronts, loco and tender steps, etc. A few pages further on you will find a varied assortment of valve gear in kit or assembled form, plus a host of individual items. Elsewhere and throughout the entire catalogue can be found innumerable superdetailing parts that will not only make your heart skip a beat or two, but will stimulate and inspire you to do things to your locomotive that you may not have thought possible. The end result, if carried out in true railroading tradition, will not only reward you for your efforts, but will no doubt draw the praise and/or envy of onlookers or other enthusiasts.

As to the methods employed for the affixing of details, the most common permanent method is soldering. Needless to say, it is advisable to use a rosin-core solder rather than an acid-core, since the latter has a habit of spitting. Flux is also handy to use, and will help make the surfaces more receptive to both heat and solder. Some rosin-core solders have the flux built in. Solder Paint made by Kemtron is especially useful and goes on as easily as the name implies. For those working with Zamac castings and boilers, Sal-Met (a liquid flux), also available from Kemtron, is very useful in soldering. Should this or other tricks fail, then the next best thing is to drill a hole at the proper location with a No. 50 drill bit. Tap the hole for a 2-56 thread, then screw in a 2-56 brass screw. You can then solder the part you are attaching directly to the head of the brass screw. Care must be taken to avoid too great a conduction of heat to immediately adjacent areas, otherwise in soldering a new superdetail on the boiler, a fitting ½ inch away might start swimming in its own soldered connection and pop off. To avoid this, try wrapping a damp (not soaking wet) rag about the entire area, leaving just the working area free for soldering. The moisture in the rag will help dissipate the heat and everything will tend to stay in place, including that which you are about to attach. Some details can be fastened in place through the use of Epoxy cements. At other times a detail featuring a projecting nub can be press-fitted into a hole drilled to accept it. Such details as sand domes, stacks, bells, and brake shoes, among others, can be screwed in place. It all depends on the item and the location of attachment. Your own ingenuity will figure greatly in technique and final outcome.

In addition to changing the outline design and ornamentation of your superstructure and boiler, pilots, lead and trailing trucks, vestibule or cab forwards, and illuminated working headlights must be considered.

One of the simplest ways of dressing up a locomotive, especially during actual operation, is through the installation and use of a working headlight. Manufacturers not including this feature on their equipment do so for reasons of economy, simplification of final assembly, or just don't think of it. Nonetheless, many brass hats prefer the realistic appearance of a working headlight as opposed to the artificiality of a jewel cemented in place of a bulb. If your loco has a jewel in place of a working bulb, the changeover can be effected without too much strain. Essentially, all that need be done is the drilling of a hole in the headlight housing and superstructure, after which you run the wire leads of a "grain of wheat" bulb to the motor for electrical hook-up. Actually, you need to solder only one of the leads to a motor terminal or point and the other to any part of the superstructure, which will serve as a ground. The only caution required is to be sure that there are no frayed ends that can cause shorts, or loose and flapping wire that can snag or foul up the working mechanisms, such as valve gears, drivers, worm, etc. Plastic tape will help keep the wires out of danger. Most headlight housings which feature jewels instead of bulbs are solid, therefore it is necessary to drill a hole large enough to accommodate and allow sufficient room for the bulb to rest within. Most modelers undertaking this form of detailing find it considerably easier to remove the headlight housing entirely (especially if it is a solid casting or part of the overall mold) and replace it with a hollow type of housing, any number of styles and sizes of which are available. If you lean toward oldtimers, you can install a headlight featuring an ornate housing. If your equipment is in the more modern vein, you can get a contemporary style. But more important than whether the headlight works or not is the fact that in comparing your locomotive with its prototype you can make up for mistakes or errors in manufacture by installing not only a more authentic-looking headlight, but the style the prototype actually used. Check Kemtron's catalogue; they have scores.

One final note for the moment concerning the application and use of working headlights: The only time the headlight will be on is when the locomotive is in motion, i.e., when electricity is being fed to the rails.

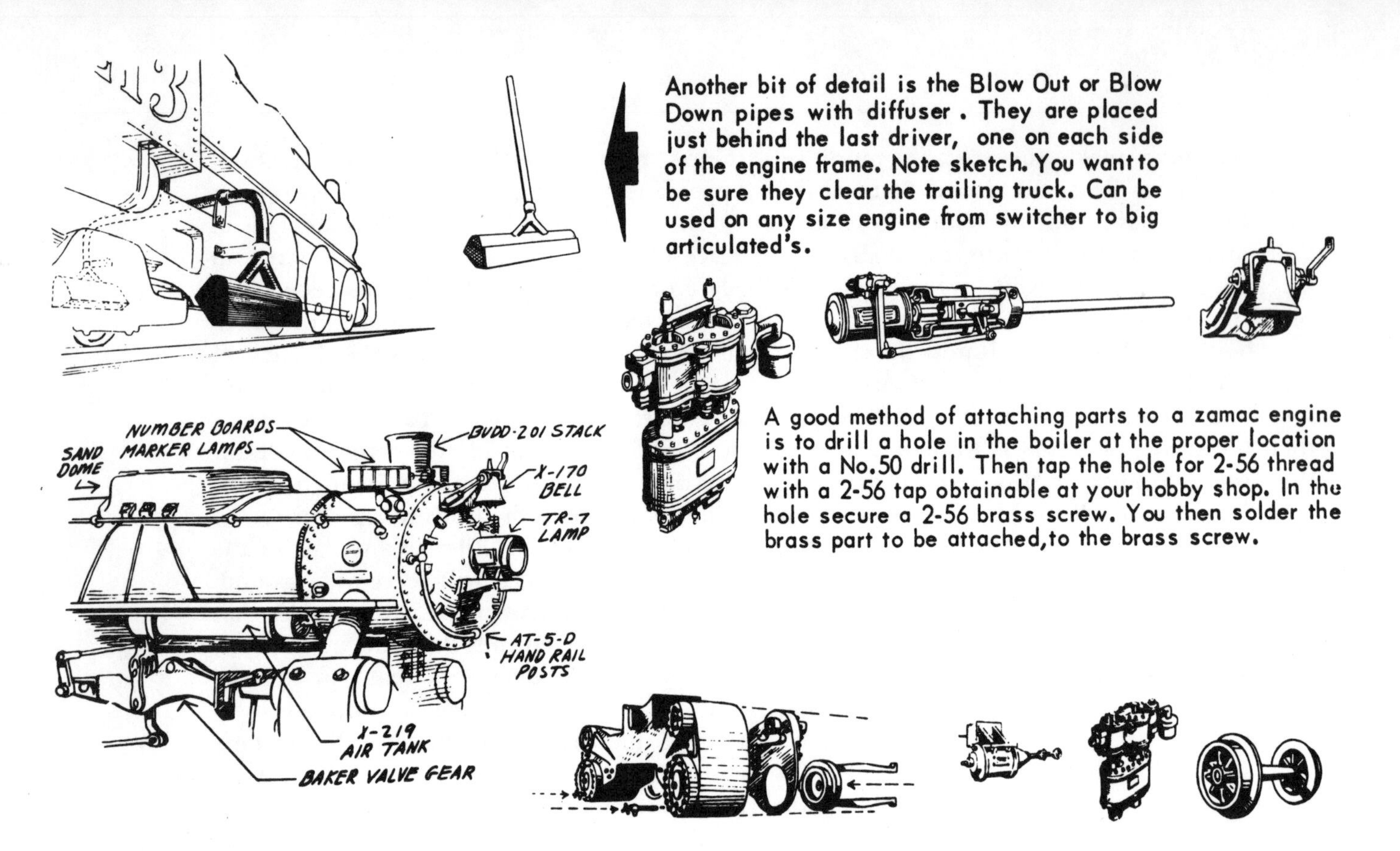

Another bit of detail is the Blow Out or Blow Down pipes with diffuser. They are placed just behind the last driver, one on each side of the engine frame. Note sketch. You want to be sure they clear the trailing truck. Can be used on any size engine from switcher to big articulated's.

A good method of attaching parts to a zamac engine is to drill a hole in the boiler at the proper location with a No.50 drill. Then tap the hole for 2-56 thread with a 2-56 tap obtainable at your hobby shop. In the hole secure a 2-56 brass screw. You then solder the brass part to be attached, to the brass screw.

Details should not be added just for the sake of dressing things up alone, but rather to impart the flavor of a prototype locomotive. A careful study of this and other diagrams will show you where certain details belong.

The 4-8-4 Northern and the 4-6-2 Pacific are among the most popular models for superdetailing. Diagrams and schematics such as these are not only helpful, but necessary. They show you what belongs where.

4-8-4 NORTHERN

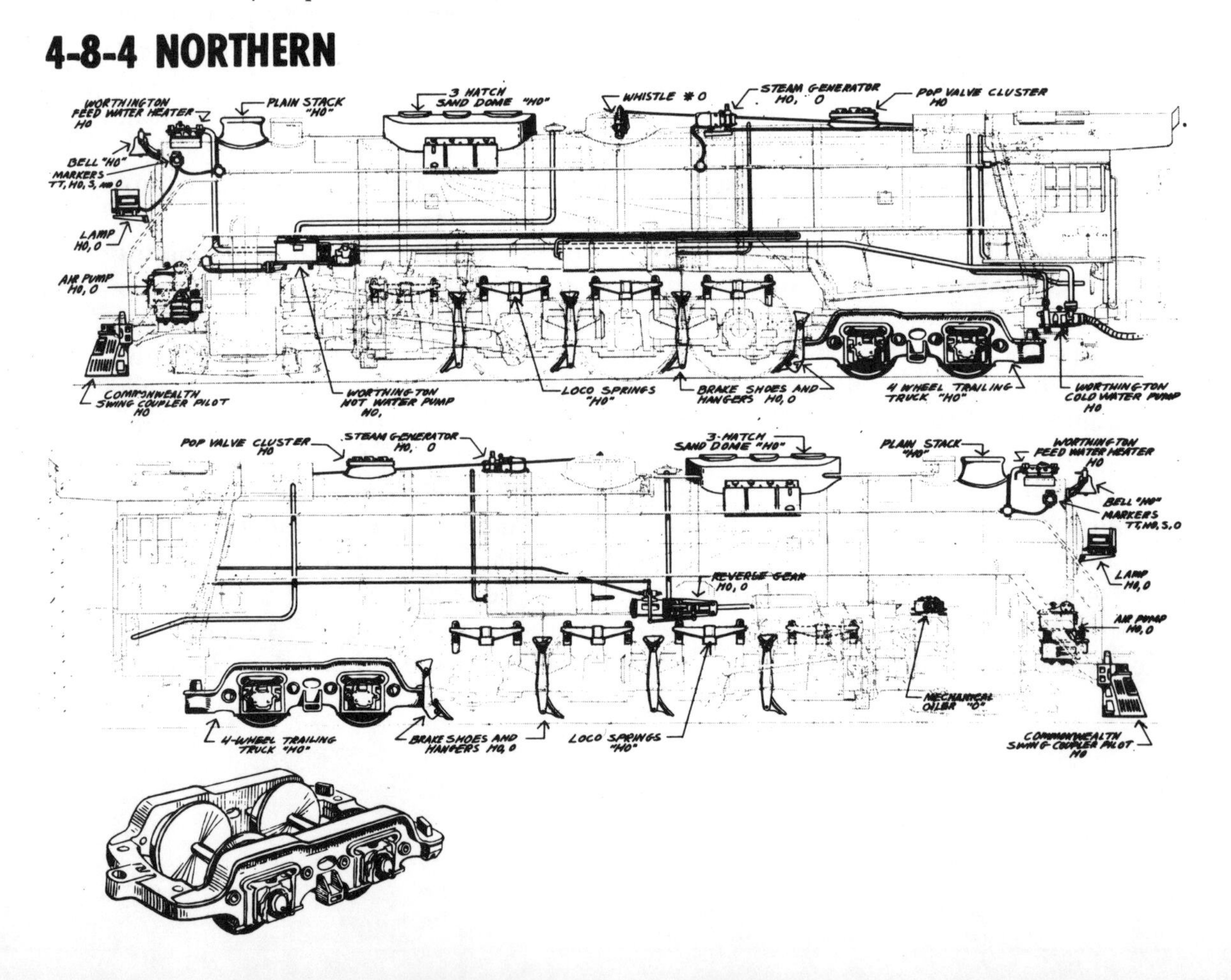

4-6-2 PACIFIC

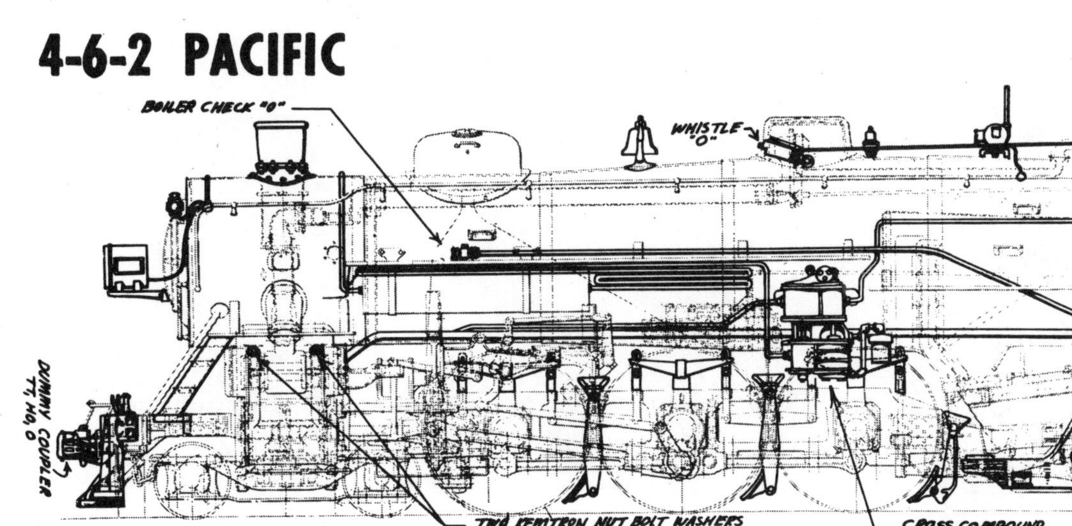

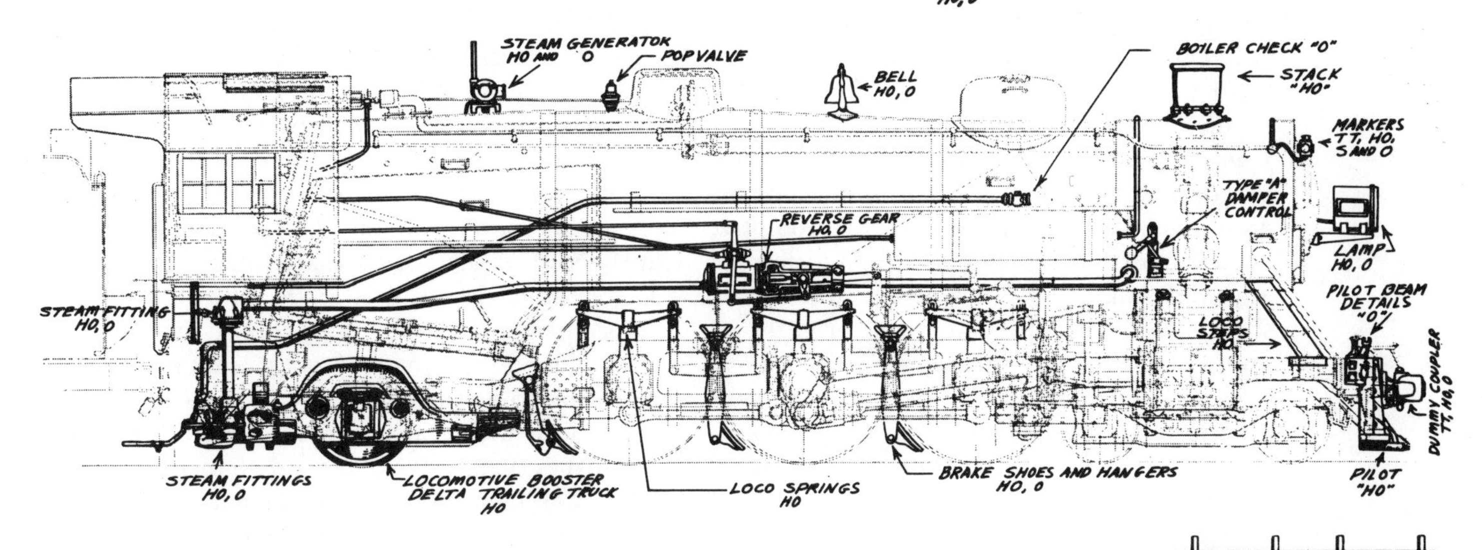

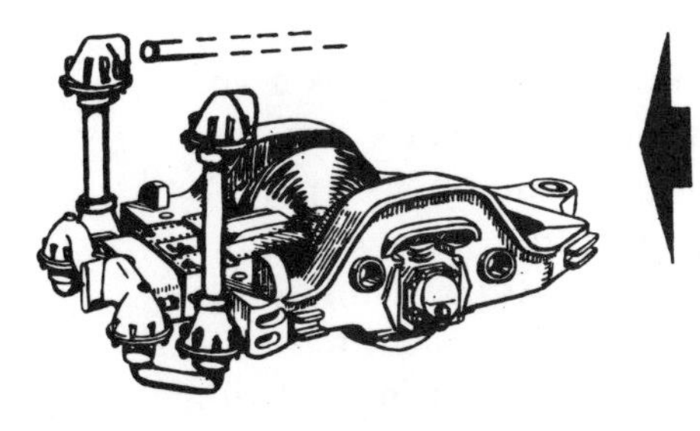

Here is a close up of the Booster Truck shown on the Pacific and Mikado drawings, so you may see the steam engine detail.

A real Booster Trailing Truck is used to assist the engine in starting a heavy train. It can then be cut out at road speed.

Every railroad has their own idea about pilots so that is up to your personal likes.

BRAKE CYLINDERS and LEVERS

X-536

Loco brake cylinders and levers normally mount on the frame, under the cab on both sides.

Brake cylinders and levers are part and parcel of superdetailing, and lend a high degree of authenticity to your motive power. Proper placement, as indicated in this diagram in a Kemtron catalogue, help overcome otherwise naked areas of a locomotive.

As you go from a dead stop and increase the speed up to and including full throttle, the bulb will burn more brightly, since juice is being fed in greater quantity to the motor. Conversely, as you decrease throttle and slow down, the bulb will grow dim proportionately and will go out when the locomotive comes to a full stop. The latter condition has annoyed many a modeler who would like to see his loco's headlight burning brightly, or at least remain on when it pulls into a station, siding, or what have you. Fortunately, there are a few ways to beat the problem, one of which is through the use of high-frequency lighting. With the aid of HFL you can maintain a constant brightness not only in your locomotive headlights, but in your passenger and other illuminated cars as well. The application of HFL to your layout and the benefit of constant brightness will be discussed in greater detail in the chapter on radio control. Suffice to say at the moment that recent developments have now made it possible to gain the benefits of high-frequency lighting with a fraction of the effort that was once involved.

Another easy chore which will do much to improve the appearance of your motive equipment is the installation of sprung trucks in place of the rigid trailing trucks frequently used on locomotives manufactured today. Why settle for a molded spring design when, for a nominal expenditure and a bit of assembly, you can install trucks featuring real springs and accompanying motion. The same can be said of the wheels, particularly in the case of the lead trucks. If a check of the prototype plans discloses that spoked wheels were used, don't worry if your lead wheels are of the solid variety. You can get a set of spoked lead wheels at your hobby shop. Kemtron makes them in 26-, 33-, and 36-inch sizes.

The aforementioned details and many others are often available from the manufacturers of particular locomotives. For example, Tyco, also known as Mantua, not only has a complete line of replacement parts for their equipment, but an equal number of parts for added detailing. The same can be said of Varney, Model Die Casting, and others. Model train makers such as United, Tenshodo, Akane, and M. B. Austin rank high among the equipment being imported from Japan. In many cases these locomotives are so well festooned with detailing and are so close to prototype plans that there remains little to do to enhance their appearance but to paint, maintain, and enjoy operating them.

Getting back to the matter of the parts themselves, I have made repeated reference to Kemtron, since this company is one of the few who specialize in the manufacture of parts and superdetails for the express purpose of dressing up your locomotives. Its catalogue, which, as I said before, is full of superdetails plus sketches and diagrams, is an essential point of reference for the superdetailer along with the *Cyclopedia* also previously mentioned. Another company, Cal-Scale, also offers a flock of well-detailed parts and accessories. Armed with a good imagination and a firm opinion of what you wish to change or add, you will find these reference materials invaluable and an assurance that your applications will be prototype in character.

The proper assortment of tools is also a prerequisite for successful superdetailing, and includes those mentioned in the chapter on kits and in other chapters throughout the book. For example, in addition to the need for various size and shape files, a razor saw, Dremel Moto Tool, X-acto knives, etc., are such extremely useful and necessary implements as needle and long-nose pliers (Xcelite No. 58 is a good bet), tweezers, and drills from No. 61 to 80. Carbon drills will handle most materials and are less expensive than high-speed drills; however, the latter will cut through easier and quicker on Zamac castings. Taps are also a tremendous help, especially where modifications or corrections are needed. Sizes 2-56, 0-72, 0-80, and 0-90 are among the most widely used in the hobby. Matching dies can also be purchased; however, hobby shops carry such a wide and varied assortment of screws to match the commonly used taps and drill sizes that it is doubtful you would have to do any of your own threading. In fact, it wouldn't hurt to have an extra supply of screws of the above-mentioned specifications so that in the event you lose one, or strip threads off the other, you will be able to reach into your supply and not delay things. Speaking of delay, it is advisable to take your time, otherwise the results might reflect sloppy workmanship in the finished project. Soldering tools are important also, and, in addition to the familiar type of soldering gun now widely used, are the Ungar pencil-type soldering irons; these feature a number of interchangeable tips and heating

These X-acto carbon twist drills, shown in actual size, are a must for the serious superdetailer and come in two assortments: small sizes, 61-80 range; and medium sizes, 45-60 range.

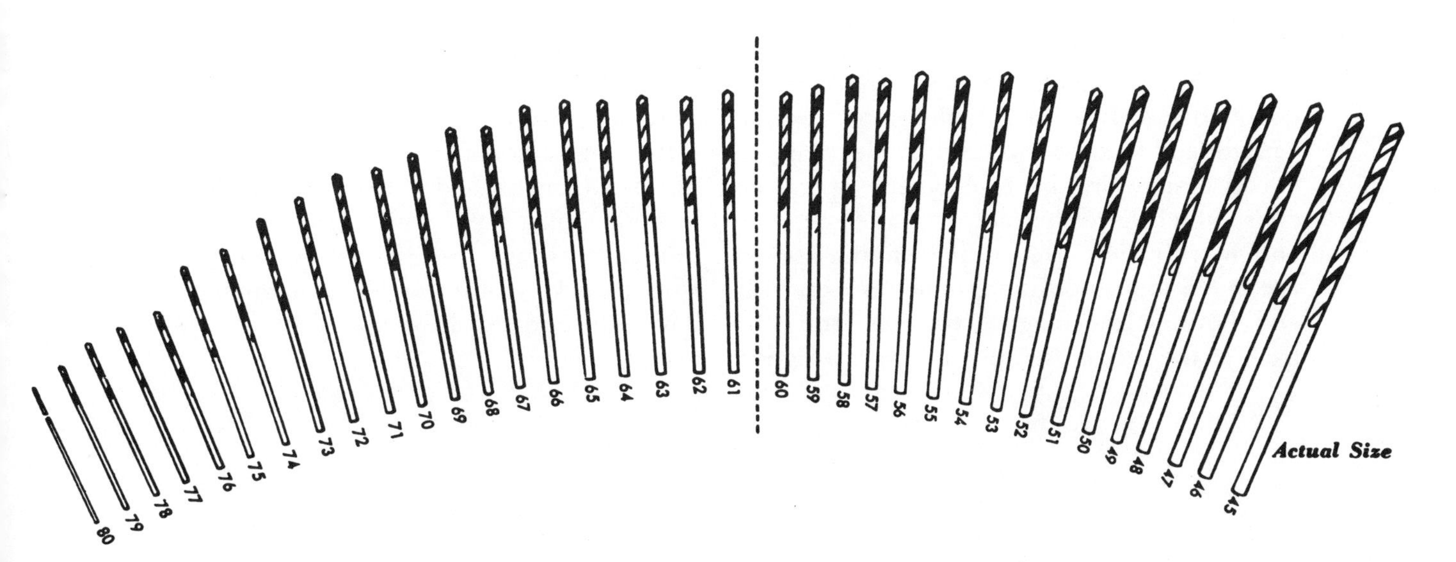

elements, and are similar in appearance and use to wood-burning tools. They will enable you to get into difficult-to-reach areas, or spots that a regular iron can't reach without melting everything in sight. Bear in mind also that a good amount of heat is needed to make the solder flow and the areas to be soldered receptive to the molten lead.

Start with simple projects, such as replacing a straight stack with a diamond stack, adding or repositioning a sand dome, installing a working bell and ornate housing from which it will hang, connecting globe valves to your water and steam pipes, and to further dress your piping, inserting L's and T's. Another simple chore, and one that will improve the appearance of your boiler, is the use of "washout plugs." In many locomotives these are represented in the form of embossed or slightly raised surfaces, which at best are not very dimensional; however, the washout plugs I am referring to are very dimensional, indeed, and exactly like the prototype. Installation is simple. At the appropriate location on the boiler drill a hole slightly smaller than the nub on the underside of the washout plug, and, by means of a press fit, attach securely. The result is both authentic and realistic. An added touch would be to run a trickle of water color from the washout plug onto the boiler and down below to simulate the effect of alkali sediment or other deposits that have been washed or flushed out (see painting and weathering in Chapter VI).

Other simple attachments include number plates and boards, marker lamps, blow-out or blow-down pipes with diffusers, power reverse, brake shoes, air tanks, steam generators, whistles, water hatches, and various details of cab interiors. In the latter respect, I might add that most locomotives leave much to be desired in the case of the open cab ends, which have the motor magnet exposed and in full view. Depending on the size of the motor and its position, sometimes the rear end housing the magnet projects from the back of the cab, presenting a rather unsightly appearance. Arrangements such as this make it difficult to detail the cab interior, though with a bit of modifying it can be done. Model Die Casting has licked this problem nicely with two of their locomotives, the Atlantic and Prairie, by having that part of the motor which extends into the cab covered by a special housing upon which have been molded realistic-looking control dials and levers. With a ready-made panel such as this, the modeler can easily add other details to the cab interior. The modeler might also bear in mind that many cab interiors and locomotive control panels were as complicated or instrumentated as many of today's jet bombers. Many cabs boasted an instrument panel featuring anywhere from fifty to one hundred levers, dials, controls, meters, and what have you. One parting shot concerning detailing cab interiors: there are few, if any, parts in HO size; however, they can be easily fabricated from tubing and brass stock—in other words, scratch built. Some modelers also insert a red "grain of wheat" bulb to provide a flamelike glow, thus heightening the effect of a working furnace.

Another avenue of detailing you can pursue is that of "conversions"—for example, converting a Ten-Wheeler to a Pacific or, in other words, a 4-6-0 to a 4-6-2, this being done by adding a two-wheel trailing truck under the cab and following the drivers. However, there is more to it than changing the wheel arrangements to create an authentic conversion. Here again, research, photographs, plans, etc., are invaluable in assisting you to make the changeover in prototype fashion. Another example would be the case of starting with a USRA 0-8-0. From there you can go to a Consolidation 2-8-0, a Mikado 2-8-2, or a Berkshire 2-8-4. Some parts will have to be discarded and/or added to. As you go heavier in both tonnage and wheel arrangement, you can keep things compatible by adding six-wheel trucks to the tender as a final touch. This will add much to the effect of a more massive engine.

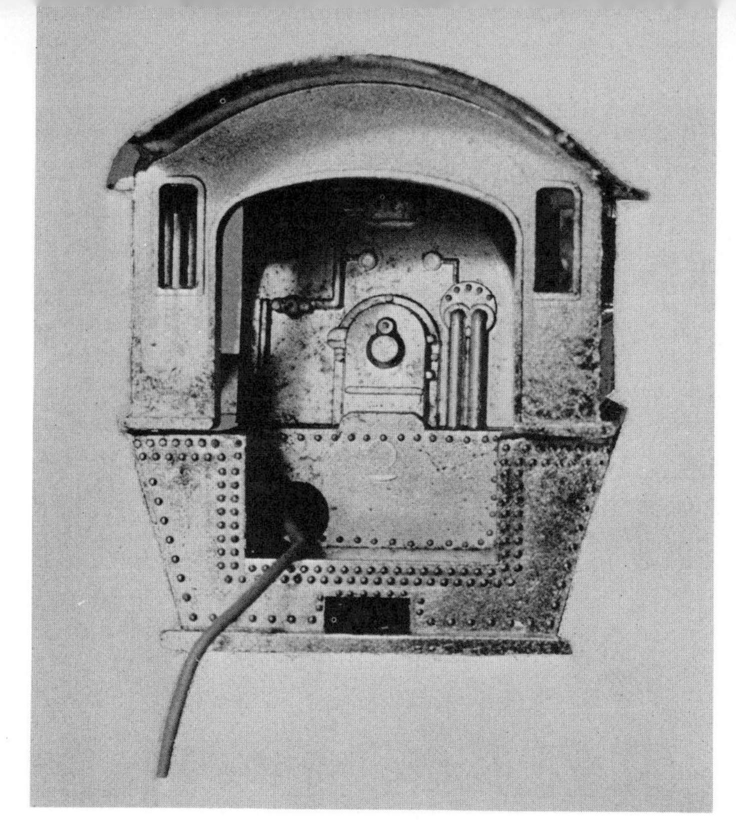

Detailing in cab interior of Model Die Casting locomotives is standard equipment and also serves as a housing which hides the motor and magnet from view.

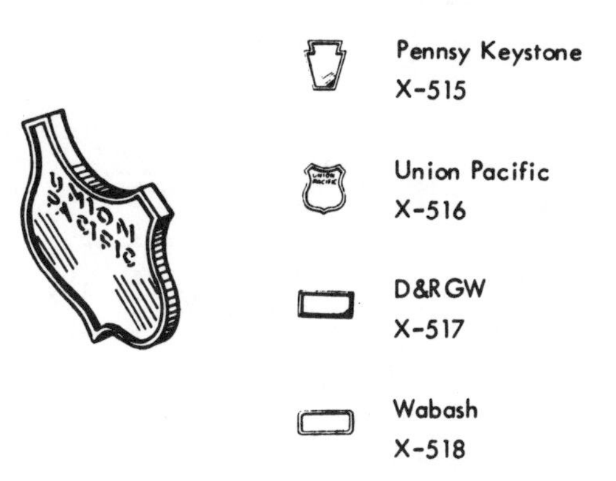

Number boards help enrich the front detail and appearance of your locomotive, and are available from Kemtron in a wide variety of styles, shapes and sizes.

There are two sides to everything—a right and a left side. Washout plugs, piping, pumps and air tanks served specific purposes and were placed at strategic areas on the superstructure. A few modifications may be needed here and there, but if you follow the prototype line in general you can't go wrong. Details and parts shown are Kemtron.

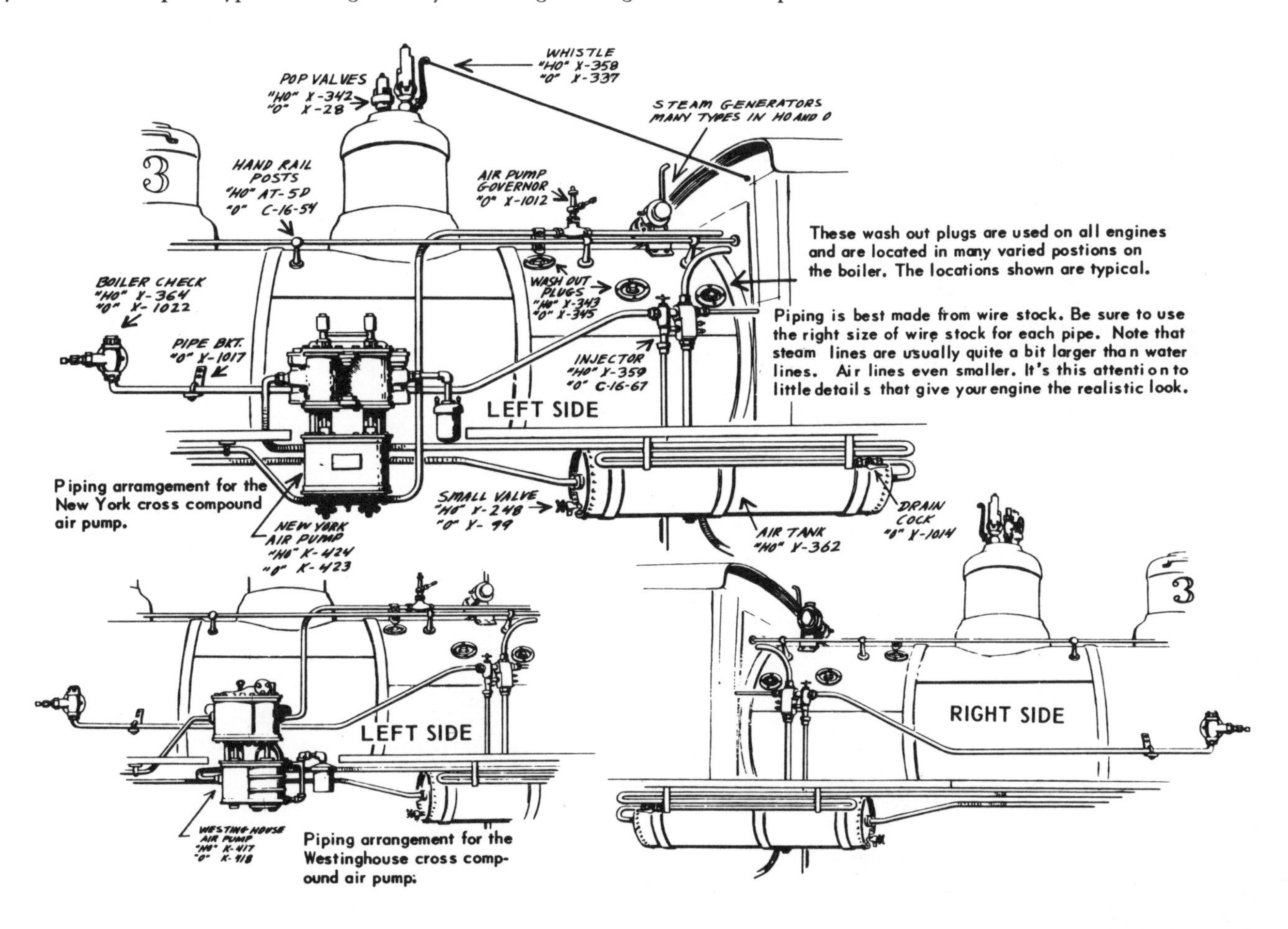

Piping arramgement for the New York cross compound air pump.

Piping arrangement for the Westinghouse cross compound air pump.

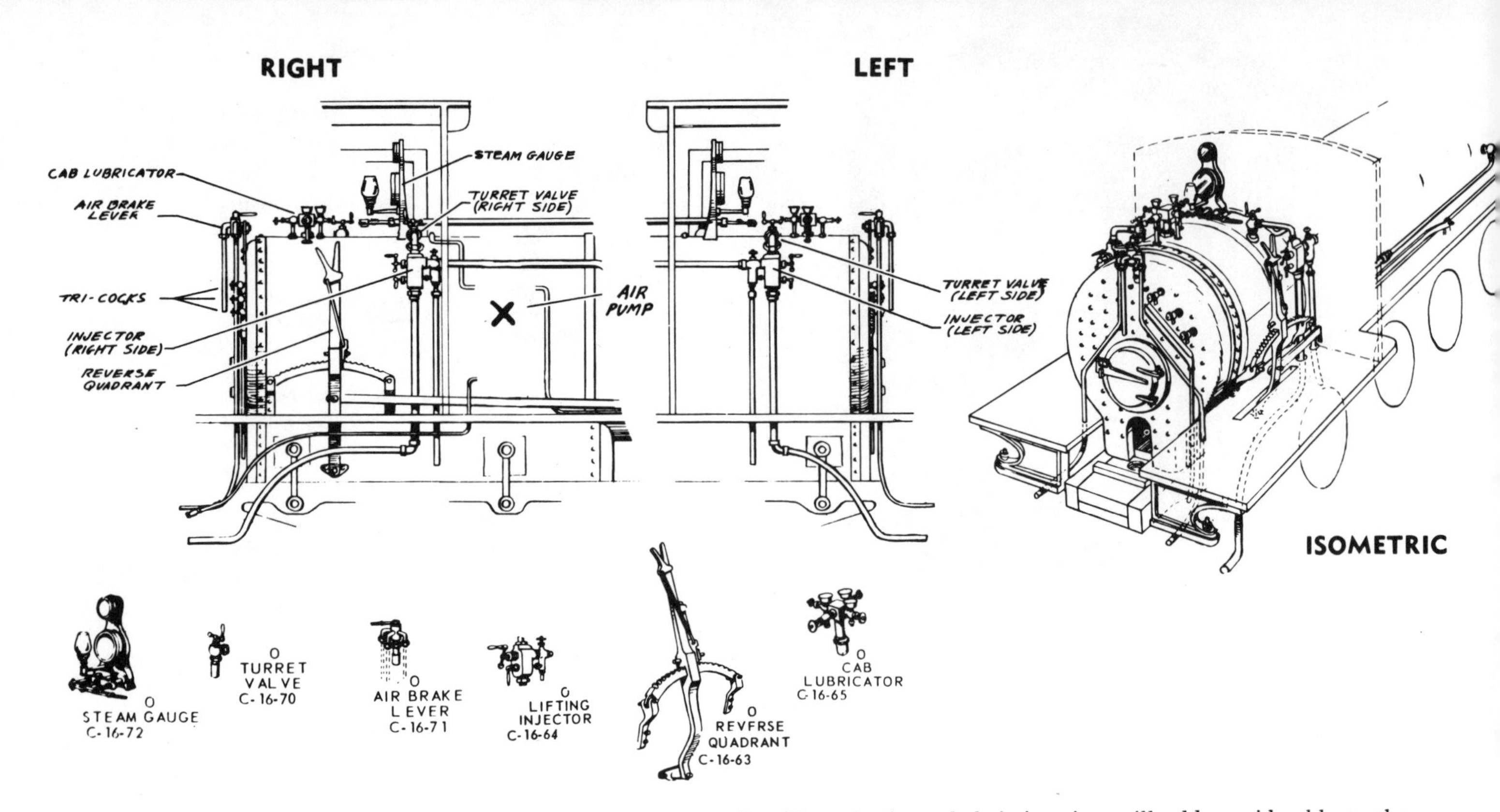

Detailing of cabs and their interiors will add considerably to the overall appearance of your locomotives. The Kemtron castings shown in this diagram have been drawn to actual size and are available in O scale only, but in some cases can also be used for S scale. While these detailed castings are too large for the HO modeler to use, they will nevertheless serve as a guide as to the possibilities where cabs and how to detail their interiors are concerned.

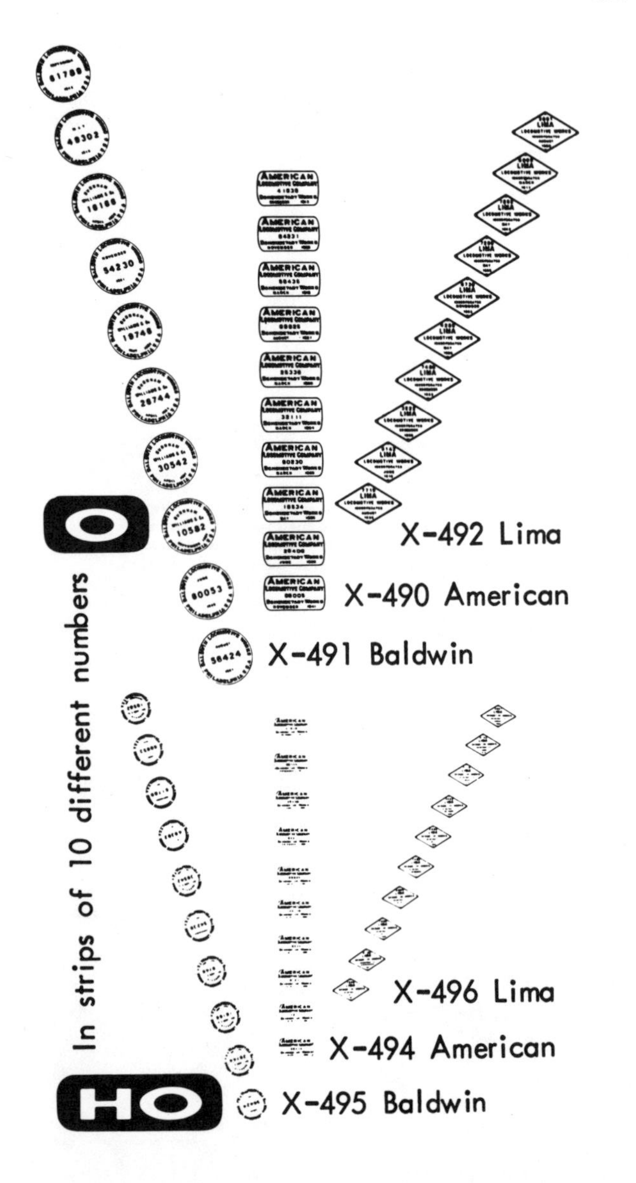

Locomotive builders usually added their nameplate to a locomotive. If your model lacks such a distinction, some of these builders' plates from Kemtron might do the trick.

For the do-it-yourself kit assembler the Mantua "Mike" (Tyco) is one of the most popular projects among model rails, novice or veteran. This particular kit-built locomotive offers a number of opportunities to add a wealth of detail with little effort required. The following photographs show some of the stages in the development of this project.

Mantua's kit-assembled "Mikado" includes a long-distance coal tender. Easy to put together and work with, this locomotive lends itself to various forms of superdetailing in which you can add various details from other "Mikes" and still remain within the bounds of prototype authenticity. It is shown here in its basic form following assembly from the kit.

Three superdetails greatly enhance the appearance of this locomotive and make for a simple project in the doing: a working bell, Delta trailing truck (sprung) and a vestibule cab specially designed by Kemtron to fit this particular locomotive. (The vestibule cab is also adaptable to most other large-sized locos.)

Although only a few details have been added at this point, the Mantua "Mike" takes on added prestige by hooking on Kemtron's all brass Vanderbilt oil tender. Simple changes and additions to follow can include a working headlight, new pilot, smokebox front and stack, back-up light, Westinghouse pump and additional piping on the boiler.

2-8-2 MIKADO

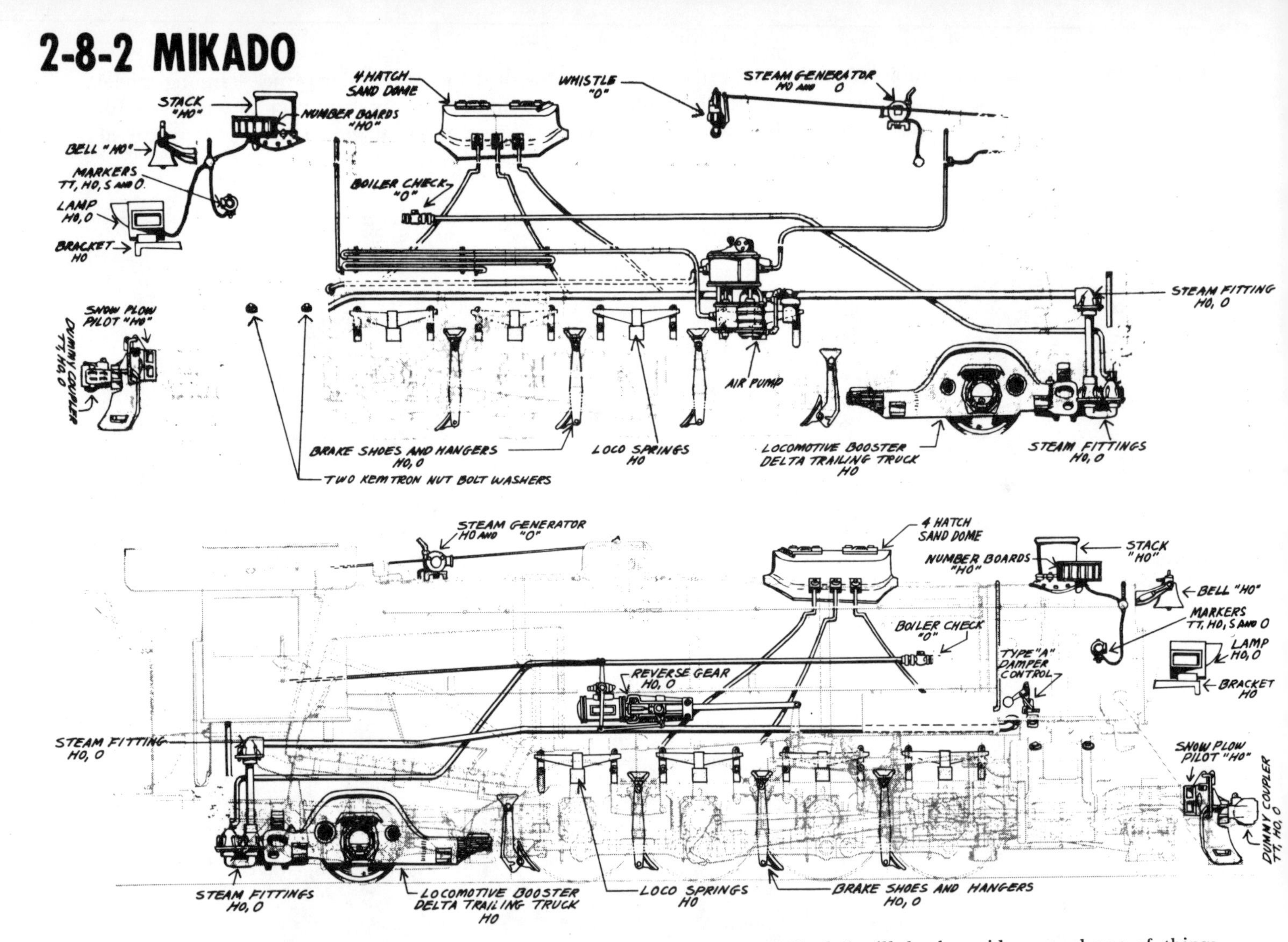

The placement of details shown in this well-detailed drawing of a 2-8-2 "Mikado" will further aid your scheme of things where superdetailing is concerned. As you can see, a number of details too numerous to mention are available. Study this diagram closely in connection with the photos showing the stages in the development and detailing of the Mantua "Mike."

A few changes and extra detail add to the prototype appearance of this switch engine: Kadee Magne-Matic delayed-action couplers for smooth hook-up and uncoupling action (replacing X2F type); a Kemtron valve gear kit adds to the monkey motion of rods and links; and a working brass bell peals the way in and about the yards. While this is just a start toward further authentication, a careful study of these before-and-after views will show you that it is a start in the right direction.

A simple project for beginners which permits the application of superdetailing and conversion as well. In prototype operation, tenders were often hooked up to saddle tank switch engines, thus minimizing the necessity for frequent stops for water and refueling during their switching operations.

Side and rear view of an 0-4-0T switch engine before conversion to a cab-forward design.

"Lost wax" casting of a cab-forward enclosure will fit most any "Docksider" and is a well-detailed part from Kemtron.

This switcher takes on a new look when converted to a cab-forward by removing tender steps and filing back end smooth. An easy project for the beginner, it can be accomplished in less than an evening. Model shown is from Revell; however, this project is equally applicable to "Docksiders" from other sources such as Varney, PFM, etc.

Additional superdetailing and conversion puts this yard hog in a class by itself. Generator replaced working headlight, which in turn is now situated in center of cab-forward cover plate. Molded plastic bell was replaced with brass working bell. Addition of a pilot truck eliminated cab-heavy appearance. Kemtron parts, such as steps, grab irons, working valve gear, etc., can yet be added. Bringing up the rear is an all-brass shorty Vanderbilt tender. Kadee couplers also add a realistic touch.

Conversions are a great source of fun and modeling pleasure, and in connection with superdetailing permit all types of modification in design and appearance. You can oldtimer-ize, modernize, industrialize, etc. Superdetailing parts and kits made by Kemtron permit numerous changes in the looks of various motive power. Not only can the modeler give his locomotive a bit more sex appeal, but he can freelance and/or alter the design from the original and still remain within the realm of prototype practice. Three conversions of a Baldwin 0-6-0T (Tenshodo side tank switcher) are shown. For the advanced model rail, these conversions require drilling and soldering for proper placement and attachment of castings. Instructions with conversion kits are easy to follow.

Modern industrial conversion kit from Kemtron helps retain that good look of steam power, yet adds a crisp modern look as well. Parts include two plastic industrial pilots, smokestack, air pump, bell, whistle, headlight, steam generator and a spotlight mounted atop the roof of the cab.

Oldtimer conversion kit from Kemtron includes two headlamps, one air pump, bell, whistle, steam generator, oil tank hatch and wood beam pilot. You can further enhance the oldtimer appearance through the use of a diamond or balloon-type smokestack.

Deluxe conversion kit from Kemtron changes the 0-6-0T to a 2-6-0T "Woods Engine" by the addition of a lead truck and some twenty-four well-detailed castings which include handrail posts, marker lamps, complete valve gear kit and six special castings that comprise the highly detailed set of cylinders. Needless to say, the purchase of a superdetailing conversion kit such as this is considerably less expensive than if you purchased the parts one at a time. This is a project which will not only give you many hours of pleasure during assembly, but an equal amount of pleasure during operation on your pike. It would look great in a timber or lumber camp area.

This 0-6-0T shown in Chapter 2 is repeated for the sake of before-and-after comparison, and while not identical to the model used in the superdetailed conversions, it can nonetheless, like others, be used with the same degree of successful change and modification. Starting with an 0-6-0T, you can convert to a 2-6-0T by adding a pilot or lead truck. The addition of a trailing truck, and you "heavy up" the appearance in the form of a 2-6-2T. You can even cut off and remove the fuel bunker and add a tender. The possibilities are endless.

Close-up view of this 4-6-2 Pacific in O scale is a good example of the extra detail that can be packed into the square inch which is afforded by the largest of the commonly used scales. By the same token however, a fair amount of detailing is necessary in O scale to keep the motive power from looking bare of accessories.

In contrast, three detailed locomotives of the smallest popularly used scales are shown in TT.

This Pacific by Hal Joyce, creator and inventor of TT scale, is a must for the TT enthusiast and can be easily superdetailed with additional parts available from H.P. Products Co. All metal, in kit or RTR.

This 4-8-4 high-wheeled Northern is beamed at the advanced TT modeler in the form of a loco and tender kit from H.P. Products. Can also be obtained custom-built, tested and RTR. Fine lines and detailing possibilities will impress the bigger gaugers as well.

A limited production model of a 4-6-6-4 Articulated is evidence of the amount of detailing and prototype design that can be packed into TT locomotives. Often referred to as a "100-car" loco because of its enormous pulling power, this particular model will handle rough grades as well. A set of parts with partial instructions requires imagination and some research on the part of the advanced hobbyist. The TT operator, if he's in a hurry, can get it RTR from H.P. Products.

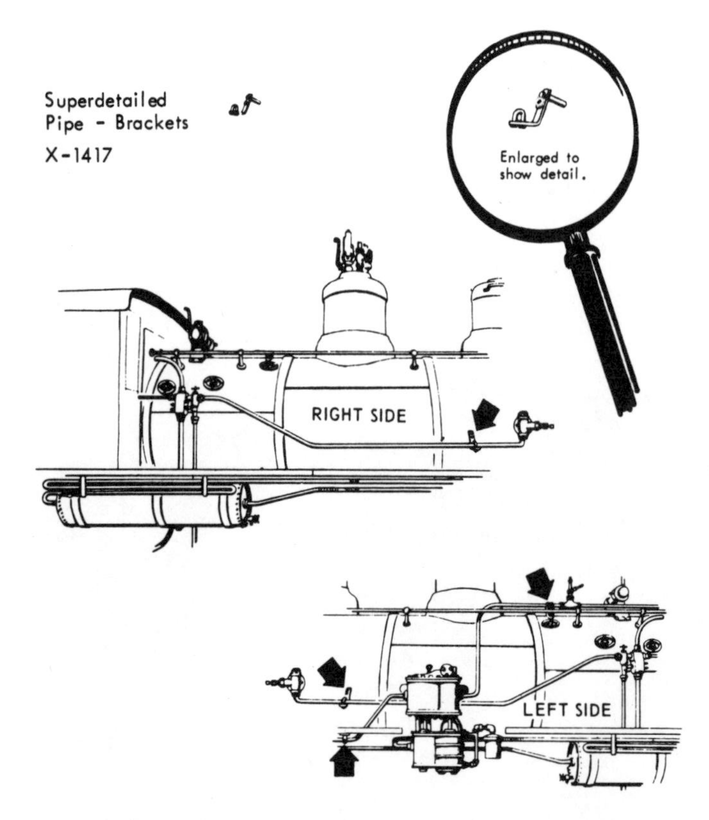

These pipe brackets from Kemtron offer greater realism, and, from a practical standpoint, are an easy means of holding piping to boilers.

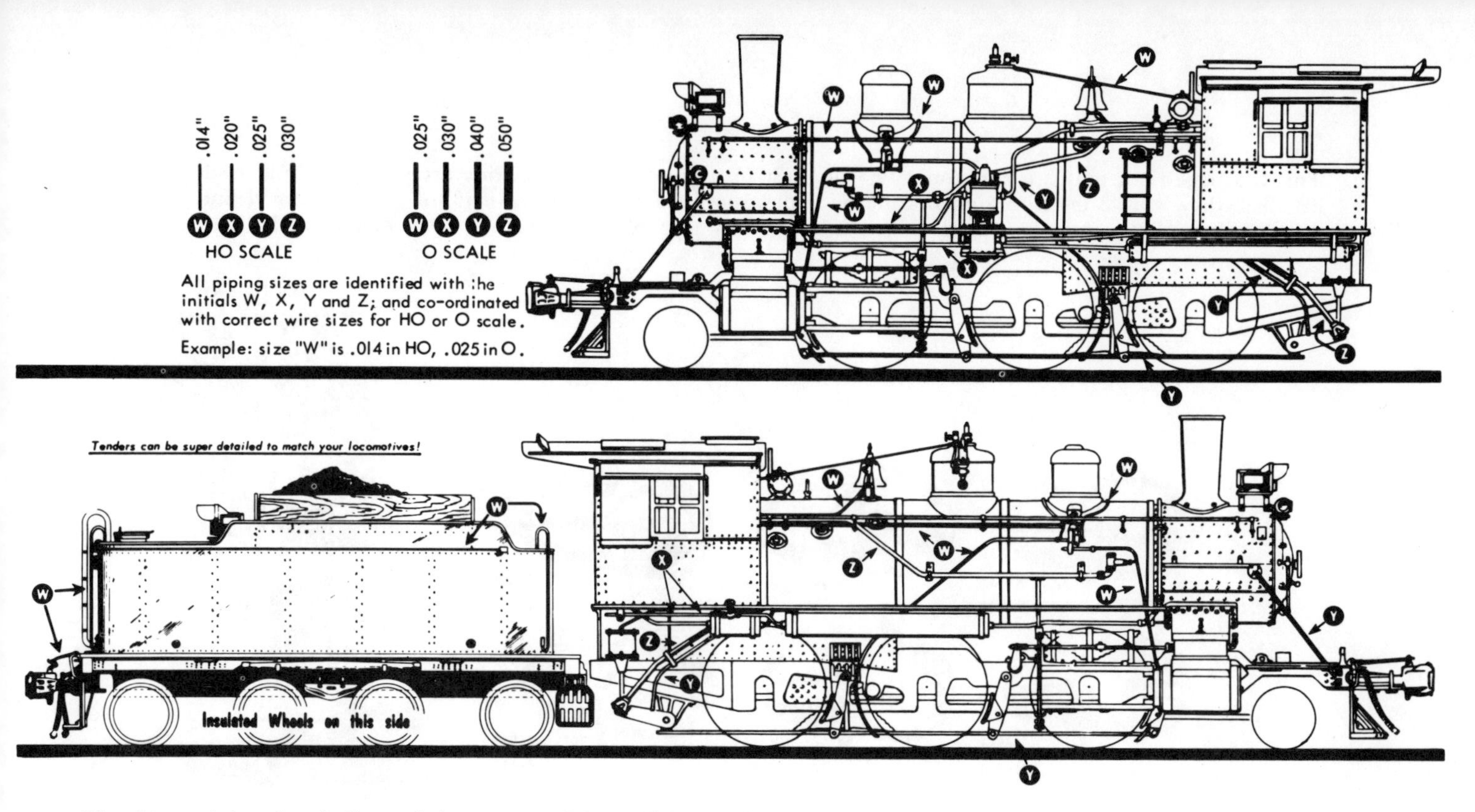

Plumbing, piping, handrails, grab irons, etc., all have different diameters. Check the correct wire sizes and code designations against other Kemtron diagrams shown in this chapter.

This "exploded" drawing of Kemtron's Wabash "Mogul" tender not only shows you the ease of assembly, but indicates just a few of the techniques possible for making the tender more striking. To make a coal pile is a simple chore, as shown in the diagram. Carve wood block to desired contours, brush on white glue, cover tacky surface with scale-sized coal and let set till dry. Or, if you want to avoid making the contoured wood block, simply pour a mound of coal onto the storage bin surface and saturate (using an eyedropper) with a mixture of white glue and water.

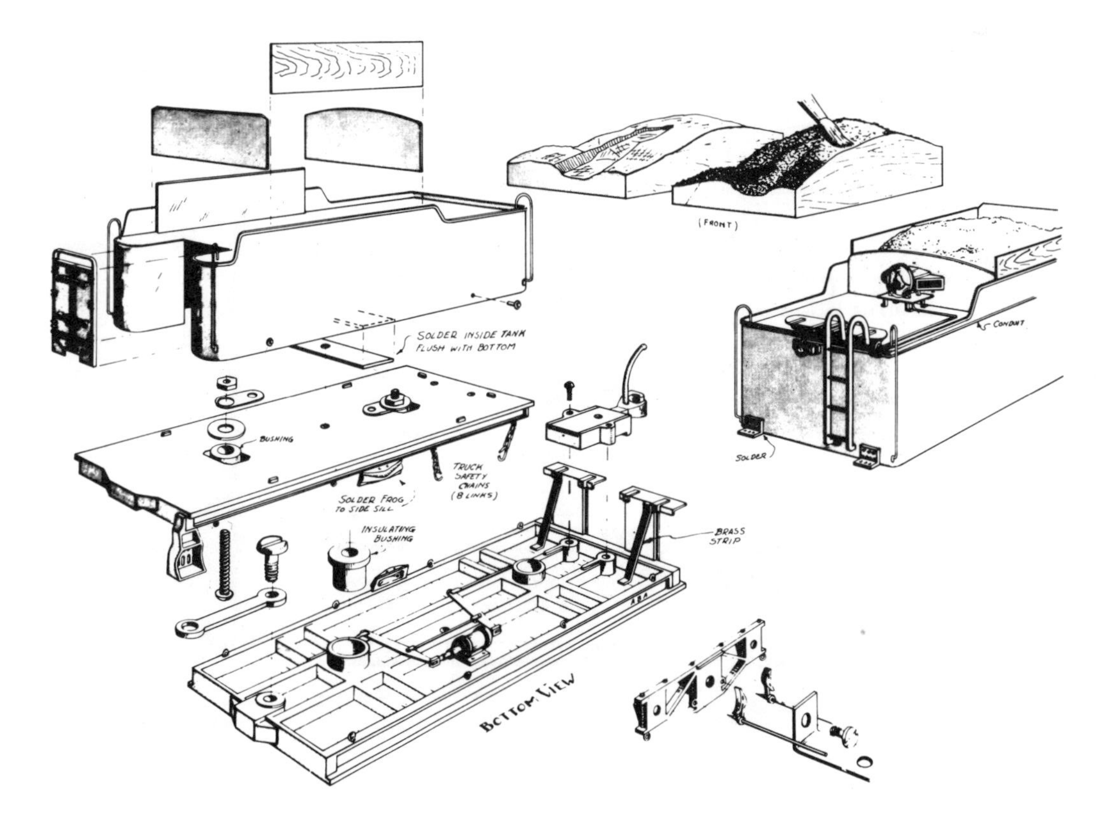

This is a page right out of a Kemtron catalogue. Just feast your eyes on the wide array of tanks and cooling coils. Easily installed, they will do much to authenticate the appearance of any locomotives and, of course, are a definite improvement over locomotives whose tanks and cooling coils are simply part of the overall mold or embossed design.

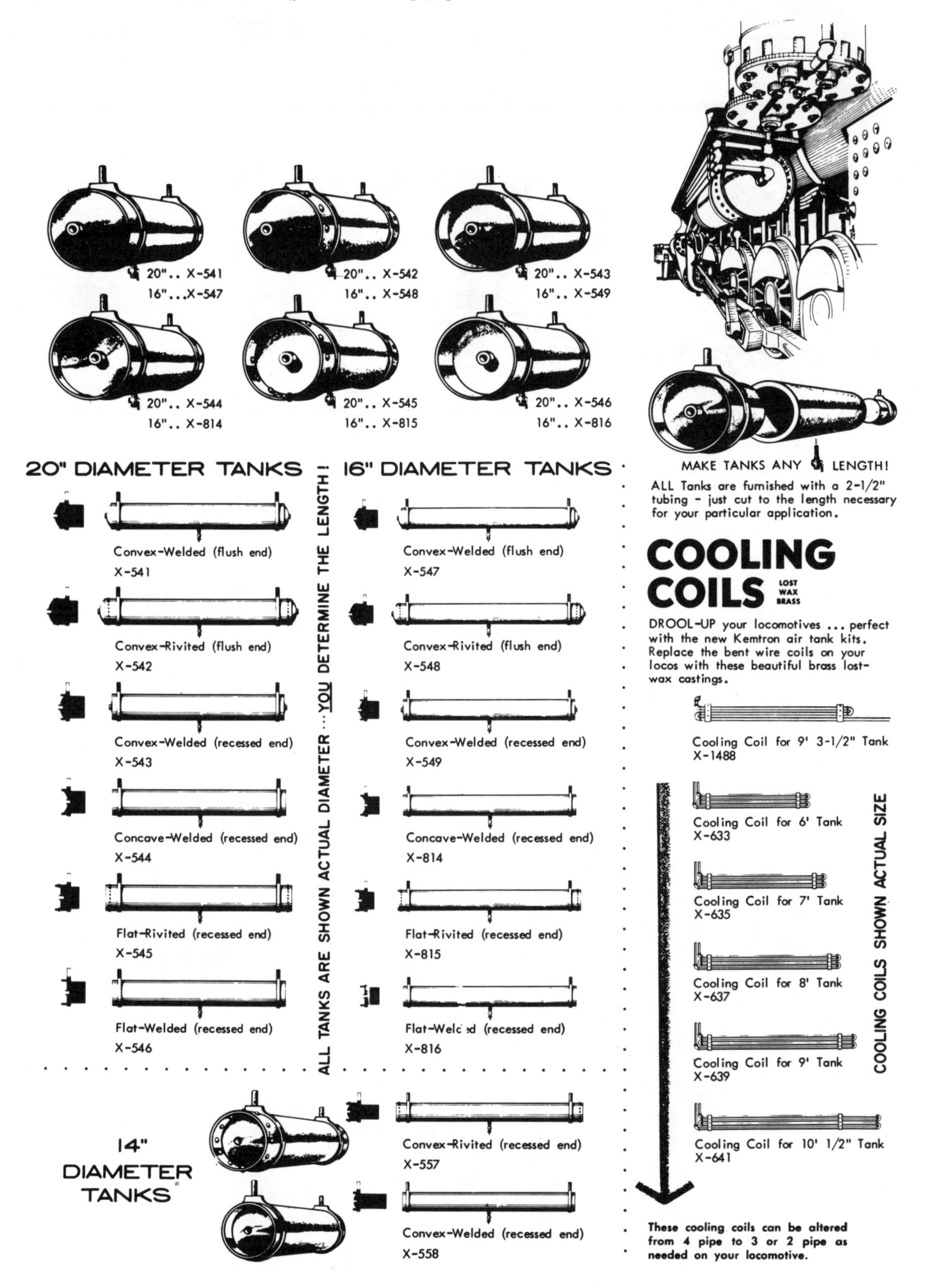

This completely detailed, all-brass Vanderbilt tender more than speaks for itself. Available from Kemtron in kit or custom-built form, it is prototype in every way and will make a handsome addition to your locomotive.

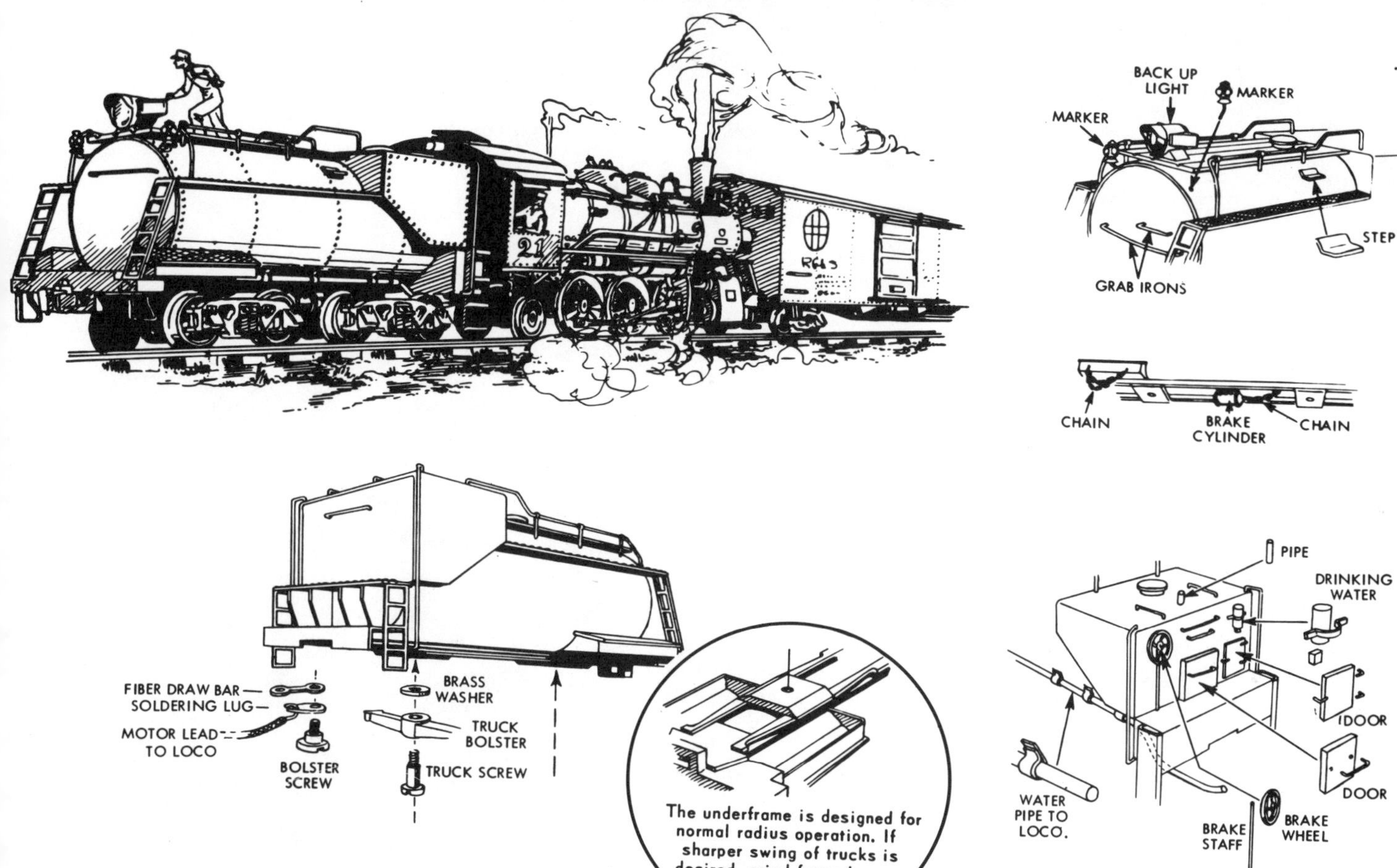

Additional parts and details available from Kemtron will add the final touch to your tender.

A fine example of scratch building at its best is this O scale reproduction of a 4-4-0 American type. Painstakingly built up by the skill and craftsmanship of William A. Cooper in 1937, it is now in the Ward Kimball Collection. When you consider that this locomotive was hand-built some three decades ago, during a period of time when scale modelers were essentially on their own, you can only marvel at the end result.

Close-up view shows excellent example of precision and hand tooling of what someday may become a lost art. Note the detailing of the drivers, brake cylinder and brake shoes, among other things.

Not every one is skillful of hand when it comes to superdetailing or, for that matter, inclined in that particular direction. A locomotive such as this Santa Fe Berkshire leaves little to be desired in the way of additional detailing. An outstanding example of scale miniaturization in HO today, this model, from United, is a handsome duplicate of the prototype locomotive built by Baldwin.

For the beginner who might be up to his elbows with his first kit, such talk of superdetailing and conversions may sound both complicated and far, far away. However, it is much easier than it appears to be and certainly worth a try if you are interested in improving or changing the appearance of your equipment. Don't forget, conversions include both a change of wheel arrangements and the era of the loco. As explained earlier, replacing a diamond stack with a straight stack, a cow-catcher with an industrial pilot (or vice versa), and other modifications which either "modernize" or "oldtimer-ize" are all part of conversion. These things happened in real railroading and still do. Wheel arrangements weren't changed merely for the sake of appearance, but rather to increase the tractive effort. Some trailing trucks also had booster engines, which are closely akin to jet-assisted takeoffs on propellor-driven planes. What was good for the prototype is certainly a fine criterion for the miniature.

Let's dwell briefly on the tender, of which there are numerous types and services performed. For example, some tenders featured wood bunkers, coal bunkers, oil tanks, etc. Some were straight-backed, others sloped. There were shorties and long-haul tenders, the latter commonly used behind anything from a 4-6-4 up to a 4-8-8-4. Then, of course, there are the Vanderbilt tenders, which are among the most attractive, popular, and widely used in model railroading today. Tenders open new vistas for detailing and conversions for modelers. Kemtron has an oil tender conversion for a Mantua old time tender in which all you have to do is install the oil tender tank in the coal bunker of the tender to update your equipment and mode of operation. And among other things that can be done to give your tender new life is the addition of backup lights, a coal pusher, ladders, water hatches, marker lights, handrails, grab irons, tool boxes, tanks, tank walks, and, last but by no means least, an automatic-working and realistic-looking coupler such as a Kadee Magnetic type.

These are but a few of the things that can be done to your locomotive equipment, and to further illustrate, you will find within these pages an assortment of photographs designed to lead you along new and more exciting frontiers of model railroading.

V

Meanwhile,
Back at the Roundhouse

There comes a time when even the heartiest locomotive has to be headed into a stall at the roundhouse for a thorough going over. Cleaning, refitting, servicing, and other chores not only keep the maintenance crew on its toes, but the equipment in top running condition. Model railroading is no exception, and after X number of operating hours your locomotives have to get the beauty treatment, too.

This should be done as a matter of course and not left until equipment is in dire need of repair. To let things go is to invite damage and/or repairs beyond your control, either of which you might not understand or be able to handle. If you get into the habit of periodic servicing and maintenance, your equipment will provide you with less trouble and more enjoyable hours of operation.

The care and maintenance of locomotive equipment involve four particular categories: *cleaning, mechanical, electrical,* and *lubrication.* We will go into these in greater detail later, but first I should like to point out that the initial hours of operation or break-in period of your locomotive have much to do with its longevity and ultimate performance. How you handle and operate your motive power in its early stages of newness, whether kit-built or ready-to-run, will reflect itself later on when it will either purr like a kitten or growl like a lion. If you were to glance over the shoulder of a veteran brass hat who was running a brand new locomotive for the first time, chances are that he would throttle the power down to see how slow the loco could creep rather than how fast it could highball. In this way the motion of the valve gear assembly can be observed more carefully, and it is easier to detect trouble spots if something should go wrong. If there is a complication, it will be right in front of you and not at some point five laps around your layout. Did you ever try to find an optical screw that has popped off somewhere along the line?

In Chapter 3 I mentioned that some locomotives are delivered without lubrication. It bears repeating, since operating a loco in this condition may not only strip the worm screw threads and the teeth of the gear, but also force the motor shaft out of alignment. An application of Lubriplate or any similar lubricant will go a long way toward preventing such a mishap. Considering the fact that locomotive break-in is, to repeat, about three

An Atlantic heads into a stall of the roundhouse for a check-up. This 18-inch turntable is a beauty and, like the engine sheds, was completely scratch-built by Dick Seydell. Turntable is powered by a low-geared (barbecue type) motor, and features an interlocking arrow device to line up and secure track on turntable ramp to respective track in the stalls of the roundhouse. Other effects in and about the yard give realistic substance to this maintenance area of Seydell's pike.

Engine house by Revell is distinctive in appearance, with operating doors opened by weight of locomotive as it enters approach track. This particular structure is one of the most popular among model rails, and can be revamped and modified in a number of ways. It is also an easily assembled kit for the enthusiast who wants a realistic-looking roundhouse but doesn't want to scratch-build it himself.

A temporary hook-up with alligator clips and the application of an abrasive stone on drivers will clean tire surfaces in a hurry, after which a pipe cleaner saturated with a contact cleaner will not only make things sparkling clean, but will do much to retard oxidation and accumulation of dirt. Baumgarten loco cradle makes a useful receptacle for holding equipment during maintenance.

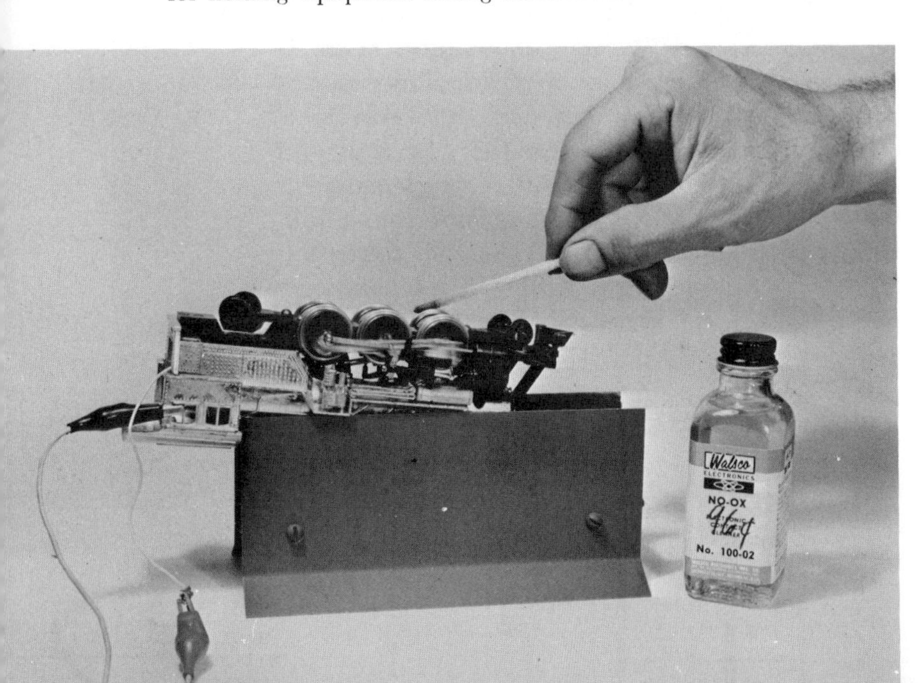

A few scraps of plywood, some soft heavy cloth, canvas or carpet and you have the ingredients for making your own locomotive cradle—a handy item to have when performing maintenance or other chores on your motive power.

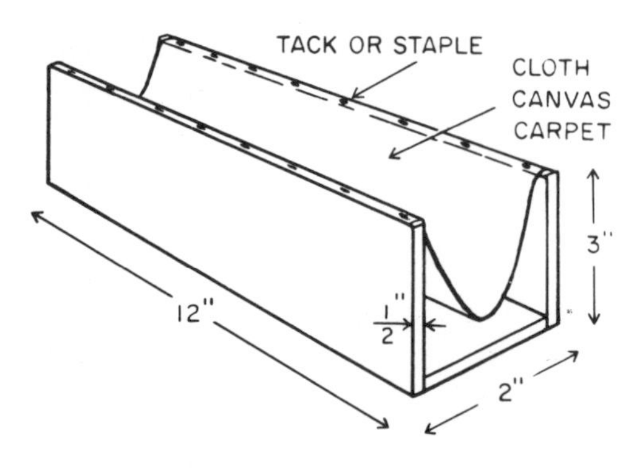

hours of operation, when you feel you have arrived at this point, double check your valve gear to be sure that free-moving parts are loose or flexible, as they should be, and those which should be securely held in place are snug. Also check to see if the break-in period of operation has vibrated loose any of the screws or rivets holding the valve gear assembly in position, re-tightening or re-riveting where necessary. Assuming that the valve gear assembly is in good working order, and shows no sign of binding or working loose, a light application of fine (thin) oil among the connecting links will aid in continued trouble-free performance. The foregoing, plus the recommendations outlined in Chapter III, are all part and parcel of preparing your motive power for future operations.

During the normal course of operations a number of things occur to thwart smooth running, despite the precautions you may have taken at the outset, and this is where regular maintenance and servicing come into play. To keep your equipment in tip-top shape you will need an assortment of tools, and the following will be of aid to you:

- Cradle for holding inverted loco and tender
- Tweezers, needle or long-nose pliers
- Set of jeweler's screwdrivers
- Brushes ½-inch wide or round, camel's hair and hard bristle
- Toothpicks (handy for lubricating and removing foreign matter from hard-to-reach places)
- Pair of test leads, with alligator clips attached at ends
- Crocus cloth and sandpaper
- Abrasive stone such as Brite Boy
- Lubriplate, or similar lubricant
- Life-like track-cleaning fluid, or kerosene
- Walsco Contact cleaner (No-Ox)
- A fine, thin oil

In addition to the above, all tools previously mentioned, such as drills, a hobby hammer, taps, and files, will be useful not only for servicing, but for repairs if they become necessary.

For regular servicing, the first thing on the agenda is a thorough cleaning of your locomotive, and this certainly means more than just a few swipes with a brush at dust which has accumulated on the exterior surfaces. Pay heed also to the condition of the wheels, cleanliness of pivot points of lead, trailing and tender trucks, foreign matter in and about wireless drawbars, etc. Use a mild solvent (one that will not mar your paint job) to remove any matter or sludge that will not easily brush away. Exterior and underbody cleaning does not require the removal of the superstructure/boiler from the frame; however, for the most part, where you have to get to the inner workings of your locomotive, you will have to separate one from the other. In so doing, remove the long screw that holds the underframe, cylinder block, and boiler in position. To keep the cylinders and valve gear assembly from flopping about on the frame, place a matching nut on the screw running up through the frame and the cylinder and secure in position temporarily (see Chapter III). In this way you will be able to run the motor and other working mechanisms in partially disassembled form, and observe the motion of motor, worm, screw, valve gear, etc., without fouling things up due to loose fit.

If the cradle or receptacle you use for holding your loco in an inverted position will also accommodate your tender, attach one of the test lead ends to a tender truck axle or metal wheel pickup and the other to the metal frame of the boiler or superstructure. Now turn the throttle of your power pack to half speed. While the drivers are turning, place an abrasive stone such as Brite Boy against the tire surface of each wheel, thus removing any accumulated gook and oxidation. Don't press too hard, otherwise the motor might stall. Since the wheels of the lead and trailing trucks are not geared, you will have to turn them by hand, and during rotation, by use of the abrasive stone, you will be able to clean these wheels in the same manner as the drivers. Following this, all drivers and wheels should be wiped clean by using a soft rag saturated with a track-cleaning fluid, kerosene, or No-Ox (a contact cleaner and oxidation retarder).

In the event the cradle will not accommodate the tender also, disconnect the tender at the drawbar and, if not of the wireless hookup type, then also disconnect the attached motor lead. You can then attach your power pack leads to the motor lead (which runs to the tender) and the underframe, or the wireless drawbar and the underframe, or whichever combination is required to power your locomotive when it is not getting juice from the rails. Do not under any circumstances use steel wool, either in conjunction with locomotive maintenance or elsewhere within your layout. This material crumbles easily, leaving small bits of metal which are easily attracted to and will weaken the permanent magnet in the motor of your locomotive. If your locomotive is tenderless and equipped with wire contact pickups which rest directly against your drivers, clean the surfaces gently with fine sandpaper to insure a better flow of juice from drivers to motor.

We now come to the mechanical end of things along the maintenance way. Since we have discussed at great length the things to look for, correct, improve on, and/or keep in good running shape concerning the valve gear assembly and other integral parts of this mechanism, we will skip over this segment —although its importance is not to be glossed over. Check the springs (if any) which, attached to lead and trailing trucks, rest against the underframe. If they are not resilient, or performing as they were intended, then replace them. Also check to see if any burrs or rough spots have developed in and about the area in which the trucks pivot on the screw holding them in place (ditto for tender trucks and bolsters). A few careful swipes with a fine file will rid you of the condition, should it exist. Also look closely to be sure that nothing has entered the scene or been removed to change the status and function of insulated and non-insulated wheels and drivers, and check for burrs and obstructions in the slots of the frame which houses the axles. Now would also be a good time to double check and readjust the height of your couplers on both the loco and tender, if necessary.

From the standpoint of electrical maintenance, the prime concern is to get a good flow of juice to the motor through the pickup wheels and other contact points. Having covered this earlier, we now get to the heart of things—the motor and connecting wires. The latter should be screwed or soldered firmly in place at both ends to provide a good electrical flow. If the leads show undue wear, frayed ends, or the possibility of shorting out against the frame or other surrounding metal areas, replace them with appropriate lengths of flexible stranded wire of similar resistance.

Check the brushes (graphite units) which ride on the copper commutators. If they are worn down to a nubbin, replace them. If the commutator appears dirty or tarnished, advance the throttle to half speed and apply a small piece of crocus cloth to the revolving commutator. One drop (no more) of contact cleaner will help reduce the possibility of arcing, and also brighten things up a bit. While you are at it, you can also check to see if the worm and gear is properly meshed —remember, neither too shallow nor too deep. The application of a lubricant, such as Lubriplate, would now be in order. If your locomotive includes a working headlight, now would be a good time to double check its performance. At a steady throttle speed of, say, half power the bulb should burn brightly and steadily. If it flickers, it could indicate a loose connection or intermittent short. Check the wire leads for frayed ends and loose soldered connecting points, remedying the causes, if any.

During the course of these maintenance chores and procedures you will note that in a given area you can clean, check mechanical and electrical sections, and lubricate at about

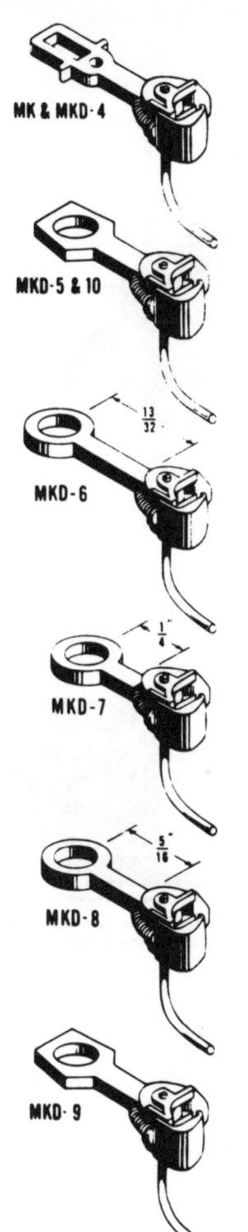

The "MKD" series of Kadee couplers shown in this diagram belong to their wide and varied assortment of delayed Magne-Matic couplers. These couplers provide smooth coupling and uncoupling. When used in conjunction with the Kadee Magnetic Uncoupler, you will be able to uncouple cars with greater ease, and by means of delayed action spot them at points away from the location of the uncoupler itself. These couplers will fit or can be adapted to all the popular makes of model locomotives, and instructions concerning their installation are specific and easy to follow.

To aid the friction-free performance of your couplers, Kadee makes a dry lubricant called "Greas-Em." It comes in a tube and is in the form of powdered graphite. A few puffs on the springs and other working parts of the coupler will provide more freedom in their action. A bit of burnishing with a metal rod will smooth away tiny burrs in and about the coupler housing compartment.

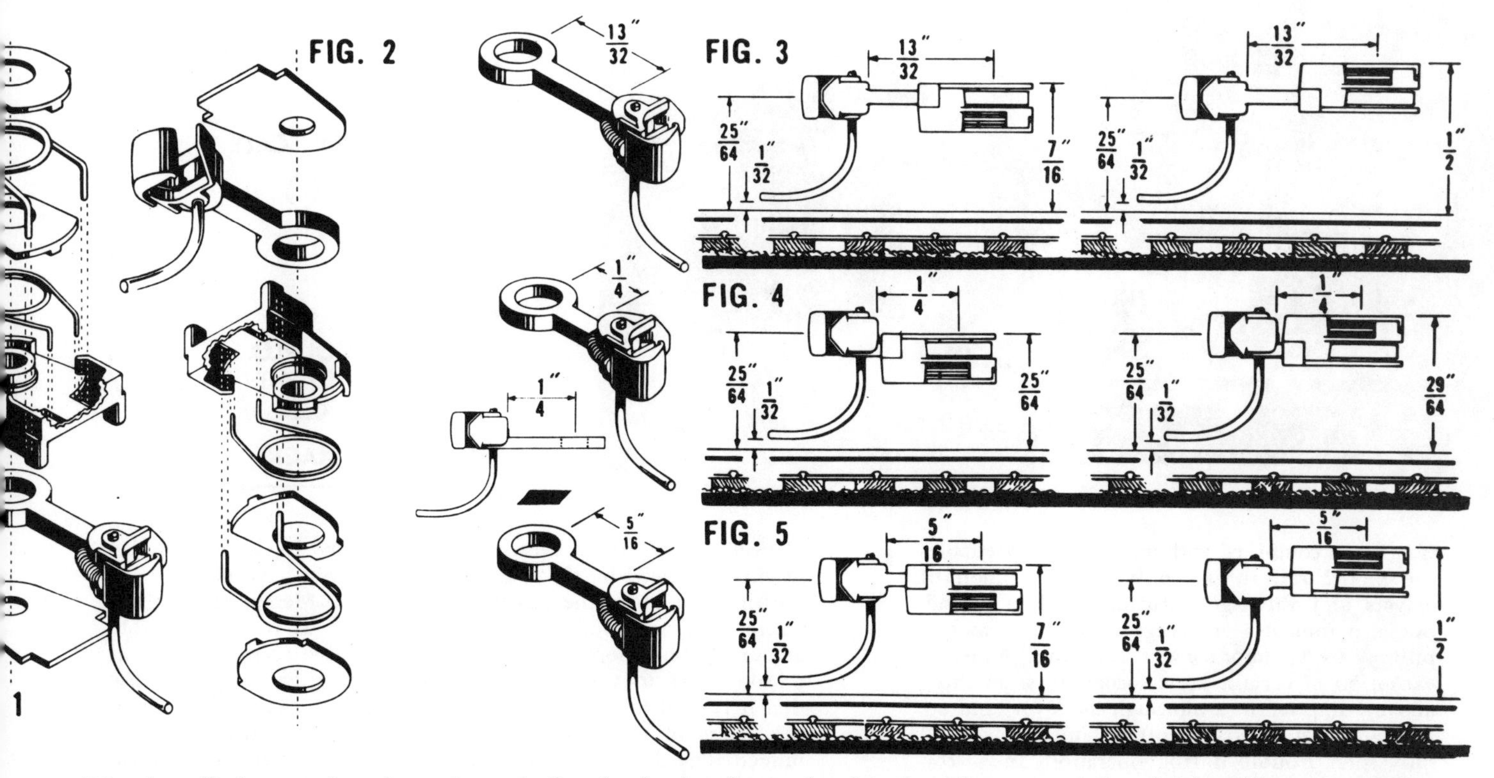

The three Kadee couplers shown have similar shanks, but in varying lengths. They were designed primarily for unusual mounting situations sometimes encountered with certain types of locomotive pilots. The three shank lengths can be assembled within the draft gear housing in two different ways, resulting in six different mounting possibilities depending on whether your pilot will require high- or low-coupler installation, as shown.

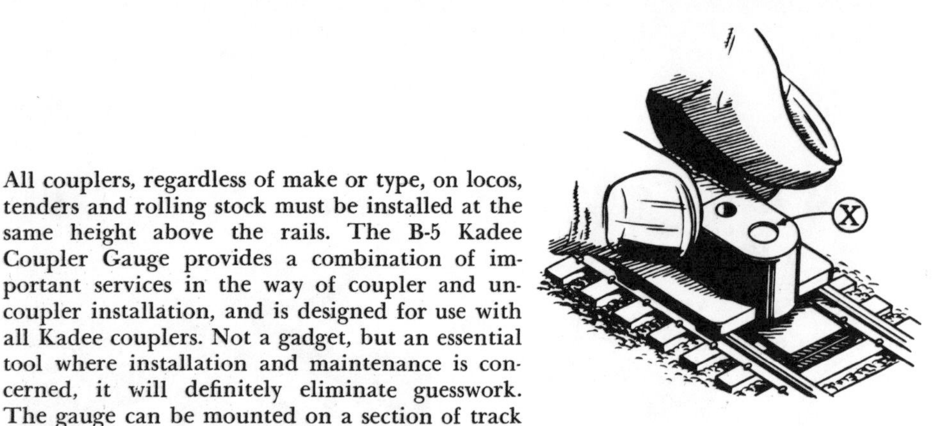

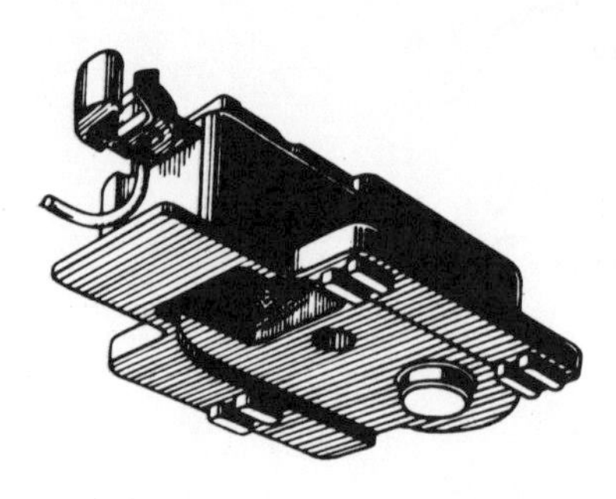

All couplers, regardless of make or type, on locos, tenders and rolling stock must be installed at the same height above the rails. The B-5 Kadee Coupler Gauge provides a combination of important services in the way of coupler and uncoupler installation, and is designed for use with all Kadee couplers. Not a gadget, but an essential tool where installation and maintenance is concerned, it will definitely eliminate guesswork. The gauge can be mounted on a section of track or moved anywhere along your trackage. You simply line it up with the coupler on your loco, tender or cars, and check and adjust coupler height accordingly. The B-5: *a*) Includes a Kadee coupler situated at proper height above the rails; *b*) Gauges height of the "glad hand"; *c*) Can be used as a track gauge; *d)* Has a movable dowel which aids in the installation of uncoupler magnet between the rails. "X" marks the spot where dowel registers flush with top of gauge when uncoupler magnet is at correct height above the rail top.

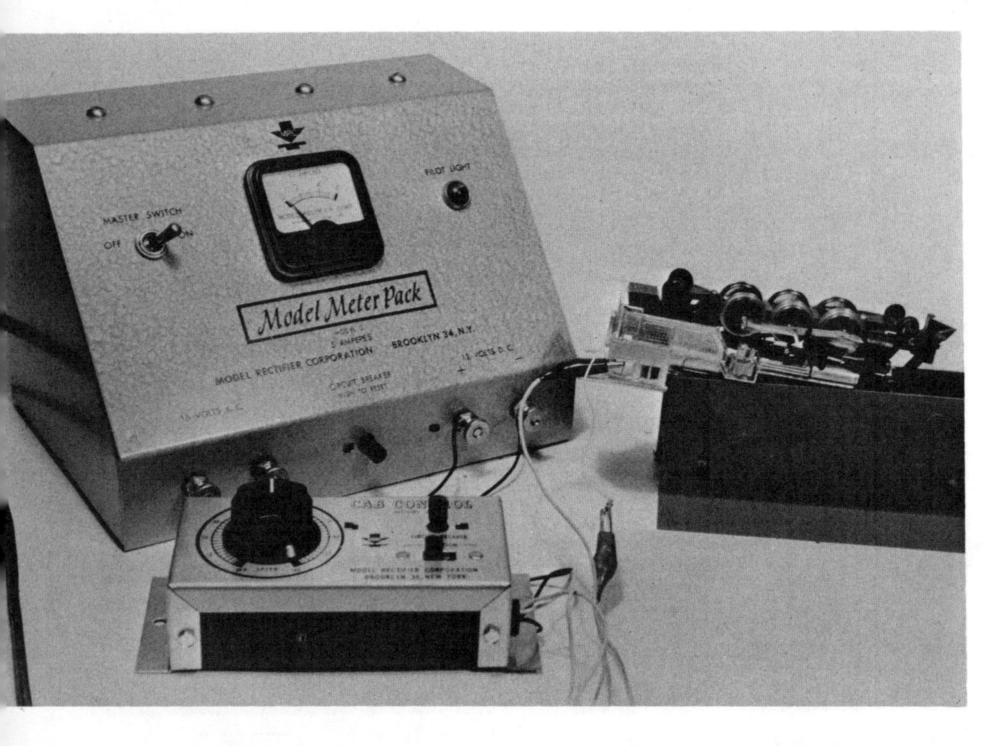

Bench test combined with ammeter check enables the model rail to not only observe action of drivers and valve gear during break-in period, but also indicates amperage draw. Most motors pull ½ to ¾ amp, some a full amp. With the exception of certain large locomotives, anything above 1 amp merits a thorough check for binding, weak magnet, shorts or other faults which will only spell trouble during operation unless corrected.

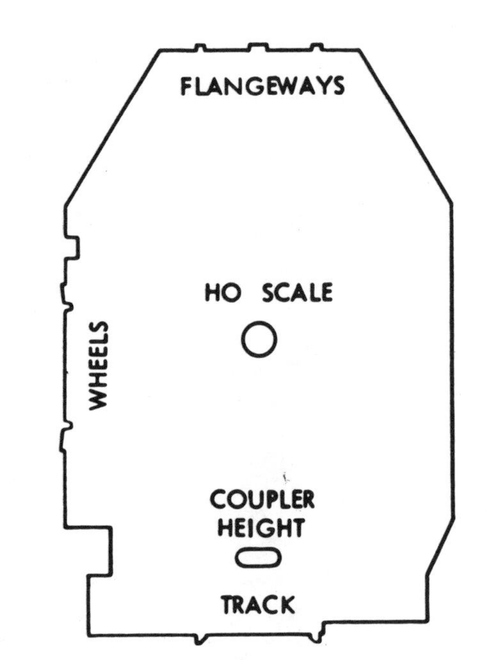

"I don't know how I ever got along without it" is the popular sentiment voiced by all model railroaders who have had the opportunity of using the NMRA Gage Check. Membership in the national organization will get you one free. It is also available at most hobby shops. This gage is as valuable to model rails as passports are to world travelers. Not a track gage in the sense that it is used to spike down rail, but rather a means of checking the gauge of track already laid. In addition, it will help you immediately determine whether your wheels and drivers conform to NMRA specifications and standards. Study the diagrams, which show application of gauge to wheels and drivers, their flange depth, tire width, etc.

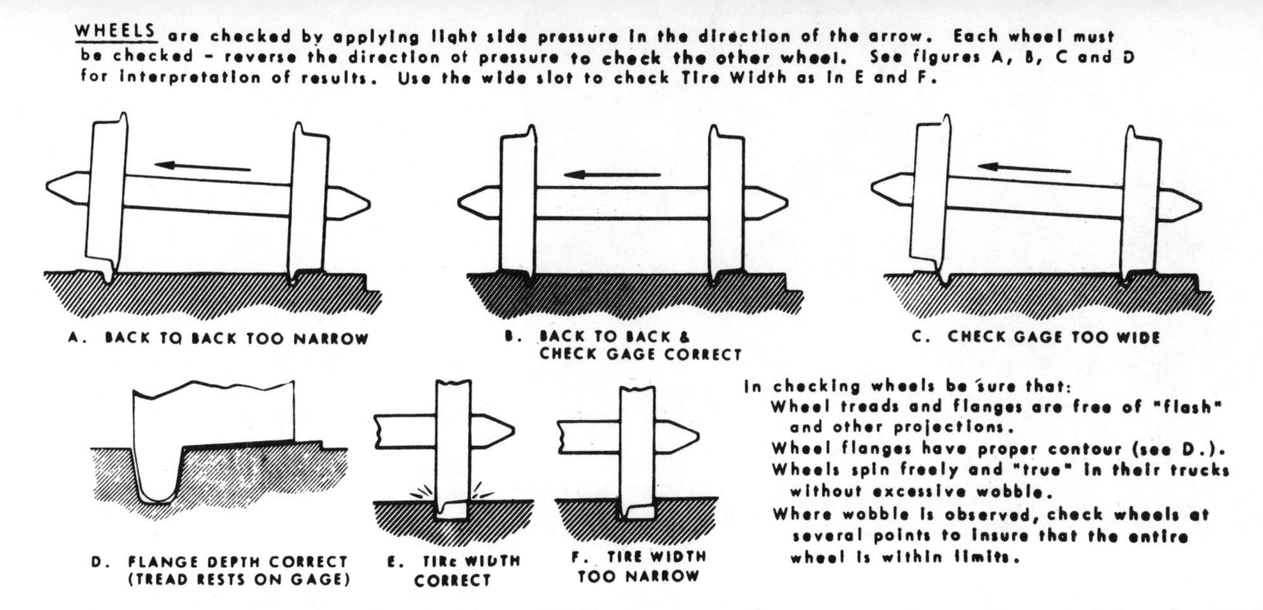

These NMRA Gage Checks on wheels and drivers will speed you on the way toward smoother running and operation. You will have less derailments, too. The various means with which the NMRA Gage Check can be put to use is shown in this diagram from an NMRA Data Sheet.

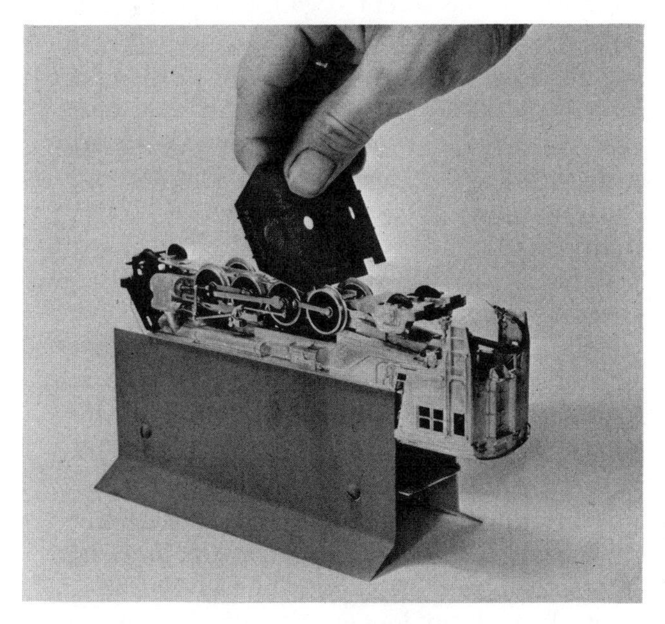

NMRA Gage Check shown in actual use will tell you at a glance if your HO gauge and depth of flanges are within prescribed tolerances.

the same time. In other words, you wouldn't remove the superstructure to get at the motor for electrical checkups, replacing it when finished, and then have to go through the whole thing moments later when you have to lubricate the worm and gear or get at something else inside, thus requiring removal of the boiler again. In short, when working on a particular area, whether within or on the exterior, try to apply as many of the maintenance categories as possible so that you won't be constantly assembling and re-assembling. For, needless to say, the less you have to take your locomotive apart the better, since you may never get it back together in its original condition. Ditto for the valve gear mechanism. As an aside to those of you who have assembled your locomotive from kit form, assuming that you kept your original instruction sheets, the importance of having them before you when working on your locomotive now becomes quite evident.

Things are in full swing in this authentic scene at the Glendale Model RR Club. A "Docksider" coupled to a Vanderbilt tender waits its turn as another loco is lined up on the turntable to head out. Look at all the details: the track-work, the switchstand, the ground cover and ballasting.

The above and other maintenance applications will serve you well and keep you on the road toward smoother operation. When the time comes—and it will—when engines won't run, or do so haltingly, when they wobble along like Donald Duck or sound like him, make erratic or jack-rabbit starts and stops, etc., then you will have a clearer idea of cause and remedy. For example, an engine that won't run and shows no current drain (or too much) on an ammeter or voltmeter can be an indication of numerous factors: lack of current on track, poor connection or dirty track, undue oxidation or dirt on wheels of loco and tender, tender trucks that have accidentally swung around so that pickup wheels are on the wrong side, and loose wires. These same conditions may exist as contributing causes for an engine that won't run because of an apparent short circuit, whereby something may be binding up, wires may be shorting out, worm and gear may be too tightly meshed, or the magnet may have attracted an unusual amount of steel filings.

Last but not least is the question of the wheels and drivers. Don't take for granted that they conform to standards. Check them with your NMRA gage. Among other things, as the accompanying diagrams indicate, the gage will accurately tell you whether your wheels and drivers conform to NMRA standards, i.e., whether they are true to gauge and conform to the accepted gauge of your track, for, if not, derailments and other mishaps will occur to plague you. In addition, you will be able to ascertain whether your wheels have the correct flange depth, a most important consideration for smooth operation through turnouts and flangeways. These and other important functions of the NMRA gage will make you wonder how you ever got along without it before.

While the foregoing is not a thorough listing of all the troubles you are likely to encounter, or of all the causes and remedial steps which must be taken, your own increased familiarity, coupled with that which has been disclosed thus far, should serve as a sufficient guide to aid you when the gremlins sneak into your locomotive and give it a hot foot. It will no longer be such a game of hide-and-seek in spotting the ailment and applying the cure. You are the doctor, and smooth trouble-free operation of your locomotive equipment is a condition for which only you can write the prescription.

VI
Painting and Special Effects

By and large, price tags on locomotives, ranging from $4.95 to $150, don't seem to disturb the model rail, but when it comes to painting such equipment, many a modeler blanches at the prospect of shelling out a dollar for a good quality sable brush, let alone investing in a quality airbrush and compressor. Yet painting and weathering of locomotive equipment is not only one of the most important considerations of the hobby, but also one of the most rewarding. Selective painting will enable you to change the "store bought" look typical of most pre-painted locos and/or give a proper finish to unpainted brass, Zamac, or other materials and surfaces. Unfortunately, it seems more the rule than the exception for a modeler to spend fifty dollars on a loco, then slap a two-dollar paint job on it. How negligent can one get, or lazy, for that matter. Essentially, there are two ways to paint locomotive equipment—airbrushing or by hand. True, the latter, in the hands of an expert, can produce a finished result that in many cases defies description and usually looks like and has that smooth quality of airbrushing. However, more often than not the average paint job done by hand is easily identifiable due to tell-tale brush marks, runs, paint streaks, and other irregularities. The most desired effect is that of a smooth painted surface free of the aforementioned.

Most modelers, in trying to achieve the effect typical of airbrushing, will generally fall quite short of their goal. This brings up a good point, to wit, if the results that an airbrush affords are what is ultimately desired, then why not use an airbrush in the first place? Well, the truth of the matter is that the discriminating modeler does use an airbrush because he knows from experience that this technique can't be beat. As for the beginner, and that includes many an average modeler, the mere mention of airbrushing conjures up visions of bulky compressors, pressure gauges, compressed-air tanks, expensive and seemingly delicate airbrush guns, many dollars, and, least of all, an artistic ability second only to that of such leading illustrators as Vargas and Norman Rockwell. True, there was a time when airbrush applications and the use of such equipment embraced the above ingredients, but it is certainly not the case today.

For example, the Paasche Airbrush Company, one of the world's leading suppliers of such equipment, has a variety of airbrush guns and power units designed to fit anyone's pocketbook. But more important, it has a particular airbrush that has been designed and developed solely for use in hobby work, model railroading included, and the price is right, as you will see.

The airbrush I make particular reference to is their H "3-in-1" Convertible Airbrush, so designated because of the availability of three sizes of interchangeable color and air cap parts, which produce adjustable ranges from a fine line to a wide spray, a prime factor where painting miniatures is concerned. Now, if the foregoing and the following sound like a commercial for Paasche, it is only because of this writer's enthusiasm following a survey of their fine product and its variety of uses. Price and ease of use are also what sold me, and I'm sure will sell you before I'm finished. The gun itself is lightweight and hand-held, like a pen or pencil. Adjustments can be made from a fine line (particularly useful when you wish to hit a small or narrow area) to the wider spray (necessary for such areas as boiler, cab, pilot, etc.). I am talking about a spray no wider than an inch, in which the airbrush is held not much farther away during the spraying. In this way you can actually see the paint going on from beginning to end of your stroke.

Instructions for use of the Paasche Airbrush are quite explicit, and within a few moments you can get the hang of things. A single button, when depressed, mixes air with paint, producing such a highly atomized spray that scant moments later the painted surface is practically dry to the touch. Other simple adjustments enable you to go from narrow to broader spray, plus such effects as spatter and stippling. Cleaning is simple and takes little of your time. As for the painting itself, all you do is pour the color you have selected into the color cup or bottle, make a few passes on a piece of paper or suitable background, spraying from right to left, or vice versa, at the same time adjusting for width and intensity of paint spray. After that it is merely a matter of technique and application, both of which will be developed far easier than you can imagine. And as I said before, the price is right, which in this case happens to be around $21. This includes the gun, 1/4-ounce color cup, 3-ounce color bottle, hanger, hose coupling, etc.

I know your next question will be, "What about the power? Do I have to rent or purchase one of those bulky oxygen tanks, or spend three times as much on a compressor?" The answer fortunately is, no, you don't have to do any of those things if you are starting from scratch. The Paasche Company seems to have anticipated the needs of model rails perfectly by offering a pocket-edition pressure tank (No. 1 Paasche Pressure Tank). It's called a pocket edition because you can virtually carry it about in your pocket—in other words, it is no larger than the average aerosol spray cans with which we have become so familiar. The beauty of it is that not only does it contain anywhere from one to three hours' supply of compressed air, depending on use, but you are not chained to a compressor. You can, therefore, spray in any part of the room, or wherever your legs will carry you, rather than in close proximity to a compressor. The initial purchase of the pressure tank also includes an air hose, various couplings and fittings, a simple tank valve, etc. Total cost is between $5 and $6; thereafter, the cost for replacement of the pressure tank is a nominal $2.

Another wonderful point in favor of this pressure tank is the fact that you can operate it in the dead of night without fear of waking the baby or disturbing your neighbors, since, except for a slight hiss of air, there is no sound—certainly a far cry from the nerve-racking rat-a-tat-tat typical of most compressors. Paasche also makes a special compressor which you could well call the silent wonder; it is the quietest compressor I have ever heard in op-

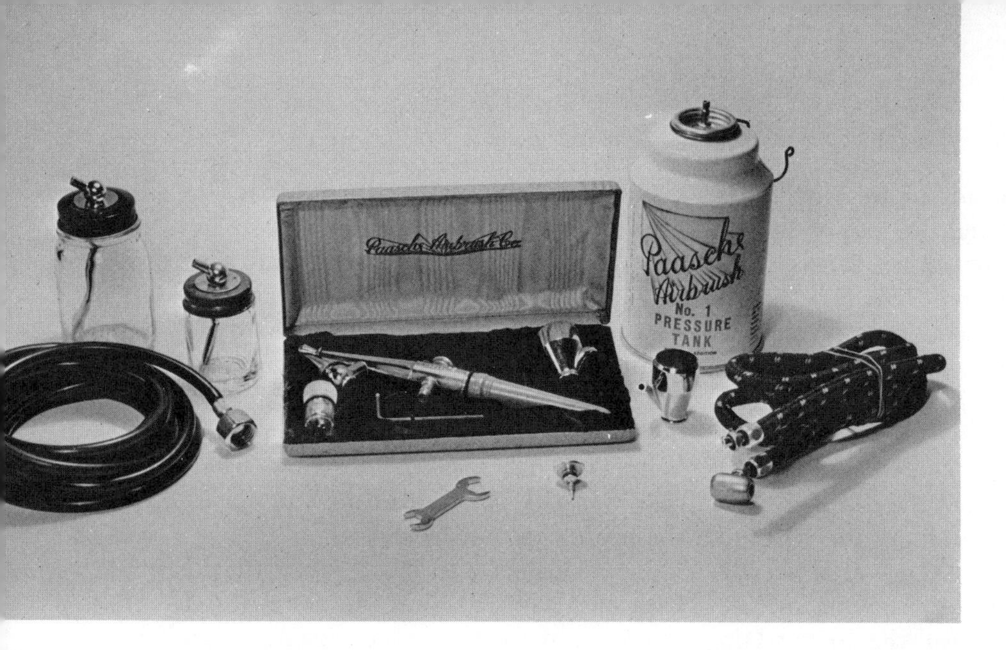

The Paasche Air Brush, shown here with some of its components and accessories, is a painting instrument which will virtually guarantee the optimum in quality and control. Range of spray is from a fine line to a 3/4 inch area with overspray at an absolute minimum. This model is the "H-3 in 1 Convertible," so called because it will accept interchangeable tips. Small paint cups are handy for fast color changeovers and when you have a minimum of painting or area to cover. Glass jars, easily attached, contain a larger quantity of paint and will save time refilling when considerable painting is in order.

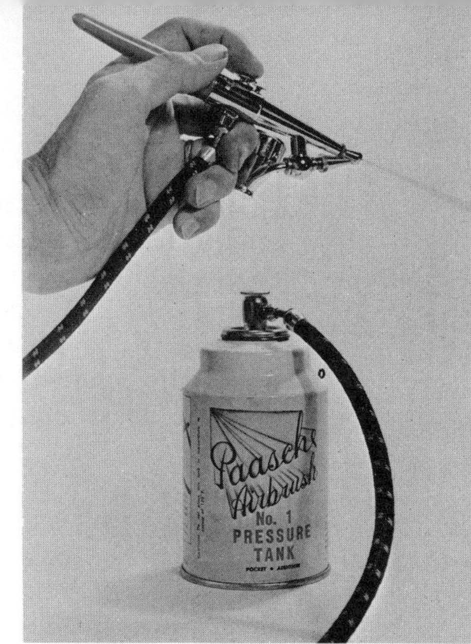

The fine controls in painting that an air brush permits will help you achieve that "professional" finish that veteran model railroaders impart to their locomotives.

eration and is moderately priced. Of course, if you happen to have an air compressor that puts out in the neighborhood of 35 pounds of pressure, then hooking up a Paasche H3 is no problem at all. In fact, for a test I hooked the H3 to the air compressor accessory of my Shopsmith, and both gun and compressor worked fine. As for hooking up to a vacuum cleaner tank, forget it; the Paasche gun won't work, for if it did, it wouldn't produce the fine and highly atomized spray that it is famous for.

That ends the commercial for the moment, but it is a pitch well worth having been delivered and, I am sure, listened to. As further evidence, carefully study some of the results pictured in the pages of this chapter and in other chapters of this book, for the Paasche airbrush certainly aided in achieving the fine finish on some of the locomotive equipment.

Having established the type of painting instrument which will afford you an optimum of quality results, we now get to the actual painting itself. First off, spraying should be done in a clean area, one which is as dust-free as possible. Secondly, there is the matter of priming the surface, or giving it tooth, so that the paint will adhere, thus minimizing the possibility of peeling, flaking, and chipping. A basic underspray coating is not sufficient, since if the undercoat doesn't grab, then it will be a poor foundation for the other layers of paint which will follow. Brass, for example, is best treated by use of a prebath in a 10 per cent solution of vinegar, or any similar acidy liquid. In fact, acetic acid, which can be purchased at your pharmacy or camera shop, will do the trick perfectly. Your pharmacist might even save you the trouble of working out the formula by pre-mixing the 10 per cent solution for you. If not, ask for it in 28 per cent solution (it comes either 99 or 28), after which you can easily dilute it to the 10 per cent required. This acid prebath will serve to produce an etching effect on the brass surface of your locomotive, which will make it more receptive for the stick-to-it quality you want in the initial and final layers of paint.

Another excellent means of treating brass prior to painting is through the use of Bright Dip, a solution used to restore brass to its natural color and condition. This is achieved by dipping the parts to be painted in the Bright Dip solution, the result being exactly what the name implies. The liquid contains various acids, and though it gives off little, if any, odor, it is slightly caustic and should be handled with care. After the dipping (use glass or earthenware container) be sure to wash and dry thoroughly, then you are ready for painting. In addition to removing surface scum, oxidation, and tarnish, the Bright Dip will also produce a slight etching effect on the surface of the brass, which will aid in the "grabability" of the paint adhering to the metal. It is $2 a gallon and will last quite a while. If you can't get it locally, you can order it direct from Hill Bros. Chemical Company, City of Industry, California.

Another thought might be to follow up the acid pre-bath with a sizing solution (glue-based) which in turn serves as a fine bond for the paint to adhere to, while it in turn adheres to the brass. Following your final paint job, as an additional precaution against scratching, chipping, peeling, etc., you can spray your locomotive with a thin coat of dull lacquer or varnish. This will serve as an outer protective film for the paint beneath. The foregoing is also applicable to other surfaces and castings, such as zinc, Zamac, etc. Model Die Casting, for example, has a zinc chromate powder which, when mixed with water, provides a tooth and primed surface on their locomotives. If you check your library, most physics books will fill you in sufficiently on both formula and application of various mixtures designed as proper treatment for different metals and alloys. You can also try "blacking" or "bluing" techniques which will darken the metal surfaces so that, if paint does chip or scrape away, a dark rather than light surface will show through, making touch-up that much easier. Now, all of this may sound extremely time-consuming, but when you consider that this is the only way you can get your paint job to hold up and last over years of handling and use, then you can appreciate that such precautions and steps employed to insure the longevity of your paint job will be well worth taking. It doesn't take as long as it might sound, and, furthermore, model railroading is not a bang-bang-bang do-it-quick type of hobby, but rather one in which the more time you spend at it, the more fun you have.

In taking things apart for both the pre-bath and painting, don't forget that you will have to put them together again, so don't be slipshod about it. If you built the loco from a kit, then dig out the original spec sheets to aid and guide you when re-assembling. If your loco is a ready-to-run job, then make careful note of how you take things apart so that they will go together the same way later on. To avoid fouling up the position of the drivers in relation to insulated and non-insulated wheels, check the correct position beforehand and make note of it (in case you happen to flop things over), or simply attach a piece of masking tape with the notation "right" or "left" side. I'm not trying to insult your intelligence by these seemingly minor suggestions, but when you are all done and you advance the throttle and nothing happens, or something goes wrong (like a short), it might be due to the fact that during the re-assembly you cross-switched the drivers, trucks, or so forth. So take the trouble to be careful and avoid the nuisances later.

If you are not inclined to take things apart, with the aid of masking tape you can block off areas that are not to be painted. You can also use cotton to stuff the open areas in and about the frame, underside, and interior of the cab to protect the motor, worm and gear, and the magnet from receiving any of the paint spray. Giving a pre-bath to an assembled locomotive is, of course, more difficult, although with a bit of time, patience, and sufficient swabs of a brush you can get adequate results.

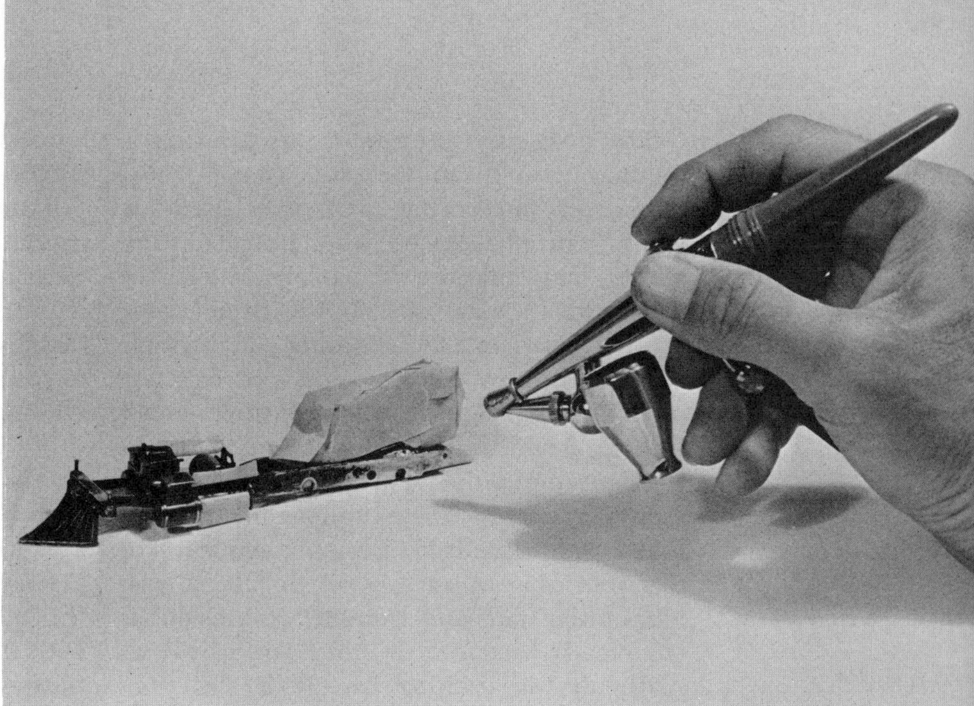

This cleaning solution called "En-Irt" has amazing properties, and cleans things really clean.

For those not wishing to remove or upset factory-positioned motor prior to painting, the use of masking tape will protect those areas that are not to receive paint. This includes cross head guides, etc. Use of an air brush such as the Paasche reduces overspray to an absolute minimum, conserves paint and affords optimum quality in final finish.

Before: Dull flat black finish of this Tyco 0-4-0 "Shifter" is adequate but uninteresting. Nevertheless, it is a start in the right direction.

After: Now this popular switcher looks like it has never seen the inside of a maintenance shed since the day it left the builder's shop. Dusty yard and service worn effect was produced by stippling and spatter application with a Paasche airbrush.

The final stage preparatory to painting is to thoroughly clean the parts free of dust, grime, oil, fingerprints, and other gremlins which will play havoc with your painting efforts. This involves the use of a solvent of which there are many, such as benzine, paint thinner, carbon tetrachloride, and what might well prove to be a wonder product for model rails in a cleaning solution called En-Irt, offered by Kyle Products. This liquid has amazing properties. Essentially a non-corrosive solvent, it is non-inflammable, non-toxic, and, aside from having a tendency to dry your skin of surface oil due to a high evaporative rate and low surface tension, is completely harmless. In other words, it dries really dry in nothing flat. It is also non-conductive, thus enabling you to completely immerse locomotive, motor and all, in the solution and fire things up. No shorting, no shock, nothing except some bubbles. Armature, brushes, wiring, wheels, and drivers will receive a thorough cleaning. Grease, sludge, oil, and accumulated gook will completely disappear, and your locomotive will be cleaner than the day it was manufactured. Of course, afterward you will have to re-lube and re-oil all working parts, worm and gear, valve gear, etc. The foregoing description is merely to point out some of the uses to which En-Irt can be put.

Getting back to painting, and we are finally a few seconds from the actual affair, a dunking, swabbing, or brushing of the locomotive parts with En-Irt will make them as pure as the driven snow, and now, at last, you are ready to paint. Airbrushing is best done in a series of strokes from left to right, or vice versa. Start the air spray before coming in line with the beginning of the part and let up on the spray after stroking past the other end. In other words, for example, assuming the boiler is 6 inches long, start your stroke a few inches before the part, depressing the air spray button about an inch away and letting up an inch after. You will, in effect, be covering an area approximately 8 inches long, with the part being painted evenly spaced within that area. In this way, the application and intensity of paint spray will be constant and even. It should be a smooth motion, not too fast—although if it is, it will only mean you will have to make a number of passes to build up sufficient layers of paint to cover the part. In short, it will take longer. On the other hand, if you stroke too slowly you will be inviting a loading up of paint on the surface resulting in runs, blobs, and what have you. In this case, speed rather than a snail-like creep is the lesser of the two evils. However, this doesn't mean you can rush things. Once you synchronize your stroke with that of depressing and letting up on the button at the right time, you will have become initiated into the fascinations of airbrushing—and, needless to say, the results will look absolutely professional. You will also find it to be far easier than you thought possible.

There are other instruments that can be used to achieve a spray-painting effect, and, while not having the refinements and high atomization of an airbrush such as the Paasche, some of them will do a creditable job. For example, there are inexpensive and simple-to-use spray guns. Some of them work on the vibrator principle and are self-contained; others are easily attached to vacuum cleaners or compressors, producing spray widths of approximately 3/8 inch to 2 inches depending on both the tip and how close or far the gun is held from the object you are painting. In short, the closer you get, the narrower the spray, and as you increase the distance, the width of the paint spray fans out in equal proportion. Of course, if you work too far from the item to be painted, chances are the paint spray will dry before it lands on the surface. The same applies to airbrushing application.

In addition, an assortment of commonly used model railroading colors are available in aerosol type spray cans. Of course, the latter can't compare to the spray gun, let alone an airbrush, but in a pinch will do the job and are especially useful and less costly when you have a minimum of painting to do. However, if you plan to have a large roster of locomotives, an airbrush is definitely your best bet, since it can also be used to paint rolling stock, structures, and scenery.

Avoid pitch-black colors, for if you check the prototypes you will find that as a rule the so-called overall black is really a smoky gray. And, of course, be sure to use a flat finish, since the dullness will add to the realism. In addition to the wide and varied assortment of model railroading paints and colors, such as those made by Ulrich 410M Styrene, Floquil, etc., there are Japan paints, water colors, caseins, and automobile surface primers. In fact, many modelers use these surface primers not only as a base or undercoat, but also for the overall finish. This is particularly so in the case of a gray primer, the finished result appearing to be a gray black or smoky effect rather than a gray. Most metal surface primers are available from auto supply stores in black, gray, red oxide, and white.

Bob Uniack, a member of the Burbank, Encino, and South Tarzana Model Railroad Club, whose prize-winning locomotives have drawn much praise, favors the use of Proxlin gray primer not only for purposes of undercoating, but overcoating as well. Bob's technique in painting and achieving roadworn, weathered effects is one of the reasons why his equipment has won such high honors in various NMRA meets. With skillful handling, you can also produce the appearance of age and service. Let's face it, no sooner does a brand new locomotive leave the shops boasting a sparkling clean paint job than shortly thereafter the elements attack the finish. Escaping steam scorches and deposits alkali sediment in and about cylinders, steam domes, etc. Smokestacks deposit soot, blackening areas of the boiler and superstructure in its immediate vicinity. Drivers and truck wheels pick up dirt and corrosion from the rails. Mud and grime lying in and about ties and track always seems to end up on the dust pans and underbelly of the locomotive equipment. Therefore, pop valves, water lines, blow downs, steam domes, and other paraphernalia make excellent and legitimate locations for aging or creating the appearance of service and operation. Aside from your own ability to mix colors to the desired tone and effect you wish to create, you will find a number of ready-mixed paints and colors to fit most occasions. Colors such as rust, grimy black, soot, dirty gray, mud, and dust are among those available for imparting the appearance of age and service. You don't have to be a Michelangelo to produce realistic effects, for a bit of experimenting and mixing of colors, coupled with the use of specially designed railroad colors, will set you in the right direction for producing the proper weathered look and appearance—an appearance which will go a long way toward making your locomotive look like a miniature duplicate of a prototype rather than a toy.

The effects you apply should be warranted; in other words, you just don't dirty up a certain area of the locomotive for the heck of it unless that particular area would be so affected in live operation. That is why I mentioned such items as blow downs, steam valves, and pop valves. The action taking place in and about these items produces on prototypes the very effects we wish to duplicate on miniatures. For example, strategically located on the boiler you may find circular projections called "washout plugs." If your loco doesn't have any, they are easy to install (see Chapter IV). These washout plugs served a special function, namely, to enable the maintenance crews to clean boilers of minerals and other accumulated gook. Removing the washout plugs, the maintenance men would insert water hoses (also rods) through the opening in an effort to dislodge sludge, grime, alkali, and other assorted material clinging to the insides of the boiler. There was always the possibility that some of this

An exciting view of a Union Pacific "Challenger" put into service shortly after it was built. Fairly bright and shiny for the moment, it won't be too long before smoke and soot, scorching steam and Mother Nature give it an aged and weathered look.

Before: Typical satin brass finish of this highly detailed Pacific is now ready for the paint shop.

After: This is a perfect example of the degree of control obtainable by the use of an airbrush in painting locomotive equipment. Using the Paasche airbrush, I first applied a basic coat of gray auto primer. Following this, darker shades and tonal gradations were introduced to produce the effect of age and weathering. The end result is what I feel to be a realistic road-travelled appearance. Light areas represent effect of steam scorching, water run-off and alkali deposits. Darker areas represent soot and rust. Spattered along the sides and underbody is the mud and grime picked up during the course of many a run.

sediment might seep or ooze out through the washout hole, thus running down the sides and onto the frame and other details below. And if that didn't do it, then the chances were quite good that the hoses or rods (now dirty) would manage to splatter the sides of the loco during removal. In drying, the remaining residue would create a discoloring on and about the prototype, and is an effect much to be desired on the miniature.

Assuming your boiler features washout plugs, the following briefly explains how to create such a special effect. Using casein colors or thinned-out paint, mix up a color effect both light and brackish in appearance. Then using an eyedropper, squeeze out a drop or two at the source of the washout plug, letting your color run down, falling wherever it may. Repeat the application till you feel you have built up a sufficient deposit of sediment, and you will have achieved a most realistic result. You can also use a sable brush to paint it on, and, for that matter, if you are so inclined, you can use an airbrush. By and large, however, the best results are obtained with an eyedropper, for this type of application will most realistically duplicate actual prototype appearance.

Lastly and most simply, you can produce a similar effect on newly painted locos by using paint thinner (full strength) and, as it seeps down and along the sides and underframe, the solvent action of thinner atop fresh paint will produce the results we are talking about. A bit of experimenting might be in order, but that is easily done on a mock-up surface.

Checking the prototypes, you will find that in a number of cases the smoke box front and ends of the boiler were painted silver, gray, or aluminum. This effect is easily created with brush and paint. Piping, water pipes, handrails, running board, and most other locomotive details, with the exception of the brass bell, were and are painted. Many modelers also paint or weather the valve gear, on the basis that this equipment also should age in appearance. Others keep it shiny and bright. Some modelers also paint wheels and drivers, and afterward wipe the tire surfaces clean so as not to retard conductivity. Many modelers use mixtures of raw sienna, umber, Tuscan red, brown, etc., to produce the rust-colored effect that is found on the underbelly and side surfaces of many a well-traveled locomotive. Many locomotives operating in desert regions have the appearance of being slightly bleached in color—at least, they are not a clean black by any means. Locos working in and about coal mines, waterfronts, steel mills, etc., all take on the particular characteristics of the area they traverse. All these things should be taken into consideration when you paint or weather your locomotive equipment. Just bear in mind the nature of your pike, operation, and the type of service your loco performs.

There are numerous other special effects which can be achieved involving locomotive equipment and they are not all restricted to that of painting alone. For example, suppose you have just finished scenicking a 3-per cent grade between mountain ranges, and you would like to enhance the appearance of your locomotive chugging along in front of a string of cars. Under prototype conditions, most iron horses would be puffing smoke like mad, but, alas, your locomotive is not a smoker, i.e., it is not equipped with one of those thingamajigs that Tyco, Revell, American Flyer, and other locomotive manufacturers install in some of their steamers. This brings up the question of why more locomotives are not manufactured containing smoke-producing units. The answer is threefold. First, it adds to the cost of the item; second, it requires a reasonable amount of room for installation and is often limited to certain types of locomotives depending on size of boilers and smokestacks; third, like a highly accessoried car, it is just another thing that can go wrong. Therefore, in many cases it is considered a useless adjunct and dies on the drawing board.

This B&O EM-1 Baldwin 2-8-8-4 articulated by Akane Models is both smooth-running and powerful in operation. Loaded with details, it features a working headlight atop the pilot, full piping and other essential equipment as in the prototype, and both sets of drivers are powered. Made entirely of brass, it comes RTR, unpainted and is shown here with typical flat black finish.

This well-detailed articulated locomotive is further enhanced by the airbrush treatment. Weathering and aging heightens road-beaten and service-worn effect, and produces more realistic appearance.

Later model of a Union Pacific "Challenger" not only boasts a sparkling clean and bright paint job, but, among other things, the relocation of the headlight, which now is situated above the pilot. This 4-6-6-4 articulated underwent numerous changes, as will your own miniature counterparts. Compare this shiny appearance with the weathered appearance of the Union Pacific "Big Boy"

An exciting view of the Union Pacific "Big Boy," a 4-8-8-4 articulated locomotive that could haul a string of freight cars for almost as far as the eye could see, and at speeds approaching 80 mph. Similar in appearance to the "Challenger," this particular locomotive once looked shiny, too.

Varney's popular "Docksider" is decked out with additional detailing, including aged and well-weathered valve gear. A loop of black thread from the working bell to the cab enables the engineer perched within to sound the way as he shuttles cars in and about the yard.

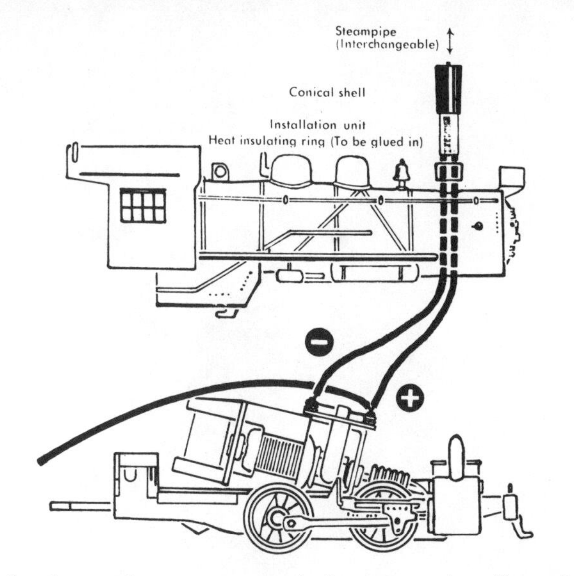

Seuthe smoke-generator unit is easy to install, and instructions are very explicit. A simple two-wire hook-up and you can puff away like the "Big Boy" —at least almost.

Smoke-producing effects in connection with your locomotives may or may not be your cup of tea. This smoke-belcher, double-headed at that, presents a stirring sight, one no longer seen along our railroads with the exception of tourist and fan excursions.

This American Flyer 0-6-0 Pennsy switcher and tender from Gilbert is quite popular among beginners and is perfectly suited to switching or light freight-hauling chores. For special effects, the loco generates its own smoke and has a "steam" sound built-in.

Revell's switch engine lumbers past the station, leaving a trail of smoke against the darkened sky. Built-in smoke unit produces an interesting effect and you can almost hear the "swoosh" as she rolls by.

However, for those of you who yearn for a touch of the old wood and coal burners, the installation of a Seuthe Smoke Generator might be desirable, and the cost is quite nominal; it will also liven things up a bit within your pike.

Essentially, the unit consists of a short length of 1/8-inch hollow tubing containing a heating element at the bottom and two wire leads to connect to your motor. You will be required to drill out your existing smokestack so there will be sufficient room to accommodate the smoke tube, or you can remove the smokestack, replacing it with the generator tube or a larger-diameter smokestack. Modifications will depend on how receptive your particular loco is to the installation. Bear in mind, however, that the finished results, whether made to fit or of a replacement nature, should conform reasonably well to both prototype and scale. By the way, the smoke does not rise in a lazy manner typical of a cigarette, but actually puffs its way up through the tube and above the locomotive. It will operate on either DC or AC. It pulls very little juice of its own and therefore does not retard the acceleration of your motor. However, it does require a good amount of juice to fire it up and, as a consequence, more often than not you will be operating at three-fourths to full throttle. In other words, to produce the smoke effect desired, you may find yourself operating at higher speeds than you actually care to. This can play havoc with rules and regulations concerning speed limits and prototype operations; however, this problem can be overcome by the application of high-frequency lighting—referred to in Chapter IV. At this point it might be wise to pause for a moment and briefly discuss HFL, which is a means of wiring in which both DC and AC current is fed to the rails—DC to the motor to run the locomotive, and AC to operate working headlights, signals, passenger car lighting, and, in this case, a smoke-producing unit for the locomotive. In HFL a provision is made whereby AC current bypasses the motor and is directed only toward the aforementioned accessories. In this way no harm is done to your DC-operated motor. Since we already have a glimmer as to how constant lighting can be achieved, we will skip over it except to say that by the same token a constant puffing of smoke can also be obtained. In short, HFL will permit the smoke generator to get enough juice to produce enough heat to create enough smoke without affecting the operation and motion of the locomotive. Therefore, if you slow down to creep speed, or come to a full stop, not only will your headlight remain lighted, but the smokestack will continue puffing away.

Getting back to the Seuthe smoke unit, you may run into problems, particularly in the case of locomotives whose boilers are attached to the underframe by means of a bolt running directly up through the smokestack. However, by means of relocation and a bit of modifying the problem can be licked. As I said, the cost of a Seuthe Generator is quite nominal and runs about $3.50 at most hobby shops. The unit also includes a supply of smoke fluid. A half dozen drops down the hatch will be enough fuel to last for quite a bit of operation, after which you can bring the loco in for refueling. When you have exhausted your supply of smoke fluid, you can purchase refills not only from Seuthe, but from other sources as well. You can also make your own mixture by using benzine, kerosene, and other solvents; add a few drops of machine oil and things will smoke like mad. A bit of smog might settle over your layout, but that's typical. If the smoke is pungent, or in any way assails your sense of smell unfavorably, you might add a drop or two of pine oil, which will add a good woodsy touch, a nice illusion and sense of smell if you happen to be operating in and about a lumber camp and sawmill. Last but not least, the smoke generator can also be used in factory smokestacks and other industrial sites such as coal mines and steel works, and as a final touch will look especially good in the chimney of a trackside shanty.

And now let's move along to other special effects. For example, a yellow-colored bulb in your headlight, rather than white, operating back-up lights which light up only when in reverse, and the installation of Kadee Magne-Matic Delayed Action Couplers. These couplers not only more closely resemble those of the prototype, but also enable you to uncouple cars and spot them at any point you wish *away from the uncoupling ramp.* This will be covered in detail in Chapter XVIII.

And while we are on the subject of couplers, we might consider the drawbar connection between the locomotive and tender. A simple way to improve the overall appearance and remove the stigma of toy trains, which results when the locomotive and tender are too far apart, is by reducing the distance. Either use a shorter drawbar or reduce its length, after which drill a new hole to accommodate the connection screw or nubbin. Don't shorten the drawbar too much, otherwise the front of the tender may make contact with the cab ends, resulting in a short. This will probably occur while rolling through sharp curves. To avoid this, a bit of experimenting is in order and can be easily accomplished by placing the loco and tender on the most minimum radius curve within your layout. Move both units through the curve while observing the closest distance they can be coupled together without actually touching each other. Measuring the space by eye will generally suffice, and after that it is merely a matter of using a drawbar of appropriate length or cutting one down as described above. Once you have done this, stand back and check the effect; you will immediately appreciate the difference and more realistic illusion of scale.

An HO scale figure of an engineer perched beside the window of the cab also adds an interesting touch. Scale figures are available from a number of sources too numerous to mention; however, the most popular model engineer in this case is made by Weston and can be purchased at most hobby shops. The figure is quite realistic looking and is replete with coveralls and cap. This little fellow is arranged in a seated pose with his arms bent forward. Assuming there is sufficient room in the cab to place the engineer in position, a few dabs of cement will keep him on the job. By inclining the figure at a slight angle and poking his head out of the window, the effect will be that of an engineer looking at the rails ahead. To avoid the illusion that the engineer is going to fall through the window, simply bend his arm so that he will assume the appearance of leaning on the window sill of the cab. Some cabs are pretty well occupied by the motor magnet, and when this happens, things get quite tight for space. In such a case, you can cut the figure just below the waist. The cab side will hide from view the fact that his legs are gone. One reason for the popularity of the Weston figure is the fact that it is made of metal and, therefore, is fairly easy to alter, a good point to consider when purchasing an engineer for your locomotive.

There are many other techniques and applications that can be employed to aid and enhance the appearance of your locomotive equipment and operation. For example, if one of your locos has trouble negotiating certain sharp curves in your layout, you can remedy this by filing down the flanges on the particular drivers which are subject to derailment, or, for that matter, you can replace them with a pair of "blind drivers." Blind drivers are wheels which have no flanges and which permit a greater lateral movement of the tires atop the rails. In prototype practice, blind drivers were commonly used in sharply curved areas where the binding and resistance of flanges against the rail sides not only could cause the locomotive to jump the track, but impede its progress as well. Check the Kemtron catalogue; they have them in various sizes, either Spoked or Boxpok of nature. If the trucks and wheels of your tender are not prototype, check those available from companies such as Cliff-Line and Central Valley, for the units these companies offer are not only among the smoothest rolling, but also prototype to the letter, and they also include wheels featuring the RP25 contour. We'll cover the RP25 wheels in greater detail further along, but for the moment take my word that they are the best.

A final note with reference to improving the appearance of your locomotive equipment, and that involves the use of road names, engine numbers, heralds, and slogans, plus other forms of identification which may be of your own personal origin or that of a particular prototype railroad which you are copying. Since the chapters which follow are devoted to the actual building of layouts and the various types of operations that can be performed, we will hold off on any lengthy discussion at the moment. Needless to say, selecting a name for your road, particular numbers to assign your engine (s), and the type of herald and slogans you wish to employ are best determined by the nature of your model railroad, the place, purpose, and era it will reflect within its operation and overall scheme of things.

Nevertheless, for those of you who are not following things chapter by chapter, or are skipping back and forth between areas which interest you the most or projects you are working on, let's get to the heart of the matter—namely the final numbering and lettering of your finished locomotive. If you are deft of hand, sensitive of touch, artistically inclined, and a good man with the brush, fine; you can letter and number by hand and leave the decals to us. Hand-lettering is quite distinctive, and offers you the flexibility of expanding and enlarging to fit almost any space or contour. It requires considerable time and patience, and should not be undertaken unless you have the proper degree of skill and experience; otherwise, you stand the chance of marring your paint job or detract-

It may be hard to tell whether this "Camelback" is coming or going, but it creates an effect all its own, and looks especially good and at home in coal mining regions. Note "blind" center drivers.

ing from its appearance. A sable or camel hair brush that can be drawn to a fine point is the basic tool, and is most effective in rendering the letters and filling them out. Drawing pens can also be used; however, a pointed brush is best. Water-based and oil-based paints are quite suitable, as are India inks. One in particular, a white ink called Snow White, is manufactured by Johnston's. If not available at your hobby shop, you will find it at most art supply stores. Select your choice of letter style carefully, for you must bear in mind that each railroad and era has a style of lettering all its own. In other words, a modern face letter applied to an oldtimer would be completely out of place. By the same token, a sleek modern streamliner bearing lettering reminiscent of years gone by will be incongruous, to say the least.

On the other hand, for those of you who have neither the time, patience, or skill, and must resort to the use of decals, don't feel ashamed; welcome to the club, for you are among the majority. I might also add that, because of the wide variety of decals that are available, you have complete freedom of choice in your final lettering. You can, therefore, select exact lettering and locomotive markings of prototype railroads. For example, Walthers offers thousands of decals for nearly one hundred railroads. They will also make up special decals of your own design and choice of lettering at a nominal cost. There are countless decal catalogues to select from, not only Walthers, but other sources, also.

By themselves, decals are quite easy to apply, and you simply follow the instructions. Unfortunately, there are certain bothersome characteristics concerning the use of decals that have plagued many model railroaders. One of them is to get the decal to lie flat and remain that way, for quite often after they are dry they will develop white spots and blisters. This condition can be avoided by using Walthers' Solvaset. A light application of Solvaset, and the decals will snuggle down and cling to the locomotive surfaces like a wet dress on Sophia Loren. It's only 50¢ a bottle and will last you a lifetime. The other problem is that of the shiny appearance that results once the decal is dry. This too, can be avoided by using Walthers' DDV. Just give the decal a final coat of DDV and the shine and glare will disappear. The end result will be a truly professional dull finish. You can also kill off the shiny toy look by using a dull varnish, but test it first to be sure that everything is compatible; otherwise, you may dissolve the decal. To put the final cap on decals and their applications for the moment, try using Walthers' Solvaset and DDV hand in hand; the total cost is only

Ore cars getting a load of coal, and a smoke-puffing locomotive emerging from a tunnel add to the dimension and depth of this dramatic and scenic special effect on the pike built and operated by Jim Foell.

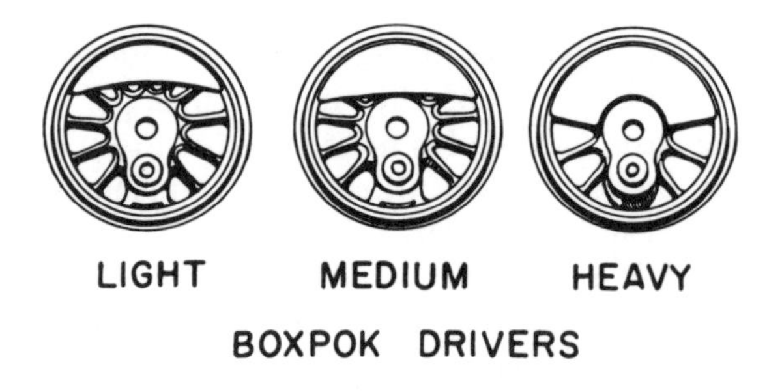

Drivers of various sizes and description are available from a number of sources, and include oldtimers or moderns, spoked or boxpok, with or without flanges, as well as light, medium or heavy, depending on the tonnage capacity and tractive force of the locomotive.

A fine sable or camel's hair brush drawn to a fine point is not only useful for lettering, but also helpful for touch-up work, and comes in handy for painting or aging small details such as steam valves. As shown, a touch of gray or white is evidence of steam-scorched metal in which the paint has been blistered away.

Looking for a name and/or herald for your locomotives and railroad? Try some of the prototypes for size. Over a hundred are shown here. For that matter, you can make up your own name, humorous, serious or otherwise. You can get a complete listing from the Association of American Railroads.

$1 and is a nominal investment that will go a long way toward retaining an authentic flavor in your finished project.

Now let's get back to the topic that started this chapter—painting. If you are an aficionado of oldtimers (and there are many), the use of an airbrush will enable you to produce startling results considering the fact that an instrument such as the Paasche Airbrush will permit easy striping, fine lines, etc. And since oldtimers boasted a variety of colors and striped effects, an airbrush is the item to help you create the appearance which will make your miniature a true rendition of its prototype. But be it painting, superdetailing, conversions, maintenance, era, and all other ingredients of locomotive practice and procedure, of one thing you can be sure—the application of these and all of the aforementioned, when combined in proper degree and proportion, will afford you the greatest degree of pride and pleasure not only for the sake of appearance, but operation as well.

If the recommendations, procedures, and ideas discussed thus far concerning locomotives seem like a lot of attention being devoted to just one phase of the hobby, then strongly bear in mind that the locomotive is the most important cog in the machinery of the train. It is the head of the drag and the main buffer as it leads the pack through wind, rain, sleet, and hail, its headlight piercing the darkness of the night, its smokestack trumpeting and billowing clouds of smoke, the valves and gears flashing as they crazily tumble through their monkey motion, the drivers pounding the rails that lay ahead, the hiss of steam, the eerie shriek of the whistle. These things make up the anatomy of your locomotive, giving life blood to your railroad. This hog, yard goat, puffer belly, peddler freight, articulated, or what have you certainly deserves all the attention you can give it. Old time iron horse or behemoth articulated, it's the grandest thing that ever ran the rails, and as you guide it out for a freight drag or a mainline passenger run, you can beam with pleasure, for you have created in authentic form a miniaturization of the real McCoy and a form of transportation that changed the face of America—and perhaps the face of your living room floor. So give it all you've got in this hobby of all hobbies, and remember the ABC's of locomotives: Appearance, Behavior, Care.

VII
Layout Design and Track Plans

Thus far, we have covered the most important aspects concerning locomotives: the basis upon which they should be selected and the various types which are available in RTR or which can be built-up from kits. We have discussed maintenance and have given locomotives the glamour treatment in the form of superdetailing, conversions, painting, weathering, and special effects. The information in the preceding chapters, while devoted solely to motive power, serves a twofold purpose:

1. To guide the hobbyist in the direction and use of scale locomotive equipment and the many avenues that can be pursued—a hobby in itself;
2. To establish the direct relationship between locomotives and the types of model railroads best suited to their operation.

There is no iron-clad rule which says that you must first establish your locomotive roster, detail them, finish them, etc., *before* building your railroad. In fact, many modelers build their railroad first, then purchase locomotives to suit their track plan or mode of operation. Others stock their roundhouse with locomotives to begin with and afterward build their railroad around the type of equipment they will be operating. On the other hand, many model railroaders combine a bit of both as they go along. Like the chicken and the egg, it isn't a question of which comes first, the loco or the railroad, but more important the compatibility of the equipment you have or wish to purchase in direct connection with the railroad you have or wish to build. Therefore, the mere fact that the opening chapters of this book have been devoted to locomotives should not be construed to mean that you should not do anything else until you have become fully indoctrinated into the why's and wherefore's of motive power. The particular subject matter of each chapter and the manner in which they follow each other has been arranged purely from an editorial and introductory standpoint, and primarily for the benefit of those who are new to the hobby. In short, set your own pace as time, money, and skills permit. The particular patterns and directions you may follow will be determined by your strongest interests. Therefore, regardless of whether you are well-stocked with many locomotives and haven't as yet built a railroad or vice versa; or if you have a little of each; or are starting from scratch; or whatever your individual situation

When Jim Foell finished laying his last stretch of track (for the time being that is) he cleverly created a section gang busily engaged in preparing to lay some new rail at the crossing. Jim figured it would serve to remind him of all the planning that went into the making of his railroad. Absolutely no featherbedding allowed, he even has a foreman on hand to keep the crew on its toes.

Standing within the open framework of his future pike, Bob Steele checks and double checks his track plans with relation to size of layout, radius of curves, type of equipment and mode of operation.

Scraps of wood are more than suitable for risers in establishing grades, and will serve as supports for the roadbed. Blocks are cut to varying heights with respect to percentage of grade being developed.

may be, the important thing to consider is that the type of layout you design, the track plan you employ, the type of railroad you build, and the manner of operations you embrace are directly related to the types of locomotives you already have or plan to purchase, and vice versa, as discussed in Chapter II.

Pursuing this one step further, I might point out that many model rails collect, build, superdetail, and maintain locomotives with no more than a passing interest as far as operating them on a well-detailed pike is concerned. Conversely, many brass hats are more interested in building a railroad for the sheer enjoyment of creating scenic effects and prototype realism in miniature and scale form. To the latter, operation is not necessarily a must, and in many cases motive power and rolling stock is at a minimum. It is simply a matter of each individual doing whatever interests him most.

Nevertheless, a happy medium in model railroading is one in which a little of everything is combined. The major ingredients are, locomotives and rolling stock, building a miniature railroad, and, finally, realistic operation. It is to this end that this book is dedicated—to provide the reader with a detailed rundown on the various facets of the hobby of model railroading and how they relate to each other. The end result, as has been said, is a well-balanced, realistic-looking miniature railroad operating authentic-looking equipment in a truly prototypical manner.

While what I am saying may appear to be repetitious and redundant, the fact remains that many favorite track plans have to be scrapped at the last minute—or during actual building. More often than not, many scale miles of previously laid track have been ripped out and relaid. Switches and turnouts have been relocated, and mountains have been torn down or moved because of one thing—lack of co-ordination in planning. Chances are that in spite of all your planning, at one point or another you will become involved in a number of changes. However, they will, no doubt, be changes for the better and probably based on accommodating additional equipment, the growth of new industries within your pike, and your advanced knowledge and techniques in operation, signalling, and wiring. Therefore, as you go along, it will not be uncommon to make the various changes I have mentioned. Far from unusual, it is actually par for the course for many model rails, who throughout a given period of time may change or rebuild half a dozen areas of their pike, if not the whole thing. In the beginning, however, it is another thing, and I, therefore, stress the importance of getting off to a good start, one that won't require any drastic changes of an immediate nature. Since you are laying the groundwork for future hours, weeks, and years of pleasure-filled railroading, make your foundation as solid as possible.

Okay, now that we have that out of the way, let's get down to the actual planning and building of your particular railroad.

The first time a beginner looks at "the other fellow's railroad," he is either consumed with the desire to rush home and start building the "pike to end all pikes," or he is ready to throw in the oil rag and call it quits. A well-proportioned, railroad-like set-up is both fascinating and inspiring to the average viewer, let alone the neophyte. Yet, there is no denying that many aspects of model railroading can easily create the impression that a rail buff has to be a combination artist, mechanic, carpenter, electronic expert, and magician—in short, some kind of genius. There is also no denying that any one or all of these qualifications will prove more than useful, but they are not absolutely necessary. Imagination, common sense, and a reasonable respect for prototype application and procedure are equally important, if not more so. True, know-how and a fair amount of money are helpful factors, but not prime requisites, for it has been established that many of the ingredients and effects that go into creating a well-scenicked pike can be accomplished with less effort and cost than the average beginner realizes. Nevertheless, most miniature railroads are the result of careful study, individual artistry, dedication, time, patience, and honest-to-goodness sweat. One thing is for sure—it can't be slapped together over night!

In taking the initial steps toward planning a layout, certain basic thoughts must be seriously considered, not only concerning the size and type of construction, but the form of operation as well. And woe unto the novice planner who, armed with no more ammunition than his own imagination, quite often will design layouts that would make the most liberal minded brass hat shake with fear, for nine times out of ten these plans wouldn't work under any circumstances. To get off to a good start, or at least a normal one, it would be best to consider some of the following fundamentals, which, by the way, go hand-in-hand toward successful construction and operation.

Space. How much do you have? Exactly, not roughly! Doodling track plans is a lot of fun, but it's a waste of time if your layout calls for a larger area than your space will allow. Measure the available room to the inch, allowing for the overall area you must occupy in both operation and maintenance. Also, consider the need for access holes, not only for ease of construction, operation, and maintenance, but for the possible presence of obstructions such as water heaters and pipes. Remember that if your railroad is too wide to reach across comfortably at arm's length, an access hole will make it possible to work the far corners without straining. While you may devise a clever way of getting around such items as ceiling supports and furnaces, you must also be able to get to them if necessary—without having to rip up half your set-up in the process. If it is a toss-up between a good amount of space plagued with obstructions, or an area smaller but free of such encumbrances, then the latter might well be the wiser choice—you can always expand if desired. Firmly establishing the exact dimensions of the area will bring you a step closer to actual construction. Many things are bound to change as you go along, so now is the time to avoid in advance a number of headaches.

Type of Construction. There are two basic techniques employed in building a foundation for your railroad. One method is the table or flat-top arrangement, and the other, the open bench or grid work. Each one has its own merits and characteristics, the choice of which is best determined by the nature of your layout design, track plan, type of operation, and the extent of scenic and terrain effect you wish to create.

If you are planning a small-to-average size railroad not exceeding 5 by 9 feet, are not planning on any elaborate scenic effects, are primarily interested in switching and freight yard operation with a branch line to service adjoining industry and perhaps a small outlying town, do not plan on any extensive grades or over-and-under crossings—in other words, operation within a flat land level—then the table top is your best bet. Another point in favor of flat-top construction is ease of handling if portability is required. Should other needs for the space arise, and your layout can no longer be free-standing, you can always remove the legs, add casters, and slide it under a bed, so to speak. For that matter, you can hinge it to a wall in bulletin-board fashion, or, by means of pulleys, suspend it from the ceiling of your garage, raising and lowering it at will. Building it is simple, requiring no more than a sheet of plywood framed by strips of 1-by-2-inch stock or larger for strength. On the underside you can add additional wood strips for crossbracing to prevent sags and warping. If not permanent, legs can be hinged, or the unit can be placed atop sawhorses. The top surface of the plywood can serve as the ground level to lay your track on, or, if noise is a factor, you can use the plywood surface as a sub-bed and

Steele's layout now starts to show some real progress as roadbed and track are laid in accordance with track plan. Solid panels covering open gridwork will serve as track bed for branch line operating in and about local community. Incorporating a "lazy-over-and-under-figure-eight" type of design, this model railroad, when finished, will offer a good amount of switching and mainline operation.

Some fellows put their scenery in before, some after. Bob Steele did it during. "It helped me get a better perspective of what I was doing," claims Bob—a point well taken. Setting a bit of a scene here and there livens things up a bit after you have built the foundation and started laying some track.

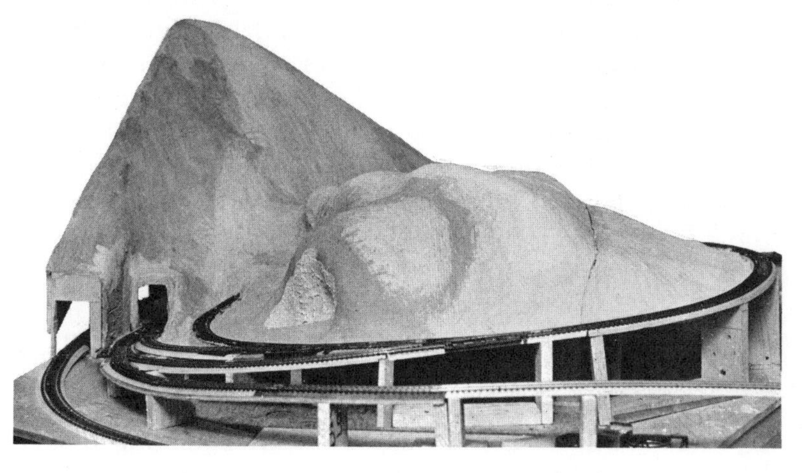

Access hole between trestle and background scenery provides means of getting to otherwise difficult-to-reach places. Access holes need not be glaring open areas and can be a hinged covering containing a scenic effect to match the surrounding area. When the need arises, you simply unlatch one end (like a trap door) and pop your arms and head through to get at any trouble spot which develops. The access hole can also be covered with a lift-out panel. If your pike suffers from "PR" (poor reachability) then access holes are a must. In this view Bob Sullivan hand wipes a section of trestle track.

Table top with center enclosure provides good spot for control panels and point of operation. Open benchwork is another excellent means of laying the foundation for your railroad.

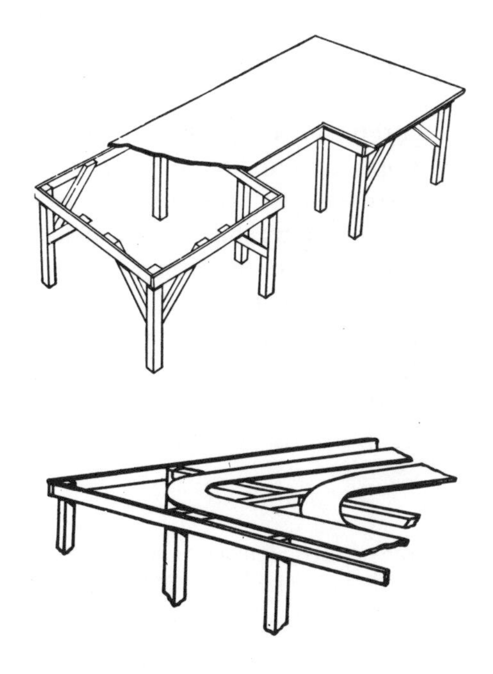

place a sheet of homosote or other fiberboard directly over it. However, most rail fans seem to prefer the firmer support of wood rather than fiberboard—it's a matter of choice. Should you wish to add a yard, loop, expand your mainline trackage, etc., you can always build another table or extension, and bolt it into position. If you decide to add a graded level, it is easily accomplished by the use of risers of graduated heights which can be made from wood scraps or purchased ready-made at your hobby shop. Remember, that while this type of foundation is nothing more than a table, it should nonetheless be firm and strong. Any wobbles or shimmies which develop will play havoc with your railroad, resulting in over- or under-gauged trackwork, kinks in the rail, and cracks in the scenery.

For the larger and more permanent type of layout, grid construction is not only more suitable, but cheaper in the long run. This form of framework offers the best advantage when embracing the use of mainline operations, sweeping curves, trackwork at different levels, mountainous or rocky terrain, and other railroad-like topography. You not only will be able to increase your operating possibilities and trackwork design, but you will have a greater opportunity to create a more believable atmosphere.

The shape of your grid foundation can assume a number of proportions, resembling a rectangle, a square, on certain letters of the alphabet, such as L, U, and C, or the doughnut-like O. It can be an island, dog bone, waterwings, or any other shape to fit the contour of the track plan you have conjured up. The L shape, for example, is quite popular, and the small part of the L makes an excellent spot for a turntable or yard to make up freight. You can also use this area for spurs to mining operations, logging industries, a railroad terminal, or departure point, leaving the balance of the layout for highballing.

Whether you choose flat top or framework as the basis of your layout construction, it is important to note that expensive lumber is not only unnecessary, but a waste of money. In the case of table tops, the plywood used for the trackbed surface can be of the common variety, not necessarily finished on either side. Just be sure it is free of knotholes and ripples, and is seasoned dry. Unless it has a very severe warp or bend, don't worry about it, for the plywood will soon straighten out when you secure it to the table foundation. Crossbraces underneath will not only straighten things out, but lend strength. So don't waste your hard-earned cash on expensive mahoganies, walnut, or other decorative plywood materials. Soon the wood will be covered with glue, paint, ballast, structures, and, let us hope, many a scale mile of track. You can get by with ¼-inch plywood, though ½-inch will give you firmer support. The same reasoning applies to grid-work construction. 1-by-4-inch pine or Douglas fir is most widely used for the framework. Ask for No. 2 common; it will do the job more than adequately and save you money in the long run. If you are lucky enough to have power tools, such as Shopsmith or Sawsmith, the building will be a snap. Any power tools, such as saber saws, skillsaws, etc., will help you do things quickly and efficiently. However, regardless of whether you have a well-equipped workshop or must rely on a hand saw, bear in mind the old wood working adage, "measure three times and cut once."

Era-Locale-Motive Power. The compatible selection of these three all-important items can spell the difference between success and failure of your best-laid track plans. It is important to determine them in advance, not only in respect to the plans you have in mind, but also in conjunction with the given area you have at your railroading disposal. If you are cramped for space and/or plan a small

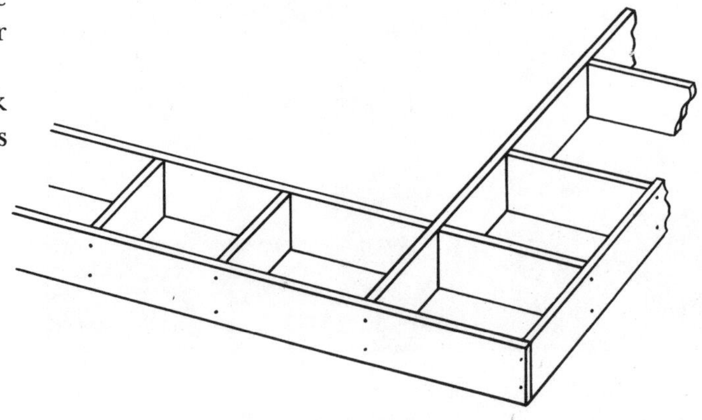

Inexpensive lumber is more than adequate for bracings and cross sections of benchwork.

That old saw, "measure three times and cut once," certainly applies during the carpentry phase of building your model railroad. A multi-purpose power tool such as a "Saw-Smith" can not only help you build your pike, but the room to house it in as well.

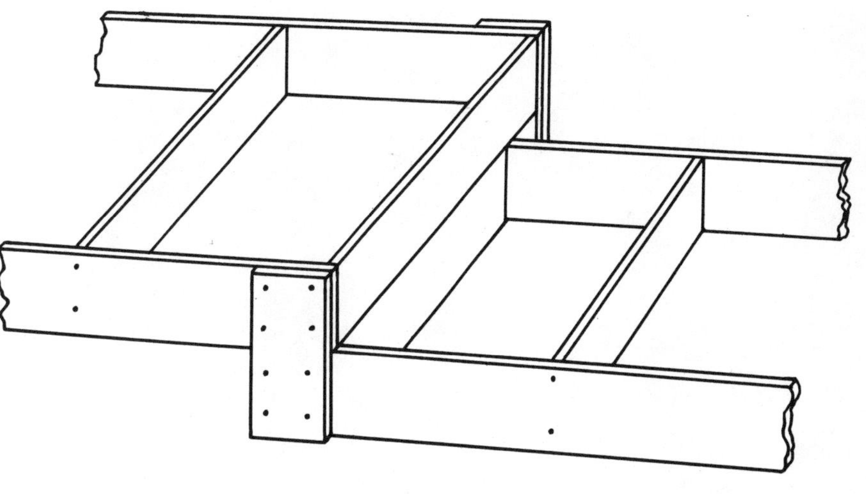

Elevations and drop-downs will offer many a scenic possibility when you reach that point. Over-and-under trackwork can be more easily installed without the need for risers.

railroad, you can pack more railroading into the square inch by embracing an oldtime period and using locomotives of earlier railroading vintage whose simpler wheel arrangements will more easily negotiate minimum track arrangements. This is why so many model railroaders design layouts with an oldtime atmosphere. To further explain, the smaller the space, the smaller the railroad, the sharper the curves, the less mainline running—in other words, the more restrictions imposed on the performance and realistic appearance of your locomotives and cars. If you have visions of heavy passenger locomotives pulling long strings of 85-foot cars in a space less than 5 by 9 feet, forget it. For even if you can manage to keep the equipment on the track, you will experience noticeable jackknifing as your cars run through turnouts and curves.

At this point it would be wise to review precisely what your locomotives can and cannot do. Determine in advance exactly what minimum radius your motive power can handle and still look realistic during the action. A perfect example is in the case of the average articulated from 2-6-6-2 and up. It may manage to roll through a No. 4 turnout and traverse a 20- to 24-inch minimum radius curve, but most likely it won't look very prototypical in doing so, for as it snakes into a turnout or curve, the boiler front and pilot trucks will part company, resulting in a severe overhang, thus producing a toylike appearance. On the other hand, a 4-6-0 or 4-6-2 will not look tintype in running through this kind of trackage.

Therefore, when drawing up your track plans, be certain that your roster of locomotives and cars (and the ones you plan to purchase) can handle the curves you have in mind, not only physically, but in a railroad-like manner. The following will aid you in designing a well-balanced track plan in which your equipment will look at home rather than out of place:

For obvious reasons, a garage is a perfect place to house a model railroad. It also presents a problem where car storage is concerned, particularly if there is more than one car for the household. The following photographs show how Jim Foell licked the problem.

When not in use, Jim Foell's pike is secured to the ceiling overhead, out of car's way. Pulley arrangement enables him to raise and lower his railroad. Getting ready to lower the first section of his pike, Jim secures legs and braces in place.

Lowering away, Jim and Dotti Foell ease gently on the rope as the pike starts its descent. Sash weights aid counterbalancing and add to ease of raising and lowering.

Almost at sea level, Jim Foell proceeds to lower his pike from the ceiling of his two-car garage. He can manage the chore by himself, but welcomes the assist from his wife, Dotti. Jim's layout consists of two sections which butt together when lowered to the floor. Each unit weighs about 250 pounds. Stress, strain and weight have been carefully and safely accounted for in the overhead pulley arrangement.

Sharp Curves	18-inch Radius	Small to medium-size locomotives
Conventional Curves	24-inch Radius	Medium-size and some larger ones
Broad Curves	30-inch Radius	All types of locomotives

(See Chapter II for a more detailed listing)

The above is simply a standard and you can go in any direction you wish, big or small, but keep it in mind when designing, and you will avoid unnecessary headaches and disappointments.

By the way, you can get down as low as 12-inch minimum radius, and although the curves will be very sharp, you can still retain prototype design and action in operation. It will simply mean that you will be limited to using small oldtimers, shorty coaches, and freight cars, but you will be prototype because that's what they used in the old days. Before continuing, just let me say that some of the finest, most excitingly scenicked home layouts in the country have been laid out within the confines of areas less than 4 by 8 feet. So don't despair if you are tight for space and must resort to sharp curves and branchline service rather than mainline running. It may get a bit hectic during operation, but it will be a challenge to your ability as a model railroader.

Track Plans. Thus far, I have said little about the track plans themselves, having placed the emphasis on a number of important aspects which must be considered before the actual construction of your design (premature doodling not being a capital offense). At the risk of being redundant, unless the foregoing factors are compatible, the plans you have in mind will be as useful as a yard hog trying to pull twenty cars up a 10-per cent grade. Neither will be successful. There has been much purple prose written concerning the why's and wherefore's surrounding the elements of track design. When you get right down to it, pen poised, paper, and straightedge before you, review everything I have said thus far. Decide what you want your railroad to do. Assuming that you are not content to watch your locomotive chasing its

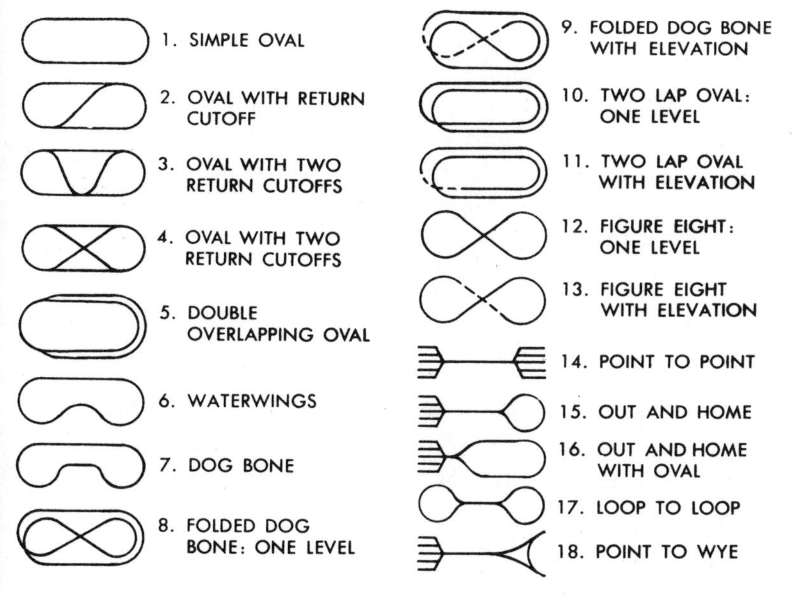

Some of the more commonly used track plan arrangements. A word of warning to the beginner: Bear in mind that any time a locomotive can return to and travel over the same section of track while headed in the opposite direction, a complete turnaround or reversing section had to be encountered somewhere along the route. This will involve the use of a "reverse loop," a wye track section, any section of track that rejoins itself whereby opposing polarities meet. This will call for special wiring, which is described in Chapter 16. Diagrams 2, 3, and 4 show this form of operation. If you trace the routes, you will see that a train leaving a given section of track and heading east arrives back at the same point and on the same section of track but heading west. If you are planning a layout for the first time and wish to avoid any wiring that is not absolutely necessary, then don't use a plan embracing a reverse loop and the wiring that goes with its use. On the other hand, there are a number of plans in which your train can appear to return in the opposite direction from which it departed *but on another or adjoining section of track.* There is many a pro and con concerning reverse loops; some swear by it, some swear at it. A turntable situated at one end of your pike will enable you to turn your locomotive around so it can return in the opposite direction. As for the train itself, you will have to break it up and re-make it for the return trip, but that's part of the fun. You will be operating rather than running trains round and round—a point to keep uppermost in mind when planning your layout and purpose of your model railroad.

caboose while making endless laps about a simple oval, you must incorporate a railroad-like function and action into your railroading scheme—picking up lumber at the mill and transporting it to the furniture factory in a neighboring town, carrying ore to a steel-works, etc. While realistic action and operation in connection with track plans will be discussed in greater detail, bear in mind for the moment that your railroad must have a purpose, and operate on the profit side of the ledger. Don't plan a complicated track design requiring equally complicated layout construction, for chances are you will be kept so busy maintaining switches, turnouts, track-work, and wiring circuits that you will never have much time to enjoy it. Keep it simple for a starter—an oval, a few industrial spurs, a passing siding, an uncomplicated yard arrangement. Of course, a simple oval is about as basic as you can get; it is also pretty boring. Even if you had all the room you wanted, could make your oval as wide and long as possible, covered various areas with mountains, tunnels, hills, and dales, your train would still be running round and round in an endless circle. The mere addition of a siding would enable you to send a slow freight onto the siding alongside the mainline and hold it there while a fast passenger rolls through. That's improvement number one. Improvement number two would be the addition of a few spurs to service an industrial area. This enables you to move off the mainline, drop a few ore cars at the coal mine, and leave a box car or two at the furniture factory. After a half dozen laps about the road, you can double back and make your pick-ups. While this is an oversimplification, it illustrates how a few additions to even the basic oval will not only add to the appearance and action, but will also give your railroad an actual function and purpose.

Throughout this chapter you will see an assortment of layout and track plans. Some are extremely simple, like the one just described, and some are more detailed, involving "point-to-point" systems. You will see arrangements for run-around track, loops, single and double crossovers, double track, and yards, plus many other forms of track-work and plans that will have you lying awake at night doing quite a bit of mental operation —at least until you have actually installed one of these track plans. For then you can operate by eye rather than imagination. Though chances are that you will still continue to lie awake at night conjuring up a mental picture of one form of operation or another, be it highballing along the mainline, switching cars or whatever, for that's part of the magic of model railroading.

In connection with the track plan you choose, or the one you develop yourself, it is of paramount importance that you also decide on the type of track material you will be using. In other words, some plans involve the use of Snap-Track (Atlas) or Tru-Track (Tru-Scale), also referred to as sectional track. Others embrace the use of Ready-Track made by Tru-Scale, while some plans are better suited to laying ties and spiking down rails. By and large, however, any of the plans can be used with any or all of the track materials that are in popular use, though a bit of modification may be necessary.

If you asked the same question of three model railroaders, you would get three different answers, for everyone has his own opinion; ideas vary, and so do techniques. Plans vary too, and usually you won't find two alike. What is good for one track planner is either too big, too small, or uninteresting to another. As you study the track plans shown, bear in mind that it doesn't take much to alter and modify according to your own space, operating plans, and the thoughts you have for scenic effects. However, proceed with caution; don't overcomplicate matters with a criss-cross of tracks and turnouts. It may look good on paper, but might well have a thousand and one hidden complications which will appear the minute things are spiked down. Don't forget that the more complicated the track-

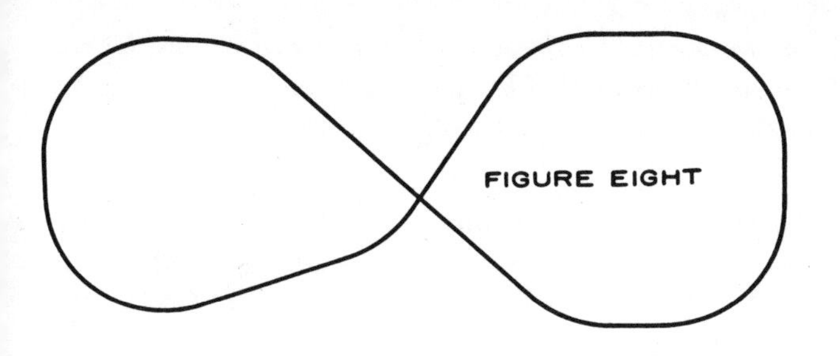

'he simple oval is pretty tame stuff, is made more inter-
sting by twisting it into a figure eight and adding the
lickety-clack of the train over a crossing. With portions
f the track hidden, the figure eight can begin to provide
pleasing reproduction of an actual railroad scene — the
·ain curves alternately to left and right in its journey and
ıe round-and-round motion isn't quite so obvious.

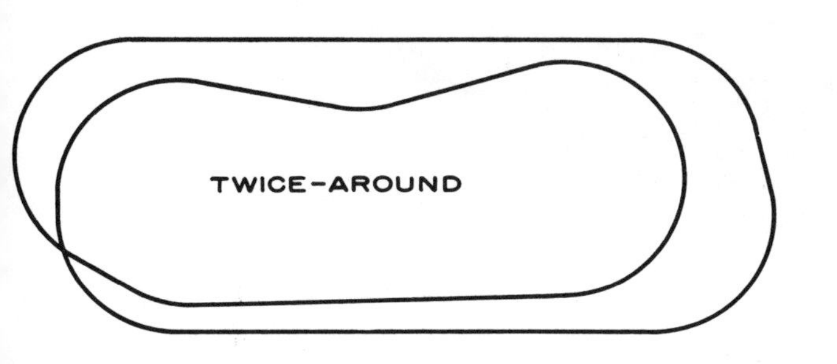

. common goal in track plans is to get a long run into the
ɔace available, and the twice-around arrangement that
esults from flipping one end of the figure eight inside the
ther and expanding it to fill the entire area does just
ıat. Larger pikes may go around three or even more
mes; care is needed in avoiding too much exactly parallel
ackage.

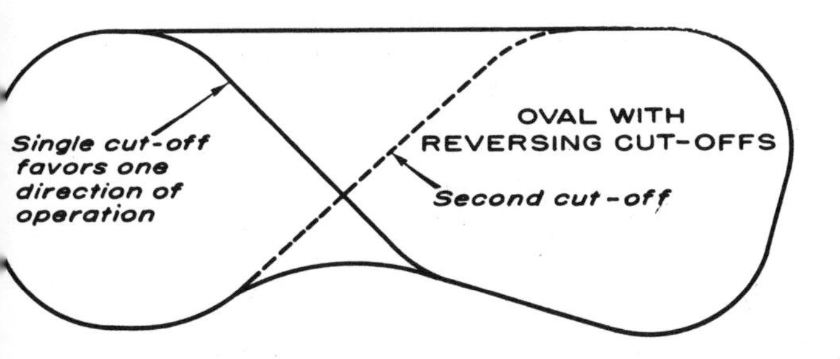

aturally, a track plan is more interesting if the direction
travel of the trains can be reversed easily. Reversing
ıtoffs are therefore a logical addition. The single cut-
f requires a backing movement for one direction of re-
ersing. Since prototype railroads don't normally run
eir trains around in circles, some ingenuity is needed
making reversing cutoffs and simple ovals look like
ırt of a real line.

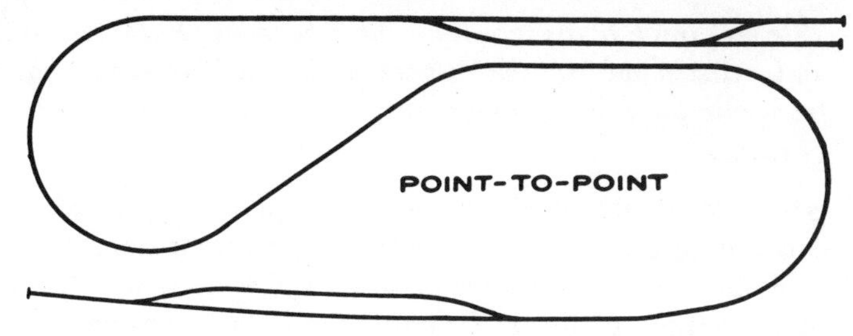

Since a real railroad extends from one point to another and runs its trains back and forth, the point-to-point arrangement is the most "correct" model possible. Even the shortest of short-line railroads can't be modeled completely, however, so there is no way in the average space to represent long-haul railroading with this type of track plan. If you like the switching involved in getting the train turned around for its next trip and want to model short-line or branch equipment and operation, the point-to-point is excellent.

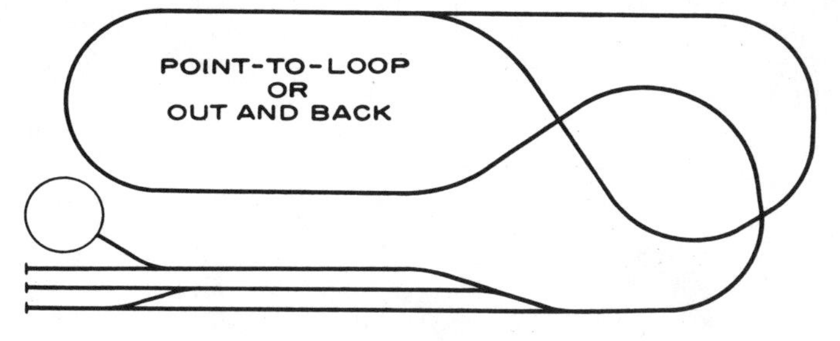

The point-to-loop or out-and-back plan lets you make a round trip before turning the train around the hard way, thus giving more main-line running for a given amount of yard work. Since only one yard is needed, it can be larger. The result is a good compromise between realism and operating practicability, making this scheme a favorite.

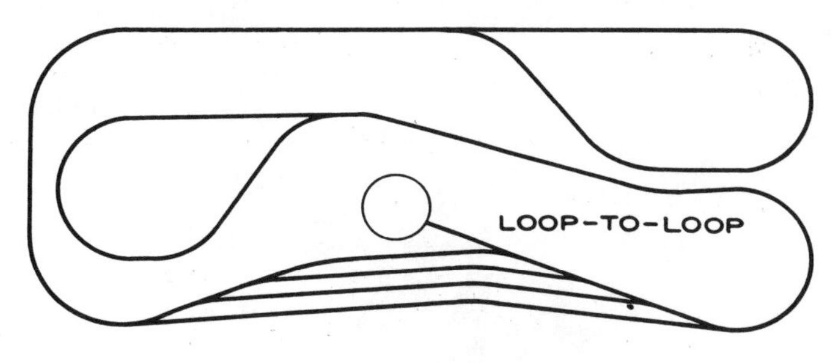

This plan allows continuous running while preserving the point-to-point idea, is thus highly flexible and interesting. Yards may be located at one or both ends of the line, or a large yard at the middle of the run may represent a "division point" yard on a main line, the point at which crews, cabooses and perhaps engines on through trains are changed and consists reshuffled.

A further expansion of layout design and track planning is more than evident in these clear-cut and informative excerpts from *Custom-Line Layouts,* by John Armstrong, and is devoted entirely to the planning and building of a model railroad involving the use of Atlas track products and materials. Definitely must reading and a highly informative addition to your model railroading library, especially if you use Atlas track. HO scale, of course.

The HO track plans shown on these pages are but a few of the many possible arrangements which can be developed and utilized within the respective dimensions indicated. Depending on available space, you can borrow ideas from one plan or the other, adding or lengthening spurs and sidings and/or broadening or narrowing the radius of curves.

Nineteen small-to-medium-sized track plans are included in Armstrong's *Custom-Line Layouts,* with full details concerning the operation in mind behind their design. The exact amount of Atlas track materials required and a host of other important information is discussed and shown as well. With the courtesy of the Atlas Tool Co., a few of their track plans are presented here and elsewhere in this chapter.

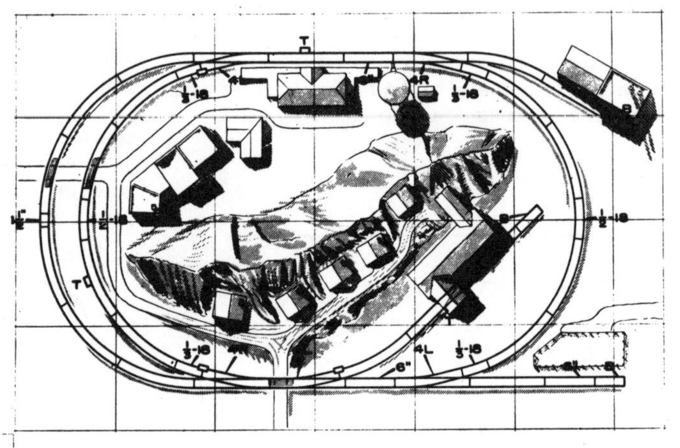

Atlas Track Plan Number 1—Simple Oval With Spurs, 4 × 6½ Feet: An effective start and a worthwhile expansion of a simple oval. Passing siding and spurs offer a good amount of switching and maneuvering. Suitable for one- or two-train operation. If the latter, however, plastic rail joiners will be required, as indicated in the diagram. Trace the routes you can take and the service you can perform. Let your imagination be your guide as to the possibilities of this small but "operational" track plan. If you are cramped for space, this plan might be right up your alley; you can always expand it into a larger system later on.

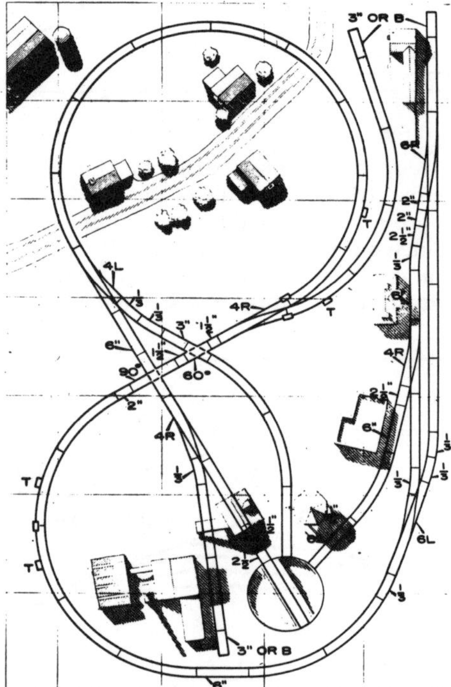

Atlas Track Plan Number 7—A Small Point-To-Point Railroad, 4½ × 7 Feet: If switching is your cup of tea, then this plan is definitely for you. It not only affords a point-to-point operation in a relatively small space, but also provides a lot of making-up and breaking-up of trains at both terminals.

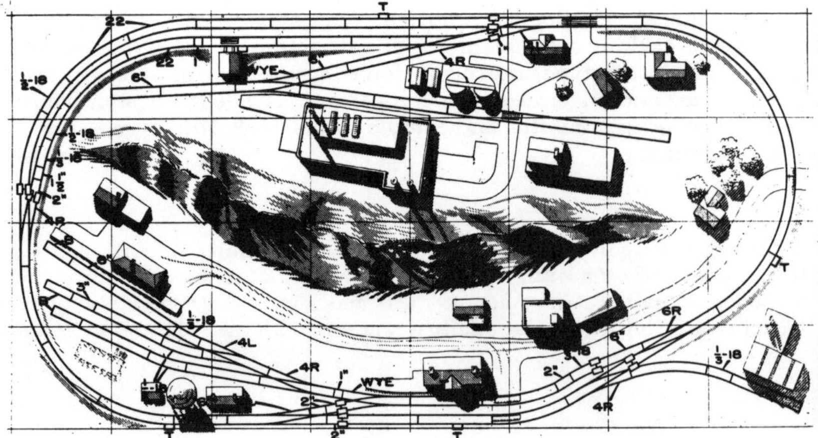

Atlas Track Plan Number 6—A Busy Single-Track Railroad, 4 × 8 Feet: Quite a bit of railroading is packed into this plan, with a number of interesting dispatching problems involved in getting one train past another during the course of operation. If you can spare the space and can build this layout within a 5 × 9-foot area you will have that much more room for scenery and background effects, and you won't be so crowded at the edges. Nevertheless, you can still manage to squeeze in an Atlas turntable to make things even busier. It may get hectic, but that's part of the fun.

work plan, the more wiring involved, so keep things fairly simple to start with.

I'm fairly sure that among the track plans shown you will find at least one that will suit you, or, with a slight change or two, will perfectly fit your scheme of things. If not, there are track plans galore available at your hobby shop. In addition, *Model Railroader* and *Railroad Model Craftsman* are constantly presenting track plans. Atlas, the makers of Snap-Track, also publishes an assortment of track plans especially designed for use with their track and turnouts. The same is true for Tru-Scale, who make Tru-Track, Ready-Track, and a host of other track materials, all of which will be covered in the next chapter. Last but by no means least is *101 Track Plans,* by Linn H. Wescott. Wescott has compiled a very formidable array of plans suitable for areas ranging from the smallest cramped space one might have to endure to the largest imaginable. It's a solid reference for all model railroaders.

Pursuing the design of track plans one step further, the actual necessity for making any final drawings will depend on two factors:

1. Whether you use published plans, such as those shown in this chapter or from other sources that were mentioned;
2. Whether you decide to design your own track plan.

Taking them one at a time, we'll start with the published plans. No additional drawing will be necessary other than marking off on the table top or benchwork where you will be laying your track and turnouts. That is, if you are going to follow the plan exactly. There will be no problem if you use the type of track materials that the plan calls for. If this is the case, simply transfer an outline of the track plan to the track surface, and before long you will be operating.

On the other hand, if you wish to make a few modifications, add, reduce, or allow

Tru-Scale, the makers of Tru-Track, also offer plans designed specifically for their Tru-Track materials, six of which are presented here. These plans are actually photographs of Tru-Track already assembled and ready for operation. Sections of track have been purposely separated for easy identification. Symbols identify odd-sized sections only. Track sections not marked are 9 inches straight and full-length 18-inch-radius curve sections of track material.

Tru-Scale Tru-Track Plan 1—4 × 6 Feet: A simple oval with an outer loop which can serve as a passing siding is accomplished simply by the installation of right- and left-hand turnouts. Pretty tame stuff, but it is a start.

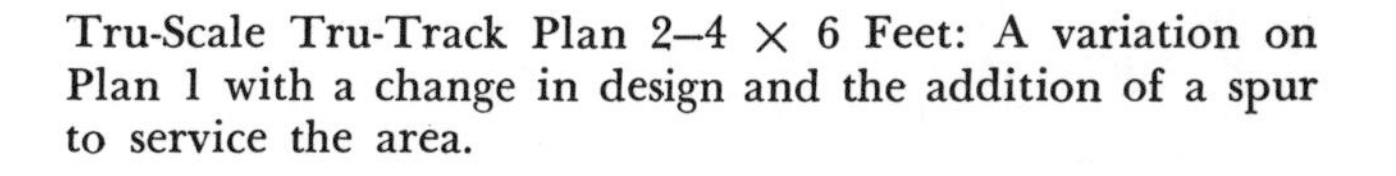

Tru-Scale Tru-Track Plan 2—4 × 6 Feet: A variation on Plan 1 with a change in design and the addition of a spur to service the area.

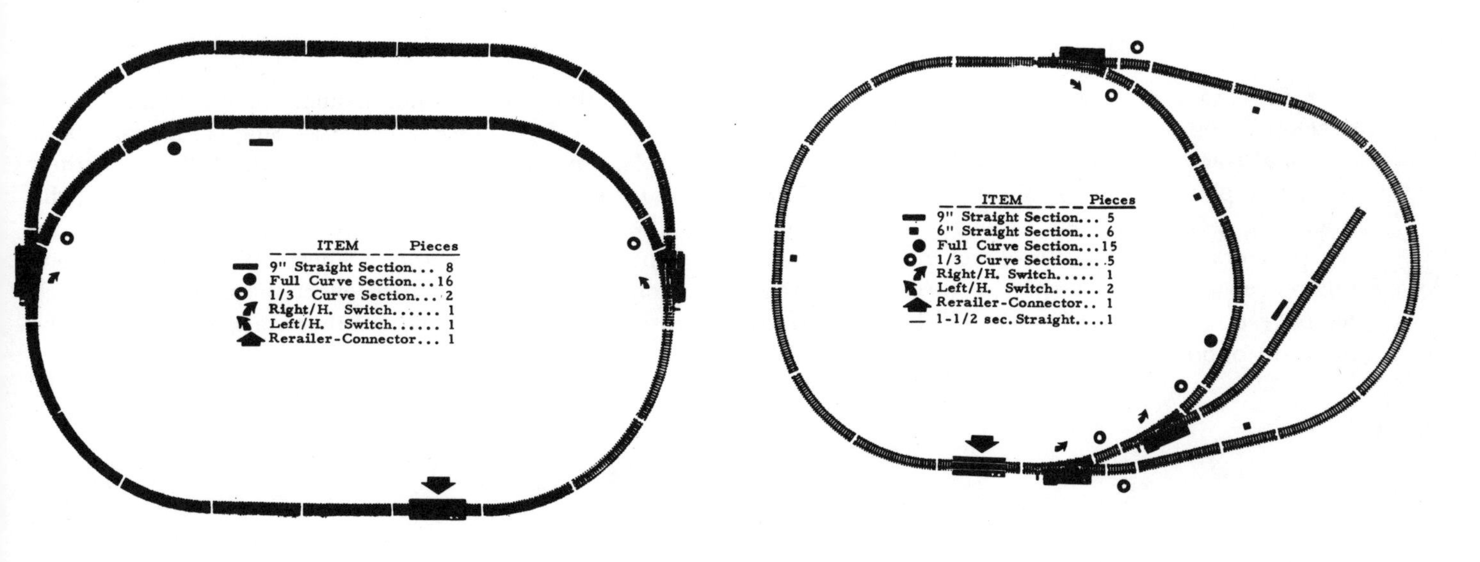

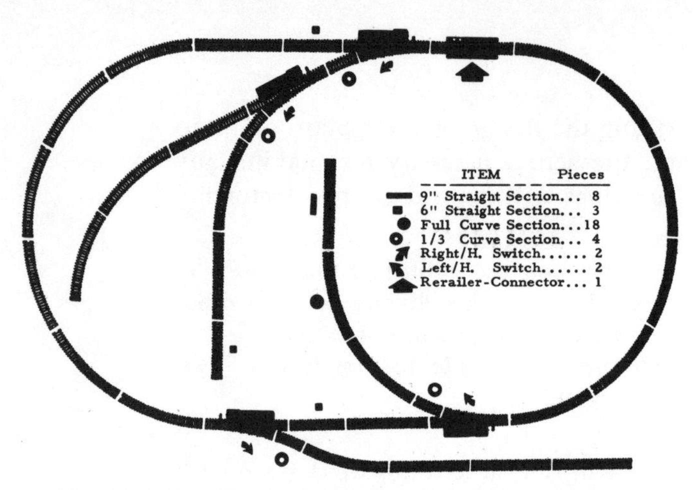

Tru-Scale Tru-Track Plan 3—4 × 6 Feet: Now things are starting to pick up with the addition of a few more spurs to service the local industries. If you can spare a few inches more, you can add a passing siding. This plan, though nothing more than a basic oval, will permit you to do a fair amount of switching.

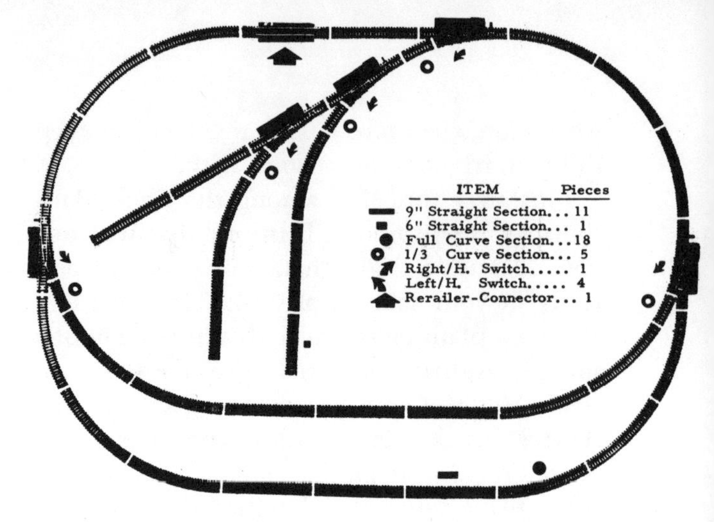

Tru-Scale Tru-Track Plan 4—4 × 6 Feet: Similar to Plan 1 with the addition of inside spurs which can be used to service adjoining industrial buildings or can serve as a small yard to make and break up trains after a run.

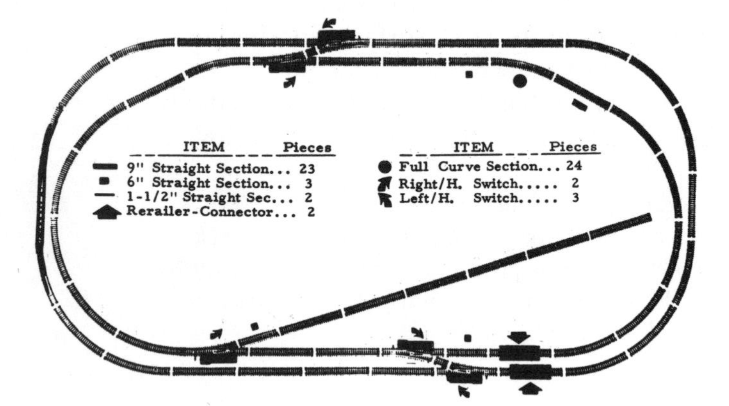

Tru-Scale Tru-Track Plan 5—4 × 8 Feet: The start of a busy two-track, twice-around railroad with a nice long spur for storage. Inner and outer loops can serve as passing sidings during two-train operation. Plenty of room inside for scenery, a town, local industries or, better yet, a yard to add to the switching fun.

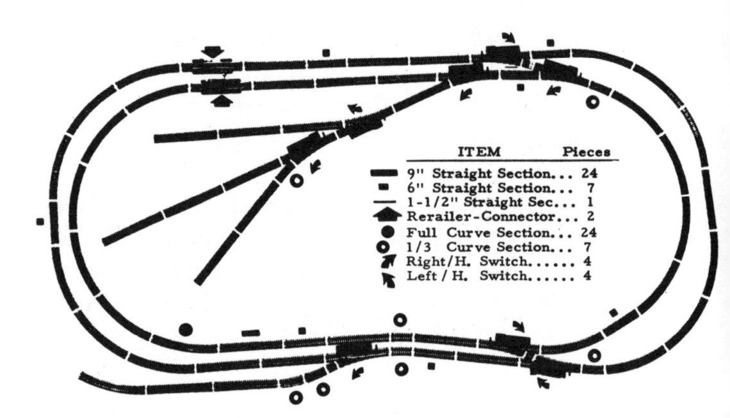

Tru-Scale Tru-Track Plan 6—4 × 8 Feet: An even busier two-track railroad, or double oval if you prefer. A variation of Plan 5 and an indication of the possibilities you have to increase your operating pleasures when you put your mind and track to task. There is still room left over for another outside spur and additional inside spurs leading in from the opposite direction, if you are switching minded.

The Tru-Track plans shown have been presented with but one thought in mind: namely, to show you how to develop a simple oval into bigger and better things. Tru-Scale's Tru-Track and Atlas Snap-Track are both sectional track materials and, by the same token, interjoinable. Since they are compatible with each other, their respective plans are also applicable regardless of whether you use Tru-Track or Snap-Track. For this reason, the operating points covered (though briefly) concerning the Atlas Snap-Track plans were not repeated in the presentation of the Tru-Track plans. In short, all things are basically equal. There are, however, a few differences where their respective turnouts (switches) are concerned, which in turn effect the manner in which Snap-Track or Tru-Track users will have to wire their railroad. Suffice to say that either track material can be hooked up, power-wise, quite easily.

for scenery that the plan might not include, a bit of artwork will be necessary. Place a sheet of tracing paper over the plan and immediately sketch in the outer lines of the railroad area your track plan will occupy. Afterward, if you wish to shorten or lengthen some of the trackage, you simply move the tracing paper to the areas in question and sketch in whatever changes you wish to make, then tie things in for continuity. Be sure that the removal of a section of track will not affect the radius of a curve, or that, by virtue of shortening, a turnout will not end up in a curve. To do the latter is to invite trouble in the form of curved points, a ticklish situation at best and a practice far better suited to the more advanced modeler; in short, it is not recommended for beginners. Increasing the length is fine if you don't exceed the dimensions that the plan area can to handle; and your straight track remains at a compatible tangent to your curves.

As for designing your own plans, that's a track of another gauge. The plan must be drawn to scale, but don't let that scare you. Most track plans are scaled at 3/4 inch to the foot. Therefore, for the sake of discussion, let us assume that your track plan and railroad scheme embraces an overall area of 4 by 8 feet —the dimensions of a standard sheet of plywood. Draw a rectangle measuring 3 by 6 inches to represent the outer edges of your benchwork or table top. Following this, draw a series of ruled lines 3/4 inch apart from top to bottom and side to side. The space between each ruled line will represent 12 inches. Therefore, the 3-by-6-inch drawing actually represents 4 by 8 feet. The boxes that result from the gridwork pattern in your drawing each represent 1 square foot and will be helpful when you start to plot your curves, straight track, turnouts, scenery, etc. If you feel that the size of the drawing is too small and confining, you can double things and make it 1 1/2 inches to the foot, but you will need a bigger piece of paper to work on. By the way, if you check the markings on your ruler, you will notice that 1/16 inch on your plan will

The five track plans that follow have been designed specifically for use with Tru-Scale Ready-Track, though with a bit of modifying these plans will also work with sectional and other track materials. Each plan is shown with an outline representing the outer edges of a plywood panel or benchwork upon which the track will be fastened down. Dotted lines are optional additions which can be used at the outset or later on, when expansion permits. They can also be rearranged depending on the type of operating activity you desire. Size of turnouts are indicated by circled numbers. Straight and curved sections of track are also shown. For example, "S-18" means a straight length of track 18 inches long, whereas "18R" indicated a length of track with an 18-inch radius curve. An extremely popular track material, widely used among many advanced model railroaders, Ready-Track will be discussed in greater detail in the next chapter.

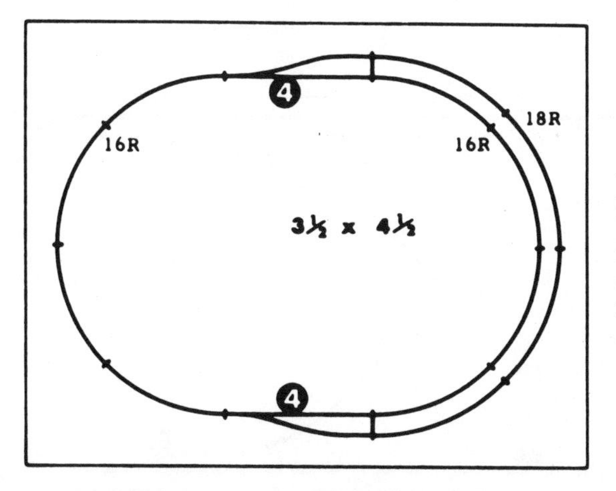

Designed for a very small space, this basic oval features an outside passing siding which will do much to relieve the monotony of the loco chasing its caboose. The addition of a tunnel (to let the train disappear for a moment) and other scenic effects will add to the illusion and dimension of this otherwise small railroad. Laying the track at an off angle to the overall space will help, too.

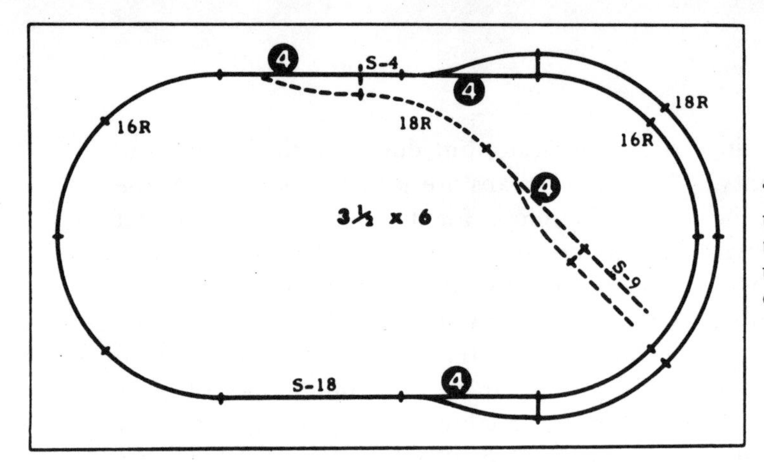

This is the same basic oval whose added length permits the use of an inside spur or two. With the aid of a few more turnouts, you can add a small yard for storing and making up freight. You will also have room left over to add an outside spur or two.

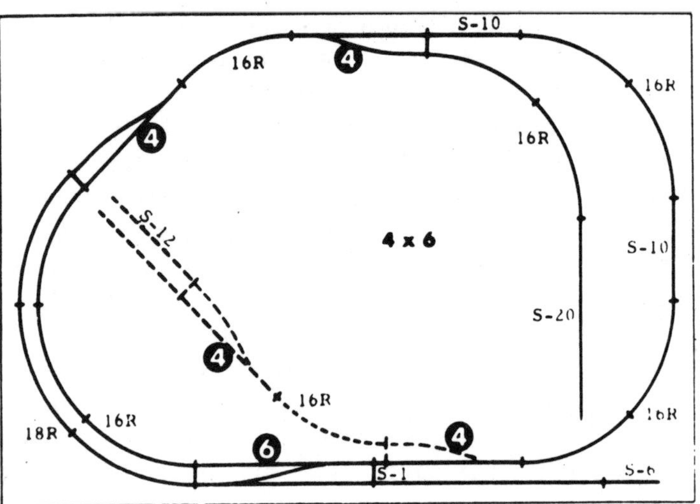

Another variation of the basic oval, with outside passing siding. This plan provides sufficient room inside for a small yard and spurs to local industry. You will also have an opportunity to flex your switching muscles a bit.

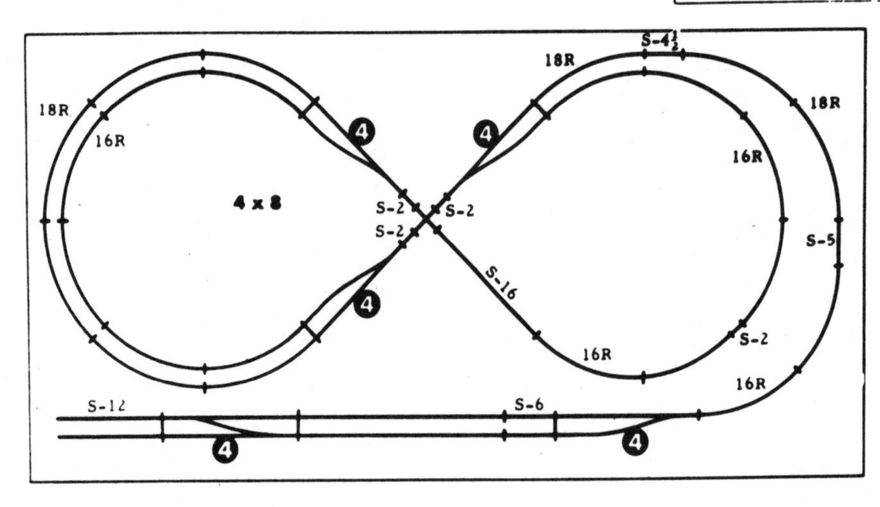

This figure-eight track plan features an outside spur with storage tracks and a "locomotive escape." If you wish, you can eliminate the use of the 90-degree crossing in the center and convert the plan to an over-and-under figure eight simply by raising one level of track above the other where they would normally join at the crossing. A mountain, tunnels, buildings and other scenic effects will add to the believability while permitting your train to disappear from view for a moment, then turn up at another point elsewhere along the line. Outside of some switching in the outside spur, and holding a train on a siding, the action will be on the continuous side.

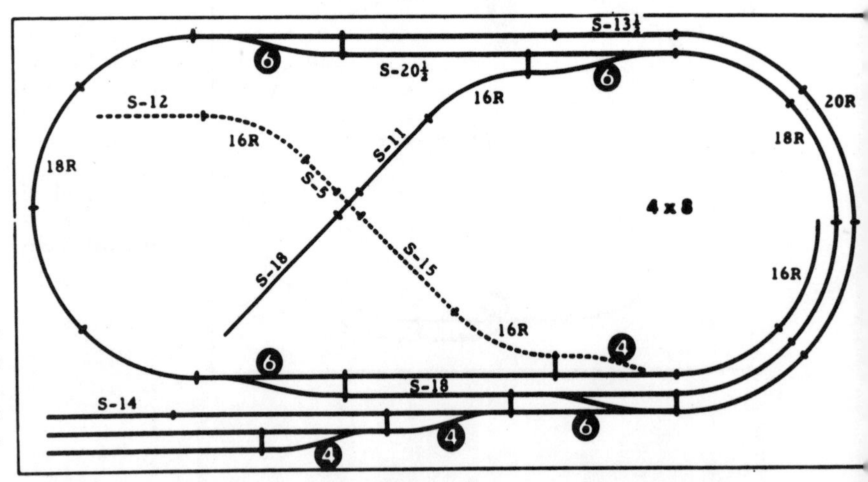

This plan not only affords numerous switching chores, but a good amount of mainline running as well. There is plenty of room left over for industrial spurs, the use of a 90-degree crossing and multi-train operation. The outside spur, storage tracks and "locomotive escape" will offer you many an hour of excitement-filled switchback operation.

be the equivalent of 1 full inch on your layout if you use the 3/4 inch-to-the-foot ratio. If you use the 1½-inch basis, then 1/8 inch on your plan will represent 1 inch in the layout. Either way, the respective measurements will help you plan things to the inch. However, since most published track plans use the 3/4 inch-to-1-foot ratio, you would be wise to do the same. In that way, if you decide to borrow something from a given plan which corresponds in scale, you won't encounter any problems in continuity. Just be sure that the plan specifies the scale, which is generally listed in the following manner and will serve to give you a comparison between HO and the other scales in use.

The rest is up to you, for when you get to the heart of things, it is difficult to tell someone else how they should design a set of track plans. It is an individual thing for each modeler. You will find that you have to make a compromise here and there; in fact, you will probably make quite a few compromises.

Returning to the question of limited space, and this seems to be a universal problem, one of the simplest solutions is to build a shelf-type railroad. Also referred to as an around-the-wall railroad, a set-up such as this will enable you to employ a number of track plans with an emphasis on switching. For example, a shelf measuring 1 by 16 feet will permit more operation than you might imagine. The length will obviously appeal to you, while the width will no doubt discourage you. But don't let the 12-inch width deceive you, for within this minimum space you can lay a number of broad curves and turnouts, and, by means of switchback methods, you will be able to run your trains a fair distance. Despite the limited space, you will be able to place many structures against the wall. You will have to slice them to perhaps one-fifth their normal depth and, in effect, end up with no more than a false front so to speak. Nevertheless, they will add to the depth of your background, creating the illusion that the railroad is wider. By means of a crossover or two you will be able to offer your locomotives an escape route, so that after dropping off cars at one end the engine can move through a crossover to an adjoining track and pick up a few cars for the return trip. Shelf railroads lend themselves perfectly to garage walls, and, as I said, are

Plans Are Drawn to:	*Multiply Figured Dimensions and Elevations by:*	*Ruled Lines Across Plans Are:*
1-inch scale for TT	¾-inch for TT	9 inches apart in TT
¾-inch scale for HO	1-inch for HO	12 inches apart in HO
½-inch scale for S	1½-inch for S	18 inches apart in S
⅜-inch scale for O	2-inch for O	24 inches apart in O

(Crossing angles are the same in all scales)

The following brief recap should also serve as a guide:

1. Draw to scale an outline of the outer limits of your table top or benchwork.
2. Do not lay any trackwork closer than 2 inches from the edges of your benchwork or table. The more the outermost edges extend beyond your track, the more room you will have for background scenery, structures, etc.
3. Be sure to allow sufficient room and clearance for turnouts, particularly if the switch motors are mounted alongside.
4. Plot your curves and mainline trackage carefully to insure a compatible and railroad-like meeting point.
5. Avoid placing turnouts on a curve.
6. If track covers screws that hold table top in place, relocate the screws.
7. Don't try to cram every bit of track you can into the smallest area possible. You will only add to your wiring woes when you get into multi-train operation.

Being cramped for space can mean a number of different things to as many model railroad builders. If you have plenty of length, but are shy of width, don't despair, for a shelf railroad will easily solve your dilemma. It will also offer more action per square foot than you could possibly imagine. True, you can't do any mainline running, but you can certainly do a whale of a lot of operating, and since prototype operation is one of the basic themes of this book, I'll let the following shelf-type railroad track plans speak for themselves.

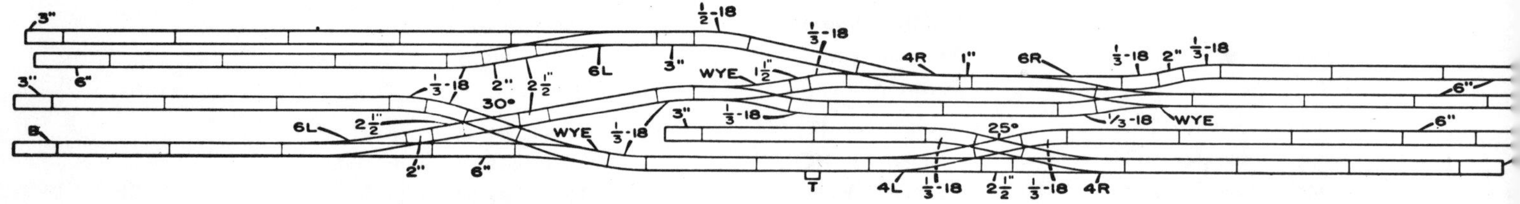

This Atlas Track Plan Number 12 is a narrow switching railroad for tight spaces. This particular plan will fit on a 10-foot shelf only 1 foot wide. A few more inches will offer you more in the way of backdrop effects, if you can spare them. If not, you can make false fronts out of the background structures by reducing their width. Don't let this plan deceive you, for it has more operating possibilities than meet the eye. As indicated in the rendering above, you can heighten the effect by introducing grades and levels from side to side and front to rear.

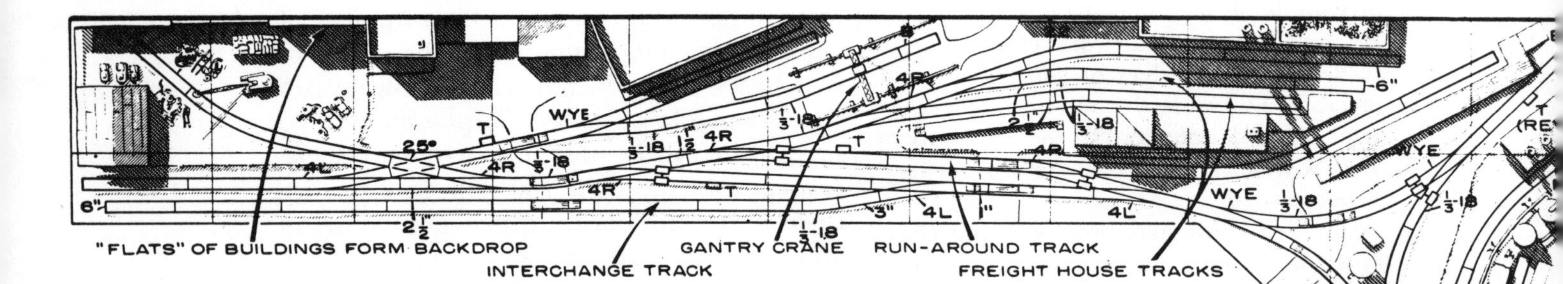

Another track plan offered by Atlas (Number 13) is yours for the making if you can manage a shelf along two sides of a room. An 18-inch width is the minimum; the wider, however, the better. Plenty of action is offered by this plan, plus a turnaround provided by the wye track in this purposeful design. You can always expand and add a loop to increase your run.

Selecting an "L"-shaped design for his model railroad, Bob Steele uses the narrow part of the "L" for his storage and freight yard area. Bob is also using a mixture of sectional, flexible and Ready-Track, a not uncommon practice. Also note the use of the Tru-Scale double crossover between the two parallel storage tracks. This provides an opportunity for a yard hog to continue its freight-spotting chores without necessarily getting boxed in. Commonly referred to as a "locomotive escape," it is an important part of switch-back operation.

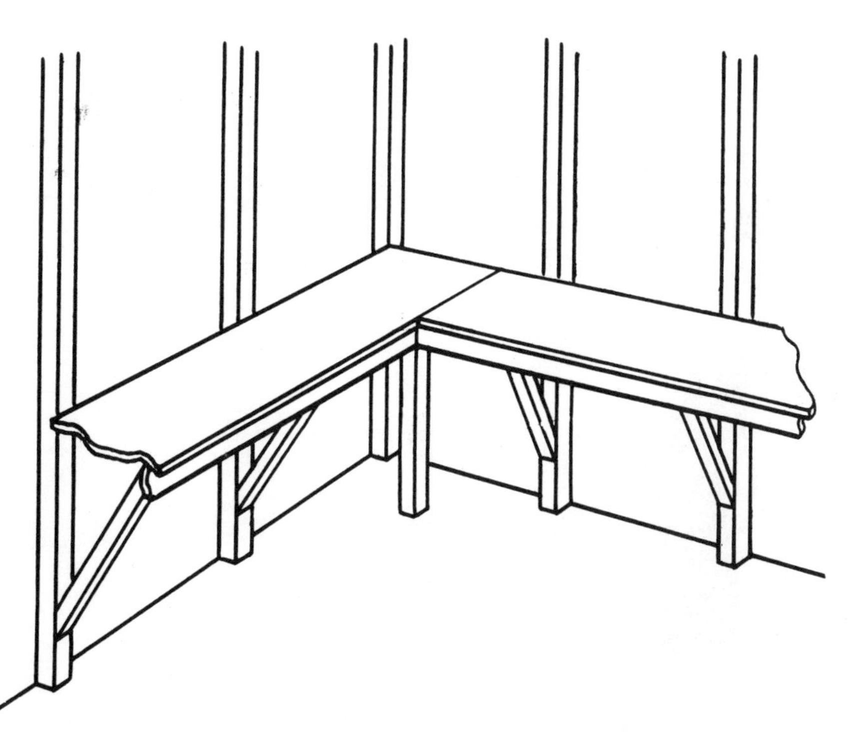

Construction of a shelf-type or around-the-wall-type railroad is quite simple. Some inexpensive shelving, plywood, braces and, before you know it, you are ready to start laying your trackwork. This type of arrangement is perfectly suited to a garage, since in most cases the studs are exposed and nailing things together presents little if any problem. You can even place it at eye level (more than enough for the hood of a car to clear) and you will be astounded by the difference in perspective during actual operation.

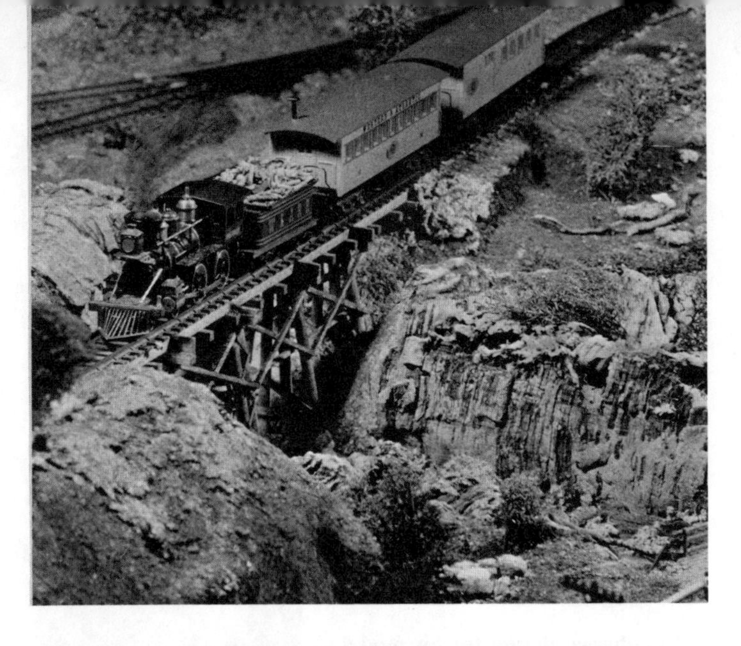

Oldtimers such as this 4-4-0 will solve many a problem for model rails who are cramped for space, yet hunger for a fair amount of mainline runs. Coupled to a few "shorty" cars such as these 1860 coaches by Mantua, the train makes up into a legitimate-looking short haul prototypical of earlier days when two- to five-car trains were par for the course. Combined with Jim Foell's scenic artistry, everything looks in its rightful place.

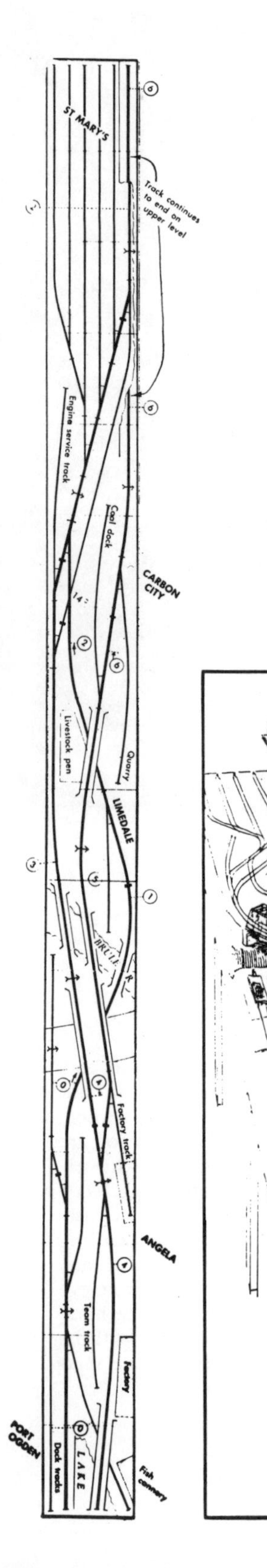

If I had to make a choice between a continuous lap about an oval, regardless of the size, shape and length of the mainline run, or a shelf type of operation such as this fascinating track plan offers, then I would probably be inclined to settle for the latter—and happily, too. This well conceived plan (Number 8) is just one of *101 Track Plans,* by Linn H. Westcott, and is reprinted here through the courtesy of the Kalmbach Publishing Co. This publication is absolutely must reading if you are seriously inclined, for it includes track plans of varied shapes, sizes and different forms of operation, in greater scope than one chapter alone can cover. This particular plan more than speaks for itself and, believe it or not, only requires a space 12 inches wide in HO. It is also 16 feet long and should fit perfectly along the wall of an average-sized garage. The dimensional rendering drawn by Linn should by itself be more than enough to whet your appetite and stimulate your imagination. It did mine!

8. Port Ogden & Northern RR. Conventional curves (24") but No. 4 turnouts.

A longer bookshelf lets you run trains a fair distance by switchback methods. To save space, many structures can be sliced and set against a wall.

primarily designed for switching. If space permits, a few more inches of width will help reduce that cramped look and will enable you to add scenery and a level or two. The wider you can make it, the more practical the possibility of adding a return loop or oval. If at the moment you are confined to a narrow width, you can go ahead and dress things up completely. Later on when space permits, you can add larger areas for mainline running and loop-to-loop operation. You can be sure that the efforts and materials of your shelf railroad will not be wasted, for it can always become a junction or yard that can be made part of a larger railroad later on.

In yards, where space is at a minimum, No. 4 turnouts are your best bet. Where space permits, the broader curve of No. 6 turnouts might be more desirable. For the broader the curve of the turnout, the wider the distance between adjoining tracks, and, as previously noted, the larger an engine you can operate realistically. In this way you can operate light switch engines of the saddle tank variety as well as heavier switch engines hauling tenders.

In summary, remember that it will be your own railroad and one that will reflect your own particular "imagineering" and ingenuity. Most track plans are intended as a guide to your own final thoughts and possibilities of application. They are also a source of ideas and an insight to model railroad practice and technique. Not all plans are applicable unless you use precisely the same type of track materials in the same amount of space as indicated. In other words, they are not necessarily the gospel and may need modifying to fit your own needs or problems. They may have to be reduced, expanded, or improved upon. Sometimes something gets lost in the transition and, by the same token, sometimes you open new horizons for operating pleasure. Certain plans offered commercially are quite attractive looking, including many forms of fancy trackwork, crossovers, freight yards, reverse loops, sidings, and the like. That is, they are attractive on paper, for quite often they do not allow enough space for locating turnouts, the installation of switch motors, or certain structures and trackside buildings that were included in the design. This is as bad as having an electrical wizard buddy wire up a super-duper control panel for you; it looks great, but afterward you don't understand it, let alone know how to use it. Therefore, rather than get caught up in the "Case of the Pre-Conceived Track Plan Caper," start with an uncomplicated track plan and expand on it as your own capabilities and experience broaden. You may tear things up once, twice, or perhaps half a dozen times until you get things exactly the way you want them. You will correct, modify, rearrange, expand, and apply a number of applications and techniques that will add to your operating pleasures. Above all, you will thoroughly enjoy it.

A realistic-looking model railroad will be the end result if you plan carefully, devote time, patience and honest to goodness sweat. It cannot be slapped together overnight. Good-looking trackwork, properly laid and conforming to prototype practice in as reasonable degree as possible, will take on added appearance when you set the scene surrounding it. In this dimensional view of Jim Foell's pike you can see that he has combined the very ingredients necessary to make a believable railroading atmosphere in miniature form. As you can see, the section crew is still working at the crossing, and will continue to be there for some time, for maintenance is part of the normal routine. A well-planned layout will go a long way toward keeping maintenance at a mininmum and provide you with more time for operating pleasures.

VIII
Track Tips

In a survey taken during the mid-fifties, the editors of *Model Railroader* estimated that there were approximately 132,000 model railroad hobbyists in the United States, who collectively operated some 2,000 statute miles of track. Placed end to end, this trackage would have stretched from New York to the western boundaries of Colorado. However, in model railroading we talk in terms of scale miles, the miniature equivalent of statute miles. Thus, 2,000 statute miles of scale track would become 134,000 miles of real track, encircling the globe almost six times. Bringing things up to date, considering the tremendous strides the hobbv has made in popularity, and the tens of thousands of new entrants into this fascinating and now respected pastime, if the collective statute miles of track were laid end to end today, it would no doubt reach deep into the Pacific Ocean. And as for scale miles, there would probably be such a crisscrossing of track around the globe that satellites would have a hard time leaving the earth's atmosphere. And bear in mind that as surveys go, even the most detailed compilation of statistics can only touch on a cross section of actual activity and, therefore, offer no more than an average estimate, which in this case could easily be considered conservative at that.

When it comes to track, the amount of material available is almost as numerous as the wheel arrangements of steam locomotives. The same can be said of the manner in which it is laid within your layout, each application not only suited to the particular track material being used, but also to the smoothness of operation and ultimate in appearance. For the benefit of those who are new to the hobby of model railroading, the following is intended to help you achieve more realism with your existing trackwork and also acquaint you with the availability of track materials other than those you may be using. I think we can safely assume that the average rail buff wants his trackwork to look as prototype as possible, and the ways to go about achieving this will be elaborated on throughout this and subsequent chapters.

Many beginners get into the hobby via the back door—they buy their youngsters a ready-to-run train set and shortly thereafter get bitten by the model railroading bug. For the most part, the track included with such sets is of the snap-together, or sectional variety. Without question, it is functional, easy to connect, and equally easy to lay on whatever trackbed surfaces are being used. Aside from the price and convenience of using such ready-to-lay track material, one particular disadvantage is the shortness of sections (9 inches) and the number of units needed for a given track plan. In other words, the more sections and resultant connecting points, the more joints; the more joints (though held in place by joiners), the greater the possibility of kinks, resulting in uneven wheel motion or derailment. The more joiners, the more possibility they will work loose, causing the connecting rails not only to get out of line, producing the unrailroad-like wobbles just mentioned, but also impeding the steady flow of power from section to section. For joiners serve not only to line up and connect one section of rail to the other, but also act as the electrical connection between them.

The appearance of the symmetrical, black plastic ties also leaves something to be desired; however, ballasting can do much to remedy the "store bought" train set look. Needless to say, the advent of sectional track has been responsible for many new model railroaders getting off not only to a good running start, but an advanced interest as well, when they discover the availability of other track products. Despite the appearance, sectional track is in widespread use today, favored mostly by beginners and/or those who want to get running in a hurry, some veterans not excepted. One particular advantage of sectional track is the fact that a given track plan can be assembled, added to, modified, and more important—*tested*—before so much as one unit of track is spiked or cemented in place. You simply join the respective units of track together as per the plan, be it a simple oval or otherwise. This preliminary procedure can be quite useful if you happen to be building your railroad on a table top. For in such a case you can move the assembled track about the surface of the table top, selecting whatever angle you prefer.

For example, a basic oval placed within the confines of a 4-by-8-foot working area will look much better in the long run

Tru-Track has certain notable features which make it different from other sectional track materials and, as a result, is quite popular among beginners. This silhouette dramatically emphasizes the irregular spacing and staggered positioning of the ties which lends a more prototypical appearance.

Good-looking trackwork will add to your operating pleasure when she's "comin' 'round the bend."

if it is arranged at off angles rather than the symmetrical fashion, wherein the straight sections of track run exactly parallel to the sides of the table or trackbed surface. This slightly cockeyed composition, or off-center arrangement, will also offer you more room at various far corners for scenic effects. At the same time you will be able to add extra track in the form of spurs and sidings, while avoiding the even appearance of toy train set-ups. Draw an outline of your railroad space on a sheet of tracing paper. Move it about your track plan, and you will get an idea of what I mean. The mere off-centering of an inch or two might well open and expand additional areas for new trackage. While the foregoing becomes more evident by shifting about a 4-by-8-foot track arrangement within a larger area such as 5 by 9 feet, even the slightest deviation from the norm will probably be an improvement. Don't overdo it, though, for while you might increase the area for laying track in one spot, you might inadvertently find yourself cramped for space at another point. However, as I said a few moments ago, this is one of the advantages of sectional track—you can move your entire trackage about the surface of your railroad and not make anything secure until you are satisfied with the overall format.

In effect, since sectional track is so relatively easy to lay, you may find it convenient to do your layout doodling with the actual units of track within your railroad area—certainly a more helpful and realistic procedure than making doodles on paper. Should you decide to broaden the radius of a given curve, lengthen a siding, spur, or mainline, you won't have to do any mathematical scaling on paper, since the results of whatever changes you make will be before your eyes.

Generally speaking, sectional track is commonly referred to as "snap-track," an obvious tag considering the fact that it is a snap to join one section to the other. Actually, Snap-Track is a trademark and product of the Atlas Tool Company and is the track material usually included with HO train sets. In recent years a new sectional track material called "Tru-Track" was introduced by Tru-Scale, a company which has long been associated with a fine line of track materials designed for and widely used by advanced modelers. Also of the snap-together variety, Tru-Track has become standard equipment for the thousands of train sets that are sold yearly, and has made great inroads with beginners for a variety of reasons. To all intents and purposes, Tru-Track and Snap-Track are basically the same and in a manner of speaking, inter-joinable. However, the introduction of Tru-Track is probably the best thing that ever happened to sectional trackers. For, while almost identical to the familiar snap-track, there are a few notable differences which are worth noting. For example, the ties and base, though plastic, have a dull finish, with a well-detailed wood grain. Tie plate ridges are on each and every tie, making the spike effect more realistic looking and, more important the ties themselves are not symmetrical but rather staggered on purpose, some shorter or longer and at off angles to each other, creating a more natural look.

A companion item to Tru-Track is the Tru-Switch turnout. Here again the improvement is quite noticeable, for the Tru-Switch embodies a "continuous-rail" design, without any electrical deadspots, featuring Tru-Scale's popular "Hi-Speed" closed frog switch components. The fact that they have been able to incorporate the function and design of their highly successful and widely used turnouts within a sectional track product goes a long way toward minimizing derailments and, more important, *eliminating wheel drop and stalling.* (In a test, we ran the smallest 0-4-0 loco we could find back and forth through a No. 4 Tru-Switch turnout, and even at the slowest throttle point the action was smooth, with no quivers at the frog points.)

For those who have advanced beyond the sectional track category, or who, from the

Logging spur alongside loading dock of sawmill embraces the use of flexible track. Logs spanning that "old mill stream" also serve as roadbed, lending a rural and authentic touch.

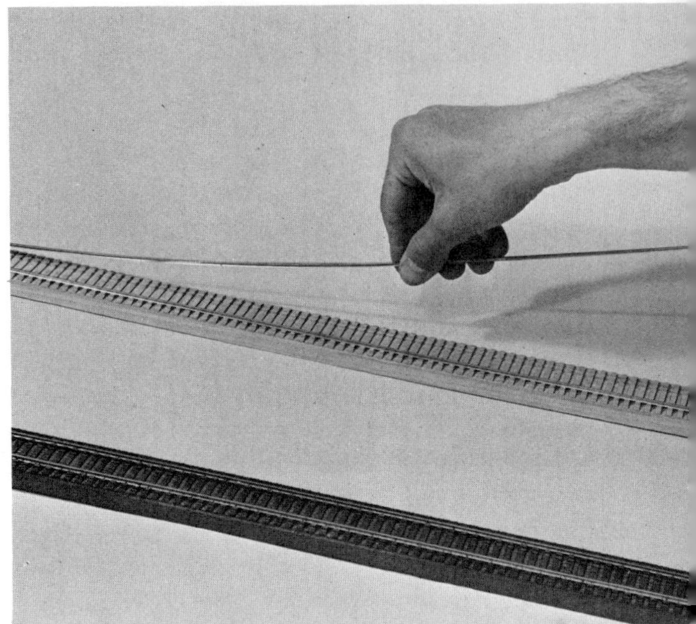

The only difference between Tru-Scale's Ready-Track and their Self-Gauging Roadbed is the fact that Ready-Track is stained, features a built-in ballast effect and is ready to use. Self-Gauging Roadbed does just as the name implies, and gives the track layer a chance to not only economize, but do-it-himself. Both materials are extremely popular with many advanced modelers.

start, are more interested not only in appearance, but in doing it themselves as well, Tru-Scale offers a more refined and advanced line of track materials which are by far the most versatile and among the most widely used in both home layouts and club operations. For, aside from the minority of scale modelers who lay their own ties and spike down their own rails (we'll get to that later), the average advanced model rail from coast to coast uses the following Tru-Scale products in one combination or another:

First, there is Ready-Track, and while this is of a ready-to-use nature, there the resemblance to sectional track ends. Ready-Track consists of rail mounted on wooden roadbed whose top surface has been milled in the form of realistic-looking ties and tie plates similar to the prototype. It comes pre-stained and ballasted, and all you have to do is screw, nail, or cement it to your sub-surface. Track joiners aid in connecting one section to another. Straight lengths come in 24-inch sections, and curves, depending on their radius, in various lengths. While the cost is a bit more than that of sectional track, when you consider the fact that Ready-Track comes already mounted on roadbed and is stained and ballasted, the saving in time is enormous. Actually, when you add the cost of sectional track and roadbed, the difference between this combination and Ready-Track is negligible, and the latter is much better looking and easier to work with. The ties of Ready-Track are stained a realistic creosote color and can be darkened if desired. The ballasting effect is a medium gray; this can be lightened or darkened, depending on your preferences.

For those who wish to spike down their own rail, Tru-Scale also has "self-gauging roadbed." This is identical to their Ready-Track, but is not stained or ballasted. Application is simple; you merely place your rail stock in the milled grooves and spike down. It isn't necessary to use a track gauge (hence the term self-gauging), but as a precaution, the use of gauge won't hurt; it will help keep the rail from moving about during spiking.

If you want to lay ties as well as spike your own rail, Tru-Scale offers plain roadbed, the details of which will be explained in a moment. This roadbed can be used also for laying tie strips or to serve as the roadbase for sectional or flex track. A liquid ballast and tie stain, also made by Tru-Scale, will add the finishing touches. They also make Super-Flex (for easements and curves), bridge stock (for trestles), switch blocks, and crossover blocks, etc. And, like other track material manufacturers, they have a full supply of turnouts, switches, crossovers, and crossings, plus switch kits. If you are interested in expanding trackwork possibilities, send for their latest catalogue or get one from your hobby shop.

In recent years there has been a growing trend among discriminating model rails to lay their own ties and rail. Among the many considerations are more prototypical appearance, smoother running, and greater flexibility, or, to put it another way, less limitations when following your track plans. Let us assume you have all your trackwork down, and then decide to add a siding or two, or perhaps rip up a section of mainline and replace it with new trackwork. Whether you have used sectional track, Ready-Track, Flex-Track, or what have you, it now might be an excellent time to try your hand at tie and track laying. I am not suggesting that you re-do your entire trackage; try your hand on a small section for a starter. Many modelers shy away from laying ties and track despite the fact that it is not as difficult as it appears. There is no question that it is time consuming; by the same token, there is no question that the rewards will more than make up for the effort involved. You will enjoy the experience of doing it yourself, and the prototypical appearance as well.

Here is how it is done: Assuming the surface in question is smooth, draw two parallel lines to represent the rails and to serve as a guide for the placement of your ties. Next comes the adhesive for keeping the ties se-

Tru-Scale offers a wide range of mounted turnouts, crossovers, switch kits, Ready-Track and a variety of roadbeds for the do-it-yourselfer.

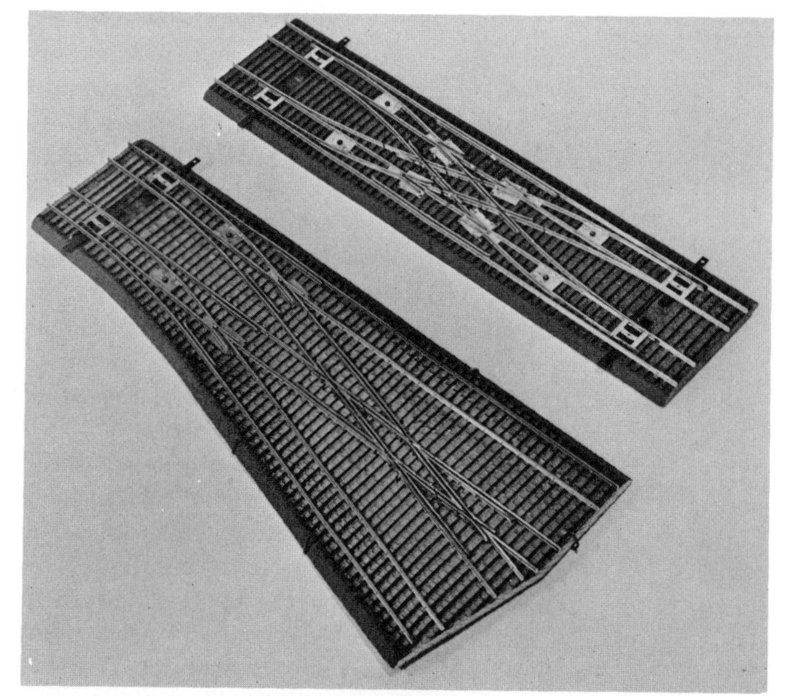

Fancy turnouts to make the hearts of brass hats beat a bit faster are Tru-Scale's Double Turnouts and Scissors X-Overs. Switch work such as this not only provides interesting and exciting action, but will also act as a stimulus when developing your track plans. Suitable for mainline, yard operation or whatever you dream up from sketch pad to actual practice. Also features a stained and ballast effect.

curely in place. A glue that sets up fairly fast is best. Plasticate, or any white vinyl-based cement, is well-suited for this particular operation. Start with an area 4 to 6 inches long. The number of ties you lay is determined by the speed with which you can place them in position before the glue sets up. If you overdo it, and lay too long an area of adhesive, you may find that at the halfway mark the adhesive is no longer tacky enough to form a bond with the tie, and you will have to add more. Placing the glue on the roadbed, or whatever surface you are working in, can be done in a number of ways. Run ribbons of glue in zigzag or straight-line fashion not only within the rail lines, but at least 1/8 inch on each side. If you don't mind a sticky finger, use your finger to spread an even film of glue over the working area, thus affording equal distribution in bonding the ties to the surface. The latter will also prevent any ridges of glue from bubbling up over the top of the ties. Now to the actual tie laying.

No straightedges or guides are necessary; in fact, they are definitely unwanted, for in this case laying the ties by eye is more desirable, and such irregularities that might result will add a more natural appearance. In fact, some modelers go out of their way to introduce slight variations rather than attempting perfect symmetry. Check the ties on the prototypes and you will find that some ties stick out a bit more than others and are not always perfectly parallel. Placing the first tie down in position, lay the next one down approximately one tie apart, and so on down the line until you reach the end of the glued area.

Following this, the ties should be weighted down so they will set at the same surface level to each other. While the first batch of ties is setting up, you can go on to the next 4- to 6-inch area, repeating the process described. As your speed and dexterity improve, you will be able to lay longer sections, and lay them faster. After all the ties are laid and have set up in the area concerned, check the top surface for irregularities and sand down any uneven spots. Don't worry about the glue showing, it will soon be covered with ballast. And there it is—a good-looking tie bed for your rail. If you have used unstained ties, it is a simple matter to stain them by using a creosote stain, such as the type made by Tru-Scale. Application is simple, just brush it on, let it seep in, then rub off the surplus with a soft rag. You can repeat the applications, depending on how deep you want the stain effect to be. Remember, however, that after ballasting not much more than the top surface of the tie will be exposed to view.

Next comes the ballasting, which can consist of your own concoction or various ballasting material you can purchase at your hobby shop. This will be elaborated on in greater detail further along. Lay a straightedge along the outside edge of the ties on whichever side is convenient to you. Using a small brush, work the ballast into the crevices, sweeping away the surplus so that the tops of the ties are clean and exposed. On the side that doesn't have the straight edge, sweep the ballast up against the ends of the ties . . . don't worry about the other side, the guide will keep the ballast intact. Next, make a mixture of one part Plasticate (or any other vinyl-type glue) and five parts water; add half an ounce of liquid detergent (Joy works fine) and stir; do not shake, otherwise you will end up with a froth of bubbles. In case you are curious as to the detergent, its use is easily explained. The detergent acts as a wetting agent, and, when mixed with the adhesive mixture, aids in seeping into every nook and cranny.

Now, with the aid of an eyedropper, lay a bead of this mixture on the ballast between each tie. The liquid will seep through, and, when dry, the ballast will appear to be lying loose and yet will be firmly anchored around the tie bed. By the way, the liquid mixture dries colorless and will not change the color or appearance of the ballast. It isn't necessary to tamp down any of the ballast while it is setting up; the next step will take care of that.

The following sequence of photographs illustrates how to lay and ballast a bed of ties. In this particular instance, a length of sectional track has been removed to be replaced by hand-laid ties and rail. This technique is applicable whether you are adding to existing trackwork or starting from scratch. It will work equally well on plywood, wood and cork roadbed and composition material such as Homosote.

Be sure tie bed surface is smooth and clean. Draw two parallel lines to represent rails. These lines will be your guide during placement of adhesive and ties.

Lay a film of cement or glue 4 to 6 inches from the starting point and extending at least ⅛ inch from the outside of each guide line. Hypodermic type of glue gun makes a useful tool in spreading the adhesive. A white vinyl-type glue which sets up fast is your best bet.

Place each tie equidistant across the guide lines and approximately one tie apart. Such irregularities as may occur from doing it by eye will add to the natural appearance. A straight edge is not necessary; in fact, it is definitely unwelcome in this type of operation. Don't be afraid to deliberately place some of the ties slightly out of position and off-center; it will add to the effect. When you are finished laying the first batch of ties, weight them down and proceed to the next section.

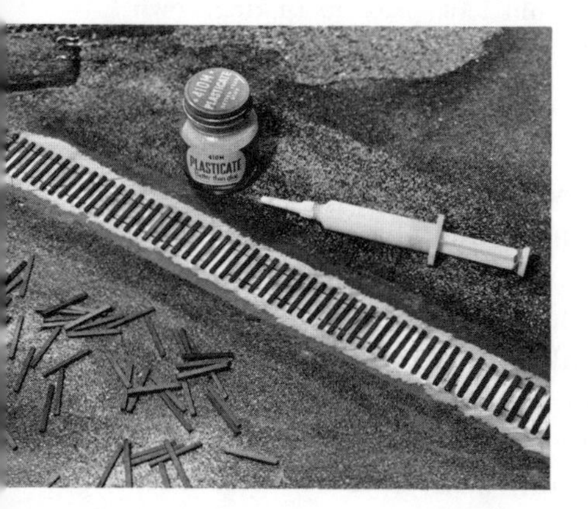

This is how your tie bed should look when you are finished. You are now ready for ballasting.

Now you can use a straight edge as a guide. Place it along one side of the ties to hold ballast in place. Sprinkle a generous amount of ballast directly over the ties.

Brush the ballast into the spaces between the ties, and also sweep away the surplus for use elsewhere. On the open side of the ties, brush the ballast with an upward motion to form a bank effect.

If you prefer to have your ballast spread and blend into the adjoining ground level, do not use the straight edge. Simply brush the surplus ballast away from the center and toward the surrounding area, smoothing or roughing up the adjacent surface as you prefer.

Using the white vinyl mixture described in the text, lay beads of the solution between the ties. You can also use the adhesive liquid to set up the loose ballast you may be blending in with the other ground fill.

When the ballast is dried in place, use a putty knife or straight edge to scrape the tops of the ties, and sand down where necessary. When finished, brush away any loose ballast that did not set up. This is how your ballasted tie bed should look prior to spiking down the rails.

When the ballast is firmly set (generally overnight), use a putty knife, or any straight edge, to scrape the surface of the ties clean of any ballast that might have adhered to them, then sweep away any surplus or loose ballast that remains; you can use it elsewhere. In Chapters X and XI, devoted to special and scenic effects, we will go into greater detail concerning ballasting and ground level cover.

Four particular items are now needed to continue the operation—long-nose pliers, spikes, rail stock, and a track gauge. The pliers are extremely important to this part of the operation and should be of good quality. In other words, avoid a cheap pair. I heartily recommend the pliers made by Xcelite. The tips assure a secure grip of the spike, which is most important in laying track. You can also use them to cut or shape wire. Your local hardware store has them or can get them for you; ask for Xcelite No. 58 pliers. They cost a bit more, but are well worth the difference.

There are any number of spikes available at your hobby shop, some of which will do the job more than adequately. There are also some which will make you wish you had never started. In purchasing spikes, look for the following: a shank not too thick, a fairly flat head, and a clean lip on the underside. This will minimize the splitting of ties, will afford a snug fit at the rail base, and will result in not only better appearance, but less chance of hanging up wheel flanges. Be sure they are HO scale. Main-Line spikes at 50¢ an ounce are available at most hobby shops, and do the job well. The same can be said of some of the excellent spikes that Kemtron has to offer.

If you are using Code 70 rail, Kemtron has a special spike for this rail size that can't be beat. Which leads us to the subject of rail size in general. We are talking about Code 100 rail regardless of whether you are using sectional track, Ready-Track, or whatever. Code 100 rail is standard and the most widely used rail size in HO model railroading. This size was adopted because it corresponded in

This is how things will look after you have spiked down rail on your hand-laid bed of ties. Prototype appearance such as this adds greatly to the railroad atmosphere of your trackwork. Weeds and other natural growth can be added for realism.

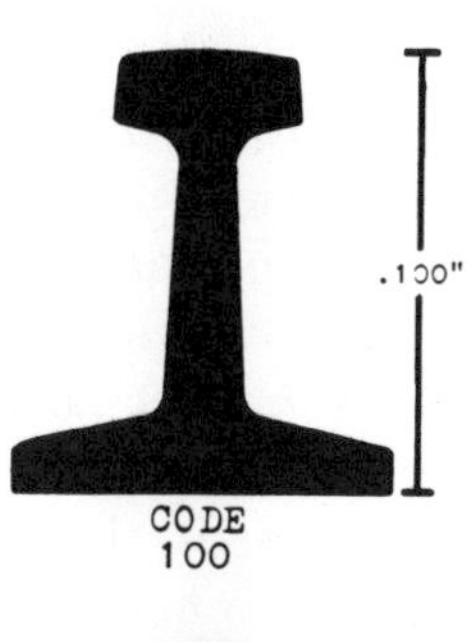

.070"
CODE
70

Greatly enlarged cross-sections show relative sizes of rail in proportion to each other.

.040"
CODE
40

Track layers will flip their spikes over this long-awaited track spiking gun from Kadee. With a tool such as this, even the most inexperienced model railroader can boast fancy trackwork to match veteran brass hats. The gun is a special-duty stapler designed specifically to drive special staples into the ties and against the rail base, thus clinching the rail securely to the tie bed. Operation is smooth and simple, and will permit laying and spiking down a section of track in no time at all. For example, in five minutes you can spike down a section of track which would normally take forty-five minutes. More important than the saving of time is the fact that the rail is laid more uniformly and accurately. These close-up views show the track-spiking gun in action with Code 100 rail stock. Where track laying is concerned, the development and introduction of this exciting tool is a credit to Kadee Quality Products and is certainly a giant step toward making life a bit more pleasant for model rails.

height to the 152-pound rail used in prototype application in mainline railroads. However, 152-pound rail is an unusually heavy rail, and, though it could take a steady pounding, many of the busiest raillines have been relaid with 110-pound track. Thus, in going from the prototype to the HO scale of things, Code 70 came into being, enabling scale enthusiasts to maintain prototypical values and appearances. Therefore, in recent years there has been a growing tendency to use Code 70 rail because it most closely approximates the size of the mainline rails used by the majority of national railroads today. However, Code 70 is an "apply-with-great-care" type of track material and is best suited to the more advanced track layer. Of even more recent note is the attention that Code 40 is starting to attract, particularly for use in mining spurs and short branch lines that are not heavily trafficked. However, this rail size is strictly for extra special effects and is quite difficult to handle even for veterans. In short, it is beyond the scope at this point of writing to pursue it any further.

Rail stock in brass and nickel silver generally comes in bundles of 36-inch lengths and is available from numerous sources such as Kemtron, Tru-Scale, and, of course, through hobby shops.

Last but not least is the track gauge. This important tool will not only set the rails the proper distance apart, but will also hold them in place during the actual spiking operation. Some of these tools are a combination gauge and coupler height adjuster, thus serving a double function. When purchasing your track gauge, be absolutely certain that it conforms to the NMRA standards.

Meanwhile, back to the tie bed that has been properly prepared and ballasted. Continue by using a straightedge, drawing parallel lines (to represent the rail stock) along the top of the ties equidistant from the outer edges. Either line can serve as the guide in laying the rail or, if you wish, you can use string pulled taut between two nails running the length of the line you have drawn.

Now, to the laying of track, spiking down one rail at a time. Lay a section of rail over the guideline; on the opposite side lay a short length to balance the track gauge, which is now fitted into position on both rails. The latter will set up the gauge and hold things in place during the spiking. Next, securely grip a spike in the tip of the pliers, leaving about one-half of the shank sticking out. Always start on the inside of the rail. Place the point of the spike slightly out from the rail base in the center of the tie and as close to the track gauge as the tip of the pliers will allow. Then make a firm downward thrust. If you are too close to the rail the lip of the spike will come to rest on the rail head. Assuming you have cleared the top of the rail, send the spike home so that it will butt directly and firmly against the rail base. Don't push too hard or you might force the rail into the tie, resulting in a lower rail surface level, in other words, a dip or a kink. If you goof, remove the spike and start over again. Now spike the outside of the rail directly opposite. Do not stagger the spikes, as this will produce wobbles in your trackwork. Continue the spiking along the entire length of rail section you are laying, spiking four ties apart inside and out, and so on down the line.

Wide view of rustic sawmill and ranch scene is a fine example of Jim Foell's scratch-building and scenic artistry. It is also a good idea of how things look when track and terrain are well blended together. The loco dragging a string of ore cars is much to big for this "bobtail" haul, but was pressed into service because the 0-4-0 was tied up at the sawmill.

Before and after ballasting of sectional track. Note how ballasting has greatly improved overall appearance of otherwise symmetrical-looking black plastic ties. Note also how wood grain effect is heightened in contrast to ballast which now covers cork roadbed. The technique for ballasting existing trackwork is identical to the method employed when ballasting hand-laid ties; however, special care must be taken to be sure that no ballast remains against the rail sides to affect or impede the motion of wheel flanges. In other words, be sure that all ballast remains at or below tie level.

When you have completely finished, you are now ready to spike the opposite rail. Start with a short section of 18 inches, or one-half the regular length. I'll explain why in a moment. Place it on the ties parallel to the newly laid rail, reverse the position of your track gauge to hold things in place and the proper distance apart, and start spiking down as outlined above. When you have finished, you can continue along, back and forth, using the regular 36-inch lengths of rail. Joiners will help keep additional sections of rail in place while you spike them down. The reason for starting with a short section of rail on the opposite side is to avoid having rail joints directly opposite each other. By this method, no matter how much rail you lay, straight or curved, the rail joints will never be opposite each other, which will result in not only a better appearance, but will lessen the possibility of kinks in your trackwork. The rail you have laid will mate up with any other track work, sectional, Ready-Track, Flex-Track, or otherwise. Depending upon the thickness of your ties, and the ties in the track work you may be joining up with, you may have to shim up the ends to make the joined rail head surfaces of equal level. Allowances will also have to be made for different heights of roadbed, or in going from roadbed trackage to flat bed trackage.

When you have completely finished your tie, ballasting, and track-laying chores, you can stand back with pride, beaming at your handiwork, for this is about the closest you can get to the real thing. I am sure you will find it easier and less time consuming than you imagined and, once accomplished, you might be prone to lay your own track on any future additions to your layout. You might also be inclined to rip out and re-do your existing trackwork. However, as I said before, I am not suggesting that you get carried away; nonetheless, I do feel that you should try it at least once. If you feel that you do not wish to devote such time and energy to the overall trackwork in your layout, then use this technique in yards, sidings, or particular sections for "show-off" track.

True, this method of laying track is more time-consuming than that of laying prefabricated track units and is definitely a delaying factor for those who are in a hurry to get operating; therefore, it is not particularly recommended unless you have already experienced the techniques and applications of building a railroad, big or small. Spiking rail is a one-spike-at-a-time proposi-

Another good example of well-blended trackwork is shown in this overall view of a whistle stop. Scratch-built, kit assembly, RTR, etc.—all of it is cleverly combined by Jim Foell in capturing the flavor of this rural mining area.

This photograph needs no caption. The trackwork speaks for itself, except to say—it was all hand laid!

tion and simply cannot be rushed. For some time the Kadee Metal Products Company has been working on a special track-laying gun which will considerably reduce the amount of time required to spike down rail. Operating on the staple-gun principle, it is expected to become available momentarily and should be a boon to those who want to give their trackwork a very sophisticated look.

In summary, sectional track—be it of the Tru-Track or Snap-Track variety—can be dressed up in a number of ways to improve its overall appearance. I have seen many well-planned model railroads that featured a combination of sectional track, Ready-Track, and hand-laid ties and rail, the latter generally in the most noticeable areas of the layout. There is no rule that says you can't combine your trackwork in whatever fashion you wish, and don't be afraid to rip out existing trackwork and replace it with improved track materials or hand-laid ties and rail. It happens all the time in prototype railroading, as well as among model railroaders. As you progress in the hobby, especially where trackwork is concerned, you will no doubt become more discriminating, and I would venture to say that ultimately your railroad will not only boast the realism of hand-laid ties and rail, but the use of Code 70 rail as well.

In the meantime, do what other advanced modelers are doing by trying this technique, not necessarily on an overall basis but along a prominent section of mainline, a siding, industrial spur—any area of your road that is subject to close scrutiny and where the most advanced and sophisticated applications will reflect in the prototype tradition of the real McCoy. One thing is certain—you will not only be thrilled with the final results of your handiwork, but you will wonder why you didn't do it sooner.

IX
Along the Maintenance Way

Smooth-running performance and trouble-free operation is a goal easily achieved by some and long sought after by others, the latter being in the majority. The initial care exercised in the building of your railroad and laying track will go a long way toward eliminating the possibility of derailments, a plague common to both beginners and experienced brass hats. But, as if that weren't enough, we are also faced with the problems arising from dirty and/or oxidized track, poor connections at rail gaps, cold solder joints, and a hundred and one other problems that frustrate model railroaders during operations. These ailments plague the live railroads, and they have a word for it which, though not a cure-all, does manage to keep things as shipshape as possible. The word, simply enough is *maintenance* and in model railroading it is a big word, too!

Without periodic checks of your pike, wiring, track, and all the other ingredients that make up your railroad empire, it is difficult to keep things running at peak performance. A few swipes at the track with an abrasive stone isn't enough, nor are a few laps about the layout with a track-cleaning car. But it is a good start and one that should be practiced regularly in addition to a number of other maintenance applications. Depending on how often you actually operate your layout, a maintenance schedule should be practiced a few times a month and should become a rule rather than an exception. Keeping things in top-flight condition is not only part of the model railroading fun, but pays off in the long run as well. The first step is to make a checklist to include not only the care of the most frequent trouble spots, but the areas where problems are quite likely to develop.

An average checklist could look like the one shown on the next page.

A brush is a handy item to help keep trackwork free of loose ballast and other obstructions which might hang up wheel flanges and, in turn, cause derailments. Dick Seydell uses the brush to good advantage to keep his pike in A-1 condition.

If you plan ahead, and carefully, you will be able to keep your maintenance at a minimum. Morton Gould checks trackwork with an eye toward scenic effects, structures and the operating which will follow. Allowances are made for accessibility in the event trouble spots develop.

MAINTENANCE CHECKLIST

1. Clean track
2. Using gauge, check through *all* trackwork and turnouts
3. Check all gaps, roadbed, framework, and joints
4. Check for, and remove, any foreign matter in and about throwbars and other working parts of turnouts and switches
5. Double check alignment and contact of point rails in turnouts
6. Check ballast to be sure it is below level of wheel flanges and couplers
7. Use gauge to check clearance of all trackside structures, signals, and other accessories
8. Thoroughly check trackwork for loose spikes that might cause shorts or hang up rolling stock
9. Check all terminals, feeder lines, and other electrical points for loose connections. Also cold solder joints, which may be secure in connection but poor in conduction
10. Clean track again!

The foregoing are the basic Ten Commandments for keeping things rolling during operation and can be expanded upon, depending on the characteristics of your particular railroad and "maintinuity." A number of these maintenance checks can be done during actual operation, i.e., by use of track-cleaning cars, gauge and clearance cars, magnet cars, etc., all part of any work train consist used for maintenance and repair. In this way you not only put your railroad to work, but embody prototype techniques as well.

To elaborate on the Ten Commandments of trouble-free operation, let's go into greater detail. Bear in mind that a number of these chores can be done at the same time, in the same area, and immediately after each other, thus saving considerable effort. But don't rush it; if you overlook an item here or there, it may come back to haunt you during operation, particularly when you are about to show things off to an awe-struck visitor.

Having a case of the *DT's* (dirty track) can cause a lot of woes to a model railroader. This is one dilemma shared by rail fans from coast to coast and is a condition responsible for many maladies that crop up during actual operation. From a scale standpoint, dust, grit, ballast, etc., can assume the physical proportions of boulders to drivers and truck wheels, thus impeding the smooth movement of your rolling stock. Oxidized track can cause uneven starts, no starts at all, or dead stops, resulting in pitted wheels and overheated or burned-out motors. Often the blame is placed on the motive power or power pack when usually it is simply a question of not getting a good flow of current to the rails and pickup

Accessibility is a key word where maintenance is concerned, and important when you wish to add an item or two. Standing within an access hole, Dick Seydell can reach across and set a telephone wire in place, reposition a dislodged building, etc., without fear of causing damage or additional maintenance chores.

wheels of your locomotives. This can result in model rails mumbling to themselves, snapping at children, leaving railroads neglected and untended, storming into hobby shops, or giving up the ghost. But there is no reason to do any of the aforementioned if you simply accept the fact that keeping track clean is part of model railroading, and no matter how much time you spend removing dirt and oxidation from the rails, it will come back. So bear in mind that the cleaner you keep the rail, the smoother the operation, and the less resistance to the flow of electricity from power supply to locomotive.

There are a number of track-cleaning cars on the market, some of which are pictured within these pages. Ulrich's track-cleaning car comes in kit form, is wood-framed, and features the use of a solvent-type fluid contained in a tank which, in turn, saturates a felt pad secured to the underbody of the car and which rides atop the railhead surface, removing dust, residue, and other accumulated gook. Revell's track cleaner is a bunk car of high impact styrene in ready-to-run form, and features "lift up" abrasive stone pads. After the cleaning chore is done, a flip of a lever raises the pads off the rail and the car becomes part of your work train consist.

Another useful track cleaner is offered by Gilbert in RTR form and includes silicon-impregnated felt rollers. These three, plus a number of other track-cleaning cars available, will greatly help reduce the problems arising out of dirty track. Coupled to a switcher, you can push your track-cleaning car over every bit of rail in your layout. Push rather than pull, so that your motive power will be picking up juice from cleaner rail as it propels the track cleaner ahead of it. Going one step further, I would suggest the following double-barreled threat to the DT's: an abrasive-type car coupled to a fluid-cleaning car, both of which are moved about by a switcher or other suitable motive power. In that way, the lead cleaning car does the abrasive job of loosening dirt, grit, and oxidation, and the fluid-type car wipes things clean.

Another track-cleaning device is offered by Baumgarten and is completely self-powered and self-propelled. Ready to go, it consists of a Mantua F9 diesel, housing special weights, and a silicon abrasive pad, the latter being removable so that when track cleaning is finished the diesel can be put into regular service. Baumgarten also offers this track-cleaning housing in kit form, and most diesels can be converted to its use. Of course, you

Dirty track is probably responsible for more railroading woes than any other ailment in the hobby. Aside from cleaning the track by hand, there are a number of maintenance cars that will make the chore easier for you and help keep the track cleaner, to boot. The following equipment is a prime example and can be incorporated into the overall maintenance scheme of things. It can also be added to your work train when you combine maintenance with operation.

Ulrich track-cleaning car is of wood construction. Tank carries a track-cleaning fluid, which saturates felt pad riding along rail heads. Track-cleaning solutions are available from Life-Like, Tru-Scale and numerous other sources.

Revell track-cleaning bunk car features lift-up abrasive pads. Note extra details such as sagging door and scribbling on sides. After track cleaning chores, a flip of the lever and the abrasive pads are raised above the rails and the car becomes part of the regular work train.

Gilbert's track-cleaning car has silicon-impregnated felt rollers, which, combined with a lead weight housed in the tank, do an excellent job of keeping track clean.

Baumgarten's self-propelled track cleaner is a Tyco F-9 diesel containing lead weights and an abrasive pad which can be removed after track-cleaning chores are done with. Following this, the diesel can be used for regular service. Weights and cleaning pad are also available in kit form and can be installed within the housing of most diesels.

can always resort to the hand technique by using an abrasive stone and following up with a soft rag saturated with a cleaning fluid, such as offered by Life-Like, Tru-Scale, etc. Still another helpful track-cleaning liquid is No-Ox, a contact cleaner used widely in the electronics field. It can be purchased at most radio parts stores. This fluid does a good job of removing grime, oil, sludge, etc. The only trouble with rubbing the track down by hand is that you have to stretch all over the place, and it is often difficult to reach those out-of-the-way places, access holes notwithstanding. It is also pretty awkward trying to clean track inside a tunnel. Your particular layout, track "reachability," and overall size will be the deciding factors in how you go about keeping rails in top-flight operating condition. If one section of track seems to oxidize or get dirty sooner than other areas, it might be wise to replace that section with nickel silver rail, since this material is less susceptible to oxidation and looks more prototype.

In summary, track-cleaning cars are useful equipment and their use can become part of the regular railroading operation. Using them will not only save time, but spare your aching back. It's all a matter of preference and finding out which method does the best job on your particular layout. Experience and results will be the deciding factors in selecting track-cleaning cars over the hand method, or vice versa.

One other thing to bear in mind when cleaning track is the fact that the use of an abrasive to clean the rail exposes a fresh surface of metal to the air. This in itself encourages a whole new cycle of oxidation and dirt accumulation, which to an extent would seem to defeat the purpose of cleaning track to begin with. It's like washing your car; sooner than later it will get dirty again. A wax job on the car helps repel dirt, grime, and dust. By the same token, a similar treatment in the form of No-Ox applied to freshly cleaned track will help retard the development of oxidation. Simply place a few drops of No-Ox on the rail heads directly ahead of your locomotive and also at a few other points about the layout. The loco drivers and wheels will pick up and distribute a fine film of the liquid all over the trackage, including those hard-to-get-at places. A few drops of fine oil used in the same manner will also leave a thin film on the surface of the rail, which in turn will help discourage dirt, dust, and grime from forming a hard residue. However, use oil sparingly, otherwise wheel slippage might result. If you prefer to rub things down by hand, a soft rag lightly saturated with No-Ox, oil, etc., will produce the same results.

Commandment No. 2 concerns maintaining the proper distance between the rails, otherwise known as "gauge." Whether you lay your own ties and rail, or use ready or sectional track, at one point or another you are likely to experience pinching or binding

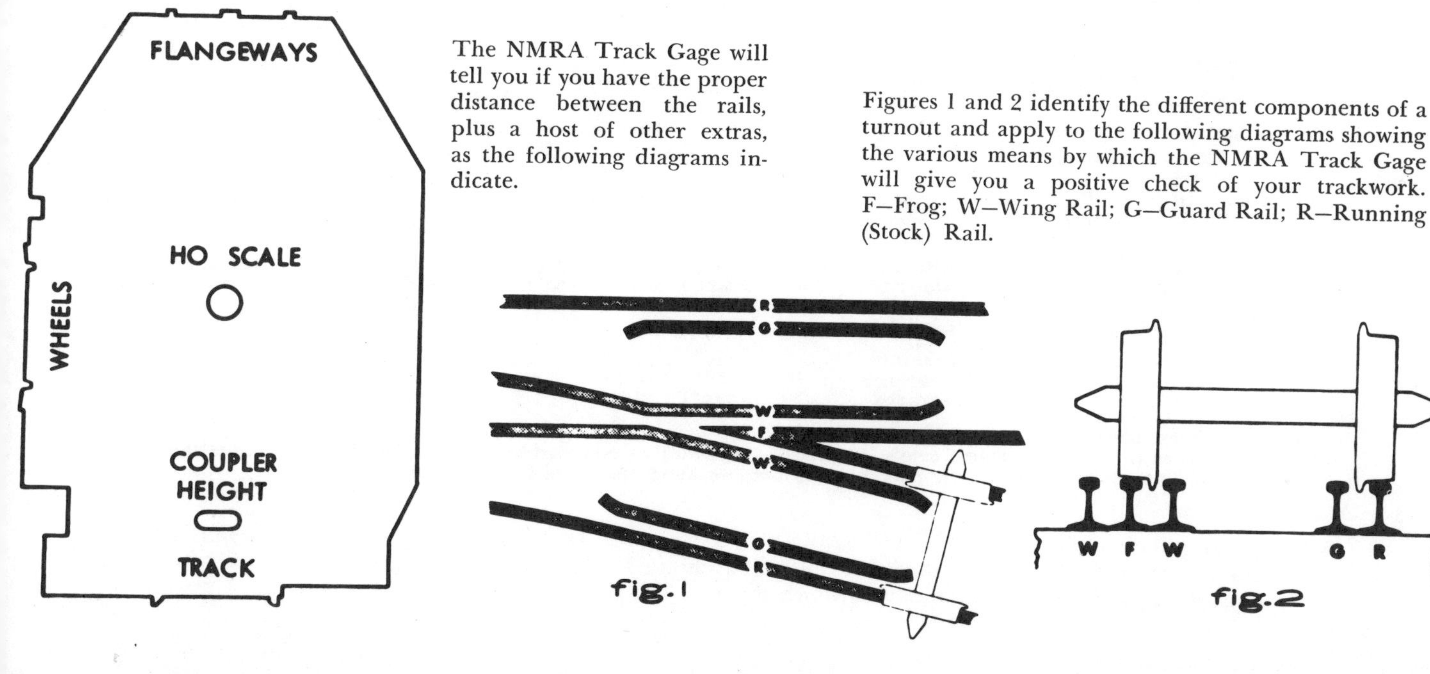

The NMRA Track Gage will tell you if you have the proper distance between the rails, plus a host of other extras, as the following diagrams indicate.

Figures 1 and 2 identify the different components of a turnout and apply to the following diagrams showing the various means by which the NMRA Track Gage will give you a positive check of your trackwork. F—Frog; W—Wing Rail; G—Guard Rail; R—Running (Stock) Rail.

1. **TRACK** marks the side of the gage used for checking Track Gage through all trackwork, including turnouts and other special work. Apply light side pressure in the direction of the arrow. See figures A, B and C for interpretation of results. (Note that the prongs of the Gage must clear spikes, throwbars and other obstructions)

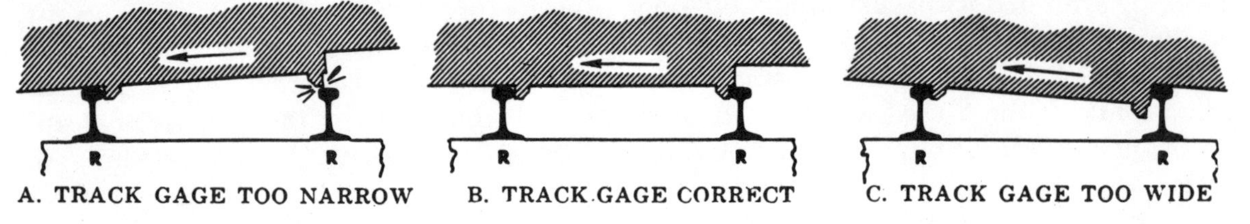

A. TRACK GAGE TOO NARROW   B. TRACK GAGE CORRECT   C. TRACK GAGE TOO WIDE

2. **FLANGEWAYS**, spacing of Guard Rails, Wing Rails and Frogs are checked with this side of the Gage. Apply light side pressure toward the Frog and against the Guard Rail (see arrow). See figures A, B and C for interpretation of results. Gage prongs must clear all obstructions below the rail head as in figure D. Use center prong of Gage to check Flangeway Width at the Frog in figure E and F.

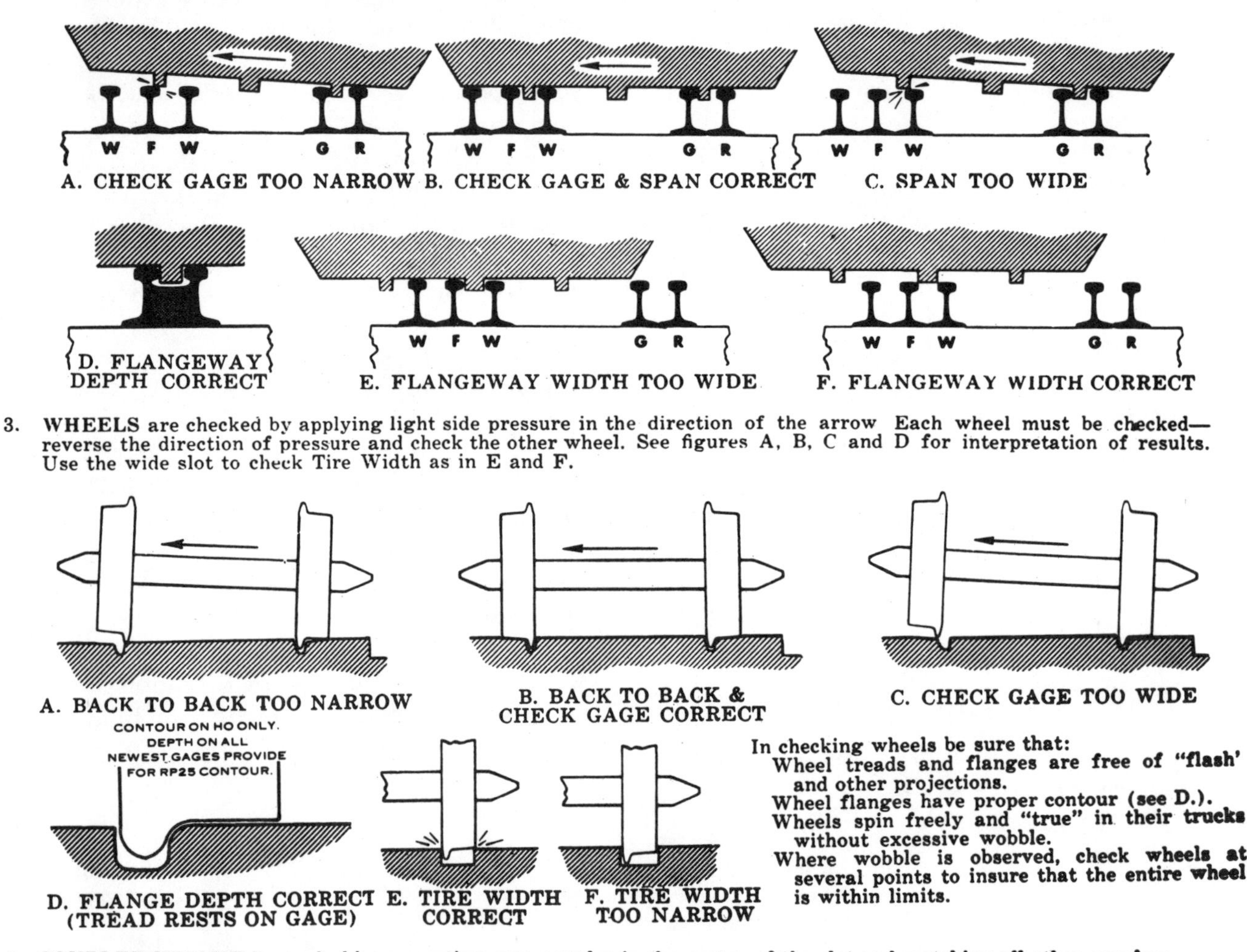

A. CHECK GAGE TOO NARROW   B. CHECK GAGE & SPAN CORRECT   C. SPAN TOO WIDE

D. FLANGEWAY DEPTH CORRECT   E. FLANGEWAY WIDTH TOO WIDE   F. FLANGEWAY WIDTH CORRECT

3. **WHEELS** are checked by applying light side pressure in the direction of the arrow Each wheel must be checked—reverse the direction of pressure and check the other wheel. See figures A, B, C and D for interpretation of results. Use the wide slot to check Tire Width as in E and F.

A. BACK TO BACK TOO NARROW   B. BACK TO BACK & CHECK GAGE CORRECT   C. CHECK GAGE TOO WIDE

D. FLANGE DEPTH CORRECT (TREAD RESTS ON GAGE)   E. TIRE WIDTH CORRECT   F. TIRE WIDTH TOO NARROW

In checking wheels be sure that:
- Wheel treads and flanges are free of "flash' and other projections.
- Wheel flanges have proper contour (see D.).
- Wheels spin freely and "true" in their trucks without excessive wobble.
- Where wobble is observed, check wheels at several points to insure that the entire wheel is within limits.

4. **COUPLER HEIGHT** is checked by cementing one coupler in the center of the slot and matching all other couplers to this height when Gage is in position of 1.B. above.

5. **CLEARANCE** is checked only with the TYPE 1 Gage in the position of 1.B. and seeing that no obstruction interferes with passage of the Gage along the track. The large notch in the side of the Gage must clear all platforms Long equipment on curved track requires additional clearance on each side of the Gage as shown in the table below (figures for HO Scale are listed for illustration).

Radius of curvature	24"	28"	36"	54"
Additional clearance	1/8"	1/16"	—	—
Platform clearance	1/4"	3/16"	1/8"	1/16"

Normally these additional clearances can be estimated by eye.
For convenience in reaching beyond arm's length the Gage may be mounted to the end of a piece of wood with a screw through the hole provided. This hole may also be used to hang the Gage in a convenient location.

A boon to beginners and veterans alike, the NMRA Track Gage will help cure many an ailment where trackwork is concerned. Instructions in its use are shown in this page from an NMRA Data Sheet, part and parcel of their recommended practices. As you can see, the uses to which the gage can be put are many.

of wheels and drivers. This can result in stalling motive power and retarding the movement of your cars. It can also cause uneven starts and other headaches. In addition, you will no doubt suffer from derailments. The pinching and binding is due to the fact that somewhere along the line your track has become undergauged, and as the rails stray from the norm, the friction developing between wheel flanges and rail produces the various woes I have been talking about. The actual derailment occurs when the wheel flanges, overcoming the bind, roll up and out of alignment with the side and head of the rails. Derailment also occurs when the rails are overgauged, but rather than pinching and binding, your rolling stock develops a few unrailroad-like wobbles, plus a few other characteristics resembling those of Toonerville Trolley scooting over hill and dale. In this case, the derailment takes place when the wheel (s) drops between the rails onto the ties.

As a rule, over- or undergauge is more prevalent on curves, though straight trackage from mainlines to sidings and spurs also suffers its share. Extremes of temperature, causing expansion and contraction, are one of the causes; sloppy trackwork is another. Inferior rail material and a track gauge not conforming to NMRA standards is another culprit causing problems. Regardless of the whys and wherefores, it does happen to both the beginner and the veteran. The first step in remedying the situation is to use an accurate "gauge check." Membership in the NMRA gets you one free (and it's a dandy). The gauge is also available to non-members for the nominal price of $1 and can be purchased at most hobby shops. The NMRA gauge, in the form of a template, features other applications such as track clearance, and wheel and flange check. There are a number of other gauges available. For example, Kemtron offers a combination track gauge and coupler height adjuster, not only for HO, but HOn3 and Code 70 rail as well. Kadee also has a combination gauge which goes hand-in-hand with their fine line of electromagnetic couplers. Using a track gauge is simple: you merely move it along the rails and the over- or undergauged areas become readily apparent by the amount of bind you experience. Once you have located the trouble spot, it is just a matter of spiking the rail securely the necessary fraction of an inch in either direction to restore the proper gauge dimensions. While you are at it, check for broken or loose ties and look for any ballasting that might be creating undue pressure against the rails. These remedial steps will speed you on the way to better railroading.

Next on the agenda is a thorough check of all terminal connections, joints, gaps, feeder lines, etc. In the latter case, railroad hobgoblins seem to work overtime, for wiring connections mysteriously loosen, insulated gaps suddenly aren't, and a few other things develop to keep the road gang on a double shift of repair and maintenance with no time for featherbedding.

Checking terminal points, screwed or soldered, is a simple chore, requiring nothing more than a screwdriver and a soldering iron. A continuity tester will help, too, but is not absolutely necessary. Remove all screws holding wire connections, and scrape the bare wire ends free of any oxidation or residue that might have accumulated, thus creating a resistance to the flow of electricity to the rails from the power pack. If the connections are soldered, place the probe of a continuity tester directly on the solder joint, also before and after the connection; the neon tube in the tester should produce equal responses. If not, then chances are you have a cold solder joint, which is simply a case of not using enough heat when making the original connection. And while solder, wire, and rail all appear to have fuzed together and the connection looks good, an insufficient amount of heat during application results in an uneven distribution of same on all surfaces concerned, so what might appear to be a good solder joint could actually be a pinpoint grab smaller

Alan Stensvold makes good use of the track gage during the course of track laying or as part of the maintenance check-up. If anything has gone awry, a few well-placed spikes will set things in order

NMRA Track Gage is shown being used to check distance between the rails and also the clearance of trackside structures.

Detailed and designed for a specific use, this clearance and check car from Tyco will help spot troubles along the maintenance way. It also makes a good candidate for your work train.

Desco's Circuitracer helps you spot trouble at the point of origin. Extra tips provide various services such as indicating shorts, poor conduction, dirty track, etc.

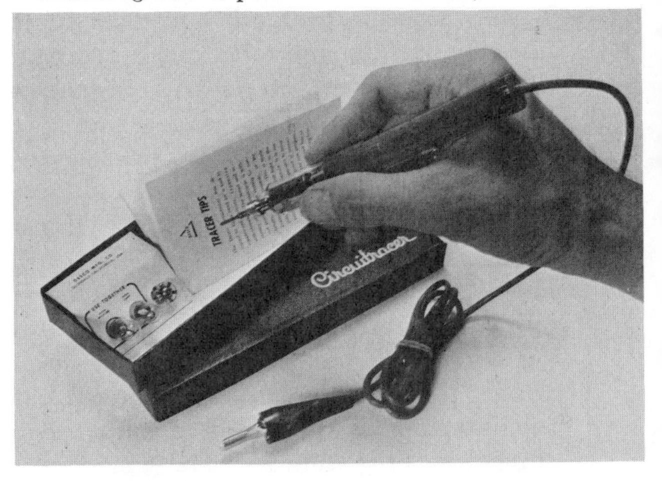

than the diameter of the wire. This, in turn, sets up a resistance similar to that which you experience with a poor water flow when you hook a 5/8-inch garden hose to a 3/4-inch faucet. Not only do you suffer from a poor flow of electricity, but the solder joint is easily vibrated and broken loose. If you do have a cold solder joint, waste no time in removing it and starting anew. Just before flowing the solder, use a dab of flux and apply heat to rail and wire, thus making them both receptive to an even flow of solder and a good sturdy electrical joint.

While you are at it, check all gaps and joints to see if any kinks or rises have developed. Some well-placed spikes and a few strokes with a smooth file will quickly restore connecting surfaces to equal level. Checking all track joiners (fishplates) will also help; crimp down any that are loose or out of whack. Needle-nose pliers will do fine. Next, check all insulated gaps to be sure they are performing as intended. Make sure that nothing has entered the scene to bridge the gap and permit a flow of power from one block to the next, otherwise you are sure to have short circuits. A discarded toothbrush is a handy item for this chore. Now would also be an excellent time to send a magnet car to pick up any stray or loose spikes, brads, or nails that might have settled in, about, or on the trackways.

One item responsible for kinks in trackwork at joints and gaps is loose or uneven bench work, road base, or table top foundations. Check all screws and bolts, tightening up those that may have worked themselves loose. Also be sure that legs or floor risers are in alignment, shimming up or straightening those which may be out of line or bowlegged. Remember that your foundation and framework may now be carrying more weight than was originally intended and, if groaning under the added load, may need bracing and/or shoring up to keep the overall layout firm and free of sagging and vibration.

As I said before, when considering the relationship of HO scale to prototype, it is easy to see that a few specks of dust, grit, or ballast, though seemingly minute, can assume the dimensions of huge rocks and boulders by comparison. Thus, any foreign matter lodging in and about throw bars, throw rods, and other working parts of your turnouts and switches, can create quite a bit of havoc. Removal of the gremlins that are thwarting the proper functions of your switches and turnouts will go a long way toward their smooth operation; thus, cleanliness in this area is an absolute must.

Remove all switch covers and clean out any flotsam or jetsam that might have accumulated. Check the area beneath and around the throw bars to be sure that there are no obstructions, such as loose ballast, to impair free movement. A bumpy or rough surface will limit the complete throw of your points against opposing rails, easily resulting in derailments every time you roll through the turnout. One stray grain of ballast can also prevent complete contact. So double check each and every part of your turnout trackage.

Thus far you have noticed that one thing seems to lead to another in maintenance, and it is understandable, since all things are directly related to one another. Items six and seven take but a few moments of your time, and it is time well worth spending. Ballast (depending on the size you use) has a habit of sometimes working loose, creating obstructions to rolling stock and couplers. Double check to see that all ballast is below the level of bolsters and underbody detail. Also be sure there is sufficient clearance for wheel flanges—in other words, that the ballast is not crowding the rail. Clearance checks are also a must where trackside structures, signals, lamps, and other accessories are concerned, whether you are just about to set them in place or not. Allowances have to be made for vibrations that might work such accessories closer to the rail than desired, and so a check of the areas in question with a clearance gauge will help.

Proper clearance is most important, especially on or about sharp and winding curves, open cuts, tunnel portals, etc. Unless you allow for a good margin of safety, you are liable to knock off a snaking pilot, plow the end of an 80-foot passenger car into a trackside building, or get tangled up with a few telephone poles. As I mentioned before, the NMRA gauge also includes the clearance check which will provide you with the minimum requirements for the right margin of safety.

Item number five, covering the care and maintenance of turnouts, is one area which should never be neglected. If you are using ready-to-run turnouts of the sectional track variety, be sure they are "floating," i.e., held down only by the track joining them at opposite ends. In other words, do not spike them down or cement to the base of roadbed. If you use remote-control switch motors, be sure the wires connecting switch to turnout have sufficient slack and do not exercise any form of pressure on the frogs or contact rails. Check the frog and flangeways for any accumulation of debris that will impede the

The following cars can not only become part of your work train consist, but also help dress things up a bit. Spot a few of them in and about your layout, and things will come alive. Later on pick them up and return them to the "rip track" area. This type of operation will provide lots of fun and will also be purposeful as well.

This is a honey of an item from Tru-Scale in the form of a well-weathered and beaten up "blacksmith car." Just dig that crazy anvil. I was tempted to put this model in Chapter 13 because it has such an authentic-looking oldtime flavor, but I couldn't resist spotting it here. You won't be able to resist it either, since it is in keeping regardless of the era and is still in use today, albeit more streamlined. It comes rarin' to go or in kit form. You'll have a ball aging this plastic (surprised?) model.

Another treat for the eyes is this domestic water car from Binkley Models. A real old fella to match that equally old work train.

This wheel car is another old-timer offered in kit form by Binkley Models. It goes together easier than you imagine. In the old days maintenance crews just slapped an open shed atop a flat car, added some wheel racks and a new prototype was born. This model lends itself to many legitimate modifications.

This derrick car from Athearn is fully operational and will look good along the maintenance way.

This 25-ton operating crane and boom car is part of Tru-Scale's work train series. A handsome addition to any maintenance section.

A maintenance area should look that way and it does on the Sierra Southern RR Club. Little touches such as this one make a model railroad not only believable, but functional as well.

Sighting down a line of cars, Dick Seydell checks curve and alignment of rolling stock. Access hole provides a ground view at eye level and is a tremendous aid in maintenance work.

Maintenance and industrial dimension of this pike built by Dick Seydell has all the earmarks of profitable activity and an enormous amount of realistic operation as well. Chimney and heating plant is an Aristo-Craft kit; coaling and water tower at left center was made from an Alexander kit; generator at trackside is scratch-built; and ladder work and plumbing was made up from the plastic flues in a Revell kit. Southern Pacific diesel stall is also scratch-built, and the area has no less than four lines of running track.

She's still comin' 'round the bend, and will continue smoothly and safely if you keep your trackwork in tip top condition.

Things are on the move within this realistic scene on Jim Foell's model railroad. Everything works smoothly and will continue that way until the gremlins act up again, then the maintenance chores become necessary. Since offense is the best defense against model railroading woes, don't wait for trouble to develop. Get into the habit of periodic maintenance checks, and when troubles do develop they will be easier to handle.

progress of wheels rolling through. Also be sure that point rails fit flush against straight stock or curved stock rails when in alternate positions. If the points are out of alignment, straighten them with needle-nose pliers; if the fit is not flush, check the surface below and about the throw bar for obstructions. Perhaps the track is out of gauge at the point of contact; if so, a few spikes will square things away. On the other hand, a bit of filing might be in order. An abrasive wheel on a Dremel Moto-Tool is one of the best means of increasing the notch in the rail. Also check the throw rod leading from your switch motor solenoid; it may be out of line or might have lost the right degree of spring tension.

Needless to say, the bigger and more complicated the layout, the more maintenance is required to keep things functioning in a railroad-like manner. The idea, of course, is to do a good and thorough job, so that the time spent in operation will give you more pleasure. However, if you spend more time maintaining than operating, obviously there is something drastically wrong with your layout and *modus operandi.*

If you stick with this basic set of rules, or any checklist that suits your particular layout, you will ultimately end up with more time to run your railroad, and less trouble in operation. And in case some of the foregoing seems alarmingly time-consuming, remember you can delegate your work train crew to do a number of chores for you, thus operating and maintaining at the same time.

So next time you get a case of the DT's, don't push the panic button, don't call Alcoholics Anonymous—*just clean your track!*

X

Mountains out of Molehills

Among other things, it takes a vivid imagination to be a model railroader. If a psychiatrist could peer into the mind of the average rail buff standing before his layout, he would probably head for his nearest colleague-analyst. For the message the mystified medico might receive from the railroader's gray matter could possibly be visions of cloud bedecked mountains, winding streams, steep grades, and all the other ingredients of a miniature railroading empire. Yet all that may actually be visible is a maze of trackwork covering a bare sheet of plywood or open framework. The model rail creates such an illusion to serve as background for the sleek motion of his favorite Mike or Mogul, until such time as he can replace these mental images with some honest-to-goodness scenery and railroad environment. Fortunately, these hallucinations are of a salubrious nature, for they stimulate the hobbyist's thinking as to where to build a particular mountain, range of hills, or other landscaping effect. Unfortunately, the hobbyist can get into a rut whereby his layout remains in skeleton form for a long time, notwithstanding the fact that a good diet of scenery and structures will go a long way toward putting some meat on them there bones. True, it is most advisable to get all the kinks and bugs out of your trackwork and wiring, and get your track plan properly proportioned and operating, so that the tunnel you have in mind does not land square over a turnout or crossing. And for that matter, it is disturbing when you find that the industrial spur you have carefully ballasted will be running clear through the factory rather than alongside it.

So, with respect to planning and the changes that undoubtedly will take place as you go along, it must be noted that *scenery is something that should not be blindly rushed into just for the sake of dressing things up a bit.* However, the time does come when a believable railroad-like atmosphere should become the order of the day, and if your locomotives and rolling stock suffer from lack of a realistic background, then now is the time to start doing something about it. The mere addition of a lineside shanty will improve the overall appearance 100 per cent. However, if your layout has heretofore been as naked as a babe, then don't settle for the random insertion of a piece of lichen here and a structure there, but concentrate on an

This breathtaking scenic effect was created by members of the Sierra Southern RR Club. It is alive with natural and realistic detailing.

Members of the Glendale Model RR Club have done a fine job of mountaineering and have added another touch of scenic grandeur to their pike. The mountain also serves to hide from view the trains on the far trackwork. A realistic illusion is created when they finally roll by and into view.

Plywood cut-outs can also serve as a basis for contour and shaping of mountain ranges and support to which cardboard strips can be stapled. Applying texture paint saturated paper to the cardboard latticework is the next step towards covering things up. In this case, Freeman Crutchfield is going from one level over the next level to the pre-contoured plywood above.

The brush wielding abilities of Freeman Crutchfield are used to simulate crags and overhangs typical of many embankments. Texture Paint was used for its ease of application and the various manners in which the plaster material can be textured and shaped.

Mountains can serve as a backdrop and need not necessarily be a complete form by themselves. In this case, Mort Gould created a mountainside effect by stapling chicken wire to the benchwork and up along the wall. Following this, he fashioned various shapes in the wire to form declivities, ridges and other outcroppings. Then he applied Texture Paint-saturated paper against the wire, adding some extra modeling during the placement.

A bit of fingertip dexterity creates small clumps and ridges. Smoothing a surface, achieving a grain-like effect or producing swirls are just some of the scenicking applications possible.

honest-to-goodness landscaping job from front to back and top to bottom.

Once you take the plunge, you will find that scenery and landscaping is one of the most fascinating aspects of model railroading. In addition, this phase of the hobby is the most important factor in creating a believable atmosphere for realistic operation, and for providing the one necessary ingredient that lifts your railroad from a toy-like setting to an authentic-looking miniature. The ingredient I am referring to is natural environment. Here is one case where it becomes a *virtue* to be able to make a "mountain out of a molehill." Back in the days when HO was a popular breakfast cereal, the average rail enthusiast had to boil up a witch's brew of water-soaked newspaper strips, after which he applied the taffy-like mixture to mountain-shaped chicken wire or other landscape foundations. Techniques involving plaster of paris were also widely used. But that was back in the dark ages of model railroading, although in fairness it can't be denied that more often than not the final results were both striking and effective. Nevertheless, it was also messy and time-consuming. Today, fortunately, there are a number of products available that are a boon to the beginner and the veteran scenic artist alike.

We'll talk about some of these creative aids a bit farther along, but for the moment let's get down to business and scale a few peaks. Mountains are among the most popular landscaping effects found in layouts, for they afford not only a formidable touch of scenic grandeur and perspective, but a backdrop to run your equipment through, around, and over. This permits your locomotive and cars to disappear for a moment or two and turn up elsewhere along the countryside, which will go a long way toward increasing the illusion of realistic operation.

There are a number of ways to build mountains and in recent years there has been a definite swing toward the use of texture paint in lieu of older methods such as plaster of paris and papier-mâché. The beauty of texture paint lies in the fact that after it hardens it will take oil- or water-based color with a striking degree of realism. Texture paint is not really a paint in the true sense of the word, but rather a type of plaster that comes in powdered form which, when combined with water, can be mixed to almost any consistency desired, depending, of course, on the amount of water you add. When dry, texture paint will not chip or crack in the manner characteristic of regular plaster, nor is it as heavy, both of which are definite advantages if weight and portability are of any concern. From a model railroading standpoint, a mountain must have a basic contour that will lend itself to the surrounding area. It should not

An embankment effect can be easily achieved without the need for any bracing or shaped forms if the levels are not too far apart. In this case a slight embankment was called for from the upper level to the ground behind the roundhouse.

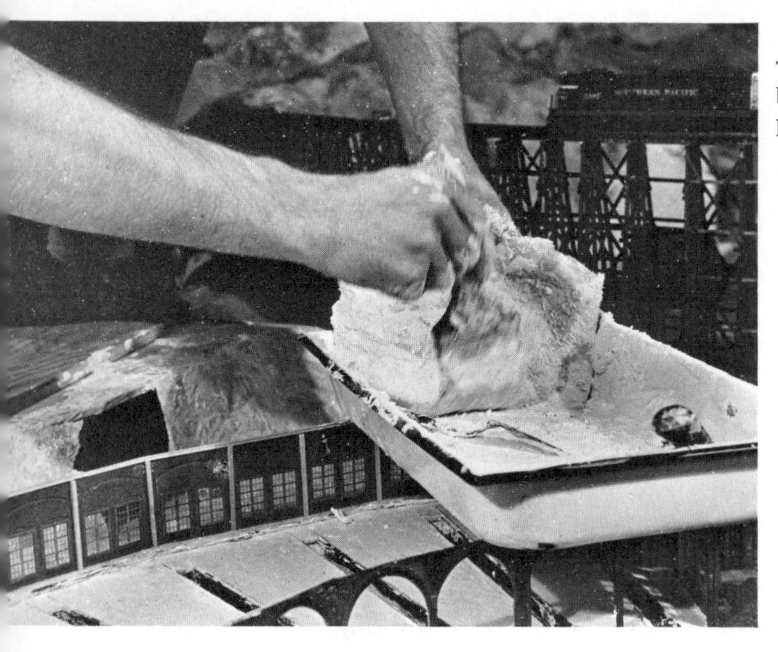

Texture Paint is brushed directly onto brown paper (shopping bags are fine). When the paper is fully saturated with the plaster, it will become pliable and easy to apply.

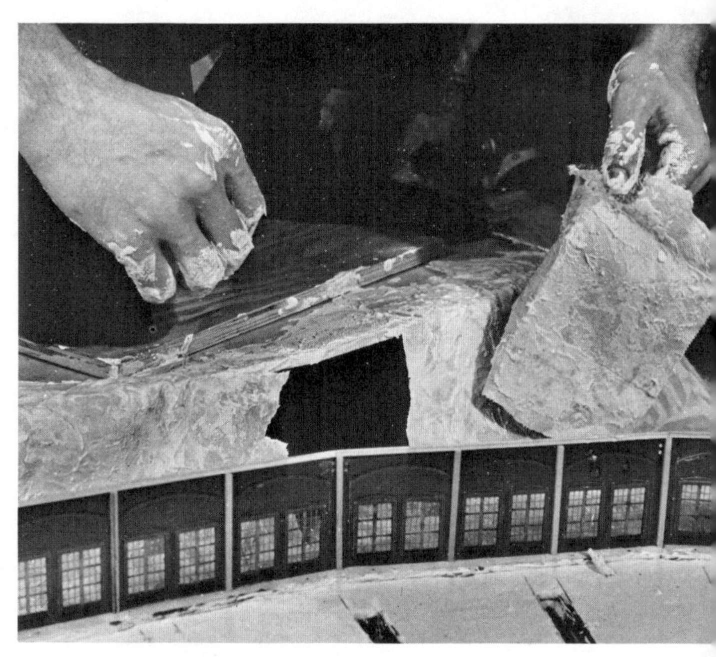

Texture-Painted paper is ready to be shaped in place over remaining opening. Note absence of supports, screening or latticework. When dry, the plastered paper will be hard and strong enough to withstand a good amount of strain.

Saturated paper is now laid in place and when dry will provide a perfect backing to receive painting and weathering effects.

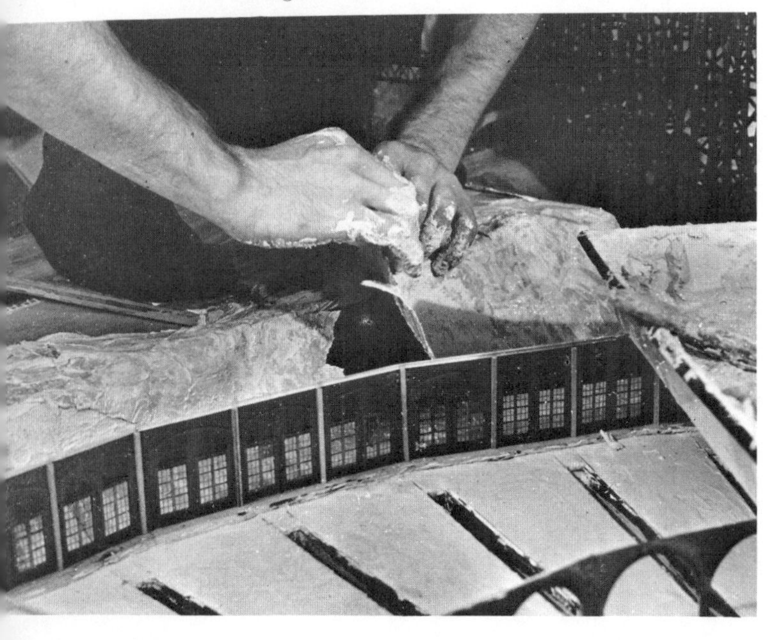

Now that the once-open area is covered, additional Texture Paint is patted on by hand. Areas are smoothed and/or roughed up depending on the effect desired.

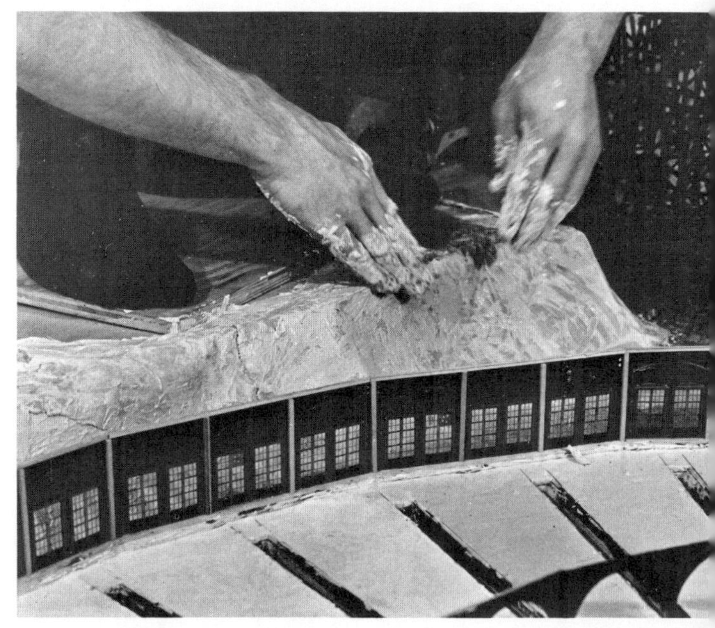

be so big that it overshadows and dwarfs everything in sight, nor should it be so small that it cannot contain a tunnel passageway without looking tinplate.

Assuming you have established the shape you want your mountain to take, the next step is to construct the basic support. This can consist of a series of wooden blocks of varying heights upon which window screening is either stapled or tacked down. Before securing the screening in place it is a good idea to bend and squeeze the wire into irregular shapes (wear work gloves to protect your hands), doing it over and over until you have created an uneven surface. The texture paint will follow such irregularities. Additional shapes, bends, and cliff-like effects can be achieved by pinching or bending when you are fastening down the screen.

When the wire covering is securely in place, mix up a batch of texture paint to a consistency similar to that of sour cream. Don't make it too thin or it will seep through the screening, nor too thick, for it will be too hard to brush on. A darkroom tray or paint bucket is a good receptacle to mix in and work from. As to the actual application of the texture paint, an inexpensive brush will do nicely. Simply dip it in the plaster and brush lightly onto the screening. The texture paint will take from twenty-four to forty-eight hours to dry hard, depending on the humidity. Too heavy a coat might take considerably longer; therefore, it is better to build up the surface of your mountain by progressive layers. As you brush on the texture paint, you can achieve a number of interesting effects by stippling, making circular swirls, or whatever the dexterity of your brush-wielding hand and imagination can dream up. With your fingertips you can form ridges, clumps, depressions, etc., depending on whether you wish to go all out the first time or do things in progressive stages before the paint finally sets up dry and hard. While it is still tacky, you can get in a few extra licks by sprinkling sand, plaster, small pebbles and other materials over various parts of the surface, further adding to the roughness of the supposedly mountainous terrain.

I could go into long dissertations on how to create carved strata in outcropping rock, the forming of gullies, cuts, and ravines; however, mountainous terrain varies from one region to another and it would only be second guessing. After all, when you consider that one modeler might be interested in ranges containing precipices and jagged cuts while another might be interested in timberline, you can see that it would require considerable wordage to go into great detail concerning the topographical features of the numerous types of physiography. Scenic effects such as the foregoing are best described as the sort of thing that improves with practice. You can slap the mixture on or smooth it on, depending on the manner of finish you are after. It's primarily a case of personal preference. By studying the photographs in this and other chapters, you will be able to glean more information than words can describe. Experience will be the best teacher.

Another method of creating a foundation to accept the texture paint is through the use of cardboard strips fashioned in the form of latice work or webbing. Sheets of brown paper (shopping bags are fine) are dipped and/or painted with the texture material, and are laid directly over the cardboard lattice work. The paper in this plaster-covered state can be squeezed, twisted, bunched up, or curved in a number of shapes and will dry hard in the same way. Apply the texture-painted paper in overlapping fashion and don't worry about the patch-quilt appearance; a finishing coat will hide the paper edges and you will have a good solid foundation and surface to paint and weather when everything has thoroughly dried. One particular advantage to this technique, as opposed to the use of screening, is (aside from economy) the fact that if there are any changes to be made, such as knocking out areas for tunnels or portals, a razor saw will cut through with surprising ease—certainly easier than cutting through wire screening.

This same technique involving the use of texture paint can be applied to creating hills, rolling or otherwise. It can be used for open cuts, gorges, buffs, plateaus, etc. The mountain effect achieved by Bob Steele, pictured in the opening chapter, was produced by window screening covered with texture paint. Unfortunately, Bob was unable to paint and weather the surface in time to photograph for this particular book.

Another good thing about texture paint is that, if you accidentally bang your elbow into the mountainside, you won't rub any of the surface away, whereas with certain other types of scenic mixtures a mishap will often result in removal of the surface, exposing the wire screening underneath. Another thing in favor of texture paint as a scenic medium is the fact that, should you happen to knock a hole in the surface or otherwise damage it, a Band-aid in the form of a sheet of brown paper dipped in the paint can be slapped over the injured area, smoothed out to hide the hole or break, and, when dry, painted to match, thus restoring things to normal again.

Here's another good example, and a quickie project at that: Suppose you have parallel tracks, but at different levels, and you wish to create a slanting fill or rocky slope from upper to lower level. You don't necessarily have to use screening or lattice work for a foundation; if the distance apart is less than 8 to 10 inches, you can probably get by with the use of paper saturated with the texture paint. You will see an illustration of this within these pages.

This particular tunnel portal and mountain slope was so close to the wall that it was difficult to blend it with the painted backdrop. The following photographs show the step-by-step remedy.

The virtual ease with which a razor saw can cut through support webbing and hardened Texture Paint is one of the reasons why this material is so popular where scenic effects are concerned.

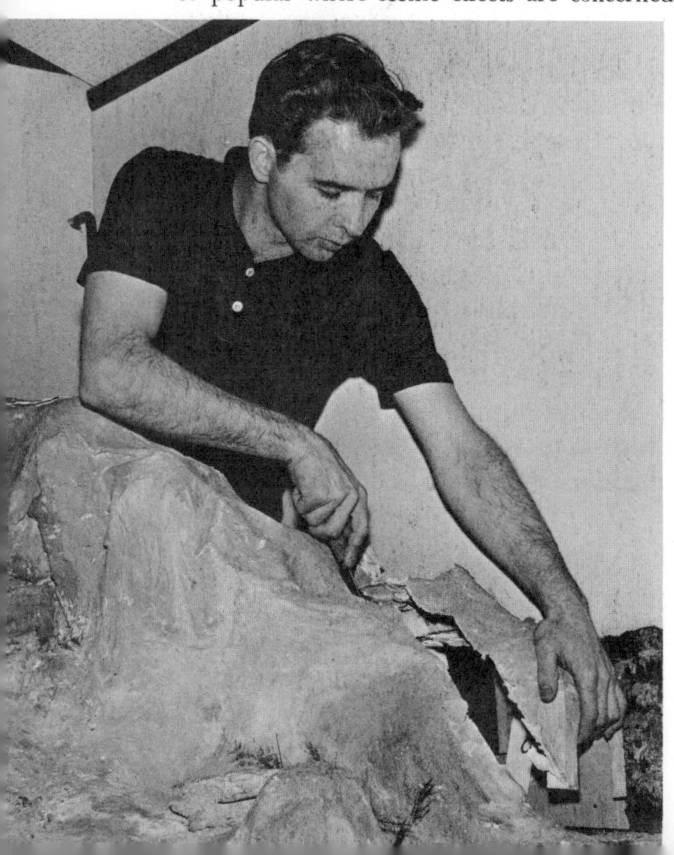

The tunnel and slope removed, cardboard strips are stapled in place to form the support for soon-to-be-applied Texture-Painted paper, which when applied will become a new canyon wall.

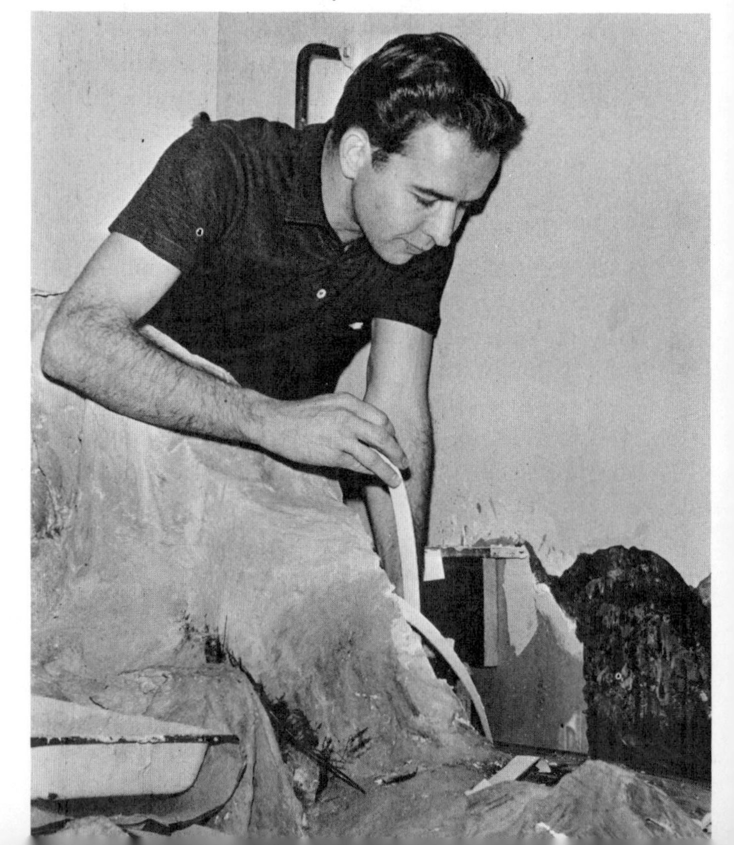

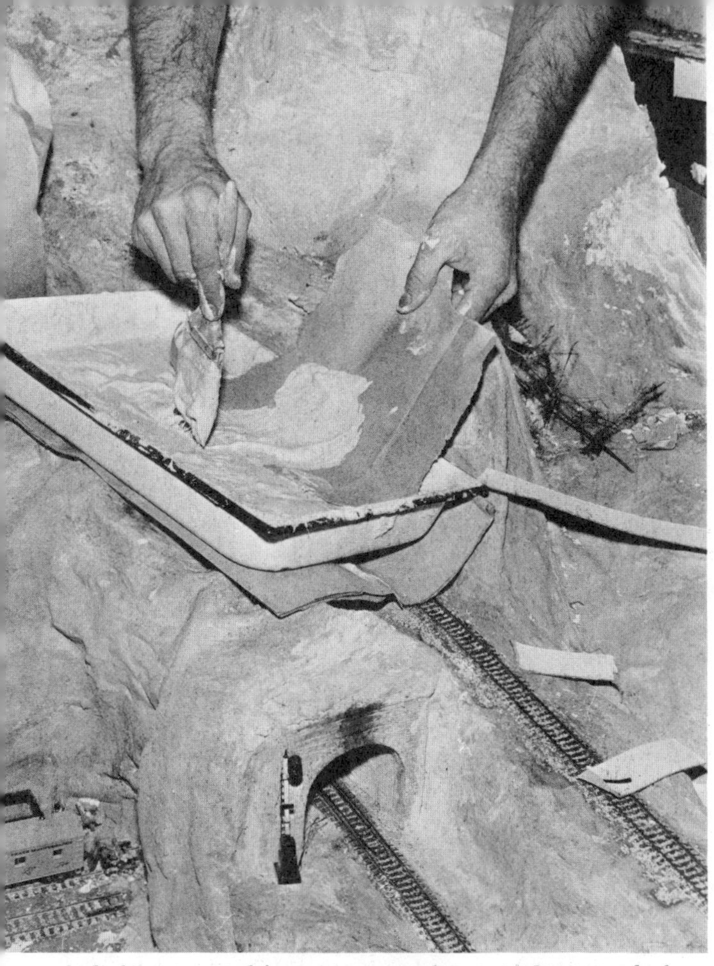

A darkroom or refrigerator tray makes a good receptacle for mixing the Texture Paint plaster. Place paper underneath to protect existing trackwork and scenery, after which simply saturate the paper.

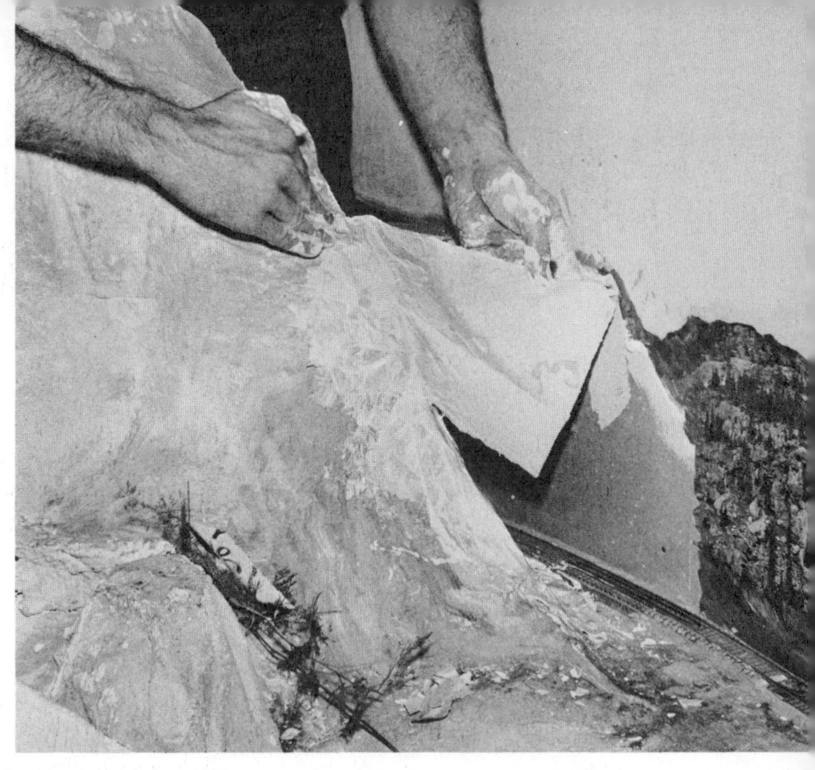

The plastered paper is applied starting at the top and working down. Additional layers of paper are added to fortify the canyon side.

Saw cuts are quickly hidden as paper is rounded over rough edges. Fingertip application of Texture Paint can produce some interesting effects at the ground level.

The project complete, this is how things look prior to painting and scenicking the new canyon wall. Background effect was achieved by pasting color scenes from magazines onto wall. Additional art work by hand not only blended one background scene into the other, but into the foreground as well. Illusion now created is that of trains disappearing between canyon walls and around mountain, rather than through it.

If you are not inclined toward creating your own background effects, these landscape background scenes from Tru-Scale will make the chore less arduous. These scenes are attractively colored, and match up perfectly to each other when placed end to end. Running size of these well-designed scenescapes are 19 × 41½ inches and will do wonders for dressing up barren backgrounds.

Town Scene

Mountain Scene

Farm Scene

At this point I think it goes without saying that there is nothing wrong with scenic effects being the figment of one's imagination providing they conform to nature. Most modelers rely not only on their imagination, but on pictures in magazines, calendar art, their own picture files, or a visit to the library for the sake of reference. A Polaroid camera can be a handy means of recording a particular scene, mountain, or area you might be driving through—just the reference you'll need for the right degree of realism. Color slides can also be of tremendous value in establishing the correct color hues and aging conditions you are trying to create. Members of the Burbank, Encino, and South Tarzana Model Railroading Club constantly have slide showings to familiarize themselves with landscaping in relation to railroading. The authenticity they have been able to achieve is attested to in the very prototype scenes pictured throughout this book. Suffice to say, the more authentic the approach, the more believable the results.

Earlier, I mentioned the fact that there were a number of scenic aids available at your hobby shops, and now seems a good time to elaborate on them. Tru-Scale offers an attractive line of trees, ornamental flowers, grass, earth, lichen, and other landscaping accessories. Life-Like also makes a varied assortment of trees, ballast, snow, coal, gravel, and other authentic-looking texture materials. Aristo-Craft has bridges of varied description, flexible surfacing sheets, a fully landscaped lake scene, and a number of scenescapes—a glance through their catalogue will fill you with enough ideas to keep you awake nights just thinking of what you can do to liven up your layout. They even have collapsible mountains for those not inclined to do-it-themselves. The shelves in the hobby shops are lined with products of many manufacturers which, for the most part, have been designed to stimulate your thinking along scenic lines and also aid you while in the process of doing-it-yourself.

This assembled timber oil derrick by Campbell Scale Models is a fine example of manufacturing with an eye toward authentic detailing. Instructions accompanying this kit are specific and to the point, enabling you to put this good-looking model together easier than you might imagine.

This is the prototype of the timber oil derrick kit by Campbell. A 1905 cable tool drilling kit, it is said to be the oldest known operative rig of its type in the United States.

Based on an authentic design and scaled down from equipment still standing in an Arizona ghost town, this mine head frame is typical of the fine kits available from Campbell Scale Models.

This is a typical deep-shaft mine—in this case, a gold mine located in the ghost town of Oatman, Arizona. It is also the prototype of the mine head frame kit available from Campbell Scale Models. A structure such as this will not only blend in well with your scenic effects, but will add a purpose to your operations.

Lichen, trees, shrubs, grass, flowering bushes, ballast, etc., are among the variety of land-covering texture materials and landscaping aids that are available from Tru-Scale and many other sources.

As you can see, there is a right way and a wrong way to set trees in place. These hints are some of many offered by Life-Like, who also make a fine array of scenic aids and landscaping materials.

Three different crossings over the same gorge in Jim Foell's pike add to the dimension of this rustic scenic effect. A combination of Perma-Scene and cork liberally garnished with lichen give things a realistic touch.

Advertisements in model railroading magazines are also a good source of ideas for planning your scene, for a thorough knowledge of what is available can be a time saver when it comes to needing a particular item to place on your layout. To further illustrate, suppose you wish to run some elevated trackage to an upper level which contains a logging camp, coal mine, etc. You can save the time of pouring over tables and diagrams that tell how to allow for grade percentage, and likewise the effort of cutting to size the risers needed for the particular grade. How? Simple. Just visit your hobby shop and purchase a set of prefabricated graduated risers. The time and effort you save can be put to better use elsewhere within your layout. Ready-to-use risers are quite inexpensive and do the job excellently. Note that in the pictures of Bob Steele's layout, in some areas he used wood blocks for risers and in other sections he used the store-bought type. The choice of one over the other is merely a matter of expedience and is entirely up to the individual modeler. It is often said among model railroaders that the trick is to do the *most detailed job in the shortest amount of time possible.* Spending umpteen hours to create a special scenic effect is not unusual, but if you can cut the time in half, or less, and still produce the same result, you would be wise to do so. Let's face it, it is not how long it takes to produce an effect that is important, but rather the final appearance of the effect itself. So to repeat, any time you can shave from scenic-building, coloring, or other chores, can be well used for such situations that might otherwise be left untended or neglected.

Two views of an open cut fashioned out of cork bark and blended into areas on each side of trackwork. Natural contours of cork offer unlimited modeling possibilities. With the aid of an X-acto knife, Moto Tool, etc., you can add extra fissures, stratification and various forms of erosion. Jim Foell did the carving.

Jim Foell's unique technique with cork, gravel and lichen provides all the earmarks of a wild and woolly setting. Note how chunk of cork bark has been used to form not only the outcrop of rock and shale, but an abutment for the overhead trestle as well.

The scratch-built trackside shanty only took Jim Foell about an hour to put together, and conveys the feeling of a log cabin outpost in this lonely looking area. In real operation many a rugged mountain pass featured roughly hewn tunnel openings, since the terrain and stone held together sufficiently enough not to require portal frames and retainers. This realistic-looking cliffwork and mountainside were created with the aid of cork.

Another view of this most desolate and starkly barren area on Jim Foell's pike finds a powerful and slow-moving geared Heisler locomotive chugging along, while an equally slow freight disappears through the tunnel.

Jim Foell, whose excellent layout is shown throughout these pages, is typical of the model railroader whose main interest is in achieving a realistic background for the operation of his equipment. I'm sure you will agree that he has done just that. Foell's layout, like many others, consists of a combination of scratch-built, pre-assembled, and kit-form structures. He has also utilized various commercial materials such as Tru-Scale lichen for shrubs and bushes, and Perma-Scene for much of his ground and scenic texture surfaces. Above all, he has taken advantage of natural material such as gnarled wood, tree bark, cork, and other items which can be found in your own backyard or not too far away. A striking example of this can be seen in the photographs of his layout which show an open cut made by placing interesting cork shapes on each side of the track. Another effect to be both admired and copied is the jutting mountain tops he fashioned out of the same material. The natural crevices and contours of the cork bark certainly lend themselves to distinctive application within his layout and they will do the same for your pike.

Trestle and bridge kits available from Campbell Scale Models come in a variety of shapes, styles and purpose. Oldtime or modern in appearance, models such as these add to the viewing and operating pleasures.

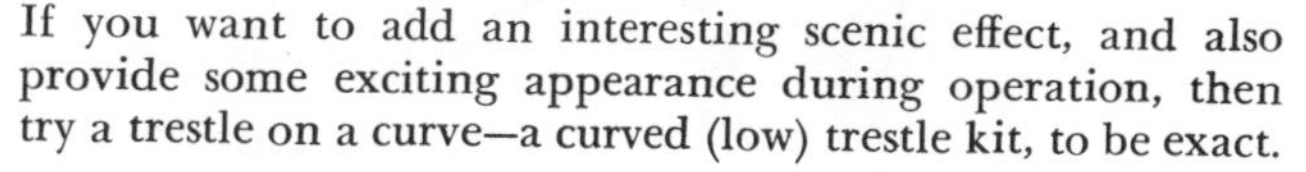

If you want to add an interesting scenic effect, and also provide some exciting appearance during operation, then try a trestle on a curve—a curved (low) trestle kit, to be exact.

This tall curved trestle offers a spindly construction and complicated appearance which will make a handsome addition to your layout. It assembles quite easily, too.

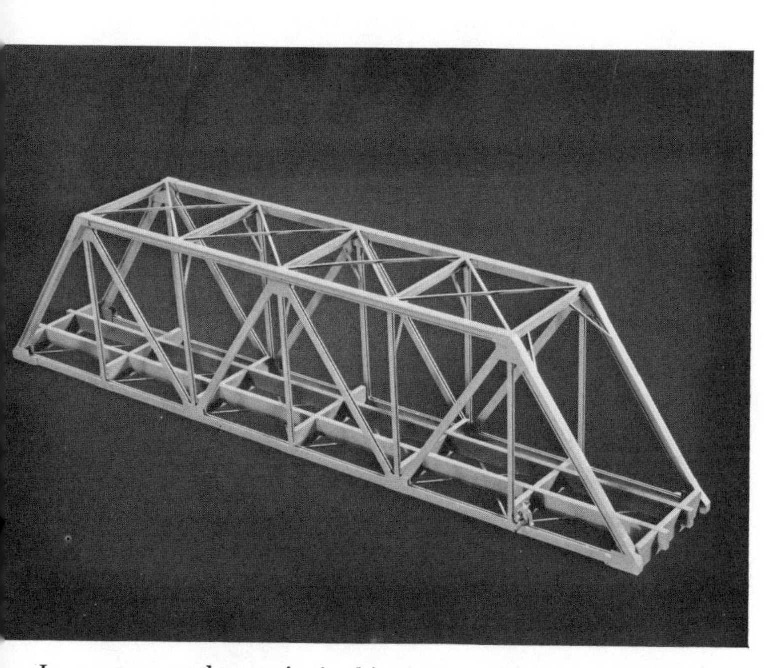

In a more modern vein is this single-track truss bridge kit.

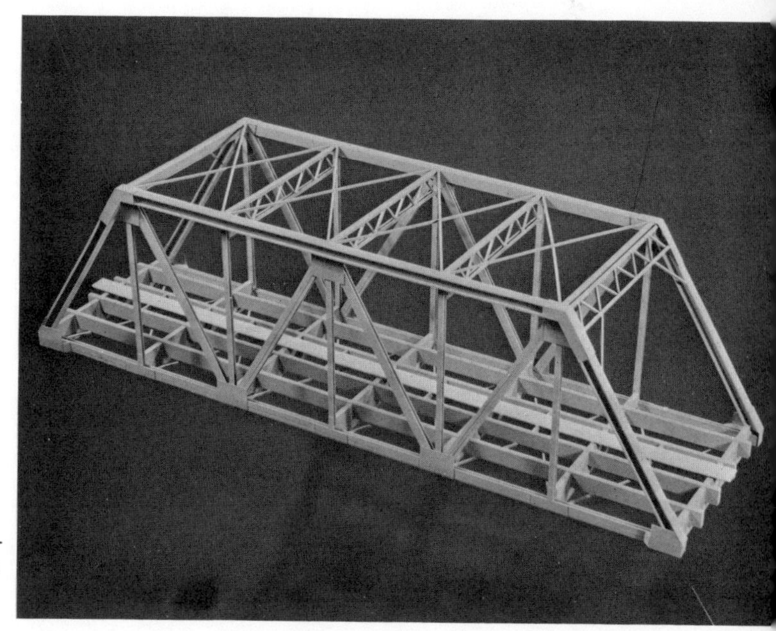

If your bridge is used to carry high-speed, double-track mainlines across valleys, rivers and highways, then this double-track truss bridge kit will fill the bill perfectly.

If you would rather do it yourself entirely, than try the technique used to good advantage by Jim Foell. With the use of bark from a cork tree, Jim was able to produce a striking sculptural effect upon the banks of the winding stream. Rough-hewn wood-beam bracings of trestle crossing were made from dried branches from a young sapling tree. Natural effects such as these contribute greatly to the overall atmosphere, and the starkly realistic and rustic scene is further enhanced by the inclusion of a horse drawn milk wagon moving over a simple crossing made of bass wood.

Another model railroader who is great at scenic effects is Dick Seydell. In fact, there isn't a section on his layout that isn't photogenic. Study some of the photos of his pike in this and other chapters and you will see what I mean. Foell's scenic applications embrace the more rustic, woodsy, and oldtime era, while Seydell's pike is more contemporary in nature, with the emphasis on industry. That leaves a wide range in between for the modeler to adopt whereby a little of everything can be combined.

It might not hurt to take a field trip to some nearby wooded area not only to look and take pictures, but also to fill a sack with interesting stones, weather-beaten wood, oddly shaped twigs, branches, and the like. Back home in your model railroad surroundings, you can go to town producing landscape, scenery, and "mountains out of molehills."

And the next time a mind reader pops his head into the realm of your miniature empire, he won't think you are some kind of a nut—just a happy model railroader throttling your trains over scenicked terrain rather than bare wood. But the visions will still be there —for they are one of the main fascinations of model railroading.

XI
Extra Special Effects

In preceding chapters we have talked about building a model railroad and decorating it with scenery. Now, among other things, let's talk about buildings which, when put in place on your pike, help bring things alive. Whether you have purchased a ready-made structure, assembled it from a kit, or made it entirely from scratch, now is a good time to give it a bit of aging and weathering before putting it in place on your layout. Not only will this enhance the appearance of the structure, but it will do much to remedy the "fresh off the shelf" look which is especially evident in the case of various plastic materials whose inherent characteristics convey that "obvious" shiny look. This is not meant to be a rap against plastic; on the contrary, for many wonderful things have been done and are being produced in styrene and other plastic materials. This is merely a suggestion that with a minimum of effort you can rid your buildings and trackside structures of that toy-like "under-the-Christmas-tree" appearance.

A light rubdown of talcum powder will kill the plastic shine. Smears of powdered graphite here and there will not only add a touch of age and weathering, but will also fill and darken cracks, greatly adding to and accentuating the surface details. Bricks and mortar will take on added dimension in a more realistic vein, and even a dab and smear of a child's crayon will give things a touch of antiquity. After all, it is to be assumed that your railroad, or at least its environs, have been there for some time, and since it is a natural thing for the elements to attack and discolor even the best paint job, it behooves us to make every effort to duplicate such an effect. A lineside shanty or any railroad structure weather-beaten and somewhat worse for wear is an effect we wish to achieve.

Aside from powder, graphite, and crayons, painting is another popular means of adding realistic appearance to your structures. Ulrich's 410M Styrene paint is a perfect medium for plastics, and works equally well with other materials such as wood and metal. In either case, full strength is not necessary, since the washed-out color obtained through thinning will aid you considerably in creating the very effect we are talking about. Casein paints, which were referred to in connection with painting and aging locomotive equipment, are also widely used, and are very popular with modelers because of the ease of application and the variety of color and tonal gradations that are obtainable. And since it is a water-soluble medium, it is easy to clean brushes and equipment. Once the painted surface is dry, the color remains permanently fixed. Another important aspect of casein paint is the fact that it does not obliterate the details it is covering. In other words, the coloring is not opaque in nature, but rather translucent; this in turn provides a somewhat transparent effect. For example, if you want to create the effect of rust and corosion streaked down the wall of a brick building —caused by an overhead rainspout—the color you applied, assuming it had a rustlike quality to it, would not hide the details of the mortar that separates one brick from another.

There is no set formula for mixing colors, for this is a matter of personal preference; however, a good rule of thumb to go by might be to *start with the thinner (or water), then add some paint.* This is one area where a bit of experimenting is definitely in order. Many hobbyists have the mistaken impression that all they have to do is slap paint on in a slipshod manner and the results will reflect age, deterioration, and weathered appearance. This is far from the case; it does nothing more than reflect a bad paint job.

Another important point is not to rush things or overload the surface with a heavy coat of paint. Build up your layers of color one coat at a time. In that way some of the underlying tones will be visible and will add to the effect of a given structure having had more than one paint job, whereby over a period of years and aging the earlier colors have started to show through. Try to duplicate prototype conditions as they exist in and about real railroads. Many trackside structures have become darkened from the soot thrown off by smoke-belching locomotives as they thunder by. Another area affected by smoke and soot is the undersurface of overhead bridges, overhangs, and tunnel portals. Don't discolor or age just for the heck of it, but rather to achieve a sense and flavor of railroading realism. In short, it should be a matter of *cause* and *effect.*

For additional information concerning the aging and weathering of railroad structures, the November 1960 issue of *Model Railroader* features an illustrated and highly enlightening article on the subject by Alan Armitage. Armitage is a wizard at this sort of thing, and you will find his expert know-how easily applicable to your own needs. Try the public library for a starter. If they don't have the issue on file, you can purchase a back copy from Kalmbach Publications. Armitage has also put together a set of plans on the building of "Railroad Structures" and also one on "Styrene Fabrication," both of which are available from Kemtron.

In recent years there has been a growing trend toward the revamping and modifying of structures, either pre-assembled or of kit origin. While this is not a new application, it has been more widely practiced in the last few years because of the rising population of rail fans throughout the country. With the increase in model railroaders, more manufacturers got into the act and, as a result, more structures and trackside accessories became available. In other words, layout upon layout from one town to the other contain identical buildings, coaling towers, station houses, etc. Since most discriminating modelers prefer to have something better, or at least different, than their brass hat brethren, they have revamped the style and architecture of various commonly used structures. Thus far I have seen twelve variations on a Revell sand and pump house and a dozen or more modifications on Tru-Scale's jailhouse. I couldn't begin to mention all of the others I have observed or have done myself.

These variations in building design and/or function are not done because the product is lacking in authenticity or detailing, but rather because the modeler wishes to fill a particular need, has to cut down on the size of a structure because of limited space, or generally because he not only wants to improve the overall appearance if possible, but avoid a sameness of building decor from one layout to the other. For example, within these

The depth and dimension achieved in this view leaves little to be desired in the way of realism, and is the result of imagination and careful planning. Jim Foell has created a tremendous feeling of natural environment by introducing special effects which are shown in close-up detail on the pages that follow. The ripples in the water close to the shoreline are about as authentic as one can get.

Revell's sand and pump house and fuel storage tank kits are quite popular among modelers, and lend themselves to modification and revamping.

Even without any great changes in design, Jim Foell has given the Revell sand and pump house a new look in the way of a fine job of painting and blending the structure into the overall effect.

The sand and pump house and fuel storage tank structures have been combined and rearranged to produce this authentic-appearing maintenance and oil storage section of the BEST Model RR Club. An Aristo-Craft single Esso storage tank placed directly alongside has the look of rightfully belonging in the scene. It is important to note that both the structures and the activities involved should be completely compatible with each other.

The Tru-Scale jail house takes on a new look once it is blended in with the surrounding ground. Careful covering of the base will do much to remove the feeling that it has just been laid in place.

With a bit of "enginuity" Bob Steele took two Revell engine house kits and butted them together, providing that extra length needed to bed down "those long jobs" he plans to operate. An imaginative touch is added by leaving the roof off the rear section and replacing it with construction workers and scaffolding. A special project, this work was done away from the layout and afterward laid in place. All that remains is to blend the edges of the base with the yard area, and the project is complete. Unlike many a static-looking area, this scene will continue to convey the feeling of activity.

pages you will see a Revell engine house that features an extra length of building, the latter designed to make possible the storage of longer locomotives—a simple project consisting of using two kits and butting one up against the other, the unused parts to be utilized elsewhere on the layout.

A more formidable example of revamping a kit is the case of the twelve-stall roundhouse shown in this chapter. Made from seven Revell engine house kits, members of the Burbank, Encino, and South Tarzana Model Railroading Club have more than demonstrated their "enginuity" and craftsmanship with as prototype a roundhouse as you will ever see. At the time of shooting, the roundhouse was not entirely finished and most of the roof was left off to give you a view of the interior. Study the effect achieved in the lower right of the photograph; the building, ballast bunker, and oil storage tanks are the end result of combining a sand and pump house with fuel storage tanks from kits made by Revell. Let's pursue the photograph a bit further. The groundfill covering in the foreground area is the result of painting the bare surface with cheap enamel and sprinkling a cinderfill ballast on top of the tacky surface. In this particular case, a Kemtron mixture was used, after which the ballast was lightly tamped down. When thoroughly dry, the surplus ballast was brushed away, to be used elsewhere. The remaining finish, as you can see, is prototypical of the coloring and ground conditions you would expect to see in most locomotive yard areas. The 2-6-0 at

The only indication of a roundhouse and locomotive yard area is the circular hole which will soon house a turntable.

It takes a bit of "imagineering" to construct a twelve-stall roundhouse from seven Revell engine house kits, but it was done in both authentic and interesting fashion. Freeman Crutchfield and Bob Uniack are shown discussing various modifications needed to complete roof. When finished, the BEST Model RR Club will boast a mighty handsome structure for locomotive storage.

the lower left was scratch-built by Bob Uniack, and this particular locomotive has been a first prize winner at past Pacific Coast regional NMRA meets. The V&T ten-wheeler atop the trestle and the 2-6-0 Southern Pacific Mogul were also scratch-built by Uniack and have won honors. Note the excellent superdetailing and weathering of these skillfully made locomotives.

Note the white areas extending from inside the roundhouse stalls to about half-way up the tracks. This represents a paved flooring and walkway for maintenance crews servicing the locomotives, and was accomplished by pouring texture paint, then troweling the top surface till level. The roundhouse will accommodate twelve locomotives, big or small. Typical of prototype practice, the engines are headed in, over open pits where the mechanics work on them. The turntable, scratch-built by members of the BEST RR, will easily handle the largest HO locomotive available—the Union Pacific "Big Boy," which is as long and articulated a locomotive as ever ran the rails.

Lined up in position to go out on a freight drag is a fine example of the better type of brass locomotives being imported from Japan. Made by Akane Models, it is a well-detailed miniature of the prototype, a B&O EM-1 Baldwin 2-8-8-4 articulated. This writer had the pleasure of aging and weathering it, though no number or road name has yet been assigned to it. Directly to the left of the engine's smoke box, and at the edge of the turntable, is a small work shed built from extra parts remaining from the Revell kits used to build the roundhouse. This is an example of how little waste is involved in setting the railroading scene. The nearby skeleton-like structure is the framework of a diesel shed in the process of being constructed. The period shown is the early thirties, when diesel motive power was beginning to be used on railroads throughout the country. Thus, in keeping with tradition, the BEST RR, while not making a complete transition from steam to diesel, is nonetheless embracing its use.

Background scenic effects are the artistry of Freeman Crutchfield who, in using the texture paint and cardboard strip technique described in Chapter X, has produced with the aid of skillful coloring a fine sculptured effect. There are other special touches such as the building inspector checking the roofing of the roundhouse and the maintenance man climbing the ladder of a Kemtron oil tank. Also note the S.P. Daylight standing alongside a Kemtron brass watering column.

You may need a magnifying glass to find everything I mention, and some I don't, for to the right rear is a coaling tower made from an Alexander kit, and also a heating plant building and tower from Aristo-Craft. Last is the trestle itself which is, I am sure you will agree, breathtaking. Bob Judson built this trestle to top all trestles. Entirely scratch-built, it took six months of Fridays to complete from top to bottom and is the longest HO trestle in the world, actually measuring 12 feet from end to end. It is equivalent to approximately 1,100 feet of actual track. Made entirely of bass wood, the sections, bracings, etc., were fastened together with a vinyl-type glue. Ties and track (including guard rails) were hand laid and spiked down, and from right to left the trestle trackage develops a 1½-per cent grade. As the railroad expanded its freight yard and mainline operations, an open cut was made in the trestle, replacing the vertical braces (bents) with a steel truss bridge and framework. Note men on scaffolding slapping a coat of paint over the metal surface. A similar open cut in the trestle was created (this one is all wood) for a mainline run, and you can see an S.P. Daylight passing through on the upper left of the picture. As the need for industrial sidings arose, additional cuts were made in the trestle, requiring nothing more than the removal of the lower "bents," which were afterward "shored up" with timber bracing. In all, this trestle presents a striking picture and an example of a challenging and rewarding accomplishment.

The Burbank, Encino, and South Tarzana Model Railroading Club not only boasts a trestle to beat all trestles, but a number of other interesting situations as well. The fifteen-man membership is 100 per cent NMRA (a prerequisite for joining their club). Secondly, they are completely open-minded in their approach to model railroading. They not only scratch build, but use ready-to-run items as well. In other words, that which will do the job properly is suitable for their use. The roundhouse, for example, is predominantly plastic (high impact styrene) whereas other structures are wood or metal. Kadee Magne-Matic Couplers are used throughout on all locos and rolling stock, and as a companion mate they also use Kadee Magne-Lectric Uncouplers (electromagnetic). They started building their layout (a combination of open bench work and flat top) using Tru-Scale's self-gauging roadbed; that is, they spiked down their own rail. However, at the half-way mark, Alan Stensvold, at whose residence the pike is housed, designed a spiking and track-laying gauge, and since then they have been laying their own ties and rail. Stensvold may someday put his special gauge on the market, and I'm sure it will sell very well.

While it may appear that I have gotten somewhat off the track concerning special effects, bear in mind that model railroading is such a multi-faceted hobby that you can talk about ten different situations and sooner

The roundhouse at the BEST RR is now starting to take shape as "I" beams and bracing are propped in place. Each stall features a pit, so that mechanics can get to underbody of locomotives for maintenance and repair. Paved flooring effect was achieved by the use of Texture Paint.

The roundhouse, almost complete, now blends perfectly with surrounding scenery, which includes the famous "biggest HO trestle in the world." The combination of activity in this scene is impressive indeed and is covered in detail in the text. A co-operative effort on the part of members of the Burbank, Encino and South Tarzana Model RR Club, it is a perfect example of what can develop when good fellows get together.

Bob Judson, who created this "trestle of all trestles," spent six month of Fridays patiently and painstakingly gluing each section of wood together. A vinyl-type glue was used as the adhesive, and small alligator clamps, clothes pins, etc., were also use to hold things in place until set. Bob is shown adding a new bracing to shore up an area of the trestle which had a "bent" removed to provide an opening for a new siding.

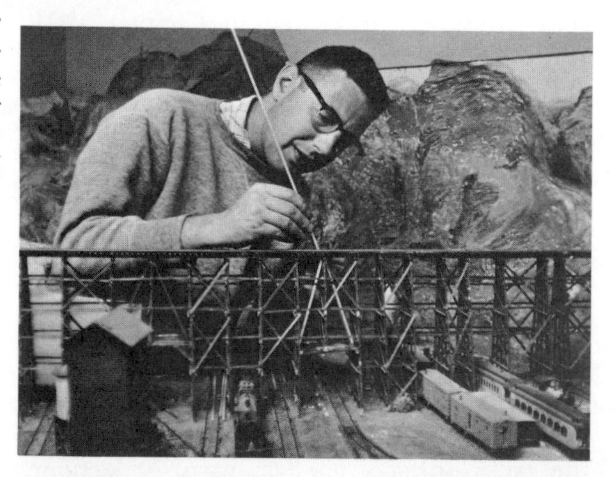

This prize-winning "Mogul" was scratch-built by Bob Uniack and contains a wealth of details which not only enhance the appearance of the locomotive itself, but any scene in which it appears.

or later you will realize they are all interconnected with each other.

The library, magazines, model railroading books, and other periodicals make excellent sources of reference and stimulation for those who need help getting ideas on how to dress things up in prototype fashion. One of the most expedient methods is to visit your closest railroad line and make a thorough study of the area. Take, for example, the question of ballasting. Aside from using commercially made scale ballast, you can resort to the use of birdseed gravel. However, many feel that the latter is out of scale, glassy, and unrealistic looking. Nonetheless, it can have other scenic applications and it should not be entirely overlooked. Sand (of the beach variety) makes a fairly prototypical-looking mixture and has a variety of uses. The silicon compound used for sandblasting has excellent possibilities, too, and can be purchased at your local building supply store. One hundred pounds costs about $2—ask for 20 or 30 weight.

Suppose you wish to create a small mound of sand. Simply pour the sand to the shape and height you desire and completely saturate it with the Plasticate, water, and the detergent mixture I described in Chapter VIII. When dry, it will be frozen in place yet appear to be lying loose.

A few pages back I mentioned the manner in which enamel was used as the adhesive in producing the ground covering in the roundhouse area of the BEST RR. To repeat, the cheapest enamel will do the job well; use a cheap brush, too. To create ground effects between parallel tracks in yard areas, mainlines, or in and around sidings, paint the bare surface with the enamel, and sprinkle the particular ground or ballast material onto the tacky surface. Shellac, varnish, lacquer, and other forms of paint will work equally well. Vinyl-based paints and/or glue will do the job also, but are usually more expensive and not as easy to apply. In selecting or mixing up your ballast or ground texture materials, bear in mind the effect you wish to achieve. As a rule, dark ballast is used in yard areas and light for mainlines. Use your local railroad as a guide by studying the composition and color of the ballast they use.

If you are modeling a particular railroad, a letter to their maintenance department should be sufficient to supply you with a knowledgeable reply. If you are creating a railroad which is not patterned after any particular prototype line, the color and composition of the crushed gravel, ballast, and other surface textures will be determined by the type of activity taking place within your pike. For example, if you plan on coaling operations, then a dark cinder-type of ballast is appropriate. Kemtron has just the mixture. If, on the other hand, your railroad is involved in freight drags to and from steel mills, mines, and similar industrial areas, then an iron rust-type of ballast will look in place. Kemtron has this too. Once the ballast or ground surface is in place, you can change the color tone with water colors to match any changes in industry or weathering that takes place. Remember that it is usually easier to darken than lighten. If in doubt, use a light-colored ballast, since it will show off your trains better by virtue of the contrast. If tracks run along mountainsides, use a mixture of crushed gravel and earth, and if you add some dried coffee grounds, you will heighten the natural effect.

As for the overall tonal effects from the ground up, don't create an eye-straining kaleidoscope of colors. Don't make your shades too strong unless you wish to accentuate pockets and crevices, such as in cliffs and mountain slopes. Try to keep the colors fairly soft and in a blend of varying tones, as in nature.

Providing structures with some form of illumination is an effect often overlooked by modelers and is a task easily undertaken. By installing a small bulb in the 16-volt range, the lighted building will take on added dimension, especially when you dim the room lights and operate at dusk or in the black of night. A sprinkling of illuminated structures situated from one end of your layout to the other will add to the believable atmosphere by adding balance and contrast to your trains as they roll by. There are any number of illuminated accessories available which will do much to liven things on your pike. Or you can do it yourself by adding a bulb or two. Power for your lighting should be fed from the AC terminals of your power pack so that you will have constant lighting. Terminal strips installed at appropriate places on the underside of your railroad and connected to your main source of power will reduce the length of wire needed for hooking up accessories. All you have to do is run feeders to the nearest terminal strip, rather than having to run wires all the way back to the power pack. On-off toggle switches will permit you to flick your lights on and off depending on the time of day or the effect you wish to create.

The best time to provide for illumination is before the structure is installed on your layout, which brings up the fact that many modelers will build an entire scene or grouping of buildings on a sheet of plywood, and after construction, painting, weathering, illuminating, etc., the entire scene is placed within the layout. If you do this, be sure to measure the overall space beforehand so that the plywood sub-base will not be larger than the area it will occupy, otherwise you will have to do some trimming. Telephone poles are a common sight on railroads, as are power lines, for they dot the landscape from coast to coast. Fine black thread is perfect for stringing from one pole to the other and adds an authentic touch to the railroad scene.

Switch motors in the sectional track category are usually mounted directly alongside their respective turnouts rather than under the table or bench work, and as a consequence are often felt to be objectionable from a viewing standpoint. This can be easily overcome by building up a small trackside structure to fit directly over the switch motor. However, be sure you have the proper clearance so that there will be no danger of sideswiping from your locomotives and rolling stock. Also, be sure to provide plenty of room for the action of the throw rods and throw bars. Depending on the number of turnouts and adjacent switch motors, it would be a good idea to vary the size and shape of the switch motor covers, thus avoiding a sameness in appearance about your layout. One covering can be in the form of a small platform, another can be a pile of ties, while another can be an oil tank or trackside quonset hut.

Another interesting special effect can be obtained by building up an area which is commonly called "rip track." This is where locomotives, rolling stock, and other railroad equipment is stored till the maintenance crews can get to them. Obvious locations for "rip track" are in and about maintenance yards, or close and adjacent to a roundhouse. The opportunities for creating a believable maintenance atmosphere is great, for on this site you can place discarded trucks, wheels, odd sections of track, piles of ties, spikes scattered here and there, oldtime box cars, reefers, and other rolling stock either in need of repairs or ready for salvage operation. In fact, a box car with trucks and wheels removed can be revamped to become a shelter or living quarters for maintenance men. Revell has such an item in kit form although it is easy to fabricate one yourself from any piece of rolling stock that has seen better days. It is scenes such as this that improve the overall appearance of your railroad by creating the feeling of function, activity, and purpose. An otherwise static-looking town can suddenly come to life with the addition of an assortment of figures and a brass band on hand to commemorate the event of a locomotive being placed on view in the town square or park. The rest is up to you, and just a little bit of imagination will go a long way toward creating a proper and believable effect.

Another interesting effect easily obtained is by means of pressing one of your oldtime

Bob Guy helps set the scene by maneuvering an Aristo-Craft heating plant into just the right position. Actually putting an item in place expedites matters when you are trying to visualize how additions will look, and whether they will fit, let alone belong.

Rock and gravel retaining wall is the handiwork of Jim Foell and was fashioned from strips of bass wood. This is the type of protective device you would expect to find against a rocky embankment. A variation on this (more likely found along mountainsides) would be electrified wire railings which transmit warning signals in the event of landslides—a good prototype practice if you have track running adjacent to foothills and sides of rocky slopes. A simple project such as this can be done in an hour.

One of the most popular trackside structures, this station house by Revell is not only widely used, but widely modified. Butting two kits together provides that extra length needed for the bigger-than-average-sized town. Cut through the middle, end to end, it can be used as a false-front effect against a wall or background—a handy gimmick where space is an important factor.

This saw mill with motorized water wheel offered by Aristo-Craft would make a handsome addition to any layout. Available in kit or assembled form, this structure has some weathering already built in. This useful accessory can become the basis of a series of realistic railroading operations by the addition of a spur. A stream directly adjacent to the water wheel side will give things the final touch.

Evening projects in the form of a water tank, and a boathouse and landing are not only fun to conceive and make, but can be tailor-made to coincide with what your railroad atmosphere calls for. A bit of scratch-building comes in mighty handy when commercial kits don't provide the very item you need. Jim Foell used manzanita wood to construct these unique additions. Shingles on roof of water tower were cut from index cards.

Maintenance shed and freight station from Revell are just some of many well-detailed trackside structures that they offer the modeler.

These well-detailed structures from Aristo-Craft are made of styrene and take to weathering and aging easily. Perfect accessories for yards and maintenance areas, they include an oil service loader, drum filling station and single and double Esso storage tanks.

locomotives into "fan trip" service. The more scenic the route, the better; in fact, you can make a situation such as this part and parcel of a branchline operation. All it takes is a bit of "imaginuity."

I have been stressing the importance of imagination and the use of photographs and drawings for reference and research so that you can apply every bit of prototypical detail possible. We can, therefore, be most thankful for the part that photography has played in prototype railroading. During the middle of the last century when the art of recording a scene with a camera began to mean more than a tintype to hang in the parlor, American railroads assigned photographers (what few there were) to capture and document their particular lines and equipment. Were it not for the graphic art of photography as employed during the earlier days of railroading and steam locomotion, valuable research and historic photographs would be lost to the world. It would be a sad plight for the scratch builder, indeed, or the researcher, historian, author, or anyone, for that matter, who desired some authentic pictured form other than sketches, blueprints, or paintings, no matter how artistic. Thus, pioneering cameramen such as Mathew L. Brady and other early colleagues of the profession set about to capture the very heart of American railroading and, with it, the golden age of steam. During the Civil War, Brady, who became famous for his documentation of the conflict, photographed a number of oldtimer Civil War trains, prints of which today would be valuable collectors' items. Glass plates were used in those days and, therefore, easily broken; as a result, early prints from the negatives are very rare.

Since that time, and as photographic techniques and equipment improved, thousands of photographs have been made of the railroad scene, capturing on film not only the early Moguls and Consols, but the brute power developed and put into use around the turn of the century and beyond until the diesel entered the scene. As the camera became a popular device for the public, millions of photographs were taken of roaring locos, streamliners, and the like. The part that photography has played in the development of American railroading is an important one, and will continue to be.

There aren't too many old smokers around that are still working, let alone seeing service, and if you should come across an "iron horse," photograph it. It might be headed for the locomotives' Valhalla, or to a neighboring town to take up residence as a permanent display. In any event, it may be the last chance you will get to shoot some action photos, and what better way is there to record the event? The rail fan can glean much from applying photography to model railroading by keeping a record of his progress while building, expanding, or adding to his pike. It can be used for research and reference in capturing the details of yards, stations, structures, and other railroad equipment. Thus, when building your own layout, you can use the pictures to authenticate things down to the last detail rather than rely on your memory.

Hills, rocks, trees, rivers—this is part of the landscaping that makes up your pike, and shooting pictures of the realism with which nature abounds will help you tremendously when you start to do your scenic effects, for after all, the aim of every model rail is to have a realistic-appearing layout. Color slides will help you to remember the color of that Drover's caboose you saw out west last year, and will capture in true tone the shaded hues of foliage and rocks under trees. One could go on and on extolling the advantages of using a camera in relation to model building and railroading, but I think it will suffice to say that by combining the two things will take on added dimensions.

You don't have to have expensive equipment, and one of the first things I learned in photography is that you could stop a speeding locomotive with a box camera. The explanation is simple. You shoot at a 45-degree angle.

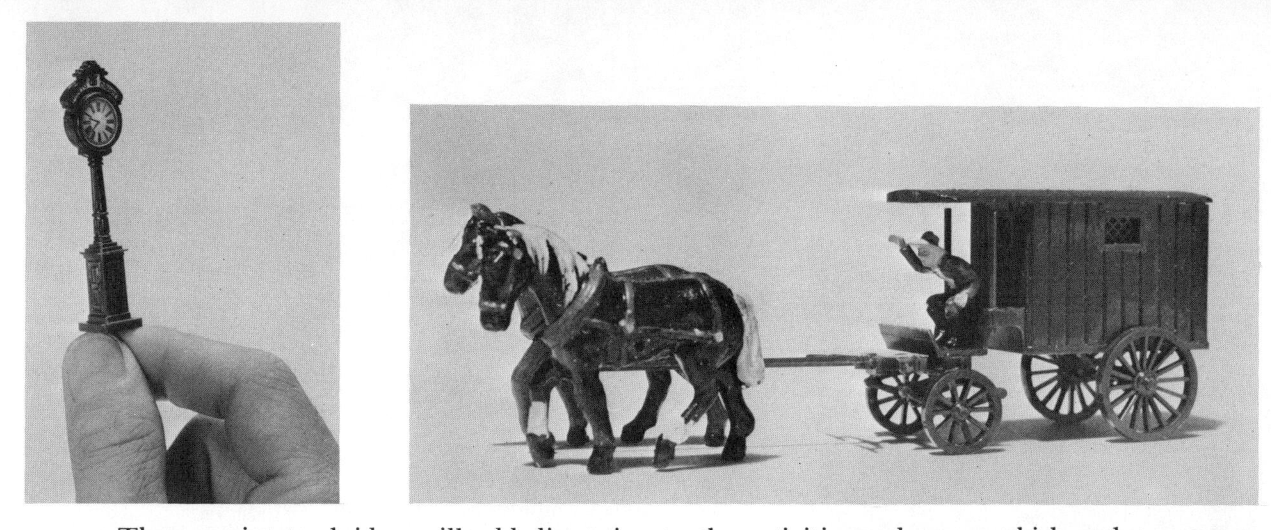

These quaint tracksiders will add dimension to the activities and scenes which make up your railroad atmosphere. The items shown are just a few of the miniatures available from Aristo-Craft and numerous other sources. An illuminated station clock is two-faced and will look perfect on the platform. The horse and wagon will look fine along a country road, and the Salvation Army band should be a natural for greeting inbound trains. To add to the festivities, a brass band can be on hand to give visiting VIP's a musical welcome, or to commemorate the unveiling of statuary in the town square (or a loco being put on permanent display). Miniature oldtimers wearing the dress of their day will add the right decor if you have chosen that era. Miniatures such as these have a charm all their own and add to the overall believability.

Polaroid close-up captures details of quaint scene created by Jim Foell. Film speed used was 3000, with existing room lighting. Note infant holding up his diapers.

The Polaroid Land Camera, or any camera, for that matter, will help capture the decisive moment. For model railroaders, the graphic reference of a finished print can be invaluable, so shoot lots of pictures. You might not get a second chance.

This Tru-Scale bank features an early day Out West design and is equally adaptable to rural areas, oldtime or more contemporary in nature.

Another interesting tracksider is this shanty house from Tru-Scale. Takes age and weathering treatment easily. Final touch is the TV antenna.

Accessories such as these trucks and trailers from Ulrich add to the feeling of transportation, activity and operation.

Two views of the Tru-Scale fire house show how the mere addition of a few trees and figures add to the dimension and blend of this building. Fire fighting apparatus will also help the scene.

Cliff-Line has a wide and varied assortment of tunnel portals in HO and other scales, modern or oldtime in design.

Polaroid film (professional size shown here) was used during cover session and this shooting session as well to provide author-photographer David Sutton with exact lighting and composition prior to final exposures. Polaroid cameras of popular and standard sizes provide model rails with a means of getting a better perspective than the eye sometimes permits. Especially useful during the creation of those special scenic effects, for you can judge your accomplishments ten seconds after the picture is taken.

Try it and see for yourself. Even with the most inexpensive camera and slowest of film, you can almost "freeze" action coming head-on, including an onrushing steamer, but I wouldn't advise it. Some of my best pictures were taken with the use of an inexpensive camera, but on the other hand, most of my best work has been done with my more expensive equipment, by virtue of the selective controls which afford me the maximum quality in enlargements for reproduction.

Over the years as a working photo-journalist I have found the single lens reflex camera to be among the most versatile and easily controlled pieces of photo equipment. For the benefit of those readers who are camera minded, I would definitely recommend the 35-millimeter single lens reflex type of camera, since the ground glass viewing screen shows you the actual size, perspective, and dimension you will get in your negative or color slide; therefore, it is easier to compose your picture before taking it. A variety of interchangeable lenses also make it possible for you to achieve different effects, and wide or close-up views of the scene you are shooting. Another ideal camera for the model railroader, who, after spending an evening producing a special effect, would like to show it to the boys in the office the following morning, is the Polaroid Land Camera which will produce a finished photograph in a matter of seconds. All types of Polaroid cameras are available, in various sizes and prices. Black and white or color, the Polaroid enables you to make a record of what you have built or viewed, but, more important, permits you to see the results of your picture-taking almost immediately thereafter. In fact, while making the cover illustration, the polaroid proved invaluable, allowing me to have a more visual and graphic check of lighting, composition, and overall effect.

Regardless of the type of camera you have or may soon purchase, new horizons for your modeling pleasure await you by applying even the simplest form of photography to model railroading.

Summing up the case of special effects and those little extra touches that lend atmosphere to your pike, I hasten to add that we have by no means exhausted the subject. For as you go along, you will invent many gimmicks and innovations of your own. The plastic flues to which parts in kits are connected will no longer be tossed into the waste, since they can be utilized for many things such as water tank piping, generator detailing, and plumbing. Odd wheels, pilots, sections of track, ties, and damaged rolling stock can all become part of your model railroading environment.

Study the photographs in this chapter and the descriptive captions which explain what other fellow rails do. And in addition to the scenic aids available at your hobby shops, I again remind you not to overlook the possibilities of using natural items which you can find in your own backyard. Small stones can become boulders, tiny twigs can serve as trees, certain flowering bushes when thoroughly dry or dormant can make effective miniatures. Just snip off scale-sized lengths, remove leaves or blossoms, and you will have what appears to be the start of springtime foliage. Actually, the techniques and applications are endless, and once you try your hand at duplicating mother nature and imparting more prototypical ingredients to your railroad scenes, you will be amazed with the success and realistic appearance of your handiwork, whether you have a natural flair or not. Don't be afraid to experiment with colors and sculptoral effects. You can always remove or cover them up. Above all, try it. You may find that you have a touch of Da Vinci after all!

XII
Rolling Stock...From A to Z

To the model rail, one of the most important parts of the railroad anatomy is rolling stock, for this classification offers both modeler and operator equal opportunity to flex their muscles in as many directions as there are different pieces of equipment. The phrase "rolling stock" has come to mean any part of rolling or movable equipment in railroad use which isn't tied down, and, like the words "prototype" and "gauge," has become all-embracing so that it not only includes freight, passenger, and maintenance cars, but motive power as well. While any and all forms of railroad equipment fitted out with wheels has come to be lumped under the one heading, the fact remains (according to many sources of research) that motive power—steam, diesel, or otherwise—is in a complete class by itself, whereas all other forms of rail running equipment is designated "rolling stock." For this reason, throughout these pages and other areas of this book, I draw the line between motive power and that of the other equipment, box cars, reefers, cabooses, *et al.*

Rolling stock is as old as railroading itself, since the whole purpose of rail lines to begin with was to transport freight or passengers from one point to another, and as quickly as locomotives were developed, various forms of rolling stock were added. Certain cars had an even earlier start than the motive power which pulled or pushed them along the rails. Years before England's "Stourbridge Lion" arrived on these shores to give birth to American railroading, ore cars atop crude wooden rails were pushed by hand from one end of a mine to the other; stubborn mules soon replaced the human horsepower, to be followed by tractive and other mechanical devices for propelling the box-like containers in either direction.

The model rail fan who likes to build or assemble his own line of rolling stock has an untapped source of design and prototype variation to keep him happily engrossed indefinitely. The fellow who likes to operate has an equal amount of opportunities because of the enormous variety of cars, functions, and procedures in use. Rolling stock offers the rail fan (regardless of category) more action per square inch than one can imagine. For example, a locomotive rolling in and about industrial areas, puffing through the outskirts of suburban communities, or highballing along the mainline takes on added significance and realistic appearance when pulling

This RTR cement hopper by Revell features "lift up" roof and can be used for other operations such as bulk grain hauling, etc.

Clean lettering and distinctive prototype design of this New York Central box car is typical of RTR rolling stock available from Varney Scale Models.

Reefer has excellent detailing and features lift-up hatches. RTR from Athearn.

Double-door auto car from Athearn is RTR and is a scale 50 feet.

Athearn's auto loader is a 50-foot flat car with superstructure designed to carry four scale-sized autos which can be unloaded. RTR.

Heinz pickle car, RTR from Revell, is perfect example of **privately** owned rolling **stock.**

RTR flat car by Revell includes removable stakes and real logs.

Chemical tank car is RTR from Athearn.

Pulpwood car by Revell is RTR and features high bulkheads at both ends to hold realistic pulpwood load in place. Removable load permits use of car for other bulkload hauls.

Another tank car in RTR form from Athearn.

a long line of freight and/or passenger equipment. Cutting off a hopper car at a cement plant, a reefer at a packing house, or a stock car at a cattleyard, are but a few of the realistic operations of rolling stock, and, moreover, the mere appearance of types and color schemes is sufficient to give the flavor of authentic railroading atmosphere. Therefore, the more rolling stock a layout can boast, the greater the illusion of real operation, which is what everyone is after ultimately.

These moving vans of the rails contain a varied amount of different designations within themselves, and, from a basic standpoint, consist of either passenger or freight equipment. Going one step further, each of these is equally divided. Passenger equipment includes coaches, pullmans, diners, baggage, and mail cars, lounge cars, observation cars, and others with many modern refinements. Freight cars embrace reefers, stock cars, box cars, flat cars, gondolas, depressed-center flat cars, auto loading cars, among many others. Cars whose primary functions are to contain freight, produce, etc., are of a specific "profit-earning" nature to the railroad.

Another branch of rolling stock is that of the "non-revenue" cars, rolling equipment which, while not performing services that add to the coffers of the railroad, more than manage to earn their keep by the chores they perform; they fall into the category of maintenance equipment, such as derrick and boom cars, track-laying cars, ballasting equipment, and rotary snow plows. Crummies, or cabooses, while bringing up the rear guard, are neither freight nor maintenance equipment, though they fall into the non-revenue status. These cars are used as living quarters for the train crew and also serve not only as a lookout or crow's nest, but as an office for the conductor as well. The caboose has an interesting history, which will be discussed shortly. There are hand cars, blacksmith cars, dynamometer cars, water cars, wheel cars, etc. A number of automobiles and small trucks or buses are fitted out with flanged wheels for use by inspectors, railroad officials, and work crews. There are flat cars carrying two- or three-story buildings which serve as movable living quarters for work crews whose functions require what might be called "living on the job." These and the aforementioned are but a few of the many forms of freight, passenger, and operating equipment used in both oldtime and modern railroading, and give you an insight into the innumerable avenues the rail fan may pursue in both building or operating.

An important point to consider in modeling, be it of the scratch or kit-assembly technique, is the fact that as far as purity of prototypical values is concerned, the field is wide open, and, in similar fashion to motive power that underwent various changes when put into service after leaving the locomotive works, rolling stock has also in many cases been changed to suit particular terrain, operating procedures, and innumerable other conditions that arise, requiring as many modifications as deemed necessary for the benefit of all concerned.

If I seem to stress this last point from time to time it is for good reason, for the beginner becomes not only confused with gauge, scale, wheel arrangements, and other ingredients, but finds fingers seeming to point at him from every direction with admonishments lest he stray from exact miniature reproduction of the prototype he is either modeling or thinking about. Thus many a veteran rail fan will look down at the beginner's efforts because a brake wheel is of the wrong design or the trucks don't have the right journal boxes, or perhaps the window on that crummy should be round rather than oval. But who is to say that such superior criticism is constructive, let alone correct? When one considers the thousands upon thousands of pieces of rolling stock that have seen or continue to see action on rail lines today, and the equal number of changes that have been wrought for one reason or another, then it is safe to assume that while in theory it is desirable to be as accurate and prototypically detailed as possible, in essence

Transformer car is RTR from Gilbert.

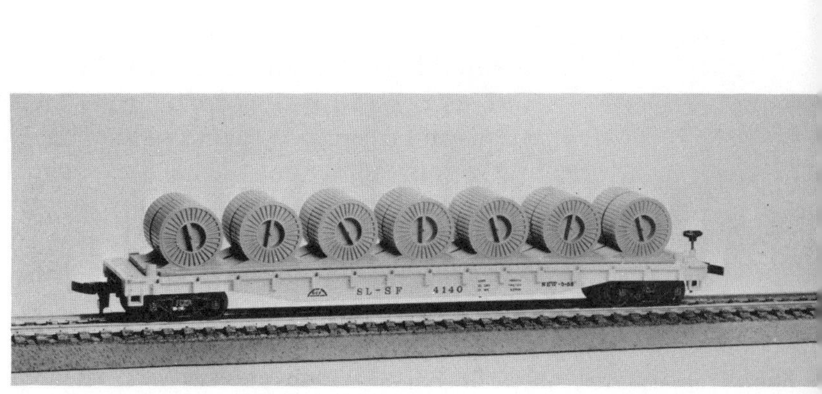

Cable reel car by Revell is RTR.

Crane car of the Pennsy Line is available RTR from Aristo-Craft.

Derrick car by Aristo-Craft is RTR. Operating mechanism raises, lowers and swings in housing.

Wedge snow plow is RTR from Aristo-Craft and includes working headlight.

Rotary snow plow is RTR from Aristo-Craft and features revolving motion of wheel as car is pushed along. Bears details and marking of Great Northern.

no two things are really alike, and if you look hard enough you will find that many modifications and changes of characteristic practiced by the railroad are, in themselves, often unprototypical in nature.

My thoughts on this matter are to play it by the ear, eyes, and interpretation. Freelancers have been doing it for years and have managed to survive the sneers and jeers of experts and theorists. Whatever suits you personally, and provides the most satisfaction and pleasure is the best direction to follow. So don't worry about the round window on the side of your caboose; I saw one like that in Oregon a few years back. In fact, during a trip East one year I spotted a caboose whose cupola contained some stained-glass windows. (Seems one of the crew, an ecclesiastical student, added the reverent touch.)

Rolling stock in the form of kits or ready-to-run equipment can no doubt boast the widest assortment of items obtainable within a given model railroading classification. Today's hobbyist can completely outfit his yards or mainline runs with both basic and offbeat equipment. This was not always the case, and in the years preceding World War II model railroading was much different from what it is today. Kits, at best, were crude affairs consisting of poorly painted cardboard; trucks made of stamped steel had their axles driven through the frames; and parts for superdetailing made of cast bronze were rough and difficult to work with. For the benefit of those of you who don't remember or were not around at the time, both American Flyer (now part of Gilbert) and Lionel not only offered their equipment assembled, but in kit form as well for the do-it-yourselfer, an important consideration in the popularity of kits and home assembly. I mention the fact that American Flyer and Lionel also offered their equipment in kit form because they have been generally associated with that of ready-made equipment, the case today.

Scratch builders had their share of problems, too, though if one was a good man on a metal lathe he could turn his own drivers and make a number of different parts from smoke boxes to headlight enclosures. Hobby and toy stores had only a fraction of that which is available today, and scale railroading was not something you could purchase by the package, but was dependent primarily on one's inventiveness, imagination, and dedicated interest. While the scarcity of equipment required and encouraged the serious enthusiast to fabricate his own parts for building or repair, it didn't encourage the incentive of the unenlightened beginner. HO soon nudged out all of the other gauges. The period that followed, now referred to as the "transition period" in model railroading, was influenced greatly by the advent of the HO gauge, and the advanced manufacturing techniques and die casting methods which were developed during the war years. This, plus the universal support given model railroading in the years that have followed, are part and parcel of the history of the rebirth and new growth of model railroading. Prior to the introduction of plastics, most rolling stock, in either kit or assembled form, was made of wood or metal, or a combination of both. Assembly required a lot of gluing and/or soldering (it still does).

Today, kits range anywhere from superdetailing assemblies to "quickie" variations, the latter of which, like some loco kits, requires a mere shake of the box to put together. Kits, simple to work with or requiring considerable skill and application, now come in a variety of materials, to include wood, metal, plastic, and sometimes a combination of all three. Some of these kits require the removal of flash, whereas others leave the factory devoid of all rough edges. Most of them include pre-painted and pre-lettered sides. In view of the coupler situation (always a controversial note), many manufacturers leave it to the option of the builder to add the type he prefers or which fits his current use. Therefore, in a number of cases, the coupler is not included among the parts. In this way,

No detailing in RTR plastic cars? Nonsense. Just study the rivets, grab irons and other detailing in this caboose from Athearn.

Caboose by Tyco is RTR and includes interior lighting.

Revell caboose is RTR and includes lamp-swinging brakeman and other detailing. Available in the colors and markings of six well-known railroads.

the modeler who employs the use of Kadee, Baker, X2F couplers, or whatever (of which he generally has an extra supply), simply adds his particular coupler choice to the built-up car so that it will be compatible with the rest of his equipment.

Repeated mention and emphasis on Kadee couplers has been made because of its great popularity. First of all, the prototypical knuckle design they employ is far more desirable than the design of the X2F, which is commonly referred to as the NMRA coupler. In addition to the knuckle shape of the Kadee couplers, you can actually lift a car out of a string of rolling stock without having to poke your fingers between the cars where they are coupled. This feature comes in handy in the event of a derailment, or when the time comes that a train or section of cars jumps the track with the dangerous possibility that they will land on the floor below your layout. Another important point to consider is the fact that Kadee Magne-Matic Couplers also offer the advantage of "delayed uncoupling," which means that you can drop cars wherever you want to spot them, even where there are no uncoupling devices. In other words, you are no longer forced to uncouple a car *only* where there is an uncoupler, an operational feat not possible a few years back. When we get to Chapter XVIII on realistic operation you will appreciate the significance of this development. It is, therefore, my opinion that Kadee couplers are your best bet, an opinion shared by many. True, in recent years the X2F coupler has undergone a number of changes for the better, and now also boasts delayed action; from the standpoint of appearance alone, however, it still suffers by comparison.

Train sets and RTR rolling stock usually feature the X2F coupler and, as a consequence, it is not unusual to find this coupler in use on layouts from coast to coast. However, as the modeler advances in the hobby, it is not uncommon for him to make the changeover to that of the Kadee couplers, which feature various length and shank designs. These couplers fall into various categories which can be installed on all the popular makes of rolling stock, whether in RTR or Kit form.

At the same time Kadee offers conversion kits for modelers whose Kadee couplers do not include delayed-action uncoupling. The uncoupling itself is accomplished by means of magnetic force rather than physical means. Two basic types of uncoupling devices in the form of bar magnets are available, one operating on the permanent magnet principle, the other electromagnetically. The latter, of course, is more preferable, since by means of a pushbutton you can energize the uncoupling magnet only when you want to. Therefore, any two coupled cars which happen to be situated directly over the electromagnetic uncoupler will not uncouple unless you press the electromagnetic uncoupler button. Conversely speaking, where the use of the permanent-magnet uncoupler is concerned, uncoupling will take place automatically in couplers that are at rest above the magnet. Therefore, when you roll out of the area you are likely to leave a few cars behind unintentionally. Of course, to prevent this, you simply back into the stranded cars and hook up again; however, uncoupling by means of the electromagnetic principle is the better of the two. Of course, no uncoupling takes place when the cars are rolling through regardless of what type of uncoupling device you use. The only other difference between the permanent magnet and the electromagnetic uncouplers is the price, the latter being slightly higher in cost. The choice is, therefore, left to your own area of economics and preference in operating techniques. So much for uncouplers for the moment. We will talk about them a bit more when we get to operation.

Another great stride and a boon to modelers has been the introduction of the RP25 wheels, which more and more are replacing those previously used. In fact, the RP25 wheels have become so popular that not only are they being included in car kits, but are used on RTR rolling stock in train sets or cars sold separately. Once again, we can thank the NMRA for their efforts in helping bring about the introduction and application of the RP25 wheel contour and design.

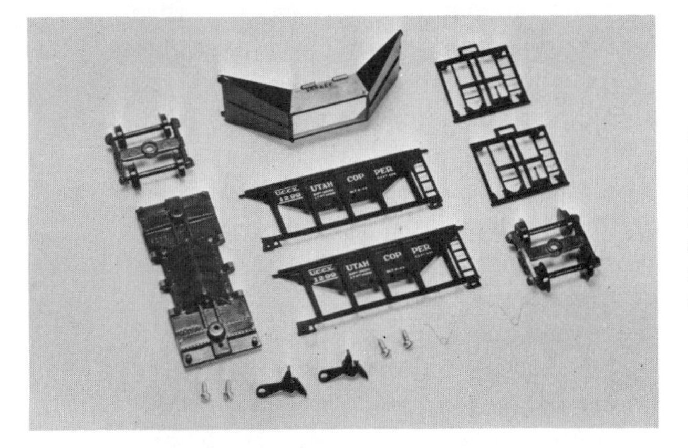

Ore car kit by Varney is a perfect example of economy without sacrifice in detail. Prototype in every way, the interlocking styrene parts go together with speed and ease, and minutes later are completely built-up and RTR. One of the least complex of today's kits, it enables the model rail to assemble and operate a long string of ore cars quickly and at a nominal cost.

These ore cars are RTR from Varney. Also available from Model Die Casting in partially assembled form, and in the lettering and colors of other railroads.

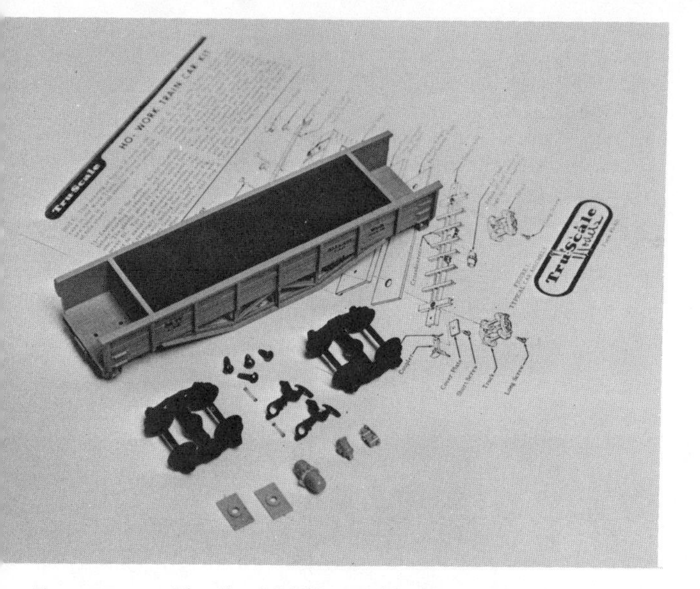

Easy-to-assemble, "quickie"-type kit from Tru -Scale is part of their work train series and almost goes together with a shake of the box.

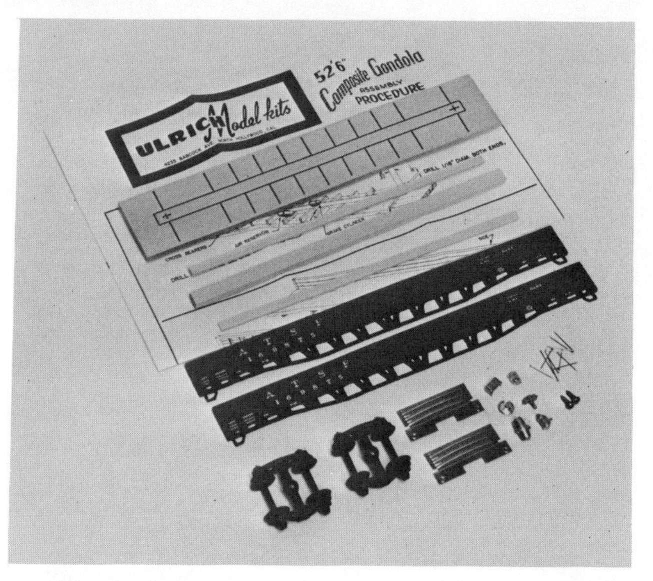

Wood-and-metal kit by Ulrich is a good project for beginners.

Composite gondola from Ulrich Models is shown in built-up form.

General service gondola is an all-metal Ulrich kit featuring eight operating doors. Photographs show open and closed positions.

Cattle car, also known as a stock car, features wood body and metal bracing, and is typical of prototype design offered in kits by Ulrich.

Off-set side-tripple hopper car by Ulrich. Kit includes factory assembled doors and linkage with door-trip mechanism for automatic and remote control dumping of coal or other loads.

Off-set side twin hopper car by Ulrich has all the rivet, angle and bracing detail of the prototype. All-metal construction includes operating doors (shown in open position). In kit form, with choice of peaked or flat ends.

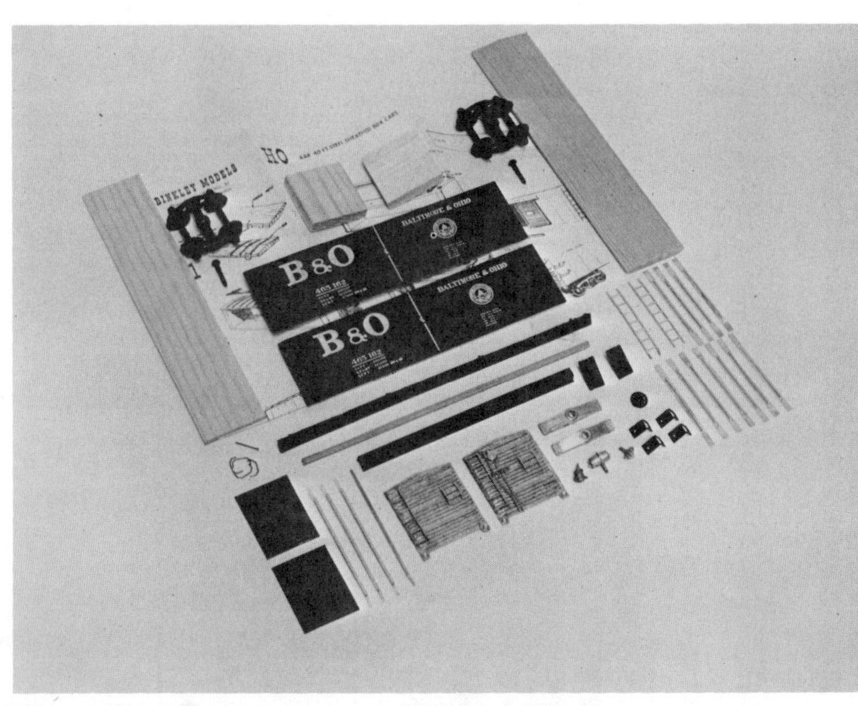

Pre-painted wooden sides, and die-cast metal parts and detailing of this 40-foot Binkley box car kit can be assembled in an evening.

Early and late model reefers of all-wood construction feature unusual lettering and prototype design typical of the Binkley kits.

For the past few decades a wheel standardized through the research and design of the NMRA and designated as the S4 has been in common use. However, the NMRA has not been content to sit back on its laurels, but rather has been hard at work down through the years in designing an improved wheel contour that offers not only more scale and prototypical appearance, but other features as well, which we shall cover in greater detail in a few moments. To also give credit where it is due, Harry Weiss of Cliff Line devoted considerable time, effort, and expense by becoming the first to present the RP25 wheels on a commercial basis. And at the moment of this writing, Cliff Line can boast the only conformance warrant issued by the NMRA on RP25 wheels. I should also point out that Cliff Line's RP25's are well within the allowable tolerances required by the NMRA.

The distinguishing differences between the old S4 and the new RP25 wheels are rather formidable, so let's review them. First, the deeper or longer flanges of S4 wheels project further ahead. Therefore, they are more subject to derailments from obstructions such as loose spikes, misaligned rail joints, turnout points, and ballast that has somehow worked its way close to the railhead surface. Because of the reduced flange design of the RP25, such derailments are greatly minimized. The reduced flange design also makes the RP25 wheels more compatible with Code 70 rail, whose rail height is closer to the ties than the commonly used Code 100 rail. And since the railhead surface of Code 70 is closer to spikes, ties, and ballast, the fact that RP25 wheels can clear these possible obstructions have endeared them to many do-it-yourself track layers, especially those using Code 70. In addition, there is no sharp intersection between the face of the flange and the wheel tread or tire surface, which in effect provides less friction due to a smaller point of surface contact between wheel and rail. This results in smoother rolling quality and reduction of dirt accumulation on the wheels, which in turn keeps wheel cleaning at a minimum.

Reduced friction also lessens binding on curves, where there is always the possibility of derailments. These all add up to obvious advantages where smoother operation is concerned, for reports have come in from the most reliable sources that following the installation of RP25 wheels it has been determined that a given locomotive can now haul at least double the length of cars it could previously handle—a conservative estimate, since there have also been reports that hauling capacities have been increased up to 75 per cent. This in itself would help minimize the need for increasing the tractive powers of locomotives by means of "weighting." Depending on the type of couplers you use, the uncoupling and dropping of cars at points distant from uncoupling ramps become a smoother operation due to the reduced friction involved in the rolling qualities of the RP25 wheels. And since less resistance is encountered during such an operation, the likelihood of accidentally recoupling is practically eliminated—an important fact to consider if your operations include lots of switching, making up of trains, and dropping off of cars at various points within your layout.

Summing up the basic features of the RP25 wheels, we have:

1. Improved scale and prototype appearance.
2. Substantial reduction of friction, permitting smoother and faster rolling quality.
3. Derailment possibility greatly minimized.
4. Less accumulation of dirt at flange and tire surface contact on the rails, thus less maintenance required in cleaning of wheel tread and flange surface.

These are just some of the points worthy of consideration concerning RP25 wheels,

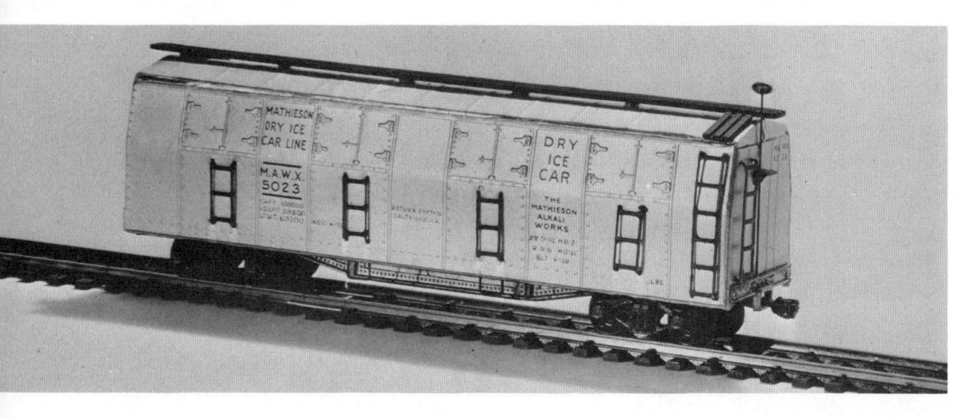

Dry ice car with pre-aluminized wooden body shows wealth of riveting and other detailing in this unusual kit offered by Binkley.

Available from Model Die Casting in kit form, this sand and gravel hopper is all metal and features tripping levers to dump the load.

A 200-ton flat car by Model Die Casting. Of all-metal construction, it can carry quite a load. Note the dual trucks.

and for those of you who seek additional information, the January 1962 issue of *Model Railroader* covers the subject in great detail.

Changeover from the use of existing equipment to that of the RP25 low-flange wheels is a simple chore, indeed. You can purchase a pair of trucks with the wheels already installed, or you can keep your trucks and merely install a wheel replacement set. In either event, you will be doing yourself a big favor and you will be keeping in step with what other model rails are doing. Of one thing you can be sure: many maintenance problems will be lessened and your operation will improve considerably. One final word concerning the RP25's. The improved performance does not become readily apparent until they have been mounted on your rolling stock, after which they will perform in the manner I have described. In other words, placing a truck featuring RP25 wheels on the track and rolling it about, or testing its rolling qualities on an inclined section of track or a grade, is not the same as the way they will perform once they are carrying the weight of a box car, reefer, or other form of rolling stock.

Another manufacturer—a pioneer, to put it mildly, and well-known in model railroading circles—is Central Valley, whose car trucks and wheels are among the most widely used, particularly where kit assembly, changeover, or replacement is concerned. In the case of any improvement in design or the performance of a given item, there is always bound to be additional improvement. This progress not only reflects the desire of some hobby manufacturers to improve their product, but also benefits the consumer. For this reason Central Valley offers their version of an improved low drag-free rolling wheel which they call the CV-3, and which they feel accomplishes as much or more than that of the RP25. Their wheels are available in a variety of truck frames which include passenger, oldtime freight, and modern freight design. Since Central Valley trucks have enjoyed such great popularity and use among many model rails, including the most discriminating, any claims they make can be taken as the gospel truth, and follow the conformance requirements of the NMRA.

Throughout the pages of this chapter you will find many glittering examples of rolling stock in various categories, shapes, and forms —not to mention function, which obviously determines the use to which certain types of cars are employed in operation. The cars and equipment shown are available RTR, in kit form, of freelance design, or can be scratchbuilt, depending on the preference of the modeler. While the equipment speaks for itself, the following is intended only to acquaint you with some of the facts which have made it possible for such an array of equipment to be available to the hobbyist.

The neophyte modeler, and not a few veterans, often take for granted the amount of detailing the manufacturer or producer of model railroading equipment includes, and yet a good amount of research and study is involved even before plans for a particular kit hits the drawing board. For example, many modelers have complained about shrinkage of parts over a period of time, where their box car or pullman seems to be coming apart at the seams, glued ends don't hold and a hearty sneeze might send the sides flying in opposite directions. This is often the case in passenger car kits featuring separate coved ends and clerestory roofs. There have been notable improvements by using various woods whose characteristic grains compensate for longitudinal and latitudinal shrinkage and/or expansion in relation to size of pieces, so that the final fit, after cementing, will always remain constant. This is another example of the detailing in research that often goes into the creating and manufacturing of kits today, and is applied by the companies making many of your favorite lines of hobby merchandise, the Binkley kit being a good illustration, samples of which you will see in both these pages and under the oldtimer heading.

Nor are such companies as Uhlrich, Central Valley, Tru-Scale, Model Die-casting, and Tyco second to any when it comes to manufacturing and placing quality equipment within the reach of the hobbyist.

With the application of plastics on the model railroading scene, many voices have been raised decrying its use, in kit or any other form, and complaints range from A to Z. Among the various gripes heard since such companies as Revell and Athearn first offered plastic models are the cries concerning a so-called lack of detail. Actually, this is not the case, for in the tooling and making of dies for plastic reproduction, skilled artists and engravers have been able to inject the minutest details, thus capturing a truly prototypical flavor in the finished product. A classic example of this is some of the equipment offered by Revell in which a well-aged appearance has been introduced by having a broken rung on a ladder, the door of a bunk car askew, scribbling on the side of a box car, and other details which create the illusion that the piece of equipment has seen a lot of service. The grooves and rivet detail of many an Athearn caboose are as detailed as one could hope for, and the string of work trains in plastic by

Central Valley Model Works offers this side-door caboose in kit form. It is loaded with fine details. You can't rush assembly on this wood-and-metal job, but the time and efforts are well spent when a result such as this is in the offing.

The same basic kit, this side-door caboose from Central Valley has been free-lanced and painted in fine weathered tone by George Hook. Among other things, note the Fox trucks—sprung, of course.

Another side-door caboose kit from Central Valley, this features variations in placement of details and windows.

Tru-Scale are loaded with extras. No detail in plastic? Nonsense. Look at Tru-Scale's Blacksmith Car; it, too, is loaded with extras and looks as weather-beaten as a yard hog that hasn't seen the inside of a roundhouse since the day it was built. There is no denying that plastic cars are easy on the scales and, as a result, might jump the rails more readily than metal cars, but they are easily weighted down.

True, the question of "weighting" rolling stock is almost as controversial a subject as that of couplers, and the pros and cons are evenly divided. For some modelers feel that adding weight to cars increases the drag and drawbar pull of locomotives, which in turn reduces the amount of cars that can be hauled at a given time, while other modelers feel that an added and even distribution of weight will make for smoother rolling and less derailments. In either event, the arguments are many and the choice is best left with each individual who knows better than anyone else the exact condition of his trackwork, the smoothness of the flangeways of his turnouts, and the ease and safety with which his equipment can navigate and negotiate the curves of his own layout. Nevertheless there is a tendency among certain plastic cars of the RTR or kit variety to be a bit on the light side, i.e., lighter than they should be under normal operating procedures. Therefore, for the benefit of those of you who may be in doubt, the following is a paraphrased excerpt from an NMRA Recommended Practices Data Sheet:

Carefully documented tests show a decided advantage past obstructions in the track for cars "weighted" to an optimum weight. Since the radial forces tending to cause derailments are greater in longer cars, this optimum weight will vary with the particular car length.

While cars of less than optimum weight will often perform satisfactorily on good trackwork, increasing weight to the optimum will improve the safety factor where operation on rougher trackwork is concerned. Mixing lightweight cars into a train of heavier cars is not recommended because of the possibility that the lighter weight cars may be pulled off the track in sharp curves.

Weight in excess of the optimum seldom adds to the ability of a car to roll down a given grade since the additional weight is almost exactly balanced by the increased friction of the axles in their journals. Extra weight simply adds to the drag of a train and in turn adds more weight to be lifted to the summit of a grade.

Cars should be constructed to keep the lowest possible center of gravity. Supplementary weight added to bring the car to optimum weight should also be kept as low as possible. (Place added weights directly over kingpins.)

These ventilated box cars from Central Valley are quite prototype in design and detailing, the latter in direct respect and reference to each particular road represented.

To find the "optimum weight" of a given car, check the table below, which lists the "initial weight" for HO. Then multiply the "additional weight" by the number of actual inches in the length of the particular car body. Add this to the "initial weight," and you will arrive at the "optimum weight" for the car.

Scale	Initial Weight	plus	Additional Weight per Inch of Car Body Length
HO	1 ounce	plus	½ ounce

This simple formula is easy to apply. For example: A box car 5 inches long would have a basic optimum weight of 3½ ounces, and so on. Note: Many factors besides car weight will affect car performance; therefore, how the foregoing applies to you will depend on how your equipment responds to your handling and operation. Thus "to weight or not to weight" is something you will have to play by ear as you go along.

As for the shiny or unmistakable look characteristic of plastic, that can be easily remedied with paints, talcum powder, and other techniques described in Chapter XI. Flash, what little there is, can be removed with a flick of a knife, or fingernail, for that matter, and the ease with which most plastic kits go together and the amount of time saved in so doing can be devoted to doing a first-class

This box car is typical of the good looks available from the wood-and-metal kits which Central Valley offers.

The same Central Valley box car now shows the ravages of time and service. It also shows what a fine aging and weathering job William Jurdan has done.

The same basic box car kit with some free-lancing and changes in detailing by George Hook. George pulled some Fox trucks out of the bin at Central Valley Models, no extra charge, though; he owns the place.

Another box car kit from Central Valley, this contains a wealth of lettering often typical of the advertising found on privately owned cars.

The same basic box car has been free-lanced during assembly by Jerry Kastka. Note the addition of the Fox trucks.

These assembled refrigerator cars show the variations obtainable in different reefer kits offered by Central Valley. They also show the different markings and detail placement of the roads they represent.

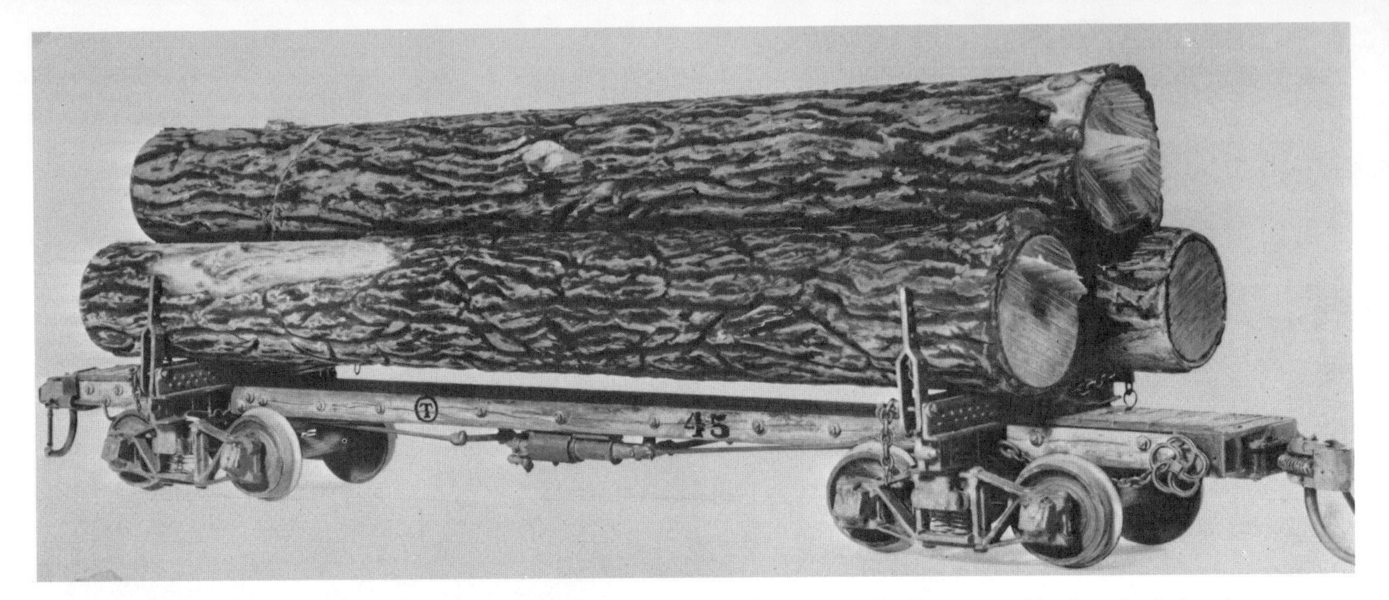

This 42-foot skeleton log flat car by Kadee has over one hundred pieces of detail to assemble, but don't let that worry you, for everything is pre-cut, pre-formed, pre-drilled, etc. The end result is an exquisitely detailed model worthy of operation in timberline areas. The logs are included, too.

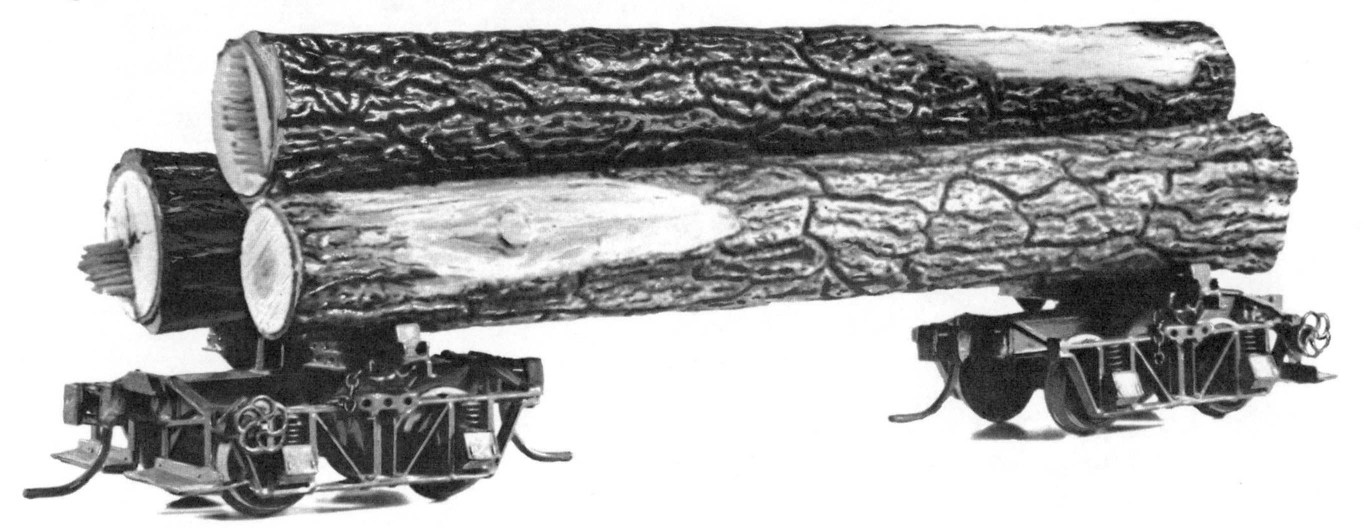

Kadee's disconnected logging car provides an end result which is bound to whet your appetite, especially if your operations involve sawmills, logging industries, etc. The curious thing about this piece of rolling stock is the fact that in essence it consists of two oldtime disconnected logging trucks. When carrying a load such as the logs, which are supplied with the kit, the trucks are kept apart; otherwise, they are coupled together, presenting an unusual, yet interesting sight.

This industrial caboose available from Kadee Quality Products is loaded with detail, and when assembled will take easily to weathering and aging, as this photograph shows. Looking like something out of "Chic Sales," a bobber caboose such as this will look great on the tail end of a line of logging cars and will also look quite at home on short line industrial and mining roads.

weathering job. Most model rails using plastic equipment do so because of speed of assembly and economy, both of which are important factors to consider when one is primarily concerned with operation, or removing the stigma of low inventory in the freight yard or other areas of his pike. A look at the layout of many veteran rail fans today will not only disclose rolling stock whose purchase and type of material dates back many years, but will include many forms of equipment in plastic as well. This is the type of enthusiast who takes the broad approach to things, which only bears out the point that in model railroading it helps if you have an open mind. Things can go from one extreme to the other in plastic. This is especially noticeable when everything seems to have come from the same mold; in other words, ladders, brake wheels, and other detailing are merely ridges, circles, or slightly raised surfaces which have no separate or added-on quality or dimension. As far as the pros and cons are concerned, I would say they were pretty much evenly divided, some swear at it while others swear by it.

Summing up the cause for plastic, I have tried to be objective about it and the best argument one can offer is the detail with which most of its products are endowed. Nevertheless, in the final analysis the choice is still left entirely up to you.

One of the most exciting things about rolling stock is the fact that, from an "imagineering" standpoint, this equipment can be put to considerable use, either legitimate or created. For example, a flat car can be changed to a wheel car simply by adding wheel and axle units to the deck, properly lashed down or held in place. A tool shed can be added and, for that matter, sides would convert it to a gondola type. The possibilities are enormous and are but a part of the fun in model railroading. As I have said before, the caboose is one of the most popular cars in railroad use. The dictionary refers to it as a

Here's as neat and compact a carrying case as you will ever see. Credit Eric Bracher for the carpentry, not to mention the nifty rolling stock which were not built by the shake of a box. Cases such as this one are available commercially; however, an evening of sawing, dadoing, gluing and what have you will result in this fine case. You can even hang it from a wall to serve as a showcase and storage area. Sections of track or grooves in the shelves will keep the cars in line, while rubber bands will hold them in place. An item such as this comes in mighty handy, particularly when you visit a fellow model rail.

"There's a prototype for everything"—this expression may be an old saw and it is often used to cover a multitude of sins; however it is not without basis. I happened to be wandering in and about a freight yard one day when, lo and behold, along rolled some trailers riding piggy-back. I did a double take, but didn't fail to take one with my camera, too. I won't explain it, for you can see for yourself. I can only figure that during a repainting of the door a few things were overlooked. See it?

"trainmen's rest car on a flat train, usually at the end," and it is also said to have received its name from the nautical terms for a ship's galley. Also referred to as a "crummy," it is one of the most colorful cars on the railroad and has had an interesting development.

Freight train crews were enjoying the privacy of cabooses long before the Civil War period in railroading, and most early cabooses, called "bobbers," were little four-wheeled affairs lacking the familiar "cupola" (dog house), which was not incorporated into the design until after the war. Among the new developments enjoyed by the railroads during and after the Civil War period was the addition of the cupola to the overall design of the caboose. While making a run on the Chicago and Northwest Freight Line, Tom Watson, the conductor, was forced to suffer the indignity of a hole in the roof of his rolling office (the result of an accident). Out of curiosity, Watson poked his head through the gaping opening to better survey the damage and was so impressed with the overall view of the train afforded him by this vantage point that he wasted no time in rigging up a chair arrangement, permitting him to sit with his head and shoulders above the level of the roof, albeit a tight squeeze. By the end of the run, however, Watson was so covered with soot and windburned of skin that he prevailed upon the maintenance department to not only enlarge the opening but to place a glass enclosure over it as well. This new "vista dome" look was soon adopted by most railroads, and has continued in use up to the present time. Cabooses featuring bay windows was another development, permitting the conductor to view the entire train's side length.

These are but a few of the changes that took place during the development of rolling stock, changes that were for the better and which reflect in part the enormous amount of progress that has taken place not only where rolling stock is concerned, but in many other areas of railroading as well. It is no wonder that we are inevitably inclined to fall back on the old bromide "what was good for the prototype is good for the modeler." Or to put it another way, we follow the prototypical scheme of things because we wish to be as authentic as possible.

Now, all this repeated talk of prototype appearance, improved performance, keeping maintenance at a minimum, and other factors involved along these lines may at times appear redundant, yet it serves the purpose of gearing you toward that time in the future when your layout has grown in size, your roster of locomotives and inventory of rolling stock has greatly increased, and you have begun to settle down to the point where you can devote most of your time to operating good-looking equipment. These are the times, especially when visitors are present, when the many applications we have talked about will pay off. I won't guarantee that your operation will go without a hitch or two, but the chances are good that you won't have to pound the track to assist a stalled locomotive, realign a derailed car, or zig when you should have zagged through a turnout. You will beam with justifiable pride and your visitor will beam with admiration.

XIII
The Forward Look-Diesels

From the standpoint of appearances, if you compare the first diesel used by an American railroad to that of today's present shape and form, the predecessor would look like a stubby, armor-plated trolley. The granddaddy of all diesels and the first one ever put into commercial use was the famous "Old 1,000" of the Central Railroad of New Jersey. Built in 1925 by the American Locomotive Company, with its box-shaped cab and paired four-wheel swivel trucks it was similar in appearance to the box cab electric locomotives called "Juice Jacks" used on the Butte, Anaconda, and Pacific runs, with the exception of the "pantagraph" used by the Juice Jacks. Primarily built for switching chores, this pioneer diesel locomotive was so successful and efficient that its power principle and potential was responsible for eventually pushing the mighty steam engine off its pinnacle as king of the rails. In general, acceptance for use other than freight yard and switching duties was slow, and railroads continued to rely on powerful and fast-running steam locomotives for mainline runs and other road service as well. In the latter respect, however, diesel designers and engineers could see into a future era in railroading power, when electrified locomotion would not only pull mile-long consists of freight and passenger equipment from coast to coast, but would span the globe as well. While the forerunners of today's diesels were too big and heavy in proportion to the power they developed, within no more than a decade the diesel emerged as the new power for locomotion.

The mid-1930s heralded the advent of two important factors in contemporary railroading: a powerful high-developing speed, lightweight diesel engine housed under a new streamlined look, both of which created a revolution in railroading the world over and led to the more refined developments of rail dieselization and appearance as we know them today. Oddly enough, the granddaddy of them all, "Old 1,000," is reportedly still in use after more than three decades of reliable service. Acceptance and widespread use of dieselization in American railroading, while not nearly as old as its big brother, the steam locomotive, nevertheless suffered a long upward climb before assuming the status it enjoys today. The first successful diesel engine (a single-cylinder 25-horsepower unit) completed in 1897 and attracting world wide attention, was the

To get the real impact of this HO scale SW-7 diesel switcher, it was placed on a rail running parallel with the Union Pacific prototype in the background. Wide-angle lens on a 35-mm. camera permitted the depth control necessary to keep the Revell model and the U.P. prototype in focus in this unretouched photograph.

The granddaddy of them all is the Jersey Central "Old 1000," the first diesel to run the rails. The Aristo-Craft model shown is a faithful miniature of its prototype and, in addition to other detailing, has working headlights fore and aft.

Far ahead of its time, this McKeen motor car is an authentic duplicate of the original which proved to be the forerunner of the gas electric diesels. One of the earliest known streamlined designs, will look great on a "turn of the century" pike and is available in both HO and O scales.

"train-child" of Dr. Rudolph Diesel, a mechanical engineer born in France of German parentage. American rights to the diesel engine were purchased by Adolphus Busch of St. Louis in 1898, and the first diesel engine built in this country was completed as far back as September of that same year. The foregoing is simply to illustrate that while dieselization in American railroading did not start to take on any formidable status until the mid-1930s, its origin and development nevertheless made an auspicious start before the turn of the century. During the years to come, in which the diesel would replace the steam locomotive as the main source of railroad motive power, many forms of energy were adapted to diesel use, including electricity, gas turbines, and oil burning.

Far ahead of its time, in the 1907-1908 period, the McKeen Motor Car was built and put into use. Revolutionary in design, the McKeen had a teardrop shape embodying the air-flow principle, and its very streamlining was the forerunner of design of diesels and passenger equipment to follow. Featuring a 100-horsepower Riotti vertical gasoline engine with mechanical transmission, it paved the way for gas electric diesels in later years. The McKeen Car featured acetylene lights and a heating system supplied by hot water from the engine's cooling system. Despite the fact that only a limited number of McKeen Cars was built, they saw substantial service, including operation and use on the Virginia-Truckee Railroad tri-weekly until it was closed down in 1950.

The development of the electric transmission finally spelled doom for the McKeen Car, but it serves to illustrate that McKeen, like many others, was instrumental in advancing railroading technique and equipment. Were it not for inventive principles, design, industrial might, and American know-how, the railroads today might still be smoke-belching, eye-cindering forms of locomotion which, while no doubt delighting steam fans the world over, would nonetheless not be in keeping with progress.

Within the accompanying pages you will find photographs of both "Old 1,000" and the McKeen Car, which are well-detailed, authentic scale versions of the prototype. Like many others, "Old 1,000" and the McKeen Car take their place in the annals of railroading history, and for the model rails whose pikes embrace the atmosphere of particular eras, especially in and around the turn of the century, or the Roaring Twenties, as it were, the addition of both of these particular models will do much to add an atmosphere of authenticity to their layout. One of the pleasures involved in model railroading comes from the warm comments made by visitors who, upon seeing your layout for the first time, will remark about the realistic appearance and effect you have created, and while they may not know a diesel from a hole in the ground, the fact that one of your visitors might recognize the McKeen Car or "Old 1,000" from a nostalgic standpoint will add to his admiration for your layout. In other words, the average visitor, unless he is blind and insensitive to any creation in miniature that has dimension and lifelike appearance, which the average well-scenicked pike offers to the viewer, is that much more enamored of what you have accomplished. Notwithstanding the fact he may know nothing about types of locomotives, diesels, interurbans, or what have you, he is quick to recognize an unusual and off-beat item in railroading such as the McKeen Car or "Old 1,000" as it whirls hither and yon throughout your layout. The possessors of such models of early motive power can feel proud in the knowledge that the equipment running on their pike is not only an authentic miniature, but has historic railroad value as well.

During the period of time when diesels began to rear their streamlined heads, steam locomotive builders made efforts in design to streamline the appearance of the "iron horses," such as the New York City "Niagara," and the Southern Pacific "Daylight" (of which some sixty modern locomotives were built by Lima). One of the most oustanding examples

The famous Milwaukee "Hiawatha" is shown again here to illustrate the streamlining that steam locomotives were given. The "diesel design" shroud was placed over the chassis of a 4-4-2 Atlantic and became a popular sight up and down the line.

The famous Southern Pacific "Daylight" was actually a 4-8-4 Northern type and is often referred to as the most beautiful of the streamlined steam locomotives. Striking and colorful superstructures such as those the "Daylight" and "Hiawatha" boasted became evident in the early 1930s.

The first streamlined diesel put into service on U.S. roads was the F-3. This scale model of the prototype was the first diesel kit (Varney) offered to the delight of HO diesel fans in 1950. Now RTR.

F-7 road diesel by Revell features working headlights and marker lights, and is a well-detailed version of the prototype. Designed for mainline passenger runs, it can be used for freight service as well. Made RTR of high impact styrene.

This RF-16 diesel by Tyco is a smooth-running and husky locomotive, and can handle a long consist of cars. All metal, it is a fine replica of the "Pennsy" prototype. RTR.

GP-9 road switcher by Athearn is a dual-purpose loco for switching and road work, and can sometimes be found hauling passenger cars. Kit available for superdetailing includes hand rails and stanchions. RTR.

Revell's SW-7 diesel switcher can handle heavy freight hauls and also negotiate narrow-radius trackage in yards for countless switching chores. RTR.

Athearn's "Hustler," an industrial switcher, can scoot through the most minimum-radius trackage. Perfect for yard chores. RTR.

Another HO model is this four-wheel diesel switcher from Aristo-Craft. It has surprising pulling power and can poke its way into those narrow industrial spurs. RTR.

The famous F-7 EMD diesel is offered with A and B units by Athearn. RTR.

Rail diesel car (RDC-3) by Athearn is a self-propelled unit used for short hauls while also serving as a combo mail and express passenger car. RTR.

RDC-1 is also a rail diesel car. However, this one is unpowered and for passenger use only. Is a perfect mate for the RDC-3 and is offered by Athearn. RTR.

of streamlining in steam is the 4-4-2 streamlined steam locomotive called the famous Class A "Hiawatha" of the Milwaukee Road. This sleek-looking locomotive emerged on May 29, 1935, as the most famous of a long line of Hiawathas which were to follow her after she made her first speedy run from Chicago to the Twin Cities. The October 1957 issue of *Railroad Model Craftsman* contains the plans for the "Hiawatha" Class A Atlantic 4-4-2 in HO. *The Steam Locomotive Plan Annual and Album,* by Harold Carstens, editor of *Railroad Model Craftsman,* in addition to devoting page after page of plans in HO and other gauges of locomotive equipment, also includes additional information and plans to scale of the famous Class A "Hiawatha." A faithful reproduction in HO scale offered by Aristo-Craft is shown within these pages, and while this section is devoted to that of diesels, for comparison's sake and historic value in connection with steam versus diesel, we include a photograph of the "Hiawatha." This is one of the few streamlined or diesel-appearing steam locomotives, which gives you a chance to have your cake and eat it at the same time. In other words, it appears to be of diesel design, yet affords the pleasure of valve gear motion from a viewing standpoint.

Most diesels have a sameness in superstructure, design, and outline though different roads vary their color schemes. Wheel ar-

GP-20 is a well-detailed Tenshodo model of the prototype, which featured a 2000-hp diesel engine, and is available RTR or in unpainted kit form.

SD-24 is another well-detailed Tenshodo model of the prototype, which was powered by a 2400-hp diesel engine. Available as an unpainted kit or RTR, and painted with the markings and coloring of various roads.

Tyco's streamlined lighted coach is RTR with a choice of roads and colors.

Tyco's streamlined lighted combine is also RTR.

Tyco's streamlined lighted observation car is RTR and, like all of the passenger equipment in this line, comes equipped with working interior lighting and choice of roads and coloring.

Coach car from Athearn is RTR and available in various roads.

Baggage car from Athearn is RTR and offered in a choice of roads.

rangements are not nearly as numerous as on steam types, and for all practical purposes the use of diesels in the model railroading scheme of things is confined to pikes whose atmosphere or era go back no further than the 1930s; therefore, if the layout bears all the earmarks of being around the turn of the century, or back to Civil War time, diesels would definitely be out of place. Of course, there are areas within the United States, or for that matter anywhere in the world, where progress, new lines of communication, and transportation have not affected the appearance of the geography, terrain, or structures. Mining and lumber camps from Maine to Oregon may look no different today than they did in the 1880s, and while it might be both uncommon and unusual to find sleek, mammoth diesels traversing such an area, the use of diesel switchers could be construed as in their proper environment from the standpoint of operation today. By the same token, areas in the Midwest and Far West, where buffalo once roamed the ground, now feel the presence of roaring diesels as they roll the rails from one coast to the other. Therefore, the operation of diesel equipment of either the passenger or freight variety is as justified running through remote and provincial areas as it is the contrasting suburban areas that dot our nation today.

The only giveaway, if one is to be concerned about criticism from the standpoint of era and equipment used, would be the vintage of accessories, such as figures and automobiles, which are included in the overall scheme. For example, an area, or, for that matter, a whole pike, which is typical of the way of life and architecture before the turn of the century, can be brought up to date by the use of figures and other equipment whose features are more contemporary in design. So, while the local station might be no different than it was fifty years before (after all, it still serves the same purpose), you could up-date things a bit by

Vista-dome car from Athearn is RTR with choice of road names.

Observation car from Athearn is RTR with choice of road names.

"Sanding her up"—a rig such as this in a maintenance yard area will do much to dress things up if you are a diesel fan.

Modern car-wash techniques are nothing new to diesels, as this photograph shows. A few figures and some simple scratch-building, and you can create your own diesel wash area similar to the one used by Union Pacific.

using figures in modern dress, and removing those miniature Tin Lizzies in the parking lot and replacing them with some miniature compact cars.

Diesels are quite husky, and will stand up under considerable operation and handling. Picking them up is not as gingerly an affair as with steam locomotives, since there is considerably less detailing to be damaged or knocked off the superstructure. When the diesels dethroned the steam locomotive in assuming the power behind, or rather in front of, passenger operation, the steam locomotive handled many of the long-haul freight chores. Thus, a pike can contain the operations of both steam- and diesel-motive equipment, and thereby add a variety of operation and switching, as a steam locomotive hauling a line of freight turns out at a siding to permit a passenger-bearing diesel to highball on through. The contrast alone is sufficient to create an exciting picture in both operation, contrasting performance, and realism. Diesels are here to stay, and while many a brass hat avoids them like the plague, they nevertheless have a magnificence all their own.

XIV
Horse Cars to Interurbans

When a fellow gets the model railroading "bug," he is embarking on a train ride which to all intents and purposes offers him a pastime of many pleasure-filled hours, weeks, and years. Once he gets the "bug" he is off and running, devouring every bit of literature he can get on the subject. Buying or building up locomotives, rolling stock, structures, planning and constructing a well-scenicked layout, are all part and parcel of becoming a dyed-in-the-wool model rail. He shares many things in common with other fans: raiding the jewelry box for that odd earring which will serve as a clamp when gluing small items together; accumulating various size tin cans and tubes which at some later date will by some magical fashion become storage tanks, gas tanks, and the like; saving sawdust, not to cover the garden ground with, but rather to become the ground cover on his pike; collecting the weirdest assortment of seemingly unimportant items which would make a young schoolboy's treasure trove seem tame by comparison.

Yes, when a fellow gets the "bug," he develops many things in common with others similarly afflicted. However, there is more to the expression than sometimes meets the eye, and the "bug," like many a modern day "virus," will floor even the healthiest hobbyist. It happens to all model railroaders at one point or another, and no medicines known to man can render a quick cure. The condition is mostly mental and is commonly called "monotonitis." This is the point where equipment is left to gather dust, track isn't wiped clean of oxidation, and once-exciting railroading chores are left untended. It isn't due to lack of time, but to waning of interest.

The malady isn't serious, and in time will surely pass, but during the period of sickness and recuperation to follow, both pike and equipment are in quarantine and the modeler conspicuous by his absence from same. Boredom sets in for many reasons, usually instigated by the sameness of operation, time in and time out, in spite of the fact that there are numerous combinations of equipment and techniques involved, not only in mainline running, but switching, and making up and/or spotting of rolling stock. Simply suggesting that the model rail cover that exposed screening with some lichen isn't enough to chase the doldrums, and giving the track a thorough cleaning has suddenly become a chore. By the same token, perhaps you have become tired

One of the many brass-crafted interurbans available from E. Suydam Co. This jewel-like HO replica of a wood coach can open new vistas in model railroading scant seconds after removing the wrappings.

Two views of a 60-foot "Niles" interurban parlor-observation car from E. Suydam Co. This car was put into service by the Oregon Electric Car Co. and was designed to attract the elite traveler by virtue of its plush interiors. Note the different window and detailing from one side to the other. RTR, unpainted.

This 57-foot "Niles" wood interurban coach is amazingly detailed in brass, and is also available as a trailer coach without power and poles from Suydam. Assembled and ready for painting, this fine model can form the nucleus of your interurban motive power or rolling stock.

of looking at that same old loco, whose simple valve gear now appears unmotion-like. You could buy a conversion kit and completely change your saddle tank to an oldtimer, but you would still be running over the same old pike and, heavens to Betsy, you're not about to change the set up at this stage of the game. Okay, you have the blues; you're slightly feverish, glassy-eyed, and down in the dumps; your tender is dragging. When the ladies get to feeling that way, they buy a new hat or visit the beauty parlor. But for model rails, a new chapeau will not do the trick, and who needs a haircut anyway?

So here it is, fellows, the antibiotic sure to cure your ills and open new vistas for your railroading pleasure. It might also clinch the deal for the beginner, who still has to determine the type of equipment he wants to build or operate. So step right up, it is yours for the asking: Trolleys and Interurbans, a form of rail transportation that is almost as old as railroading itself, and certainly one that has had its share of growing pains among the millions of hobbyists down through the ages. To get a clearer insight into the modeling and operation of interurban railways, I visited with Ed Suydam, a name quite familiar to model rail fans as a manufacturer of a fine line of model railroading equipment and accessories. Ed also happens to be one of the foremost authorities on trolleys and interurbans, and was more than happy to discuss his favorite subject. The following information, excerpts of which have appeared in the NMRA *Bulletin,* plus my own comments and observations, might well start you in new directions, and if the commentary doesn't dent your sensibilities, then the gleaming brass-crafted equipment offered by E. Suydam & Co., and pictured within these pages, surely will.

In many railroad circles, the mere mention of the word "traction" is cause for raised eyebrows, yet those same fellows model diesel locos. This is what is called the fine line of distinction, for when you come right down to it, what else is a diesel but an outgrowth of the trolley car carrying its own generating plant? Generalizing can often be misleading, and to one group the word "traction" creates a picture of tiny trolley cars darting here and there with no apparent purpose. With the other extreme, however, it includes anything powered by the so-called "traction motor." Somewhere between these two is a happy medium. Few modelers would be satisfied with a single-track trolley line running a Birney or two, but this same line, added to a model pike, becomes one of those details that helps round out the overall picture. Few modelers would have the time, means, or space to model a complete interurban empire, one covering hundreds of miles and operating freight and passenger trains anywhere near the volume of many an old interurban system. For example, the Pacific Electric at its peak dispatched some 6,000 runs a day. All these modes of transit have their place in the overall transportation picture. In many cases, they were closely related to what we think of as conventional railroading. The small town with its one carline usually connected with the railroad at the depot and handled the local traffic. The larger interurban lines covered an infinite variety of purposes, from direct competition with the steam railroad to co-operation, being feeders in both passenger and freight service, and, in a number of cases, the interurban line was actually part of the railroad.

To narrow our sights, let's consider the interurban railway itself, how it came into being, and what it was like in its more active years. The best place to begin is with the old horsecars of the past century. Here we find a common ancester, for early railroads had their start with horse-drawn carriages on a crude form of track. If we picture what it must have been like without automobiles and paved roads, and with rutted and muddy cowpaths for a main street, we'll get some idea of how great an improvement it was to lay rails through the heart of town and run the

This 1370-Class P.E. interurban combine makes a compatible running mate with other HO steel coaches and was used for early morning runs, carrying sacked mail and newspapers. On the return route it would carry fresh eggs, milk, etc. It could also head a five-car boat train to the harbor. In satiny brass finish, it is RTR from Suydam.

New York Central "T"-Class electric locomotive is all-brass construction and is one of the most popular of the electric prototypes. Available from Model Engineering Works, this well-detailed RTR gem offers super-smooth running and the opportunity to have a change of pace in your regular operations.

This Butte-Anaconda-Pacific (known as a "BAP") is a box cab electric loco with smooth eight-wheel drive, an exciting brass replica of its prototype which saw considerable passenger-hauling service, though in later days has been put into freight service. RTR from Suydam, it includes working pantagraph and headlights.

This model of a Class "B" interurban electric locomotive was used on the Illinois Terminal System, and is all brass with impressed rivet detail and turned or forged brass fittings and details. It can negotiate the sharpest curves and minimum radius. Smaller than the average box motor, this husky interurban is RTR from Suydam.

Pacific Electric 55-foot wood interurban coach in powered or trailer form is perfect for branchline operation and would make a fine "commuter special." Designated as P.E. "Tens," the prototypes had unusual ventilating strips along both sides of the clerestory coved roofing which has been duplicated in this RTR model painted by Ed Suydam.

This scene on the P.E. empire of Richard Keegan of Goodland, Kansas, shows a P.E. train of steel cars taking the turnout for Pasadena at Oneonta Junction. Catenery and overhead wires supply the power in this layout.

P.E. Class "1200" steel coach, like all the Suydam brass models shown, is HO scale and contains a wealth of detailing. Can be used as a powered or trailer unit, and is a perfect match for its 57-foot prototype. RTR.

This photo shows the same coach after painting and decals have been administered by the deft hand of interurban expert Ed Suydam.

Perfect for mail runs, this all-brass box motor is a well-authenticated version of the P.E. steel railway Post Office cars offered by Suydam Co. RTR.

This exciting looking box cab electric locomotive is perfectly detailed and scaled after the prototype used on the Great Northern RR. Pantagraphs are insulated and wired to the motor, permitting "juice draw" from overhead wiring as well as from "two-rail." A husky motor is geared to power all eight drivers, which are individually sprung for maximum rail contact. Suydam offers this gem in RTR form.

This steeple cab electric from Suydam is all brass and RTR, and only needs breaking in and painting, as the finished item in the photo shows. With husky pulling power and eight-wheel drive, this beauty can easily negotiate a minimum radius down to 8 inches. This is a P.E. version of the Baldwin steeple cabs, the major differences being the shorter frame and end railings. Like all the interurban equipment shown, prototype decals are also included.

flanged-wheeled vehicles on them. The best power then was a horse or mule, despite the fact that they were a bit reluctant with their chore. In the 1880s a new power was being developed, the electric motor. It followed that some bright inventors would try to power the horsecar with this new form of energy, and the trials and tribulations in this connection are a story in itself. Nevertheless, the first successful electric street cars were four-wheeled horsecars with a huge electric motor on the front platform connected to one set of wheels by a chain drive. The brave soul who risked life and limb by running this noisy, sparking contraption stood by and controlled it with a lever, not knowing whether he would be electrocuted within a moment or so. He was known as the "motorman." Current was at first taken from two overhead wires with a four-wheeled gadget that rode on top of the wire on grooved wheels connected to the car by a cable and called a "troller." It had the mean habit of jumping off the wire and crashing down on the roof, making such a racket that passengers would take off right out the windows. Even before this, two-rail circuits were tried, just like our models, but imagine the danger to trespassers.

At any rate, the upward-sprung pole soon replaced the troller. This was called the trolley pole, from the word troller, or trolley. With all that juice bouncing about, one way or another, one might have thought it was a shocking state of affairs. However, this form of transportation managed to survive the dangers of a shock or two here and there, which was never really a serious threat to begin with. Soon, motor developments permitted the motor to be hung on an axle under the car and geared direct to the wheels. This was the first traction motor. Before long, the trolley car became a practical means of public transit, and any town worth its salt boasted a trolley line. As time went on, these lines branched out to connect neighboring towns, and transit companies began to see an opportunity in faster service between towns and cities to compete with the steam railroads. The city cars built for start-and-stop service were not particularly suited to this new concept in transportation and freight service.

It was at this point that the larger and faster interurban cars came into the picture. From here on there was a more or less definite split between the "city" and "suburban" service, and the "interurban" service, with equipment development following the requirements of each. Before long, many interurban lines were operating cars that bore little resemblance to the streetcar, other than the fact that they took their power from an overhead wire. In the city they ran on street trackage, but once out of town their character abruptly changed as the train of interurban cars took to their own private right-of-way and the motorman opened up the controller. With air horns blowing for grade crossings, the cars would accelerate up to 60 or 70 miles per hour, some even faster. Naturally, for this type of operation the tracks had to be built along conventional railroad design with wide sweeping curves, railroad-type switches, crossing and block signals, and railroad operating rules. In time, the cars were built for a wide variety of services, as well as for carrying passengers. The interurbans carried package freight, railway express, mail, newspapers, eggs, produce, etc. The Pacific Express Line in the Los Angeles area even hauled iced, fresh fish on an express basis from the harbor. This variety of service gave rise to many different types of cars that had cause to be built. In addition to the regular passenger coaches, there were combination baggage-passenger cars for baggage, called "combos," package freight and railway express, also the all-baggage (box motors) cars for all mail or all freight and express. There were many others, including diners, sleepers, and even observation cars for deluxe service or excursions. There was an extremely wide variety of line cars and maintenance equipment. Then there were the freight locomotives for regular

These photographs show some of the possibilities of interurban modeling and operation. The E. Suydam Co. offers a number of car barns and other structures to fit in with the scheme of things, plus special overhead wiring rigs and other useful accessories to round things out. You can set up a catenery system for overhead wiring or simply take the power from the rails.

freight trains, as more and more industry located in and about the interurban lines. Most electric locos were the steeple cabs, though quite a few box cabs were also used. In recent years, as interurban traffic has ceased to exist, many of the interurban lines still continue as freight railroads.

Considering this background, from the modeling standpoint, one can see that the interurbans did play a considerable part in the overall transportation picture, either in competition with, or in co-operation with the regular steam railroads. More often, it was the latter, with localized short-haul types of operation fanning out from major rail points; for example, the Pacific Electric in the Los Angeles area, which, in addition to the regular interurban commuter, also served to distribute the incoming railroad passengers to the surrounding towns. Freight was also similarly distributed. Unfortunately, there was very little standardization of body design, there was some more or less production-type cars, but more often each road developed its own particular design, and thus models will assume the identity of that particular line, which is not a far cry from regular railroading, considering the fact that each rail line distinguishes itself from the others not only in lettering and painting, but in certain rolling-stock design. An example of this is Pacific Electric, most of whose cars were strictly "PE." Others, such as the Chicago North Shore and Milwaukee, or the Illinois Terminal, also had particular characteristics. While this might be a drawback from a model manufacturing standpoint, it is an advantage to the fellow who wants something different or distinctive. Perhaps this is why there are so many scratch builders in traction modeling.

An important point to make is that, in modeling railways, some thought should be given to the part played by the interurban line and local streetcars. There are all sorts of combinations possible and the fellow whose pike consists of a streetcar line is doing what many branch line modelers do; they simply model a portion of the overall picture. Ed's personal view is that a combination of a railroad and an interurban is highly desirable; that is to say, the steam railroad handles long-haul traffic and the quick interurban handles the short-haul traffic. Here, there can be interchanging of freight, local switching to industry, main-line and branch line interurban passenger traffic (often crossing and recrossing the steam road), thus rounding out a comprehensive picture of rail transportation and one that adds much more in the way of both facility and operation.

Often the unused portions of a layout can be very nicely filled with the interurban or trolley trackage, as smaller radius curves are possible, similar to that of prototype operation and procedure. For the fellow with limited space, yet with a yen for "railroading," the interurban model pike offers him a good chance to work out his ideas in smaller space without getting that cramped or foreshortened appearance that often occurs when too much is attempted in too small an area. The interurban line had fewer and more modest facilities, and didn't require huge terminals, yards, and roundhouses, shops and pace-consuming facilities of the steam road. Thus, smaller radius curves typical of the prototype can be well applied to such limited space and at the same time obtain a great deal of operation. Short-haul passenger trains of interurban cars can operate between extreme points, with a circuitous route that was often quite typical of this type of operation, a case in point being the "Pasadena viz Oaknoll." The interurbans can run up the main street and turn in a 6- or 8-inch radius curve into a combination car barn and terminal. The freighters using the same trackage work back and forth on a "peddler" basis, and many times come right into town, down the streets, supplying industries downtown, where sidings nestle between factories and can only be reached by sharp curves from the street.

An interesting scheme for such a pike and one that could be well adapted to an around-

Where steam locomotives once ran the rails of some 170 miles of circular running track at the Kennicot Copper Mine in Bingham Canyon, Utah, electric locomotives now handle the chores. If you think that overhead wiring is too much of a chore, then just consider the maintenance required for the prototypes. For effect you can make your overhead wiring a strictly dummy affair and take your power from the rails. In either event, even a small amount of electric locomotion on your layout will add to your operating fun.

the-room or garage, L or U shape, is two towns, one at each end, connected by a rural motif in between, where some real running can be enjoyed. When one considers the diversity of services offered by the old interurbans, you begin to see just how much real operation can be worked up along this particular type of railroading, where the foreshortening necessary in modeling is much less apparent. As far as wiring is concerned, there are no problems involved, you can either take the juice from overhead lines or from the rails as in your regular line of equipment. Again, as in many other facets of model railroading, the biggest selection of equipment is obtainable in that of the HO gauge. You don't have any needs for reverse loops either, since, like many modern automobiles, the interurban or trolley will look the same going backward or forward. You can, therefore, go into the narrowest of areas without worrying about turning around to get out. You simply back out, and as far as prototype appearances are concerned, you are safe there, since that is how they operated in the old days and continue to do so today. There are occasions where turntables might be put into use; they still are in use throughout the country where this type of service is employed. And if you want to give things an oldtime touch, Cliff Line has an excellent kit in the form of a gallows turntable that would make a splendid addition to your pike and to the interurban railway line of things.

Like diesels, the trolleys and interurbans have more than their share of colorful paint schemes, and you can take many liberties in that respect. Red car line, yellow car line, blue car line—they all look attractive as they speed along the main line, dart in and out of industrial sidings, and perform their tasks in the true tradition of railroading. Not a toy or a gadget, but a most useful and operational addition to your present pike, and a wonderful way to get started in a hobby that has many facets. Try it and see, or at least explore the possibilities further by looking at some of the equipment available in your local hobby shop. You have to look at them first-hand to really appreciate them. To the modeler well ensconced in the mysteries and pleasure of model railroading this might be just what the doctor ordered to get out of a rut; to the beginner who still hasn't decided in what direction he will go, this might be the means with which to get rolling.

XV
Civil War–Old Timers–Historic Locomotives

The most colorful period in the history of American railroading, and certainly the most romantic, existed from the Civil War to the turn of the century. For during this span of years railroading was surrounded with an aura of intrigue, adventure, pioneering background, and many forms of historical accomplishment. For this reason the possession and operation of oldtimers is one of the most widely followed pursuits in model railroading, particularly in the case of models whose prototypes have historic value and have been immortalized in railroading's hall of fame.

When you stop to consider that imagination plays an important role in the art and skill of scale and prototype modeling, then you can easily understand how the ownership and operation of a particular locomotive whose prototype has a historic label attached to it takes on added significance. The same pride and affection that engineers in the past lavished on their locomotives is in no less manner reflected by today's model railroader. Putting it another way, let us assume that your railroad is other than contemporary in nature; in other words, it is not modern in scheme, but, rather, generates a rural atmosphere or era of years long gone. Your motive power includes an exact replica of one of the many famous trains that carved a niche for itself in railroad annals. Immediately, your working scale model becomes more than a wheel arrangement or type, but a locomotive with a story behind it, be it legend, fact, or otherwise—and the knowledge that it was the first engine to haul a load of freight over the Alleghenies, or established speed runs from Philadelphia to Chicago, adds much to your owning and operating pleasure, for there is a bit of the "collector" in all of us, and collecting is based not so much on value from a monetary standpoint, but value from the standpoint of background and history attached to the particular item involved.

A classic example of being both operator and collector is in the famous "999 Empire State Express," which for a number of years was referred to as the "fastest thing on wheels." Here was a steam locomotive beautiful to behold, and whose superstructure, perched atop gleaming 86-inch drivers, seemed to suggest Milady lifting her skirts to cross a rainsoaked thoroughfare. Yet, in the story behind the story, this trim, dainty-appearing locomotive captured the hearts of the entire

There is nothing more eye-arresting than the charm, gay coloring and fancy ornamentation and detailing of an oldtimer. This fascinating rendition of the "General" is the result of the artistry of Jerome C. Biederman, one of the foremost illustrators of American transportation. This completely authentic rendering reflects the glory of the famous locomotive before the ravages of the Civil War took its toll. A natural for history buffs, it should also make super-detailers sit up and drool while taking careful notice.

Another fine and exciting illustration by Jerome C. Biederman is this exact rendition of the "fastest thing on wheels"—"999," the pride of the New York Central, circa 1893. Just imagine—112.5 mph!

A new paint job, a new pilot and brake shoes and hangers are just the start of the super-detailing this dainty appearing HO model of "999" will undergo.

No doubt you have seen the widely published photograph of the famous "C. P. Huntington" alongside a giant diesel. Here it is in HO scale. The oldtimer is by M. B. Austin, the streamliner by Athearn.

The "C. P. Huntington," one of the most colorful of the oldtimers, is known as Southern Pacific's No. 1. Originally No. 3 on the Central Pacific, it was shipped round the "horn" in 1863 in life-sized kit form and, upon arriving in Sacramento a year later, was assembled and immediately put into service. Needless to say, it wasted no time carving out a name for itself in early California railroading. It is now on display at the S.P. depot in Sacramento. The HO scale model shown captures all the flavor of the prototype. This puffer-belly type measures only 4¾ inches in length, yet can haul the same complement of cars as did the live one. In addition, it will easily traverse a minimum radius curve down to 10 inches, making it exceedingly popular with history buffs who can pack a lot of railroading into old era layouts. Shown in satin brass, it is RTR and also comes painted in the true colorful S.P. tradition. Available from M. B. Austin, it would make a worthy addition to your pike.

If you are cramped for space and must resort to minimum-radius trackage, then oldtimers will not only solve your operating problems, but add considerable color as well.

The "Atlantic" (1832) was one of the earliest of the ancient steam locomotives and is shown here in re-created form during a pageant. This might give you an idea of the pomp and ceremony that accompanied the launching of the "Best Friend of Charleston."

Many a tiny, early vintage steam locomotive goes powerless because there is no room for motor installation in the boiler or even on a "tender drive" basis. This "teaspoon of power" from Kemtron can be placed in a box car to not only power dummy equipment, but tiny locos as well.

world in establishing an unprecedented speed record. Turning back the calendar for an eyewitness approach to an exciting event in railroad history, the year is 1893, the day May 10th, and "999," the pride of the New York Central and Hudson River Railroad, has just glided out of the roundhouse for a special run between Batavia and Buffalo. Up and down the line for as far as the eye can see throngs of curious spectators have gathered in and about the right of way in anxious anticipation of witnessing an astounding episode in steam locomotion. At the halfway point Engineer Charles H. Hogan has opened his throttle to the last notch and held it there, and what at first appears to be a small speck dotting the horizon along the straightaway suddenly looms up with the brute force of a cannonball, yet with the majestic grace of an Olympic runner. The people on hand crane their necks for a better look and start to murmur excitedly, and the air, though silent a moment ago to the point of becoming almost stifling, is now suddenly shattered with the roar of "999" as she comes thundering and shrieking into full view, at an incredible speed of 112.5 miles per hour, then disappears as quickly from view, as her high-stepping drivers swallow up the rails before her.

Veteran railroaders and laymen alike gasp in astonishment and near disbelief, and not a few ladies swoon, upon being eyewitness to the first man-made machine to exceed 100 miles per hour. Of such deeds are heroes made, and henceforth "999" became classified as a historic locomotive by virtue of fearlessly establishing a speed record which remained unbroken for the remainder of the decade. In addition to the historical insight into the background of this locomotive, "999" also falls into the category of an oldtimer, since she was of a vintage prior to the turn of the last century. For the model railroader whose interest lies in the direction of history-making locomotives and oldtimers, feast your eyes on the authentic miniature of "the fastest thing on wheels" within the accompanying pages.

During the growth of American railroading, many "firsts" took place with respect to accomplishment and daring exploit, and in the decade preceding the Civil War to the turn of the last century this nation's railroading gave birth to many locomotives glamourously symbolic of the speed and romance attached to the golden age of steam. Prior to the middle of the last century, most of the motive power was seemingly crude in appearance and an offshoot of irregular metamorphosis. In the years that followed, however, motive power took on a more colorful and exciting appearance, decked out and liberally garnished with piping, flagposts, ornate headlamps, and grills, and other sorts of superdetailed finery. Color schemes were both gaudy and aristocratic in nature, ranging from blues, greens, yellows, reds, and whatever suited the companies' particular tastes, and engineers administered loving care in keeping their equipment shiny and bright. Coal and wood-burning engines, which were widely used at that time, and whose diamond-shaped smokestacks belched clouds of smoke into the air above, were commonly referred to as "puffer bellies," a name that still clings.

In those good old days, rolling stock rarely exceeded 64 feet in the passenger class, and the average coach of the time measured under 50 feet in length. Flat cars and box cars ranged from 22 to 35 feet, and the locomotives, if placed side by side with later developments in motive power, would be easily dwarfed by comparison. (See the photo of the S.P. "Huntington" against the giant diesel.) Pulling power capacities of the early Moguls, Prairies, and Consols generally amounted to a fifteen- to twenty-five-train haul and that was considered quite formidable. Yet the average consist of trains embraced only five to ten pieces of rolling equipment, closely approximating what today would be considered a "bobtail" haul. The latter brings up one of the most striking characteristics and reasons behind the popularity of oldtimers among model railroaders today. In short,

The ten-wheeler, a 4-6-0 type popular in American railroading around the turn of the century, is a fine example of the brass-crafted well-detailed oldtimers available in HO today. This model is a duplicate of the Illinois Central "Cannonball" which the famous "Casey Jones" rode into song and saga on his farewell trip to the promised land. A most historic locomotive, it is available from Aristo-Craft and other sources.

Partial superdetailing of the "Casey Jones." Note changes from the basic assembly of the locomotive. Safety tread running board has been cut off before the cylinder rather than running over it. Also note the addition of lower piping from pump to smokebox, connected at both ends with a Kemtron union and elbow. Additional details such as handrails and grab irons on the cab and boiler add to the authentication along prototype lines, as do the free-lanced water and steam lines running beneath the cab. The original "Cannonball" had Fox trucks on the tender. Central Valley provided the exact type. A bit more detailing such as tender straps, painting, lettering, etc., and this loco will be an exact miniature of the immortal prototype.

The famous "General" of Civil War fame. Tyco, RTR.

The not-quite-so-famous "Texas." which chased and caught up with the "General." Aristo-Craft, RTR.

Scenes from the Walt Disney motion picture "The Great Locomotive Chase" show the "General" thundering along a trestle and the "Texas" pursuing her.

Very early movie makers also produced their version of "The Great Locomotive Chase" and, with the flair for authenticity that has made Walt Disney famous, these early movie makers tried their hand at superdetailing on a large scale. This is a 4-4-0 Cooke locomotive, circa 1886, which operated on the Corvallis and Eastern RR and was later sold to the J. H. Lumber Company. This is also how she looked before being made up to resemble the "General."

The "General" ready for the "take." Note the covering over the air brakes, the addition of spoked pilot wheels and the dome and stack changes. The camera crew worked from the bed of a flat car coupled at the rear.

where space is at a premium oldtimers will accomplish what later-developed motive power cannot. Since these pioneers of the rails were smaller than their later-developed brethren, and embraced simpler wheel arrangements, such as 4-4-0 and 4-6-0, they were able to negotiate the sharpest of curves and track routes, which in the days of laying track to fit the contour of the terrain often resembled roller coaster designs, a result of the frantic race to open new frontiers. Nor can you overlook the operating limitations of these relatively underpowered locomotives which, though pulling comparatively short lengths of trains, in many cases had to be double- or triple-headed, further adding to the pleasures of running "iron horse" miniatures.

Thus, what was good for the prototype becomes applicable to the scale operation, and, as a result, the model rail who is cramped for space can pack lots of scale railroading into a relatively small area because the models, like their life-sized counterparts, can negotiate a minimum radius of trackage. On the other hand, the chap with room to spare can go all out in producing not only a well-scenicked pike, but, through the use of oldtimers, enjoying a type of prototypical operation such as running in and about mountainsides, up and down steep grades, traversing sharp curves, and many other railroading procedures (which would be taboo from a prototypical standpoint where the more modern type of pike and equipment is concerned) thereby using many areas of the layout for actual railroading rather than effect. And to those who might scoff at the crowded conditions, all I can add is that in the earlier days of railroading these were the conditions that prevailed.

Oldtimer models have their drawbacks too, and if you like to pull a train of twenty or thirty cars (and lucky is the chap whose pike will accommodate such a haul) then you will soon find that the average model is not equal to the task and, whether you like it or not, you are almost forced to observe authentic operating procedure. First of all, as I mentioned earlier, the locomotives are smaller and, as a result, lighter. Thus, the traction is impaired. Careful weighting, however, will increase the pulling power, but it would be a good idea to use an ammeter to check the extra current draw required to pull the additional cars; it will save burning up or overheating the motor. A number of the oldtimers, such as the early 4-4-0's, in being reduced down to scale proportions required that the motor drive be mounted in the tender. Upon occasion the tender will appear to be having fits of St. Vitus dance, if not properly balanced and weighted, but as a rule the performance is more than satisfactory. Of course, the manufacturer, if he wished, could simply make the boiler oversized to accommodate the motor, and thus dispense with the tender drive application; however, it would not be scale and true to type or design. PFM, Tyco, M. B. Austin, Aristo-Craft, Akane, and others who offer a variety of oldtimers have employed this "tender drive" so as to conform to prototypical standards from the standpoint of scale.

In reviewing for the moment some of the advantages of oldtimer and historic locomotive operation, we find colorful, eye-arresting, and excitingly different superstructure outlines and designs—superdetailing possibilities galore, action-filled railroading techniques, and, last but by no means least, the historic backgrounds with which a number of these early gems were blessed.

The collectors, for example, would revel in the possession of a miniature of the "Best Friend of Charleston;" for flashing back to the latter part of 1830, an event was taking place at Charleston, South Carolina, which was to inaugurate the operation of the first pioneer railroad of the South and the first scheduled steam-passenger service to be introduced in America. This important event, a milestone in the growth of railroading in this country, was not without its mishaps, however, and as the "Best Friend of Charles-

A locomotive of the O.R. & N. RR (later the U.P.) was fixed up to represent the "Texas." This was a 4-4-0 built by Manchester in 1881. Note the typical U.P. domes. A locomotive similar to this was sent to the bottom of a creek in the film for the bridge-burning scene. (She's still there.)

Typical of Walt Disney authenticity and showmanship, the "Texas" is shown following a rebirth for a re-filming of the same story several decades later. Check your TV logs every once in a while: "The Great Locomotive Chase" is shown on the late late show.

This rare old photograph found in Santa Barbara, California, is now part of the Ward Kimball Collection and shows The "General" on exhibition shortly after the Civil War. Laden down with bunting, flags and floral wreaths, the famous locomotive stands ready to haul sight-seeing excursionists to the battle-fields. The sign in the upper left corner reads "Cheap Excursions To The Battle Fields," a somewhat dubious honor for the most heralded locomotive of all times. The "General" has been rebuilt and looks much the same today as she proudly stands in honorable retirement at the Union Station in Chattanooga, Tennessee.

This 0-6-6-0 articulated is an authentic scale model of "Old Maud," the first Mallet introduced to American railroading in 1904. Originally offered by Aristo-Craft as part of their Crown-Jewel series, you might come across one if you look hard enough. Both sets of drivers feature full working valve gear. Steam pipe in front follows motion of forward drivers, which swivel independently, adding much realism when led into curves. The prototype was originally designed for heavy freight duties; however, for greater tonnage and tractive effort the locomotives that followed were converted to 2-6-6-2 and up.

Tyco makes these 1860 coach and combine cars RTR with the markings of Western & Atlantic or Central & Pacific Railroad.

One of many operating collector's items offered by Aristo-Craft is this distinctive European-styled dining car. Particularly noteworthy is the fact that it is a miniature of the "Armistice car" which was used to sign the cessation of hostilities in 1918, and again in 1940 when France was overrun.

The ultimate in scratch-building is shown in these two photographs of Wells Fargo equipment in O scale by the president of the "Grizzly Flats" RR, Ward Kimball. Ward devoted much time and research when building these 100 per cent prototype scale models. Look at the terrific detailing, right down to the brake shoes and chain guides.

ton" courageously puffed her way through the countryside to the extreme pleasure of railroad officials and the delight of merry making passengers, fate dealt a foul blow in the shape of an inexperienced helper who had been hurriedly pressed into service as a "fireman" for the maiden journey. The greenhorn became exasperated and somewhat frightened by the hiss of steam escaping from the safety valve and unthinkingly snatched up an oil rag and held it tightly over the opening from whence the seemingly ominous sound effect was emanating. The rest, of course, is history. The boiler blew up, scattering pieces hither and yon, and the next moment the "Best Friend of Charleston" ground to an unceremonious stop. Fortunately, no one was seriously hurt, and indignant passengers, their festivities abruptly curtailed, swore at railroad officials who, in turn, did a bit of swearing in the direction of the novice "fireman."

Ordinarily, this might have had a catastrophic effect on the future of our nation's railroading, or, at the least, have been cause for considerable delay in its growth. However, undaunted by this unexpected setback, the Southern Railroad immediately ordered another locomotive from the West Point Foundry in New York, which they named the "West Point," and which proved to be a better friend to Charleston and the railroad than her late sister. On the second inaugural run, the railroad took the precaution of piling bales of cotton on a flat car between the locomotive and the passenger cars to protect the occupants in the event the boiler blew up again. However, there were no more novice firemen and no more explosions, and railroading in the South was well on its way toward the day when it would be linked to a network of railroads spanning the nation.

In the century that followed, the railroad became a giant among industries and certainly the most formidable means of transportation the world had ever seen. During this period, a score of locomotives engaged in daring test runs, established unheard-of speed records and, like "Casey Jones," were

Pennsy lo-board flat car and New York Central convertible gondola available in kit form from Binkley Models. A string of these will certainly lend an oldtime touch.

Some of the detailing in the oldtimer car kits available from Binkley: die-cast metal, pre-contoured and scribed wood, grillwork and fabricated sides, etc.

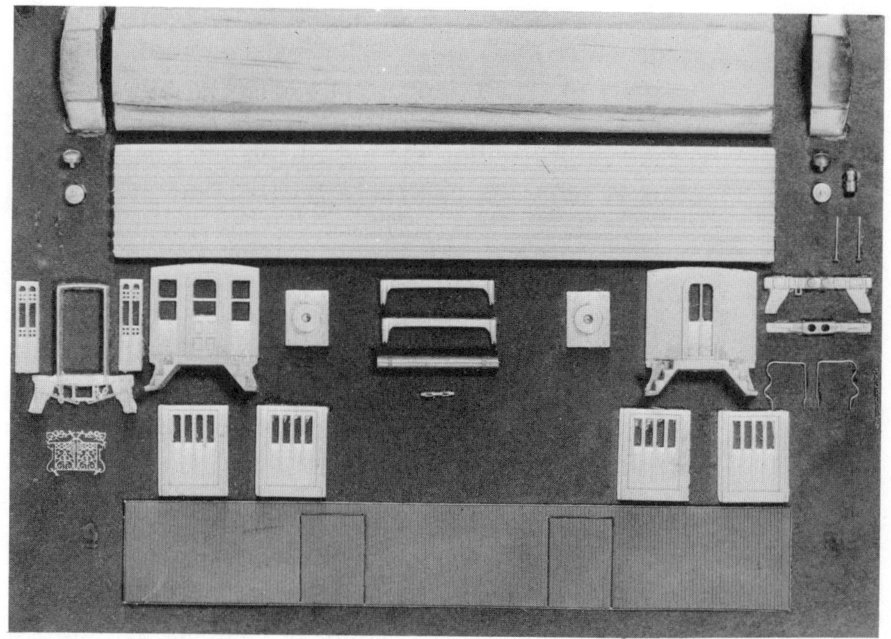

Shorty coach car kit from Binkley.

Pay car by Binkley Models is as much a part of the old West as cactus, and just as sharp.

captured in both saga and song for their many deeds and accomplishments. However, the most immortal locomotive of them all, and one that has been the subject of more stories in published form than all of the other locomotives combined, is the "General" of Civil War fame. In the last hundred years innumerable paintings, cover illustrations, and other forms of visual media have kept alive the daring exploit of a band of intrepid Union soldiers deep in the heart of Confederate territory, who, following the unique capture of the "General," proceeded to head north, laying a swath of destruction in their wake and providing the ingredients for what proved to be the greatest locomotive chase of all times. No book on railroading, model or otherwise, would be complete without even a brief insight concerning the events surrounding this famed oldtimer and her pursuer, the "Texas," for had the raiding party been successful in their mission, the Civil War might have ended some three years sooner, and the course of history might have been changed.

On the day of the raid, the Chattanooga-bound "General" was making a breakfast stop at Big Shanty, Georgia, about 27 miles north of Atlanta. As Conductor William A. Fuller and his crew sat down to eat breakfast, the raiding party, consisting of twenty-one Union soldiers led by James J. Andrews, innocently boarded the train. Their mission was to capture the engine and race north along the circuitous Western and Atlantic Railroad, destroying communications and a number of high-trestled bridges spanning the winding Chickamauga River.

As the "General" rolled away from Big Shanty without so much as a by-your-leave, the surprised conductor and his crew took off in hot pursuit, despite the fact that they were on foot and certainly no match for the "General," which was fast developing a good head of steam. About a mile ahead, Fuller and his men came across a hand car and, pumping vigorously, made a gallant attempt to overtake the captured train. Further down the line, the pursuers came across an old yard engine, the "Yonah," and literally tore up the tracks in an attempt to catch up with the "General." Meanwhile, Andrews and his men paused whenever possible to not only wreak havoc as per military plan, but to harass the oncoming Confederates as well.

During the 86-mile run, the persistent Confederate conductor laid his hands on additional motive power, climaxing the home stretch of this fantastic race in the "Texas," which he had commandeered along the way. "Along the way" happened to be in the opposite direction, and so the "Texas" stayed on the tail of the "General," while being driven backward, a mean feat in those times, considering that the locomotives of that day did not have any brakes with the exception of a rather inadequate hand brake on the tenders. If that was not hazardous enough, considering the tortuous grades and curves that were being traversed, then dwell on the fact that locomotives at that time did not have trailing wheels to serve as lead trucks when moving in reverse. Despite these handicaps, the "Texas" thundered on furiously at unheard-of speeds, and as the race continued, during which telephone lines were cut and track was destroyed, the gap between the two locomotives narrowed—even though Andrews and his men took precious time from their dangerous task to pile logs on the rails and set afire some of the box cars they had been hauling, which they uncoupled and left on the track behind them to further delay the oncoming "Texas." To Andrews and his men fuel had become a severe problem since, while they had not expected to make a leisurely trip while destroying the lines between Big Shanty and Chattanooga, they certainly had not expected such energetic and vigorous pursuit as that displayed by Fuller and his crew. Thus, they had to keep up a full head of steam at all times so as to stop for their destruction and take off again immediately each time their pursuers hove into view. An

Shorty combine offered by Binkley Models was used extensively on short hauls and branchline service, and fits in well on small pikes particularly.

This combine served as a passenger car, baggage car, smoker and tonsorial parlor.

Pullman palace sleeper by Binkley is finished with bright red sides and gold trim. Originally called the "Pioneer," it was the first successful sleeping car built in spite of the fact that railroads had to alter their station platforms and trackside structures to accommodate the clearance this car required.

Cutaway section of a Binkley car shows detailed interior, which includes a pot-bellied stove, coal pail, shovel and a sleepy conductor trying to catch forty winks on one of those straightbacked chairs.

unexpected amount of fuel was consumed, to a point where they were using every bit of combustible material, including most of the clothing on their backs, to keep the fire going and make good their escape. Finally, the "General" ran out of fuel and had to be abandoned after the fantastic 86-mile run. Within the next few days all members of the raiding party were captured, and on June 7, 1862, Andrews and seven others were hanged as spies, thus bringing to a climax one of the most daring raids and railroad episodes of all time.

When one reviews all the circumstances of this historic event, it almost seems incredible that the "Texas" achieved little if any fame in comparison to the "General," though one can easily see that, had the Confederacy won the Civil War, the tables would have been completely reversed and, obviously, the "Texas" would have received all the accolades in the years that followed. Nevertheless, in all fairness, and considering the railroading feats accomplished by the "Texas" against seemingly unsurmountable odds, this gallant train should be accorded a greater place in railroad history.

One can easily see why these two models are among the most sought after within the realm of model railroading. Tyco (Mantua) the only model railroading manufacturer to produce the "General" in HO, is reported to have spent more money tooling up for the scale miniaturization of the prototype than the famous oldtimer originally cost the builders. The "Texas," available from Aristo-Craft, is also no slouch when it comes to research, tooling-up, and overall investment. Both HO models are as close to their prototypes as is economically feasible.

As I said earlier, the "General" is top dog not only when it comes to fame, but also when it comes to lore, both fact or fiction, and those model rails who own a "General" might be interested in an excellent article by Bill Schopp in the June 1959 issue of *Railroad Model Craftsman.* The article contains additional historical information concerning the "General," and a step-by-step description of how to age and further authenticate its appearance. Last but not least, in recent years Walt Disney produced a feature-length motion picture which delighted a number of model rails and the moviegoing public as well. The film, appropriately called "The Great Locomotive Chase," and starring Fess Parker and Jeff Hunter, is a dramatization of the historic raid involving the "General" and the "Texas," and in true Disney tradition, every conceivable bit of authenticity was employed to embrace a true accounting of event and equipment.

There is yet another aspect to the term "historic locomotives," and it refers not only to the background of the prototype, but the scale model as well. For example, one of the reasons why the Dockside Switcher called "Li'l' Joe," first offered by Varney Scale Models, became one of the most popular models in scale railroading, and at last report had sold well over the quarter of the million mark, is not because this model 0-4-0 switcher was an exact replica of the B & O Docksider, but simply because it was the first motive power in HO scale produced in the United States, introduced by Varney in kit form as far back as 1937. Prior to this time, which was just witnessing the birth of HO, the only motive power one could secure in this new scale had to be imported from the Reed-Pathe Company in England and, as I reported earlier, the only HO materials produced on our shores were rolling stock kits. The advent of Varney's die-cast 0-4-0 Docksider was a pioneering feat that has kept the name Varney a familiar word among brass hats, old and new.

The model of the 0-6-6-0 Mallet offered by Aristo-Craft has the added significance of not only being a fine example of distinctive model craftsmanship, but when put into use on American railroads in 1904 in commemoration of the one-hundredth anniversary of the steam locomotive, it also represented the most

This Shorty baggage car, like all the other Binkley models shown, has been assembled from a kit. Oldtime rolling stock such as this is available from a number of other sources, such as Walthers, etc. Needless to say, it doesn't take more than a half dozen or so of these cars to give you the length of train that was hauled about in the old days. In fact, two- or three-car hauls were far from unusual and it had to be a mighty strong loco to pull many more.

The "A" frame-type and the "gallows"-type turntables are manually operated, just like in the old days. These HO scale models are available in kit form from Cliff Line and are patterned after the wood-frame turntables used by Southern Pacific in small engine terminals and branchlines. For remote control, they can be actuated by a small motor (slow-geared barbecue type) and will look perfect at home in oldtime and rural areas. If you are short on space for a return loop—or wish to avoid one—and still wish to have some way of turning your locomotive around for a return trip, either one of these turntables will fill the bill perfectly for oldtimer locos.

Do it the way the prototypes did. Here, a Southern Pacific gets the turnaround on the former Owenyo Branch Narrow Gauge Line.

From the earliest days of railroading to the turn of the century many a locomotive headlight has pierced the darkness that lay ahead, traversing newly laid track in newly opened frontiers and carving out a niche for itself in railroading's Hall of Fame.

powerful American locomotive then in use. While the Mallets quickly developed into 2-6-6-2's . . . 2-8-8-2's and more powerful and complex articulateds, the original 0-6-6-0 Mallets more than served their purpose on the railroading scene, and that knowledge adds to the ownership and operation. In this particular section you will find an assortment of well-detailed models, not only representative of earlier days in railroading, but in many cases exact duplicates of their prototypes down to the last rivet. Also pictured within these pages are locomotives of historic note both in legend and in fact, plus some of the "firsts" in the early and later days of HO.

As charter members of the age of steam locomotion, oldtimers will continue to attract a good share of the new entrants into the fellowship of model railroading, and rightfully so, for the "Puffer Bellies," "Diamond Stacks," Moguls, and other examples of earlier steam locomotion are part of the most exciting and romantic heritage of American railroading, and therefore deserve the attention and honor shown them in railroading annals. There is far more to it than meets the eye. For example, "Balloon Stacks" were not designed for ornamental purposes, but rather to catch the sparks thrown by the wood burners. Cow catchers, now called "pilots," were designed to fend off stray cattle, which on occasion saw fit to stop a locomotive in its tracks. Were it not for an edict issued by Cornelius Vanderbilt, whose New York Central and Hudson River Railroad boasted the greatest four-track line in the world, oldtimers of the 1870s, '80s, and '90s, plus the behemoths which saw service up until the advent of the diesels, might have continued to be bedecked and adorned with colorful paint schemes and trappings. However, in 1869, in the interests of economy, Vanderbilt imposed an order that the locomotives of his line were to abandon their many colors and ornate brass fittings, and were henceforth to be painted black. Fortunately for both steam and oldtimer enthusiasts, the adoption of a color scheme devoid of sex appeal was an eventual process, for railroads here and there continued to operate in their Sunday best. Thus, the modeler has a wide variety of both color and ornamentation to both modify and superdetail with, and certainly can take a few liberties here and there without detracting from authenticity.

Oldtimers offer the most flexible system and combination of model railroading representative of the early days when each turn of the driver often spelled a challenge to the engineer as he highballed along newly laid track that appeared before him for the very first time.

XVI
Supplying the Power—An Introduction to Wiring

We have now reached the point where we must devote time and comment to a source of power which is not only an important part of everyday living but is also the staff of life for any model railroad—in short, *electricity,* the very means by which our layouts are energized. In the introduction we traced the evolution of miniature trains from the most primitive wooden block pull toys to friction drive, clockwork mechanisms, and steam-powered models, finally arriving at the point where electricity entered the scene, permitting the refinements that have followed over the decades. Fortunately, those very early forms of motive power are far behind us. I mention this only to impress upon you that we sometimes take for granted the why's and wherefore's of the power that enables us to run our model railroads. By the same token, many articles, books, instruction sheets, and what have you also take for granted that the reader knows exactly what is being said and described, no matter how complicated the schematic or circuitry involved—a mistake this writer would like to avoid, for not everyone is knowledgeable about electricity, or for that matter is really interested. There are any number of books and articles devoted specifically to this subject, and for the sake of reference and additional research they will be dutifully listed. For bear in mind that if you started out as the rankest of beginners and have had to hook up the simplest of ovals, it only required two wires from power pack to rails to provide the juice needed to operate your locomotive. Therefore, it is not absolutely essential that you have a thorough knowledge of electricity, at least not at the outset, although the more informed you are, the easier it will be to wire your layout when you advance beyond the simple oval to the more operational track plans. As for the advanced modeler, if you have arrived at that stage, you certainly have done considerable reading and research on the subject of electricity and wiring, especially in relation to the needs of your own layout. And where the veteran is concerned, I don't know of any to speak of who can't cope with even the most complicated wiring plans.

I shall endeavor to give you a basic background on how to wire your trackwork in as simple and uncomplicated a manner as possible; in the hope that it will help you avoid a rat's nest of wires beneath your railroad that would probably defy the description and understanding of an electrical wizard. I will talk about and show you some of the primary ABC's, do's and don'ts, how to operate more than one locomotive at a time, and how to add to your operating pleasures through the use of simple relays, detection units, and signaling devices. This is not an attempt to excuse the omission of a long treatise on wiring and electricity, for when you stop to consider that the type of track plan you employ, the nature of the track materials you use, and the type of operation you have in mind will definitely determine the best method in which your railroad should be wired, you can easily see that a volume in itself would be required to cover the subject adequately. And this has already been done, as I will cite later on.

For example, while Tru-Track and Snap-Track are both sectional track materials, there are a few notable differences in how they need to be hooked up in relation to the type of operation their respective track plans call for. A Tru-Switch turnout will power the track (complete a connection) *only* in the direction the turnout has been thrown. This is part of the system involving the use of Tru-Track components. On the other hand, where Snap-Track is concerned, their Snap-Switch and Custom-Line turnouts are compatible with a wiring system whereby there is electricity in the rails at all times regardless of the turnout position. In other words, a basic track wiring plan involving the use of an oval, siding, and spur is just as applicable to either type of track material, but will require gaps and insulated sections of track depending on the material you use. *No discussion of electricity and wiring will be automatically applicable down to the last wire unless you use a specific wiring plan that has been devised for a specific type of track material and turnout.* Therefore, chances are that you will have to make a number of modifications here and there, and cut a few gaps in the rail to avoid shorts. And if you haven't already experienced it, I can assure you that you will know why and when to do it—when you get to it.

It is, therefore, our aim that the space and illustrations devoted to wiring will help the beginners over the hump from hooking up a simple oval to wiring a more advanced track plan; will reacquaint the advanced modelers with wiring ideas that have either escaped their attention or have been avoided; and, lastly, might even suggest an idea or two to the wiring veteran despite his knowledgeable bag of tricks.

Since certain electrical terms and expressions are best understood at the outset, the following list explains some of the most commonly used jargon within the framework of model railroad wiring:

Ammeter	A device used to measure the strength of current.
Amp	The unit of strength of electric current.
Block	A length of track isolated (by gaps or insulated breaks) from all adjoining track.
Cab	The electrical equipment provided for one operator to control one train. Facilities might include a throttle (rheostat), reverse lever, traffic direction controller, etc.
Gap	A cut or break in the rail which interrupts the flow of current.
Power Pack	A transformer combined with a rectifier which reduces the intensity of standard household alternating current and also converts it to direct current for model railroading use.

Members of the California Central Model RR Club take time out from their regular chores during a "shakedown test" to check their wiring. Eric Bracher, at the control panel, brings a train down the line while Jim Webb keeps an eye on things. Bob Semichy, laying track on an upper level, takes a look, too. When completely finished, the club will boast a four-cab control dispatch system.

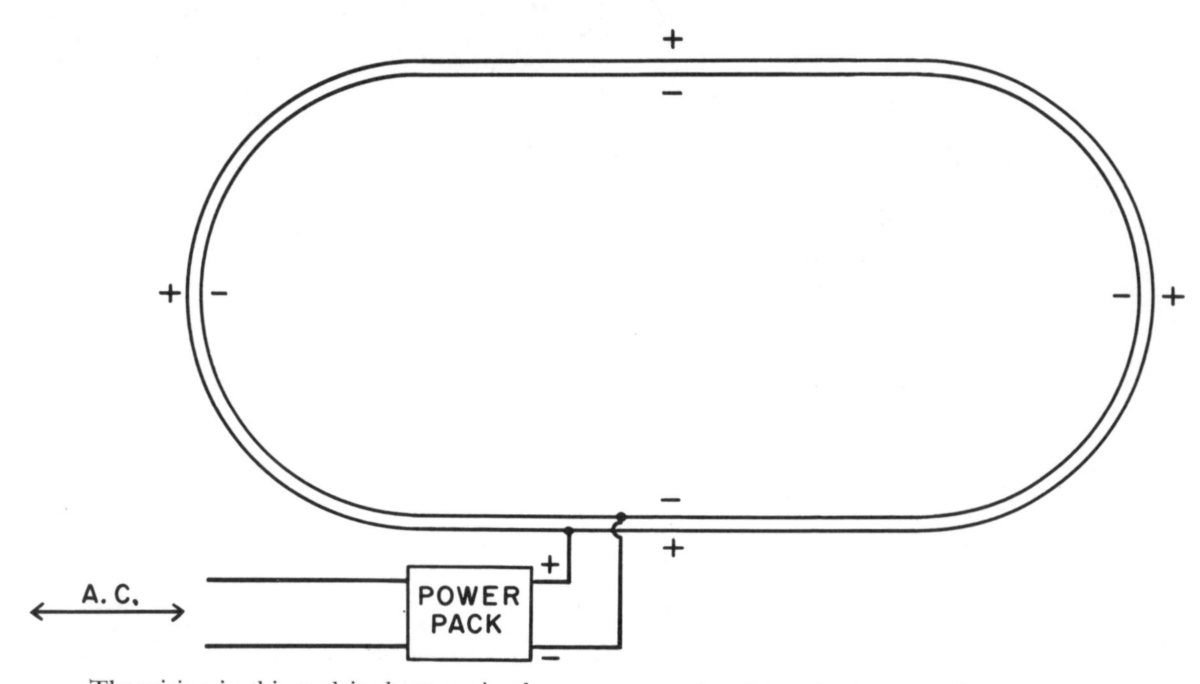

The wiring in this oval is about as simple as you can get and is only the start of things to come. No matter how big a layout you design, you can keep wiring relatively simple by avoiding built-in booby traps such as reverse loops, the meeting of opposite polarities, improper location of feeder wires and other situations which will set the electrical demons to work.

The type of turnouts you use will have a definite influence on the amount of wiring that will be required for even the most basic plan. This arrangement involves the use of Tru-Track and Tru-Switches. Only two wires from power pack to track connections are required, yet you can hold a train on the inner loop and move a train around the outer loop (and vice-versa) without the need for any extra wiring or isolating of the track involved.

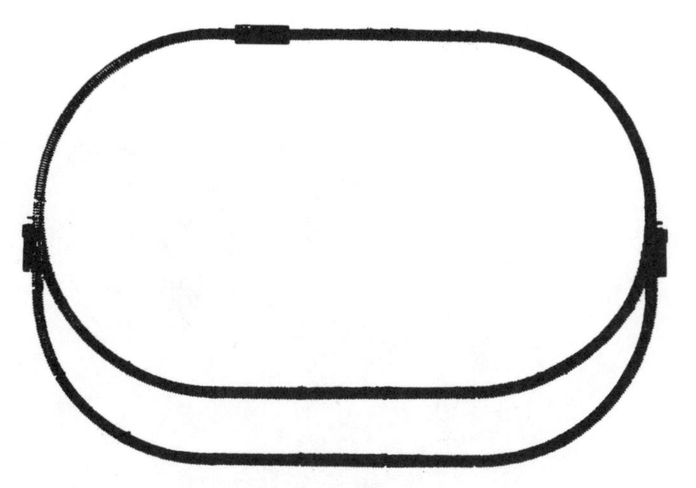

Insulated wire comes in a variety of colors, enabling you to keep a record of your connections. This color coding will be of enormous help to you later on when you have to troubleshoot an area to find shorts, etc. It will also make it easy to track down particular connections when you expand or add jumpers or extend feeders. Tagging wires with masking tape will also remind you at a glance where particular wires go. For example, black can be for negative feeds and red for positive feeds. Therefore BB1 and RB1 can be for Block 1 respectively, etc. Marking these designations on masking tape and tagging appropriate wires will help eliminate trial-by-error searching later on. Harry Dardis, beneath layout, is shown pulling wires through from trackwork above.

The Marnold C-25B Power Pack (available from Walthers) delivers $2\frac{1}{2}$ amp. of power and includes throttle-controlled pulse power. It can handle up to four average HO locomotives. Has built-in terminal connections for reverse loop wiring, and provisions for expansion and cab control.

The Aristo-Pack from Aristo-Craft has one knob to control speed and direction. Two-amp. output with AC and DC on separate circuits. Respective warning lights flash when there is trouble on the line. Center on-off control makes you come to a full stop before changing direction—a mighty useful aid if you forget.

Golden Throttle Pack offered by Model Rectifier Corp. is perfect for beginners and advanced hobbyists as well. Two-amp. output will drive three average HO locos and dual-range switch permits choice of full or pulse power. Also has provision for another cab control throttle, direction control and circuit breaker.

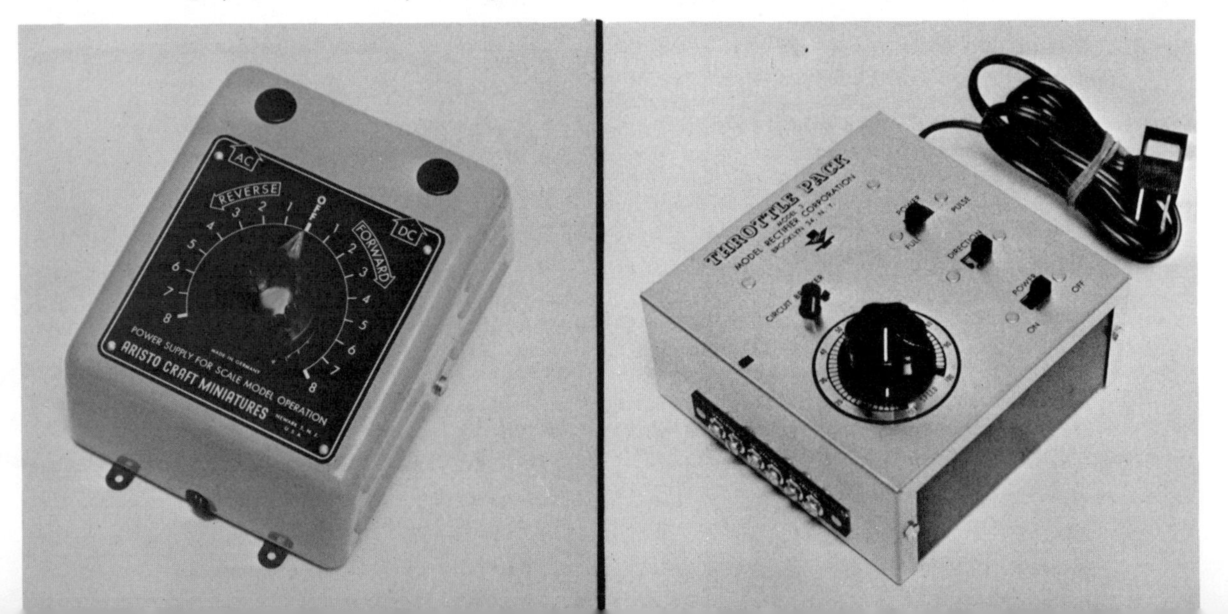

This Tri-Pack from Model Rectifier Corp. is loaded with many extras. It includes three complete cab controls providing operation of trains in three separate sections of track. A $4\frac{1}{2}$-amp. output, this unit will handle up to six locos.

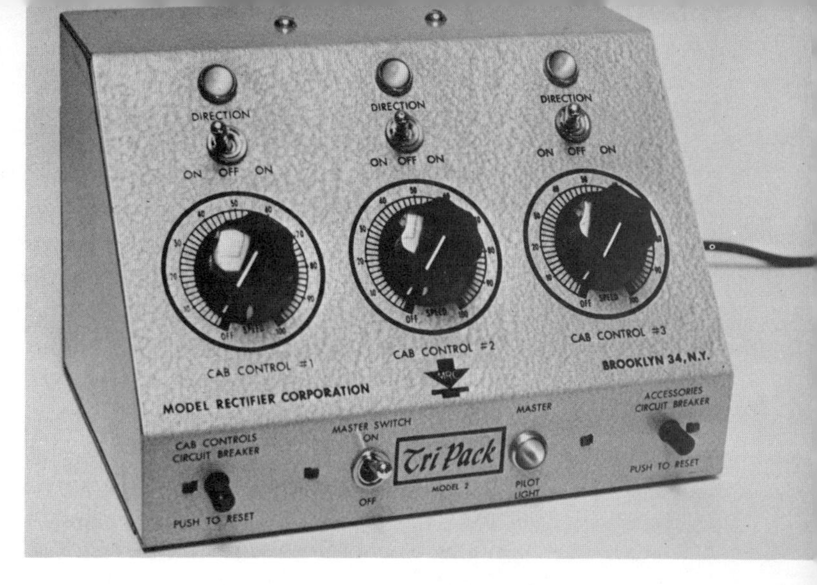

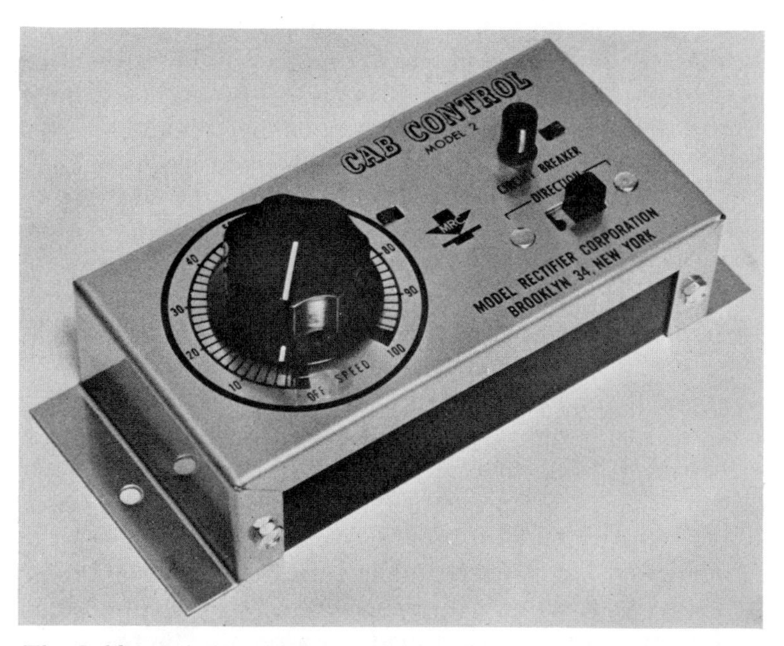

The Golden Cab Control throttle unit will work in conjunction with any of the Model Rectifier Corp. power supplies, such as the Model Meter Pack, Tri-Pack or any MRC rectifier, etc. This unit will control speed and direction in any additional track section and enables the operator to install it in a control panel while placing the power supply elsewhere out of the way. A useful accessory and an aid during expansion.

The Model Meter Pack offered by Model Rectifier Corp. is a 5-amp. power source and works in conjunction with their Golden Cab Control throttle units. Ammeter continuously shows current draw of locomotives. Will handle seven HO locos, and is the basis of use with an external control panel for the selection and operation of motive power within a number of track sections independent of each other.

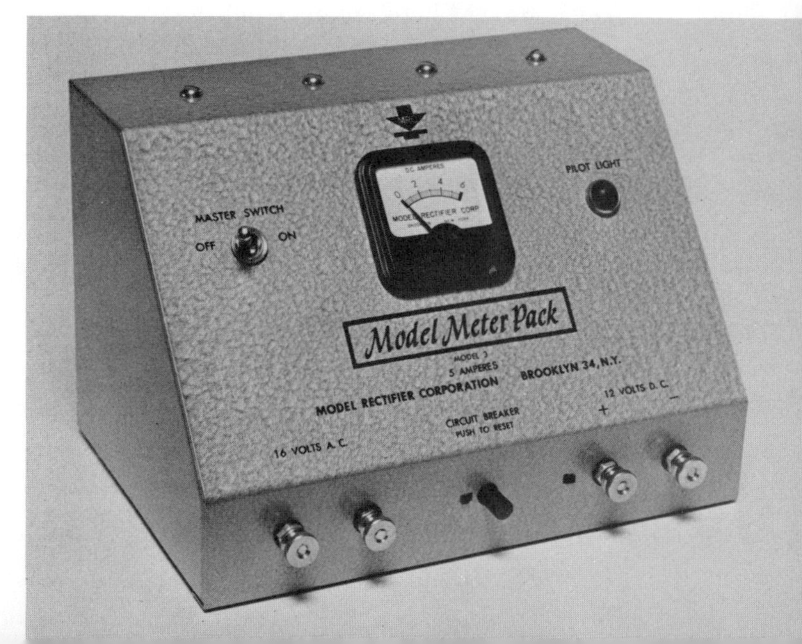

These are just some of the expressions that are constantly used in wiring, and along with numerous others will be elaborated upon as we go along. In addition, numerous words, classifications, and special terms are defined in the glossary at the back of the book.

To repeat, a thorough knowledge of electricity isn't essential, though it will help. Certain basic information is all that is required to get you started in the right direction, for as you move along your knowledge of the why's and wherefore's of model railroad wiring will increase. Common household power is alternating current, whose characteristics involve a positive and negative flow which changes direction every one-sixtieth of a second. It is generally referred to as 110 volts, 60-cycle AC, certainly far too powerful for model railroad operation. Therefore, all HO and other scale-model railroads are operated on direct current, DC being used because of the better control obtainable at lower voltages, and because with DC the current always flows in the same direction, except when reversed.

In addition to powering locomotives, juice must be provided for switch motors (to change the position of turnouts), lighting equipment, and other electrically operated units whose source of current should be independent from your motive power. The advisability of separate and independent sources of current is explained thusly: If, for example, you used DC to power both your locomotive and switch motors, then every time you flipped a toggle switch to change the position of a turnout the drain of electricity would cause your locomotive to falter while running. Therefore, to avoid the draining of current from one operation to another, it is customary to use DC for motive power and AC for accessories. Fortunately, most power packs include two sets of terminals as follows:

12-Volt DC terminals for locomotives.
16-Volt AC terminals for switch motors, lighting, etc.

This listing is only part of what the power pack does, and now I'll elaborate. The little black box that supplies the energy to your model railroad, first of all, is not a black box like that of many years ago—it is no longer oily and smoky in appearance or smell. True, this description aptly fits many transformers that powered toy trains and tin plate equipment of past decades; however, today's power packs are sleek paneled instruments ranging in cost from $5 to $50. Yet with all the improvements that have been administered in the producing of modern power supplies, they are one of the most sorely neglected items among model railroaders.

A rail fan will think nothing of shelling out $50 for a Berkshire, but when it comes to spending a quarter of that amount for the very power that will move it about, he acts like he just saw a flying box car. And why is it that some fans will spend considerable time building up equipment, an equal amount of time doing the woodwork and scenery, spending an equal amount of cash, yet when it comes to the power pack, the pursestrings tighten? And woe unto the railroader who hooks a ten- or fifteen-car train to his favorite loco, then bemoans the fact that it won't pull it. Chances are that the pack has been overrated. In other words, it is supposedly a 1-amp pack, but puts out only half or three-fourths of its rated power. So be sure you buy a power pack made by a reliable source, bearing in mind that a power pack that puts out an actual (not just rated) 1 amp is the very minimum, and depending on the extent of your trackage, blocks, and motive power, higher amperages will be necessary. Some packs include pulse power, a power application followed by some and avoided by others. In overcoming the inertia of a still locomotive, instead of a jerky forward motion (or jack rabbit start), pulse power can accomplish the same forward movement with a series of gentle shoves. As you increase the throttle speed, you attain a believable rolling action, and in slowing down you can literally

From an electrical standpoint the more important parts of the "turnout nomenclature" are the frog, wing rails, closure rails and points. These parts affect the electrical scene. Understanding their functions will help you when you get to various wiring chores.

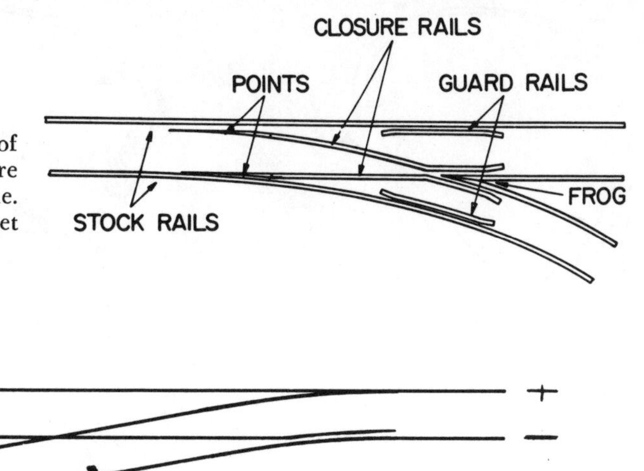

When two turnouts connect to form a single crossover, the unit must be gapped as illustrated. Connect feeder wires to the rails ahead of the points in the same way as for a single turnout. Before throwing switches for moving a train through the crossover, be certain to set polarity in the same direction for both tracks. The Tru-Scale (regular) single crossover comes as a mounted unit and is pre-gapped. Combining the Tru-Track turnouts to make a single crossover will not require any gapping on your part, since these turnouts feature an almost invisible form of insulation at the frog point. Custom Line and Snap Switches will require the use of plastic-insulated rail joiners at the gap points.

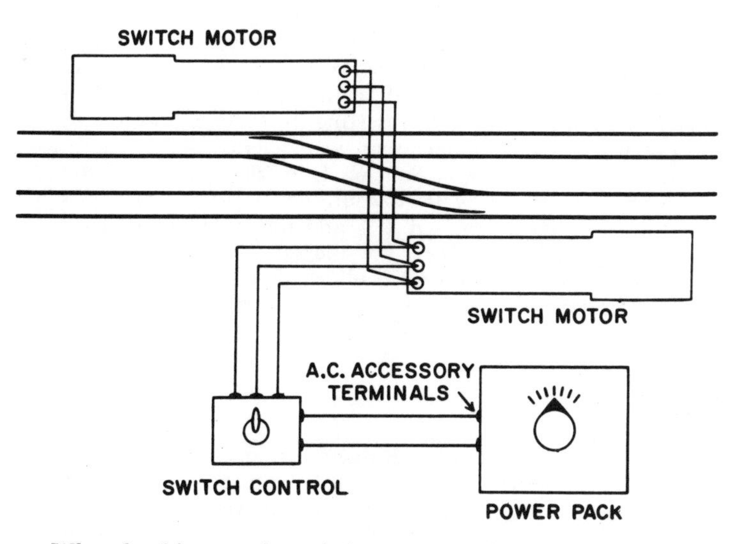

When hooking up the switch motors used to actuate turnouts for a single crossover, you can cut the wiring in half by means of jumpers from one unit to another. Both turnouts will respond accordingly when you flip the toggle.

Always supply current to the points of the switches, thus the direction in which the switch points are thrown will energize the frog properly. When turnouts point away from each other, such as in the single cross-over, gaps have to be cut in both rails of the track or tracks that connect them. For a passing siding, also gap rails at points marked "G." This primarily applies to the use of regular turnouts.

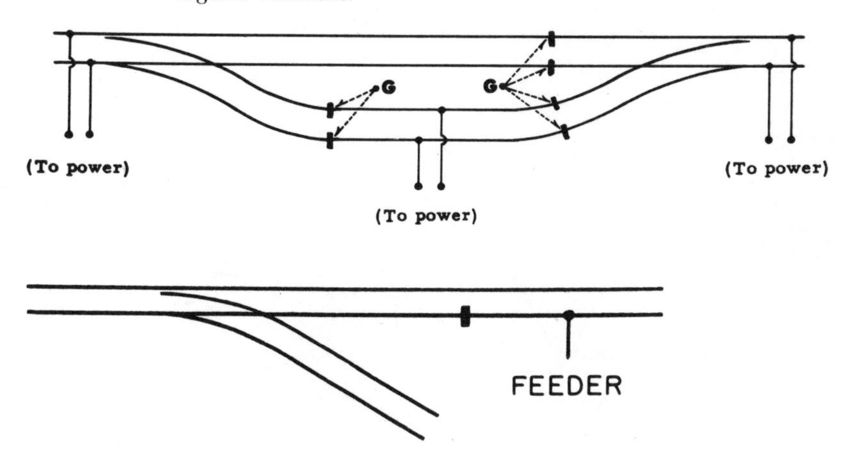

Never locate a feeder on a rail which leads directly to or from the frog of a turnout. If the occasion arises when you must, then cut a gap in the rail to separate the feeder from the frog.

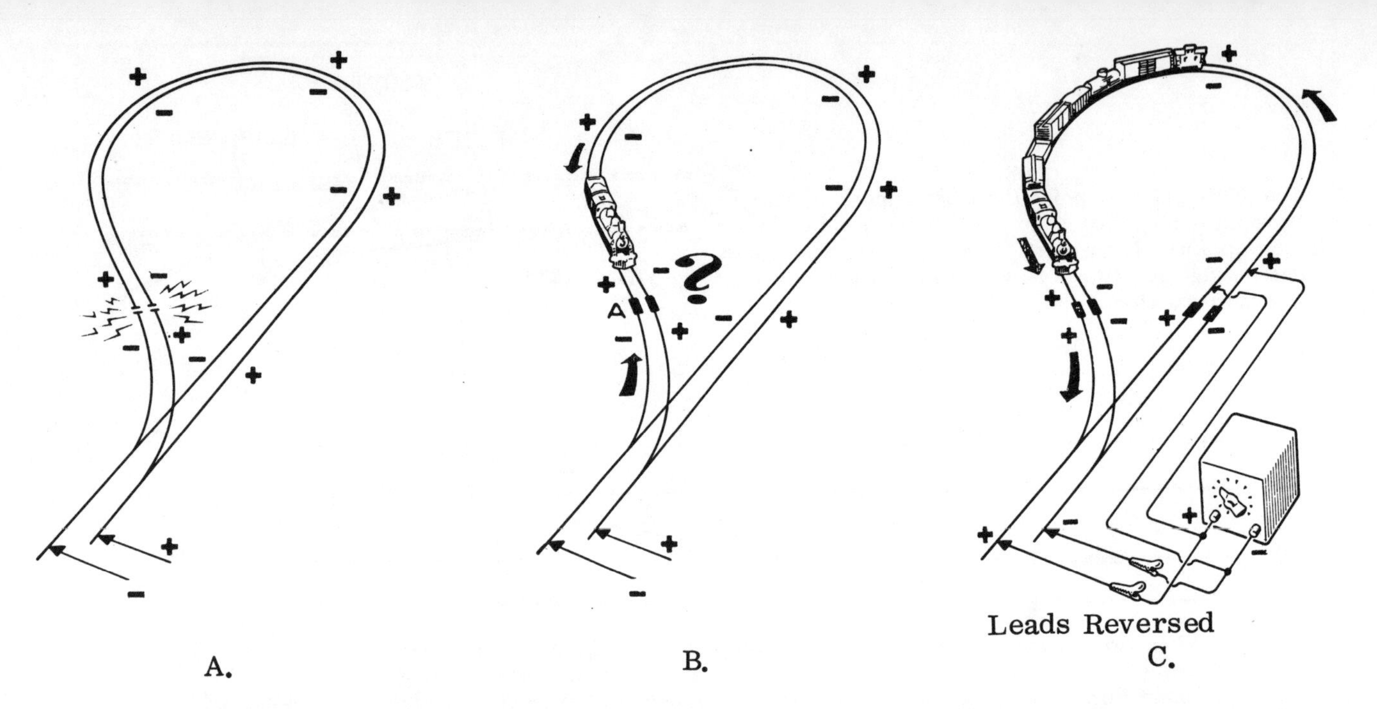

You might call a reverse loop a necessary evil, at least with respect to the problems that accompany its use and the wiring that goes with it. Some swear by it, other swear at it. Nevertheless, the fact remains that it is probably the least complicated means of turning an *entire* train around so that it can make a return trip along the same stretch of track while headed in the opposite direction. One of the best ways of describing and illustrating reverse loop problems is shown in these three diagrams from *Atlas Layouts* by John Armstrong. Note that in trying to hook up a loop of return track you will immediately encounter a short circuit (A) since opposing polarities will be johnny-on-the-spot to raise an electrical fuss. This problem can be avoided by gapping and/or inserting plastic rail joiners (B). Now the train can enter the loop, since the opposite polarities have been kept apart by the electrical break at the joint. The train can continue around the loop, since for the moment there is no polarity conflict. However, when it reaches the insulated joint, it will suddenly meet up with those opposing polarities and ordinarily would buck backward, except for the fact that a short occurs the moment its wheels cross over the joint—to wit, it stops dead in it tracks. This problem is overcome by isolating the loop section completely by gapping and/or inserting two more plastic rail joiners (C). However, be sure that the loop section of track is a bit longer than your average train length. This section of track can now be connected directly to the power pack. Starting from the beginning, the train enters the loop and, since things are status quo polarity-wise, the train continues around. Once it is completely within the isolated loop section, the mainline polarity is reversed (C) and the train can re-enter the mainline (come out of the loop) without hesitation or causing a short. For the sake of simplicity, the change in mainline polarity is shown by means of reversing the power feed leads to that section of track. Prior to entering the loop again with another train, all polarities must be made equal with respect to each other and the direction of travel.

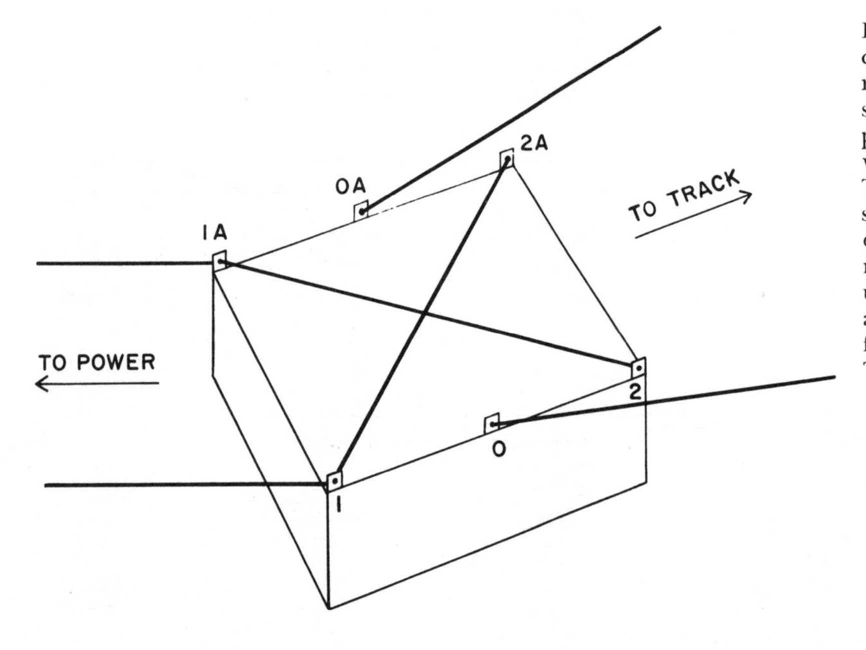

In the reverse loop diagrams we showed how to change the polarity in the mainline by means of reversing the position of the power leads to that section of track. However to repeat, this was done purely for the sake of illustration, for this method would be impractical during actual operation. Therefore, a double-pole double-throw toggle, slide switch or reasonable facsimile is introduced. However, before installation a bit of revamping is necessary. To convert the switch so that it can be used to reverse polarity, crossed wires would be added, as shown in this rear view. Solder a wire from Terminals 1 to 2A and another wire from Terminals 1A to 2.

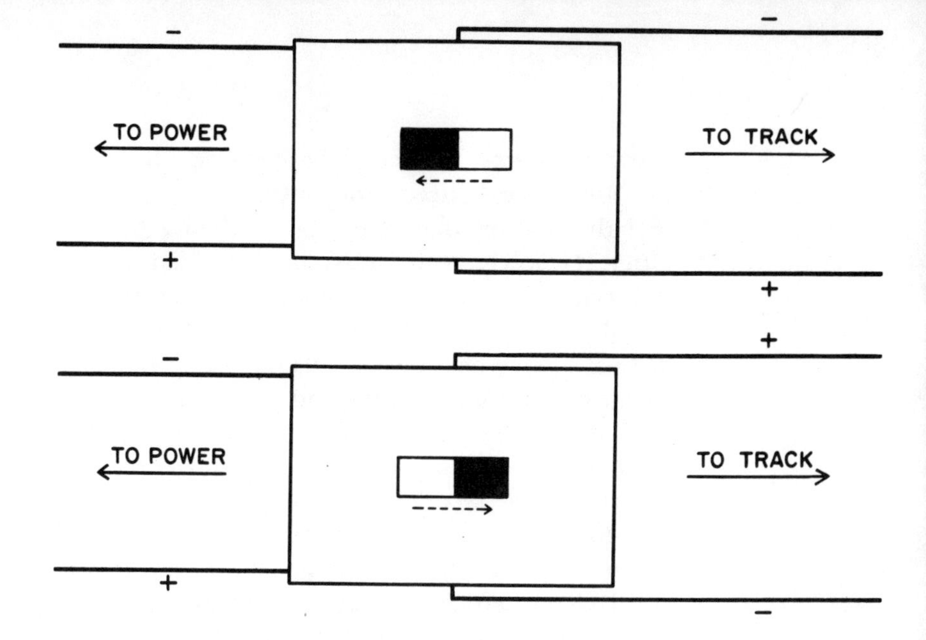

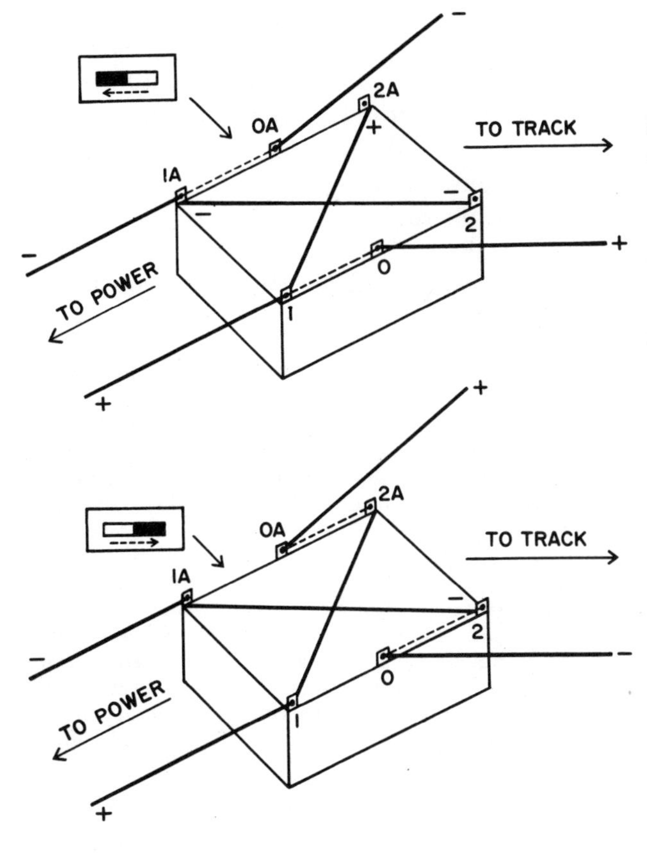

These top and bottom views show you precisely what happens when you add the crossed wires and flip the switch in either direction. When the switch is thrown to the left, Terminals 1 and 0 are connected, as are Terminals 0A and 1A. Throwing the switch to the right connects Terminals 0 and 2, as well as 0A and 2A. Thus the polarity of the current fed through the switch, and in turn to the track, can be changed depending on the position of the switch when thrown. Also note that Terminals 2 and 2A remain constant with a fixed polarity and can be used as a connecting point to feed an area of track that will not require reversing.

Meanwhile, back at the loop we are now hooked up and as indicated two double-pole double-throw switches are installed, one feeding the mainline trackage, the other the isolated loop section. Both switches are set the same way and polarity is matching, which permits the train to enter the loop free of problems.

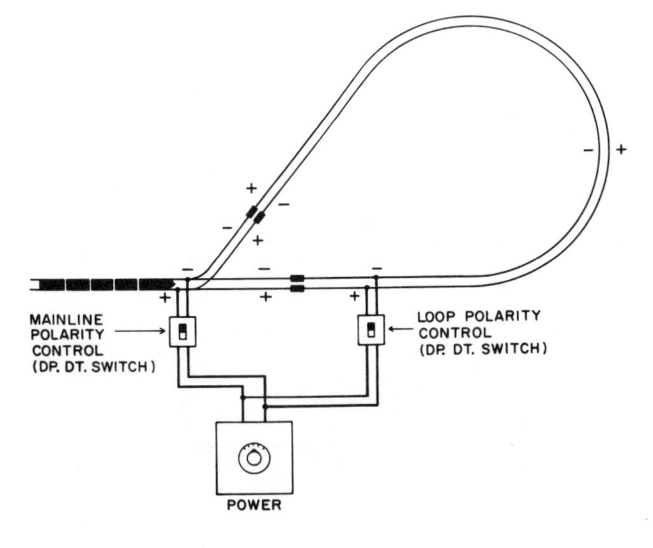

crawl to a stop. Technically speaking, it is the difference between the output of a full- or half-wave rectifier, pulse power being the latter. However, care must be exercised in this type of power usage, since it is not advisable to run your engine at high speed for danger of overheating or burnout. The best application is for starting and stopping.

The Marnold power pack has pulse power built in rather uniquely. As you move the throttle from starting position, you have the benefit of pulse forward motion; as you increase throttle, the power switches over to full DC, so there is no danger of running your engine into a heart condition. As you throttle down again, the pulse power cuts back in at the lower pulse range, and the engine can glide to a smooth stop. Model Rectifier Corporation has a similar provision for pulse power built into some of their accurately rated packs. The Golden Throttle pack, for example, features a two-position power switch: full or pulse. When used in the pulse-power position, the pack is delivering only half the voltage output and, therefore, the locomotive does not attain maximum speed, thereby eliminating the danger of burnout or overheating, since the maximum voltage when pulse power is being used is not in excess of 6 volts. In full position, you have the 12-volt output and the regular power operation. A flick of the switch will bring in the pulse power whenever you want it for starting, stopping, or whenever the occasion might arise. Dead stop position on both the Model Rectifier and Marnold packs is about 97 per cent minus power—in other words, just the slightest bit of juice is left flowing so that the train can come to a smooth, gradual slowdown and stop. Slamming on the brakes can still result in a touch of realistic stopping (depending on a locomotive's coasting abilities) and while the engine is idle, the amount of electricity still flowing is too minor to be of any consequence.

Other features of power packs include "on" and "off" switches, and a direction switch or lever which will enable you to op-

Once the train is completely within the loop, the mainline switch is thrown. This reverses the polarity in the mainline and at the same time makes it match the polarity in the loop. Now the train can come out of the loop and re-enter the mainline. You will note that the loop toggle switch has not been touched at all during this operation, and if you are wondering why it is necessary, simply bear in mind that it has a number of uses. For example, if you wanted to change the direction of travel around the loop from counterclockwise to clockwise, the loop toggle would enable you to match the polarity of the mainline at the other end. In short, it enables you to match polarity of the loop with respect to either point of entrance and route of travel and direction. You will also find additional uses for it if you should happen to add another section of track to the loop. There is one rub to the whole situation, and that is the fact that when you change the polarity of the mainline trackage prior to coming out of the loop, you also affect any other equipment operating on that particular mainline at that time. A system of blocks, cab controls, holding track, etc., are some of the refinements that can be added to avoid changing the direction of other equipment when you reverse the polarity of the mainline. (See reverse loop wiring for ASTRAC in the next chapter.) If you are not inclined toward revamping toggle switches as indicated, there are a number of commercial units available which are designed for direction and polarity control. For example, Atlas makes a dual-control unit called a "twin." A simple affair, it is easy to connect and does away with the need for two separate switches.

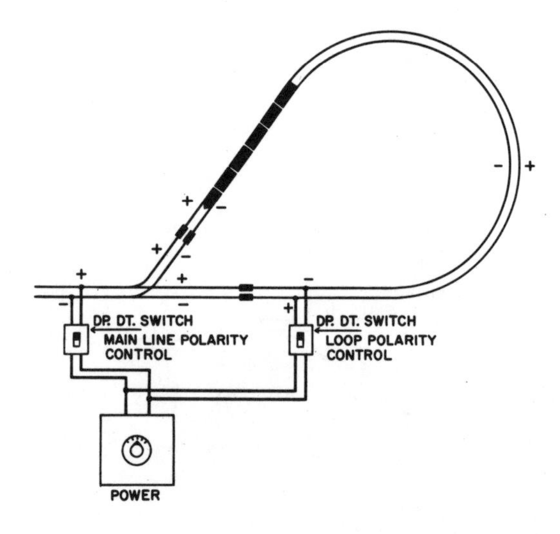

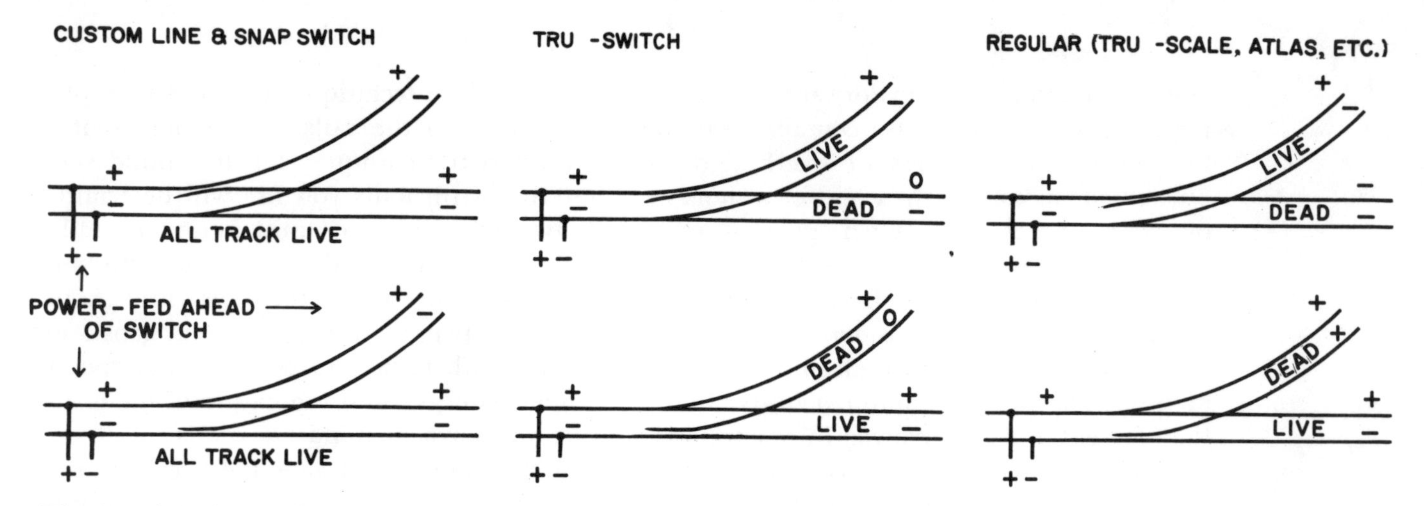

The electrical characteristics of the commonly used turnouts are shown in these diagrams. Note that in all cases the power has been fed ahead of the switch points. To "power route" or not to "power route" is a decision best determined by the type of operation you have in mind.

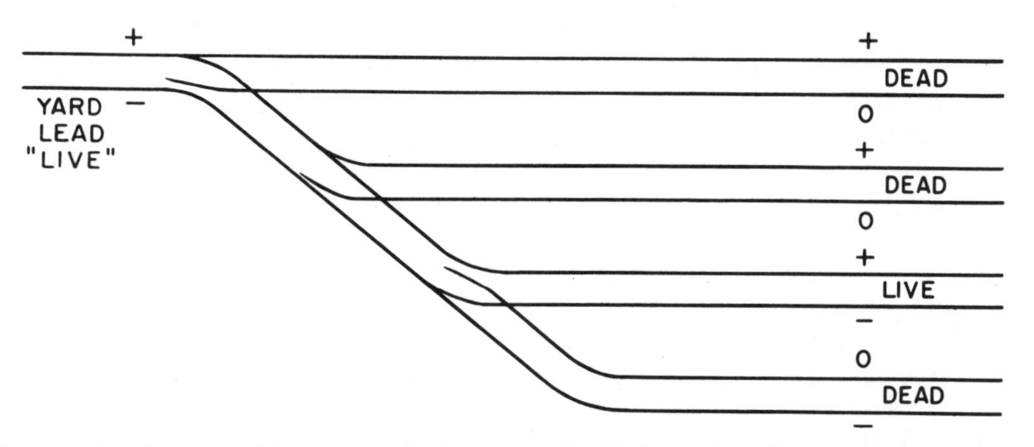

In this diagram the advantage of "power routing" turnouts should be obvious. If not, then simply bear in mind that in the case of using Tru-Track turnouts in a yard arrangement such as this no additional wiring is needed, since the position of the turnout powers the track it is facing. A yard hog can run up and down the line, and the only toggling required will be that of actuating the switch machines connected to the respective turnouts.

By means of gaps and the insertion of on-off single-pole single-throw toggle switches you can liven or deaden yard trackage, spurs, etc.

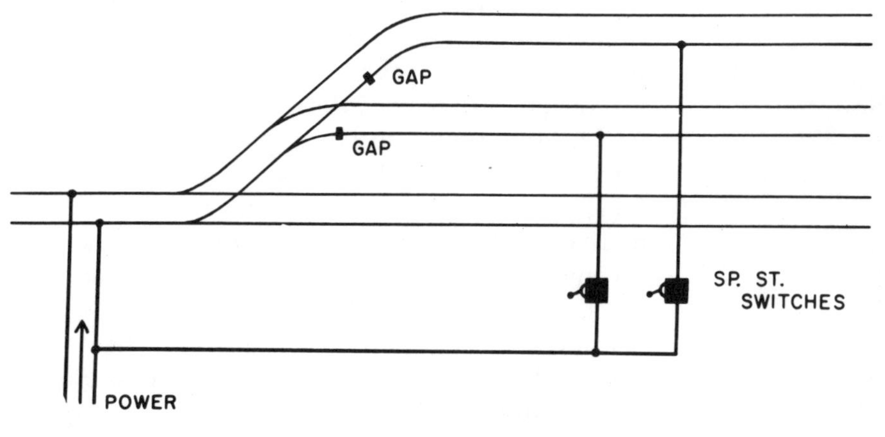

Simple terminal strips such as this will enable you to eliminate long stretches of wire from point of feed to point of power. They are available at most hobby shops or radio parts stores, and are an absolute must if you want to keep things neat and easy to check out when troubles arise.

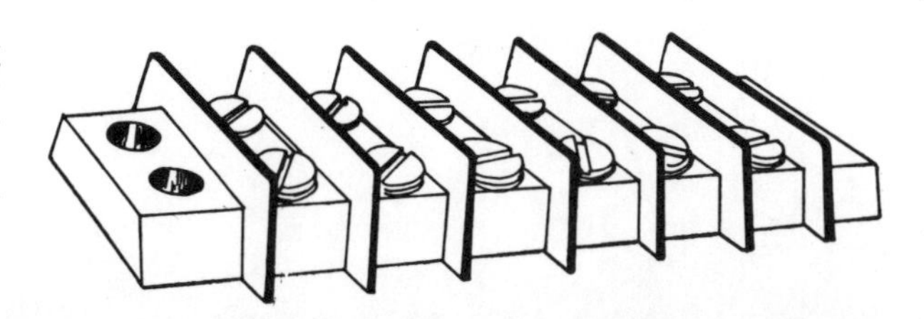

erate your locomotives in forward or reverse position. They should also contain a circuit breaker or fuse to prevent overheated or burned-out motors in the event of a short or overload of current. When purchasing a power pack be sure that the one you select has this safety feature, otherwise don't buy it. Another thing to consider is the power output, which will reflect itself in the number of trains you can run simultaneously. If for the moment you are involved in one-train-at-a-time operation, a pack which will produce a 1-amp output will be sufficient. Most locomotives will draw anywhere from half an amp to three-fourths of an amp, and quite a few locos will draw a full amp. Anything over that is cause for checking into the roundhouse to see what is wrong. Generally speaking, a 1-amp power pack will more than handle your needs at the moment, although once you get into multi-train operation, the need for additional amperage will become quite evident.

In recent years these sleek power packs have become quite sophisticated not only in appearance, but in some of the refinements that have been added. Such things as transistorized circuits, overload compensators, coasting, and realistic braking, and numerous other touches which add to one's operating pleasure. Within these pages you will see an assortment of power packs which will illustrate the ingredients we have been talking about. And for those who are do-it-yourself-minded the bibliography at the back of the book will list various sources of information and plans for building your own power packs. So much for power packs at the moment. As you become more involved in operating your locomotives, and as the need for additional power becomes important, you will appreciate what we have covered thus far and, more important, you will realize the necessity of having reliable, safe, and accurately rated power pack equipment.

Now that we have the power in hand for the moment, let's spend a bit of time exploring the various techniques involved in applying current to the rails. Please note that I said different techniques, for, to remind you, the type of turnouts you use will determine the type of wiring you must follow. In addition to auxiliary feeder wires to help distribute the current to the rails throughout your track plan, you will also need gaps and jumpers with respect to polarity, the type of turnouts you use, and the nature of the operating you have in mind.

Why all this talk of gaps and breaks in the track? Simply because electricity is a mischievous force comprised of two primary factors: negative and positive. When these are mixed, mysterious things happen, trains grind to unceremonious halts, shorts occur, and other miseries descend upon you. These opposing forces are called "polarity" and must be kept separated under all circumstances. They also determine the direction in which your trains will run, depending on which way the direction control lever is set—in other words, the arrangement of polarity in your rails. It is for this reason that gapping of trackwork by means of cuts or breaks in the rail, or the use of insulated plastic joiners, becomes necessary, particularly in such instances where sections of track rejoin each other—reverse loops being a case in point—or any areas of your trackwork where a change in polarity is encountered. Therefore, the need for gapping will depend on the nature of the track plan you choose or the one you design yourself. There is nothing wrong in having a complicated track plan providing it embraces a realistic and railroad-like operation, and assuming you don't mind the effort and time involved in hooking things up properly. Complications add to the challenge, but only if they can be resolved.

The accompanying diagrams indicate where gaps in the rails are required. The absolute necessity for many of these gaps will depend on not only the track plan you employ, but also whether you are involved in one train or multi-train operation. In other words, if yours is a one-train railroad, or your trains are operated one at a time rather than simultaneously, then the need for gaps is lessened. If, on the other hand, you have trains running simultaneously, utilize a number of turnouts, have a return loop, etc., then the need for strategic location of gaps becomes a matter of vital importance. Therefore, study the diagrams, which are the fundamental ABC's of hooking things up correctly. And since most commercial track and wiring plans indicate where gaps are needed, you will better understand their functions.

Pursuing the question of gaps a few steps further, once you have become acquainted with their use and accept the fact that under certain circumstances there must be gaps in the rail, you can at your own option select a track plan in which the need for gapping does not arise. This, of course, is a matter of personal preference, and let me point out quickly that avoiding gapping, which is necessitated by the more complicated arrangements of turnouts, reversing track, etc., does not necessarily mean that your operation and railroading fun will be curtailed. On the contrary, for there are a number of plans where breaks in the rail are not needed and where plenty of fascinating action can be obtained. Certain yards and switching arrangements are a prime example. In addition, certain commercial turnouts and crossovers are already gapped or insulated for you and you are, therefore, relieved of the chores of doing it yourself. For example, in connecting two parallel tracks, a pair of turnouts is required, as are appropriate gaps—this is called a single crossover. In making an installation of this nature, plastic joiners will be necessary if you are using Snap-Switches. In the case of Tru-Switches you don't have to do any gapping yourself since the necessary electrical breaks in the rail are part of the unique design of the Tru-Switch turnouts. And if you should decide to use an already mounted crossover, Tru-Scale has just the thing, which is pre-gapped at the factory for your convenience. In the case of all commercially made crossings, the necessary gapping is taken care of at the time of manufacture in one manner or another.

All of which adds up to one thing—don't let the needs for gapping frighten, discourage, or confound you. The diagrams shown are the very pointers that will keep you out of trouble and, depending on the type of trackwork you purchase, you may or may not have to do it yourself.

Creating a gap in the rail can be accomplished in two ways:

1. With the use of insulated joiners. These joiners connect sections of track to each other in the same manner as metal joiners, with the exception that they are plastic and, therefore, prevent the flow of current between one section of rail to the other. Plastic joiners are commonly used with sectional track materials.
2. By cutting a break in the rail. This can be done with the aid of a razor saw, although an abrasive cut-off wheel on a Dremel Moto-Tool is faster. (Afterward, a few swipes with a file will remove any burrs you may have created.) A squirt of model cement in the newly formed gap between the now-separated rails will keep them from touching each other if they expand during hot weather. This technique is commonly used with Tru-Scale Ready-Track or when laying one's own ties and rail, as previously explained.

The important thing to remember is that once you have become acquainted with the why's and wherefore's of gaps, and where they should be located in respect to your overall scheme of things in relation to polarity, half your electrical battle will be over. As changes within your layout or scheme of operation take place, you may find that certain gaps are no longer needed. When this happens, a jumper wire is your best means of restoring a flow of current from one gapped section to the next.

Another means of keeping your wiring simplified is through the use of "common rail" wiring, otherwise known as "common power return." In essence, this simply means a type of track wiring in which only one running rail will have to be gapped when the need for separate blocks arise. The number of toggle switches and wiring is, therefore, greatly reduced—a case in point being the powering of an otherwise dead siding, spur, or yard lead, and, of course, vice versa. There are exceptions to this rule, however, and in certain cases both rails sometimes have to be gapped to offset short circuits which result when opposite polarities meet, a prime example being that of the "reverse loop."

Next on the agenda are the different electrical characteristics of various turnouts and, in view of these differences, we offer the following concerning the types of turnouts commonly used:

1. Regular switches (primarily used by modelers who lay their own track) made by Tru-Scale, Atlas, etc. These switches have only the track for which the turnout is set "live" with electricity. In other words, *the track facing the position for which the turnout has been thrown becomes powered.* This method of "power routing" is handy where sidings, spurs, and yards are concerned.
2. Tru-Switches (for modelers using Tru-Track or other sectional track) made by Tru-Scale. *The track is live only in the direction the switch is set, as in the case of "regular switches."* Therefore, in like fashion, the track the switch is *against* is "dead" when using either regular or Tru-Switch turnouts. In the case of regular switches, "dead" means that both rails of the particular track section have the same polarity, both negative or positive. In the case of Tru-Switches, "dead" means that one rail is either negative or positive, and the other is devoid of current, electrically neutral. In short, no polarity.
3. Custom-Line and Snap-Switches (for modelers using Snap-Track or other sectional track material) made by Atlas. *In this case, the track is live at all times regardless of which way the turnout has been thrown.* I might also mention that these switches can be converted for "power routing." (See reference in Bibliography.)

The following book should be read in connection with the foregoing and following information. Linn H. Westcott's *How to Wire Your Model Railroad* covers everything from A to Z in a book devoted exclusively to model railroad wiring and in far greater scope than one chapter alone can provide.

The why's and wherefore's of wiring are as simple or complex as you wish to make them. The various ways in which a given track plan can be wired are many, any one of which will do the job properly. In other words, a given track plan, though wired in different ways, some more complicated than the other, will still provide you with similar operating possibilities. One wiring arrangement may accomplish the same thing for a given track plan as another wiring arrangement, and, yet, might eliminate a fair amount of wiring, toggle switches, etc. These short cuts are all part and parcel of knowing how to hook things up; therefore, the importance of additional reading is stressed. Westcott's book is quite complete in this respect and offers many variations. For your edification and through the courtesy of Kalmbach Publishing Co., certain diagrams from *How to Wire Your Model Railroad* are shown in this chapter. *Wiring Your HO Layout,* by Paul Mallery, is devoted exclusively to Atlas Snap-Track and turnout materials, and will be helpful to snap-trackers. These and other areas of reference cover the subject in far greater detail than this chapter permits. Now, let's get back to our discussion concerning turnouts.

By way of summarizing the foregoing, when using regular or Tru-Switches, you can route power to a siding or spur by simply throwing the turnout to that position, and by returning to mainline or straight-through position,

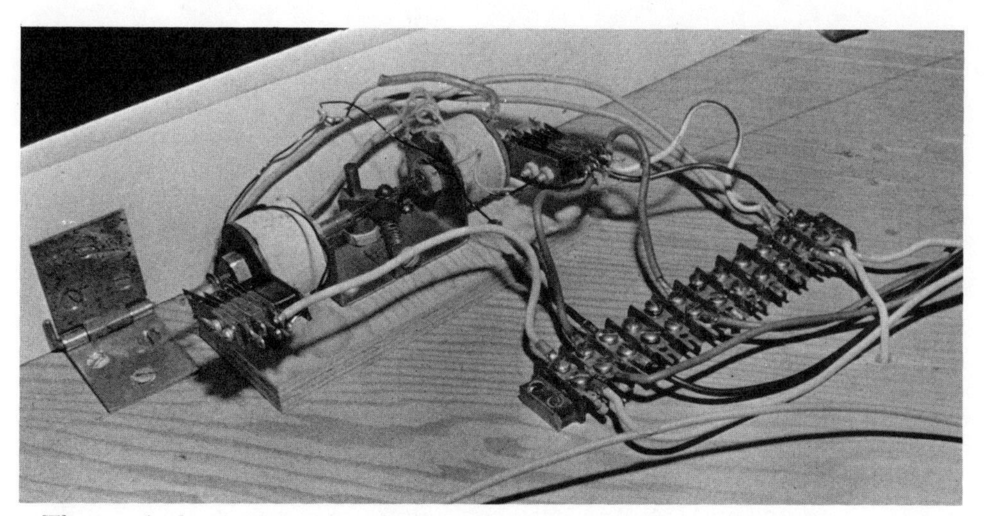

The terminal strip serves as a feeder and connecting point to the twin-coil switch machine, track and signal lights above (upside-down view).

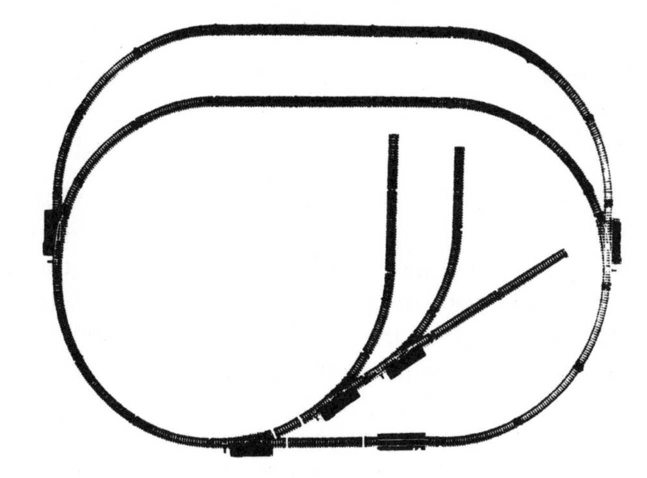

This Tru-Scale plan involving the use of Tru-Track and Tru-Switch components only requires connecting two wires to the track, yet it gives the beginner a chance to operate up to four locomotives individually without the need for gapping (a built-in feature of the turnout) or the use of any plastic rail joiners.

Snap-Track users can get off to a quick start in this plan, which permits the operation of two locomotives simultaneously or one at a time. Since only one power pack is being used, both locos will run at the same relative speed, stopping and starting at the same time. However, since each oval is isolated, they can be likened to blocks and in effect you have a form of block control with a minimum of wiring and gapping, as shown in this Atlas wiring plan, one of the many from *Wiring Your HO Layout,* by Paul Mallery Associates. The Atlas twin switch enables the operator to select single- or dual-train operation.

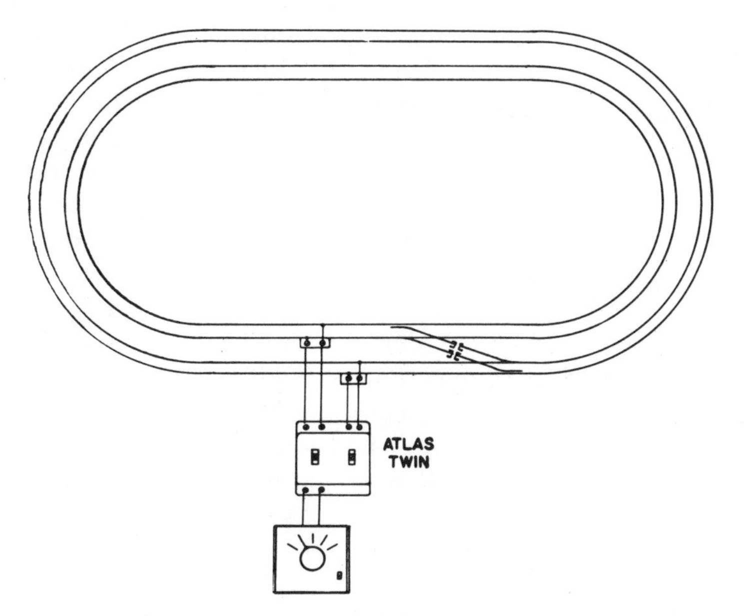

TWO-TRAIN OPERATION FROM ONE POWER SOURCE WITH INDEPENDENT DIRECTION CONTROL

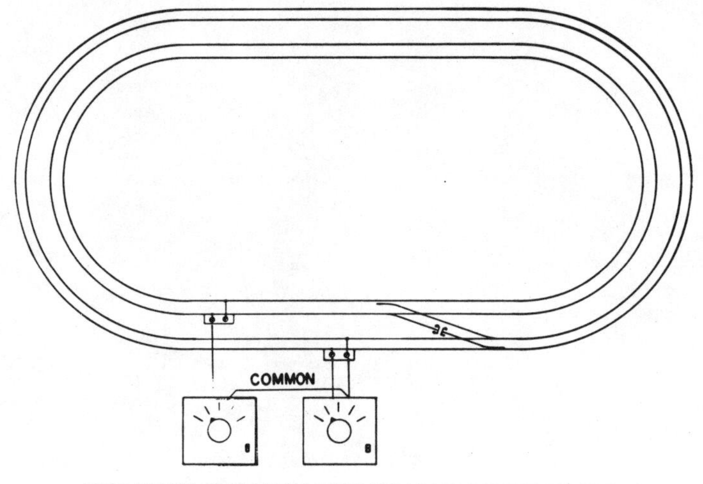

TWO-TRAIN OPERATION WITH SEPARATE POWER SUPPLIES

The same Atlas plan now involves the use of two power packs on a "common" wiring basis, permitting a simple form of cab control in which two locos may now be operated simultaneously and independently of each other's actions. Note also that less wiring is involved, which only goes to prove that sometimes you can expand the operating potential without necessarily increasing the amount of wiring.

you deaden the spur or siding, etc. However, if you wished to retain power in an otherwise dead spur or siding, a few alterations would be necessary. Regular switches would require gapping and auxiliary feeders (of proper polarity), whereas, in the case of Tru-Switches (featuring an almost invisible gap), a jumper wire (of proper polarity) would have to be fed to the neutral rail in question. In either case, the additional feeder, when connected to and controlled by an off-on toggle switch, would enable you to keep power in this particular trackage even though the turnout is thrown to the main. The value of such an arrangement will become more evident when we discuss multi-train operation.

On the other hand, where Custom-Line and Snap-Switches are concerned, the fact that all tracks are powered regardless of turnout position precludes the need for any additional feeders to power any trackage off the mainline. But, should you wish to deaden those particular areas when so desired, then gaps or insulated joiners would be necessary, along with auxiliary feeders and off-on toggle switches. If you have suddenly concluded that all in all it is six of one or a half dozen of the other, and it doesn't really make much difference which type of turnout is used, then pay heed to the following, for you will see that although all things may appear equal, they really aren't—not by a long shot.

For the beginner who wishes to operate as much as possible and with the least amount of wiring (and that includes most of us at the start), the use of "power routing" turnouts will help keep wiring not only at a minimum, but will permit more prototypical operating possibilities. That's why the average advanced model railroader uses this type of turnout. And if you are a sectional tracker, you might consider the fact that Tru-Switches, when combined with Tru-Track or other sectional track material, will virtually provide you with a wireless no-gap-it-yourself hook-up other than the two basic power feeds from pack to rail. To appreciate this, let us consider a typical small-sized layout consisting of a simple oval, a passing siding, and three spurs or storage areas. Let us also assume that for the moment you are content to operate one locomotive at a time while two or three other engines are standing by in various storage and holding areas of your layout, such as the siding and spurs I mentioned. Ordinarily, the passing siding and spurs would have to be isolated from the mainline or basic oval. Additional wiring in the way of auxiliary feeders and no less than four toggle switches would be required if your turnouts permitted the flow of current in all directions, turnout position notwithstanding. Immediately, a simple plan such as this suddenly needs a bit of gapping, power-feeding, and toggle-switching to deaden the areas in question, and liven them as desired. Yet with the power-routing capabilities such as Tru-Switches afford, you could operate four locomotives, and in this given track plan only two hook-up wires would be needed. No gapping (it's taken care of in the switch), no feeders to liven or deaden track away from the mainline (the switch does that, too), and, of course, no extra toggle switches either.

True, such an operating arrangement involving regular turnouts would require a bit more wiring and gapping even though they are power-routing in nature. However, if you are a sectional tracker and plan to eventually change over to the more sophisticated track materials and power-routing regular switch turnouts, then Tru-Switches are a perfect means of getting off to a flying start and having the opportunity of operating in prototype fashion without having to wire specially for it. Finally, it is in terminal areas and yards where this Tru-Switch no-special-wiring feature becomes so useful. And at this point, the reason should be obvious. So much for turnouts for the moment, and bear in mind that the foregoing has been presented in an effort to call to your attenton the functions and electrical characteristics of various turnouts. The choice is entirely your own and will be determined by your own needs, skills, and plan of operation.

Now, let's talk about feeders, which in their initial use and form represent the basic wiring connection between your power pack and trackwork. On a small layout involving single train operation, one pair of feeders is generally sufficient to power the overall trackwork. However, as you expand your track plan and extend the distance of trackwork from the power feeding point, a certain amount of current resistance is likely to be encountered due to loose rail joiners, poor connections, and size of wire, etc. To overcome this loss in power, and to affect an even distribution of current throughout your entire trackage, the use of auxiliary feeder wires is employed.

Now is a good time to digress for a moment and consider a few important characteristics about wire, and the types most suitable for model railroad hook-ups. Naturally, it should be insulated—plastic preferably, since this material is easily scraped off when baring wire ends to wrap around screws or for soldering. The diameter of the wire is equally important, for the thickness (size) will determine how easily the current will flow from one point to another without any appreciable loss in power. For example, size 14 wire has a larger diameter than size 18 wire, and thus offers less resistance to the flow of current. For this reason, size 14 wire is popularly used, especially where long feeder connections and heavy current is required. In the case of shorter lengths of wire, such as would be needed within control panels, jumpers, etc., size 18 will be more than adequate. By using terminal strips, you can avoid having wires running back and forth and every which way from power source to point of connection. Terminal strips are quite inexpensive and, if not available at your hobby shop, are easily obtainable at radio and electronics parts stores. Another nice thing about terminal strips is the fact that they will enable you to keep wires connected to their respective mates, and, by means of numbering and color coding, not only help do away with a mumble-jumble rat's nest of wires clumped together, but are an easy means of changing connections and trouble-shooting should the need

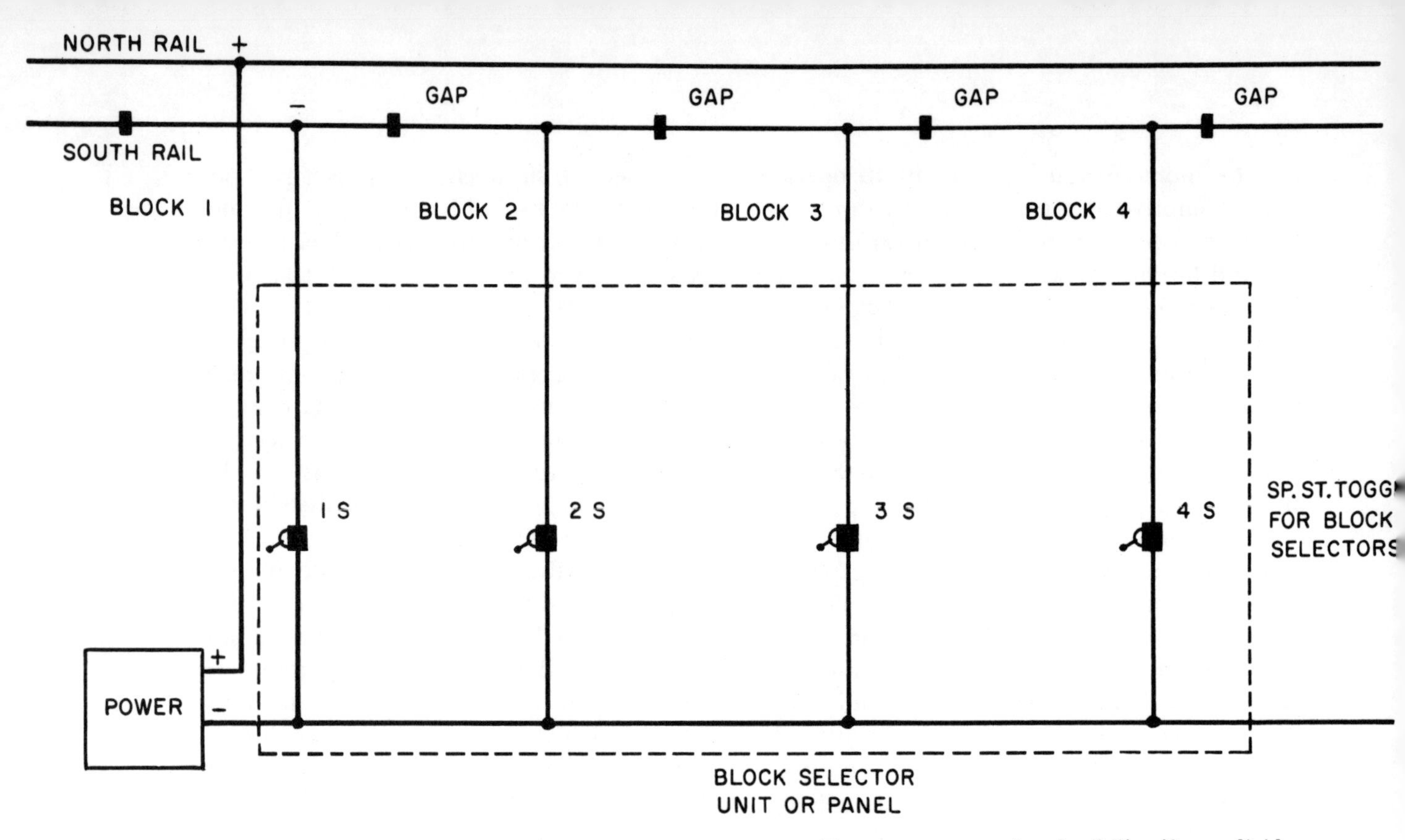

Regardless of the type of track plan you use, you will get more operating flexibility if you divide your track plan into a number of blocks. A common rail of each block featuring a single-pole single-throw toggle switch will enable you to operate one train after the other throughout the trackage of your plan. Block wiring will also help you quickly find trouble spots when they develop. Each block should be slightly longer than the average train length.

arise. Auxiliary feeders can run directly from the power pack terminals to that troublesome far-reaching stretch of track, or they can tap off current from a terminal strip or track-work at some point in between. Of course, all things must be equal, current-wise, so be sure you don't accidentally reverse or mix the polarity.

Now, let's get back to that simple oval and one power pack. To all intents and purposes, this permits the operation of one locomotive at a time. By placing another engine on the track, you can operate both of them simultaneously—that is, if you don't mind them chasing each other around the track, running at the same relative speed, and starting and stopping at the same time, since they are controlled by the same throttle. Therefore, the next step toward more realistic operation would be to divide your oval into various blocks, sections of track that are isolated from each other electrically by means of gaps. Then, by connecting auxiliary feeders and simple single-pole single-throw off-on toggle switches, you can control the current in the respective blocks so wired. In this manner, two locomotives can run or stand still independent of each other *when they are in separate blocks.* Oversimplified as this may be, this is the essence of block control, which, to repeat, is a means of wiring and isolating one area of track from another (each no less than a train's length long) so that one train can operate in one part of the layout independent of the action of another train elsewhere on the layout. However, since only one power pack is being used to power the blocks when both trains operate at the same time, their speeds will be relatively the same, along with the other considerations mentioned above. Nevertheless, by means of block control and selective toggling, you can run one train at a time or both, whichever you prefer, and while the disadvantage of having two trains operated by the same throttle becomes painfully and increasingly obvious, it is still an improvement, since you at least have a form of selective control whereby one train can be held in a passing siding while another train rolls by, or, to put it quite plainly, both trains can be operated on a stop-or-go basis.

After awhile this can become pretty monotonous—generally sooner than later—but it is a good start and not a waste of time, as you will see in what follows. So you decide that you would like to operate two trains at the same time (or different times) independent of each other's action and *at different speeds.* In other words, each train would be powered by its own throttle. Well, to put it mildly, thousands of other model rails felt the same way and that is how cab control came about, whereby two trains could operate independently of each other, at different speeds, stopping and starting without affecting each other, and certainly offering more possibilities where prototype operation is concerned. This is accomplished through the use of an additional power pack—now we have two—wherein each throttle is fed to each block or section of trackwork (group of blocks) by means of separate feeder wires. Therefore, with the aid of off-on switches of the single-pole single-throw variety, the operator can power one or all blocks with whichever throttle (cab) he so desires, whenever the occasion demands with respect to his mode of operation. Accompanying diagrams show the basic wiring of this type of hook-up. The results obtainable through cab control arrangements are quite obvious and are a definite refinement of block control.

Within the framework and concept of cab control technique and operation are various applications, some more advanced and complicated than others. For, in addition to plain cab control, we have systems involving the use of block-control panels, dual-throttle control panels, power-routing panels, and a host of other sophisticated ingredients all designed to guide you in the direction of the highest plateaus in model railroad operation.

True, this all adds up to quite a bit of wiring, numerous switches, power packs, toggles, wire, terminal strips, and other electrical equipment—not to mention time, effort, and expense. Of course, it also adds up to the commonly accepted, proven, and tried method of obtaining a high degree of flexibility and authentic-appearing action and operation—to wit, the end certainly justifies the means.

It also adds up to the fact that wiring, complex or otherwise, has an infinite variety of techniques, applications, do's and don'ts, short cuts, etc., and is a subject so broad and with more detailed avenues than one can pursue, let alone write about in one given chapter. How you wire your layout will depend on your knowledge of what it is all about. On the other hand, there is no set rule stating that you must follow the procedures that are prescribed, and you can wire things in any manner, shape, or form you wish, providing that the forces of electricity don't challenge you. Chances are that you will come up with a few short cuts of your own, not to mention an experimental innovation or two which will do much to eliminate conventional wiring as we have known it to be employed up to this point.

Therefore, if someone were to ask, "What about radio control?", the unanimous reply no doubt would be, "great!" However, that would entail each locomotive containing its own receiver tuned or sensitive to its own special frequency, which, when transmitted, would be received by this particular locomotive alone, and no other. In like fashion, other locomotives would have similar receivers tuned to their respective frequencies, all different and separated from each other. The master control panel would, therefore, feature a transmitter for beaming frequencies to the receivers of respective locomotives, and the end result would be that any number of locos could operate in any direction, speed, or action completely independent of each other. This sounds fine and would certainly

The following diagrams (courtesy of Kalmbach Publishing) are a sample of the information available in *How To Wire Your Model Railroad,* by Linn H. Westcott. Chock-full of extremely useful and informative material, it is definitely recommended reading for beginners, advanced hobbyists and veteran brass hats. The simple oval in these plans involves the use of a reverse loop, passing siding and spur track leading to a turntable. Also note the fact that the throttle controls have been separated from the power supply—a common practice among advanced model railroaders.

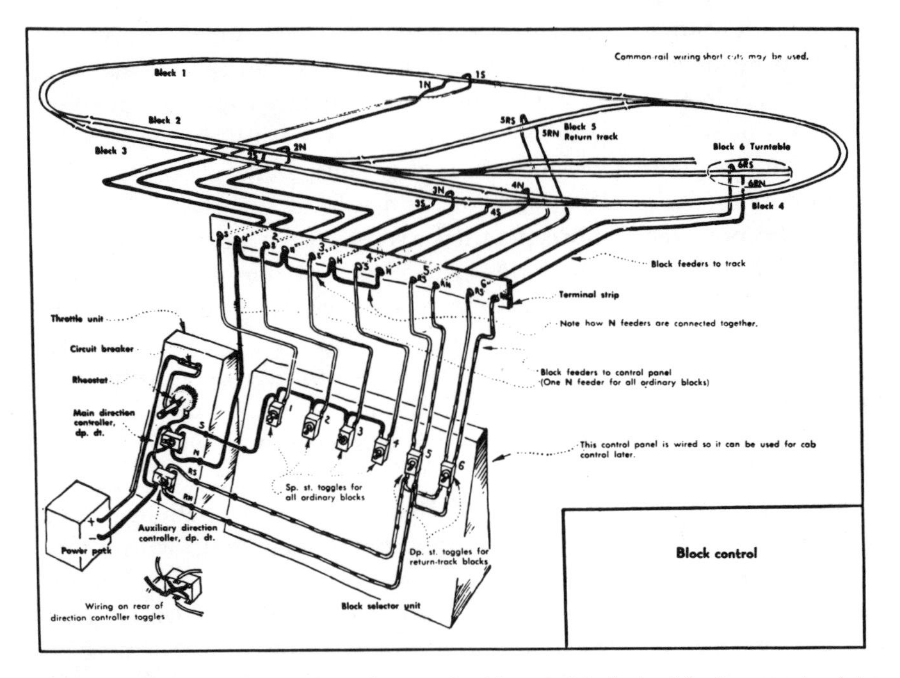

This dimensional schematic embraces the ideas behind the block-control wiring plan shown within these pages; however, circuits have been added for turntable, turning track and other trackage. In these particular blocks, double-pole toggle switches are used to prevent short circuits (via N feeders) which might occur between two panels if you use this type of wiring for cab control later on. This is just the start of a more sophisticated approach toward wiring and the more flexible operation it permits.

This is the essence of plain cab control using a single power supply. But it is an improvement over block control, for it offers more versatile operation. Since only one power supply is being used for more than one control panel, all N feeders as well as S feeders must be broken through the block toggles. This requires one more pole on each toggle, and N feeders cannot be connected in common. There must also be gaps between both rails at every end of each block. This same doubled-wiring scheme can be adapted to the twin-throttle type of panel if you want to use the same power pack for both throttles.

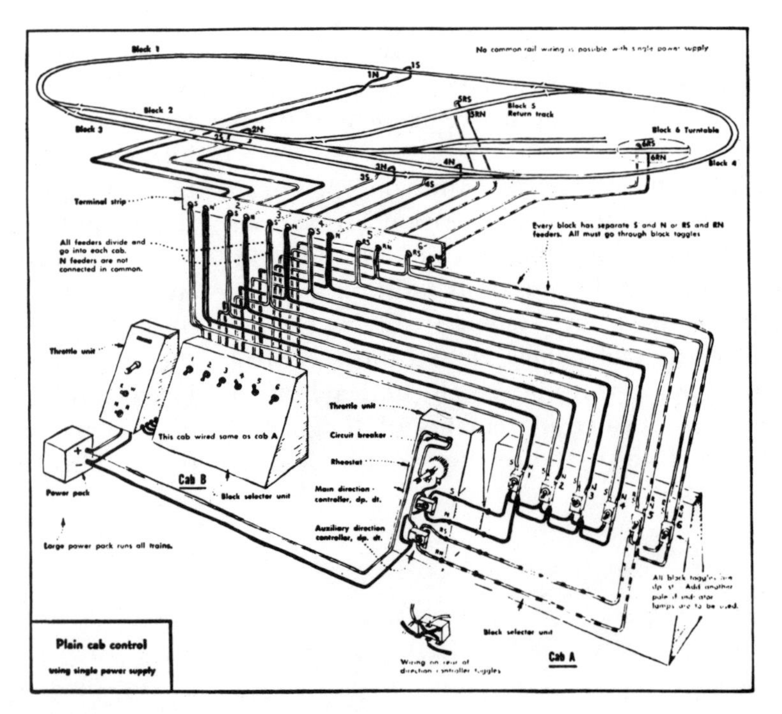

By providing a block control-type panel for each train, you can operate a railroad by cab control. The wiring in each cab is exactly the same as in the block control panel. This is a refinement over the plain cab-control wiring plan.

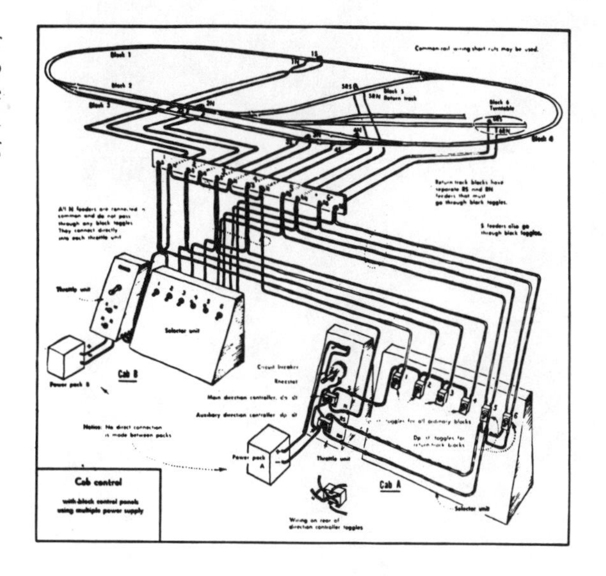

Cab control with dual-throttle panel and multiple power supply is the most commonly and widely used form of wiring for dual-train operation. For more detailed information, see Westcott's *How To Wire Your Model Railroad*.

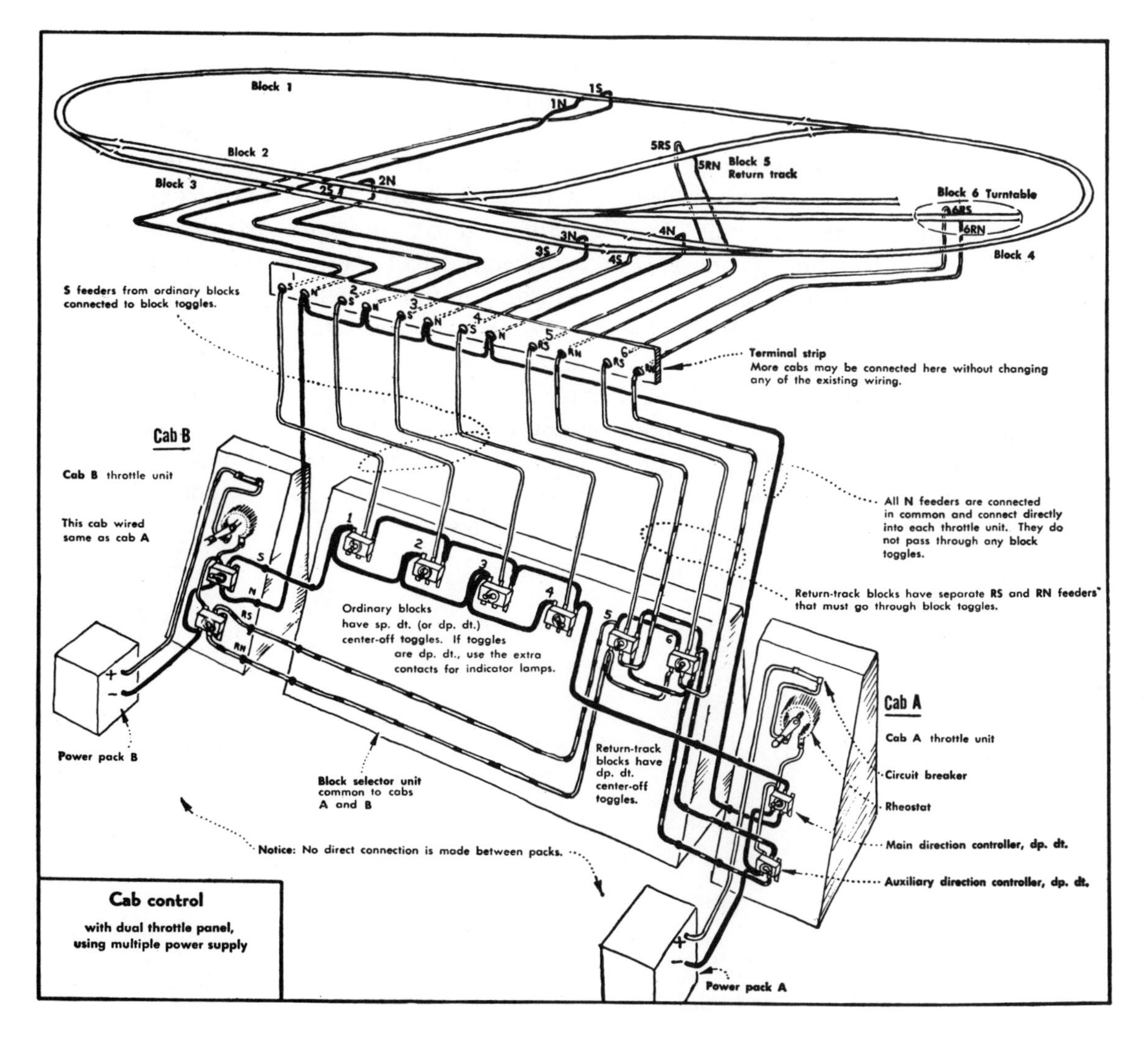

Cab control with dual throttle panel, using multiple power supply

Don Thompson has done a thorough job of carefully integrating his wiring so that he can quickly locate trouble spots in his swing-out control panel.

minimize the amount of wiring for blocks, sections, cabs, toggles, etc., if not completely eliminate them. However, the locomotives would also need good-sized antennae, and miniaturized though things may be in today's space age, "there ain't no such animal" yet—at least where model railroading is concerned.

However, there is something close to it and it is one of the giant steps the hobby has taken since HO was first introduced.

It is in view of this scientific breakthrough and electronic achievement that I am about to slam on the brakes and bring this chapter to a close. At this moment, I won't say that the information and revolutionary applications which follow will make all of the foregoing obsolete or of minimum necessity, for what we have discussed thus far is absolutely essential in any event—not only for the sake of model railroad wiring knowledge, but to enable you to appreciate what the next chapter offers. It will also explain why I stressed certain points and generalized about others.

So, prepare yourself for a journey into a new world of micro-receivers, kilocycles, radio frequencies, power control transmitters, and, most important, the possible elimination of up to 75 per cent of conventional model railroad wiring. No, the trip is not fantasy or make-believe, but actual fact.

XVII

ASTRAC–A New Concept for Radio Frequency Control

ASTRAC—it's here at last. It is one of the greatest developments in model railroading, and the first successful and commercial presentation of what model rails have been waiting for the world over. ASTRAC—Automatic Simultaneous Train Control—is a product of General Electric research, electronic engineering, and radio frequency miniaturization which now offers new and unlimited horizons for prototype model train operation whereby different locomotives can be controlled anywhere on the layout, in close proximity to each other or far apart, and completely independent of each other's speed, direction of operation, or action.

Using high-frequency current to control model trains is not a new idea and, in fact, hobbyists have been dreaming of it for years. Model plane enthusiasts have been enjoying various forms of remote radio control for quite some time, but, unfortunately, model railroaders have not been so blessed. Now, however, through the advent of miniature electronic devices capable of handling high power, the use of intermediate-frequency radio waves (on a "carrier control" basis) within the framework of model railroads has become possible—and more important, is *finally available!* Equally important is the fact that model rail fans can now enjoy all the refinements of block and cab control without having to become involved in complicated wiring plans and sophisticated control panels.

True, the wiring involved in the ASTRAC system is also quite complicated, and includes many exotic components and parts. But *ASTRAC is available pre-wired* and, complex though its circuitry may be, you don't have to do anything more than connect tiny receivers to your locomotives, add only two extra wires to your track, and you are underway to new adventures, and unlimited control and operating possibilities. The operating possibilities permit you to operate five different locomotives on one or more stretches of trackwork, one at a time or simultaneously; at different speeds and in opposite directions, and without so much as one single gap, plastic joiner, or toggle switch (depending on your track plan and turnout arrangement).

Five trains on one track? Sounds unbelievable. Just picture it—a system that would permit you to operate so many trains simultaneously and independently on one electrically continuous track without requiring insulated rail joiners, gaps, miles of wiring,

This is the most important load a tender ever carried. Fuel in the form of radio-frequency propulsion, received and distributed by this micro-receiver, will enable you to guide your locomotive into any number of unlimited operating procedures. ASTRAC-equipped locomotives can be operated simultaneously or singly, completely independent of one another's actions and movements in a manner which has heretofore been virtually impossible without resorting to the most sophisticated and complex of wiring arrangements, and even then there would be limitations. Where ASTRAC is concerned, there are no limitations in operation. Three wires connected to your locomotive, two extra wires fed to your track-work and new adventures in model railroading await you.

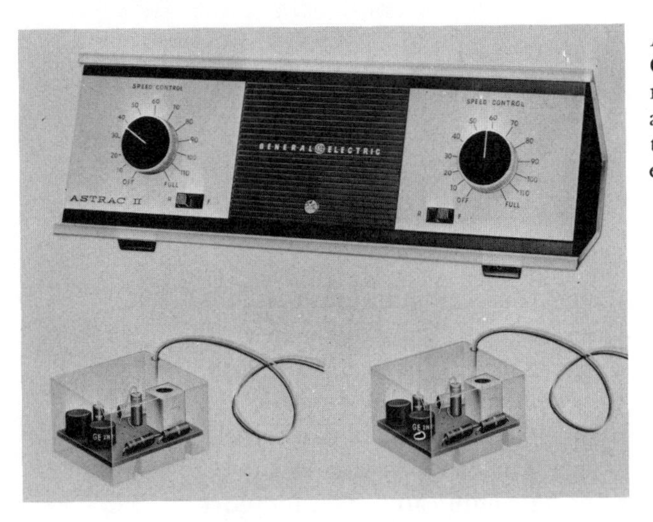

ASTRAC, Automatic Simultaneous Train Controls, such as this General Electric K2 or K4 unit, opens new vistas for model railroad operation. Transmission unit includes two micro-receivers and easy-to-read hook-up instructions. Separate speed and direction controls permit dual or single operation of two receiver-equipped locos.

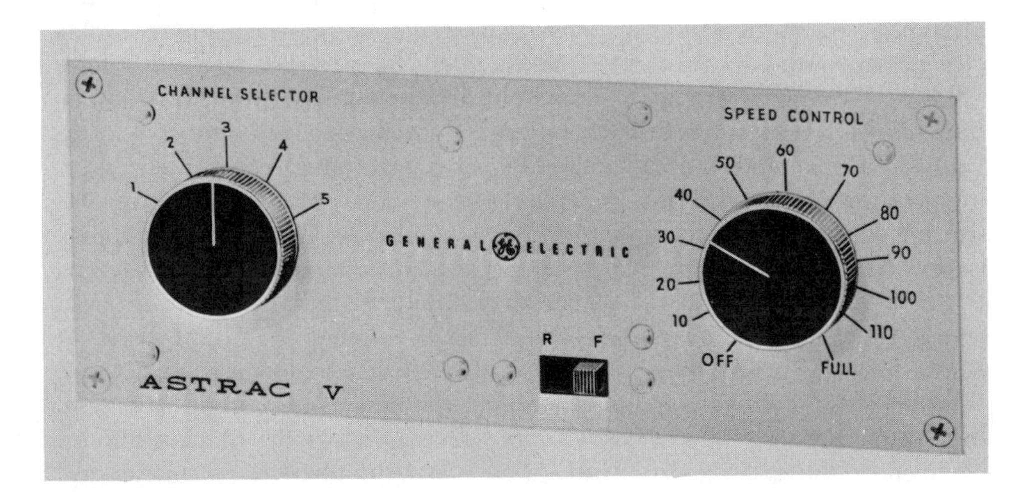

Five-channel ASTRAC Model K5 permits selective operation and control of any one of five channels. Identical to Model K7, which transmits to five other channels.

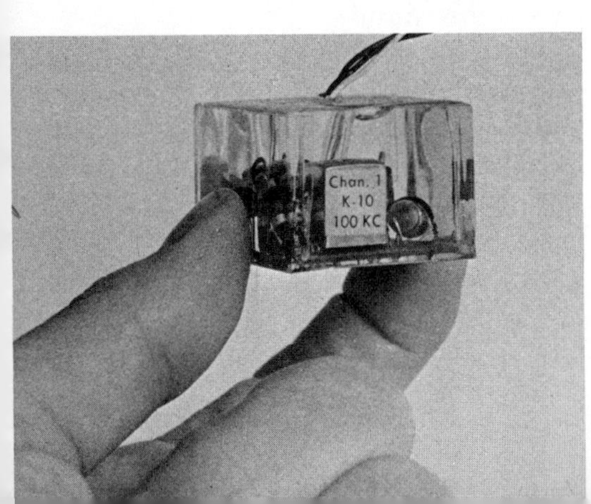

The heart of the matter is the micro-receiver. Two silicon rectifiers prevent AC power in the rails from getting to the motor and, in fact, convert the AC to DC. The rectifiers also act as switches and, though they are "solid state" devices, turn on and off, permitting not only the flow of current to the loco motor when the ASTRAC signal is transmitted, but control of the direction of the locomotive for forward or reverse operation.

toggle switches, and separate power-controlled cabs and blocks. Each train could go forward or backward, or stand still regardless of what the other four were doing. And this is only one of the many advantages of the ASTRAC system, for, in addition to the automatic operation of as many as five trains, there are numerous other benefits which we shall go into later. And bear in mind that all this can be accomplished by means of the most simple hook-up and, conversely speaking, the *elimination of up to, or at least, 75 per cent of what would normally be needed in the way of wiring.*

The basic idea behind the ASTRAC system is the use of high-frequency signals to control the operation of different locomotives which are powered by low voltage AC fed to the track in the same manner that we normally connect DC power. I know that many eyebrows are being raised at the mere mention of AC current, low voltage notwithstanding, being used as the main source of current and power. However, be patient; the explanation is quite simple and we'll get to the technical aspects in a few moments. The flexibility of this system permits the control of different trains by different high-frequency signals, making multiple-train operation no longer the wiring problem it used to be, and, to repeat, enabling you to eliminate all the conventional wiring that would be required under normal circumstances. However, these are not normal circumstances, for each locomotive is fitted out with a receiver—a *tiny* receiver, at that. And, in turn, transmitter control units replace the rheostat or throttle in your power pack. The power pack is still used, of course, but only to supply the AC power, not to control it.

The feasibility of such a system depends largely on the size and power requirements of the respective receivers. They have to be small enough to fit inside the boiler or tender of their respective locomotives, since space is at a premium. Furthermore, the receivers have to be capable of handling the high current demanded and required by the motors, and, in addition, they have to be shockproof, heat-proof, collision-proof, and, most of all, completely reliable. And I'm happy to say that since these receivers feature all the above-named ingredients, General Electric has been able to offer the ASTRAC system of virtually wireless multi-train operation to the model railroader.

Permit me to digress for a moment, for if I sound repetitive, it is only because I wish to stress the significance of this achievement. For, over the years there have been many abortive attempts at radio-frequency control for model railroading. The reasons for previous failures have been many, including lack of proper technique, lack of sufficient miniaturization with respect to practical application and installation where HO scale is concerned, and, among other things, lack of proper financing. Fortunately for us the ASTRAC system is one in which many of the problems that have eluded other companies in the past have been solved.

I have mentioned that the characteristics and integral wiring of ASTRAC and the circuitry involved are complicated, and embrace a number of exotic components in miniature and transistorized form. However, the seeming complexity should be no more disturbing to a potential ASTRAC user than to one who uses a ready-made power pack, transistorized or otherwise. Outside of one's own curiosity, there is no reason to open things up, for, to repeat, ASTRAC comes with the complicated wiring already done for you. You can also expect repairs or replacement of parts to be at a minimum, since the controlling devices are transistors (rather than vacuum tubes) and a well-designed transistorized circuit such as ASTRAC employs should last for a number of years if not mistreated. Should repairs become necessary, a knowledge of how to check electronic circuits will be required, or you can enlist the aid and services of a knowledgeable repairman or, for that matter, send the unit or whatever to General Electric for repair, replacement, etc. So don't concern yourself with the wiring involved, for despite its complications all you have to be concerned with is the pleasant fact that it only takes two extra wires to connect an ASTRAC control unit to your layout, and only three wires to connect a receiver to a locomotive. However, for the benefit of those who are technically minded, and for the sake of having at least a general idea of how and why ASTRAC can do what it does, let us pursue these why's and wherefore's.

Earlier, I mentioned that, with ASTRAC, the power fed to the rails is AC rather than DC. Under ordinary circumstances this would be impossible, for the nature of the permanent magnet motors used in HO locomotives is such that any more than a few seconds of AC would burn them up. However, within the heart of a given receiver are two SCR's (silicon controlled rectifiers), which are recently developed miniature electronic devices, small as transistors, but capable of handling hundreds of times the power. In addition to this, they are also capable of transforming the AC current to DC current in a fashion similar to that of a power pack. In other words, although the ASTRAC system utilizes AC voltage on the tracks, the SCR's within the micro-receivers prevent any of the AC track voltage from reaching the DC motor. Therefore, while there is constant AC power in the rails at all times, only DC current actually reaches the motor. The SCR's also control the direction of the locomotive by performing the service of tiny switches. One SCR controls the forward motion of the locomotive, and the other the reverse motion. The SCR's, however, have no moving parts, since they are "solid state" devices, but nonetheless can turn themselves on and off when the signal to which they are tuned is beamed to them by means of this "carrier control" system. Thus, the position of the direction switch on the transmitter control unit will trigger the action of the SCR's, which respond accordingly; to wit, the locomotive will run either forward or in reverse. I feel that no particular benefit can be derived from any further detailed technical aspects of why these components behave the way they do. Suffice to say that they work, and work well.

Please note that I wasted no time in establishing the fact that ASTRAC provides simultaneous and independent train control on the basis of "carrier control." In short, we are not talking of radio control, for in radio control the operation of one or more locomotives would be a completely wireless affair in which they would be powered and controlled by the transmission of different radio waves through the air, whereas in carrier control, which is actually better suited to our purposes, the control of one or more given locomotives is accomplished by superimposing higher-frequency current (intermediate radio frequencies if you prefer) on the rails. In other words, a control transmitter unit feeds a specific signal to the rails, which in turn carry it to a receiver which has been connected to and controls the action of the motor in the locomotive.

Thus, by way of summary for the moment, the ASTRAC system, in addition to controlling the action of locomotives appropriately equipped with receivers, also utilizes AC voltage on the tracks. This AC can be supplied from the accessory terminals of your present power pack. The DC portion of the power pack is not used, nor is the rheostat, which can be left at zero and ignored, since it has no affect whatsoever on the AC output. If perchance your power pack does not include AC accessory terminals—highly unlikely—you can use any AC transformer that produces an output voltage in the 16- to 20-volt range. ASTRAC receivers can be operated in the 3-30-volt range; however, 16-20 volts AC is recommended by G.E., and will usually produce sufficient and maximum speed for average operation. However, some locomotives may respond to ASTRAC differently than others, and we will get to that shortly. Also,

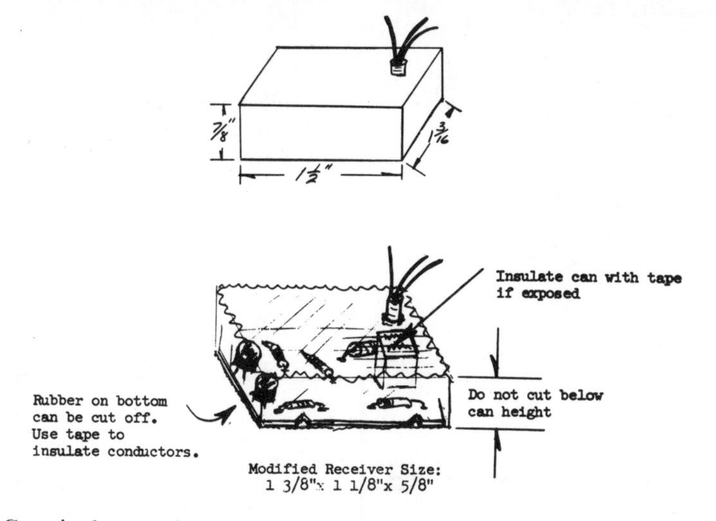

Certain locomotives, particularly oldtimers, are simply too small to accommodate receiver installation, more often than not, the tender will house the receiver. If necessary, the receiver can be cut down in size, as indicated in this diagram. Relative and modified sizes are shown.

Actual size and modified size of micro-receivers. In time, they will be even smaller.

in line with the latter is the fact that while creep speeds are possible with ASTRAC, the smoothness of operation will depend on whether a locomotive operates well at creep speeds to begin with. Some do and some don't, regardless of how they are powered. Also bear in mind that at creep speeds the motor's armature is not turning fast enough to produce good air circulation; as a result, you are quite likely to encounter a bit of motor overheating if you operate at very low running speeds for extended periods. A bit further along we will cover in greater detail the actual performance capabilities of locomotive equipment and how they respond while under the influence of ASTRAC. For the moment, however, let us turn to the actual equipment itself for a brief rundown on the various units and their uses.

The ASTRAC system embraces the use of micro-receivers and various control units which can be used singly or combined.

MICRO-RECEIVER models, channels, and frequencies are:

K-10	Channel 1	100 KC
K-20	Channel 2	140 KC
K-30	Channel 3	180 KC
K-40	Channel 4	220 KC
K-50	Channel 5	255 KC

As you can see from this listing, each receiver operates on a separate channel which, in turn, is tuned to and receptive only to its own special frequency or signal.

Control unit models and channel controls are:

Model K-2—A dual-control unit providing independent operation of two locomotives on Channels 1 and 5. Separate speed controls and separate forward-reverse switches are provided for each train. Also includes an indicator light to tell when the system is on.

Model K-4—Identical to Model K-2 except that it controls Channels 2 and 4. By connecting the K-2 and K-4 models in series with each other, you can operate up to four trains simultaneously in different directions and completely independent of each other.

Model K-5—This unit has one speed control and one forward-reverse switch, but is capable of transmitting power to all five channels. With the aid of a five-channel selector switch, the operator is able to control any one of five trains on the track by merely switching to its particular channel. In other words, the K-5 unit permits the operation of up to five ASTRAC-equipped trains, *one at a time.*

To control five trains simultaneously you would need the combination of Models K-2,

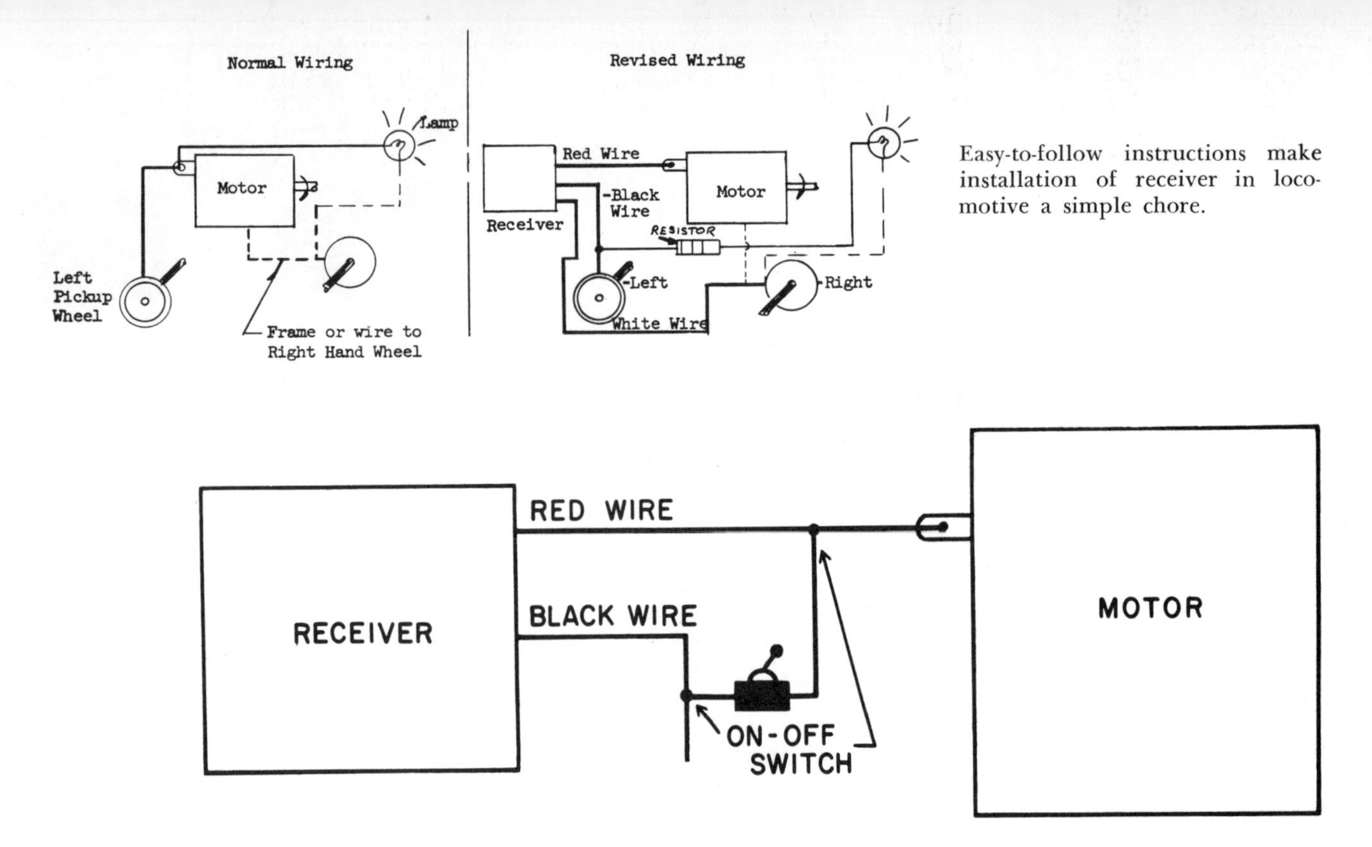

Easy-to-follow instructions make installation of receiver in locomotive a simple chore.

Installing a sub-miniature or small on-off toggle switch between the red and black wires (other wiring omitted for clarity) will enable you to switch from ASTRAC back to normal operation of the loco. This comes in handy when you wish to operate your receiver-equipped loco on a layout wired for and powered by DC. It will also enable you to operate on sections of your own trackage which do not receive the ASTRAC signals. The best time to provide for this option is at the time of initial receiver installation. Caution: When a receiver-equipped loco is switched back to normal operation, do not attempt to operate it on ASTRAC-AC-powered track, otherwise you will overheat and burn out your motor.

A typical installation is shown in this receiver-equipped diesel locomotive. Receiver resting on chassis can be held in place by masking tape and will easily fit within the housing of the average diesel.

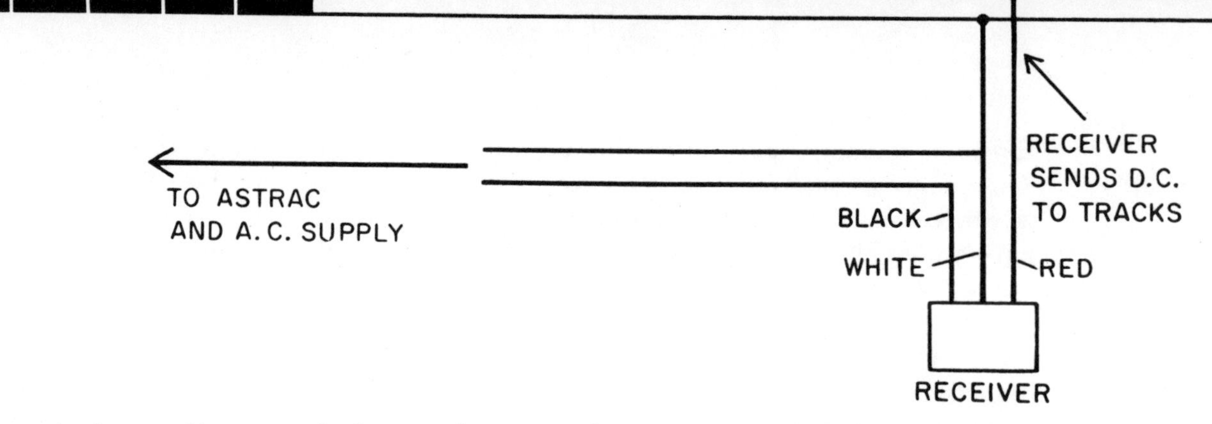

This simple test hook-up enables you to check out performance and response to an ASTRAC signal without having to actually install a receiver in a given locomotive. Silicon rectifiers in the receiver only allow DC to get to the rails, permitting operation in the conventional manner, but controlled by the transmitted signal from an ASTRAC unit.

K-4, and K-5. K-2 would handle Channels 1 and 5, K-4 would handle Channels 2 and 4, and K-5 would handle Channel 3. Of course, it goes without saying that you would have to have five locomotives equipped with individual receivers corresponding to the respective channels. There are a few other combinations for multi-train operation within the framework of the ASTRAC system. For example, a K-2 or K-4 combined with a K-5 will permit simultaneous or independent operation of three ASTRAC-equipped locomotives. Two K-5's combined will handle any two of five trains simultaneously, three will handle three, etc.

As far as electrical hook-up is concerned, the installation of a receiver in a locomotive is a fairly simple affair and only requires the connecting of three wires. All you have to do is follow the directions in the instruction sheets. Excerpts and diagrams from these instruction sheets are shown in this chapter, so study them carefully and check the caption information, for they contain all the details. As for the physical installation of the receiver in the locomotive, it will depend, of course, on whether or not there is sufficient room within the boiler to accommodate it. For, in spite of the small size of the micro-receiver, in a number of cases you will find that there just isn't any room in the locomotive itself to house the receiver. This is particularly evident in the case of oldtimers. Should this be the case, then, you can install the receiver in the tender and run your wires forward through the cab to the motor. Diesels present little if any problem for receiver installation, since there is generally sufficient room within the superstructure. If not, you can use the "B" unit of your diesel to house the receiver.

Hooking up the control unit to your layout is a snap, requiring the connection of only two wires from the terminals on the back of the unit to the terminals on your track or points of power feed. Two wires from the AC terminals of your power pack or transformer also connect to the track leads. And that is all there is to it in the way of wiring and connection.

And that is the essence of ASTRAC—as neat and trim a means of controlling one or more trains as is not only dreamable, but, thanks to General Electric, believable as well. However, don't loosen your safety belts yet, for there is more to come. For example, some of those fringe benefits I was talking about.

The information discussed thus far points up one important factor—namely, that through the application of ASTRAC you have the benefit of block control, cab control, and many of the other sophisticated refinements of prototype operation without wiring for it as described in the preceding chapter. In addition, you automatically get a bonus in the way of constant lighting of locomotive headlights and other lighting equipment, since the AC power is in the rails at all times and is not affected by the operation of your motive power or throttles. This means that headlights will remain on whether the locomotive is running or standing still—quite the opposite where conventional operation of locomotives is concerned. For, in that case you would have to install and wire a special high-frequency lighting set-up into your railroad which would involve the use of capacitors and/or condensors plus other doohickeys too numerous to mention, and which, in view of the circumstances, would make it pointless to delve into any further. So as fringe benefits go, HFL is a handsome bonus, especially since it is free. The advantage of having current in the rail at all times manifests itself in a number of other pleasant ways, also. It not only offers an opportunity to keep our lights on all the time, but also provides a handy supply line by sending power through the tracks to lights and other accessories near or far. In other words, it is like having one power outlet after the other all over the layout. For wherever there is track, there is power.

To power an accessory or supply juice to an otherwise dark structure, you simply tap current from the nearest section of track, and, lo and behold—oil wells pump oil, structures glow with illumination, factory smokestacks puff clouds of smog into the air (if equipped with smoke generators), and otherwise quiet and static-looking areas of your layout come alive. And you didn't have to run any auxiliary wires back to terminal strips or power pack. This certainly saves a lot of time, wiring, effort, and expense. The same goes for supplying the power to the toggle switches which control the switch machines, which in turn change the position of your turnouts. I'll stop right here and go on to other things, for your imagination does not have to work overtime to think up dozens of ways in which you can utilize the fact that your trackwork also serves as a power supply line. Last, but not least, passenger cars, parlor cars, any illuminated cars will now stay lighted. One last word concerning the trackwork acting as a common carrier for both the AC power and the ASTRAC signals: The signals will, when transmitted, travel to all areas of the track in the same manner as the AC power, and during a series of exhaustive tests I did not encounter any weakening or loss of signal power; likewise for the AC current. However, depending on the size of one's layout, it wouldn't hurt to have a few auxiliary feeders as described in the preceding chapter, for they will help produce a more even distribution of power and signal, especially for those troublesome and far-reaching stretches of track. To all intents and purposes the signals will travel to any area of trackwork that the running current can reach; nevertheless, a few extra feeders won't hurt.

For those of you who have already wired your layout for block control (see Chapter XVI), leave things as they are. The addition or conversion to ASTRAC operation is a simple matter, for all you have to do is connect the ASTRAC unit and the AC terminals of your present power pack to the track leads, flip the toggles of all blocks to "on" position, and you are ready to operate. If the AC side of your present power pack does not provide sufficient voltage for the ASTRAC-equipped locomotives, then simply replace it with a new source of AC power. The advantage of retaining the existing wiring is twofold. First off, it will enable you to locate trouble spots in your trackwork by the process of elimination, and, should a short circuit occur in a particular block, you can still keep operation on the move within the other areas of your railroad. Secondly, it will permit you to test and run non-ASTRAC-equipped locomotives by turning off the AC power to a block or section, and powering them with DC in the conventional manner. This could make for an interesting project in the form of a simple control panel featuring two toggle switches, one controlling the power feed of AC and ASTRAC, and one for DC. Finally, and for the sake of comparison, if under a given block-control system you employ the use of a dual-control ASTRAC unit (Model K-2 or K-4) and install corresponding receivers in two of your locomotives, you will have im-

ASTRAC control units can be combined and hooked up to provide you with various forms of single, dual- or multi-train operation. Bear in mind that the application of ASTRAC control signals to the rails only requires the connecting of two additional wires. You get the benefit of block and cab control without having to wire for it.

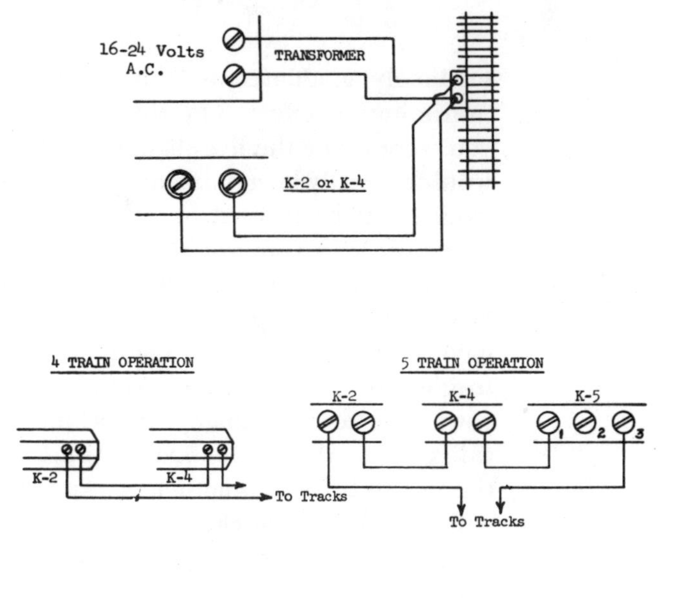

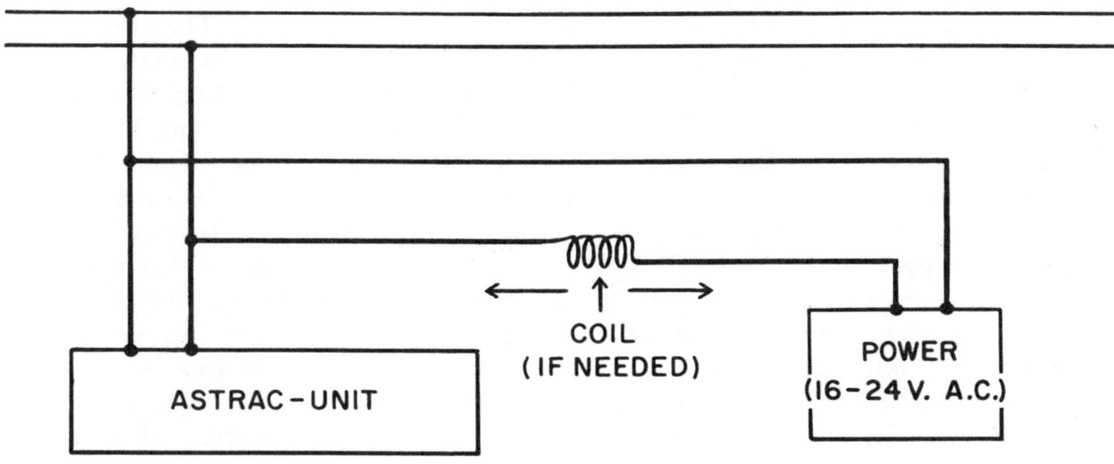

Rectifiers in power packs may sometimes have a tendency to short circuit the ASTRAC signals. If this happens, a "choke-coil" inserted at the point shown in the diagram will help remedy the situation.

Since power in the rails is constant at all times, a resistor inserted as shown in the diagram will lessen the tendency for smoke generators to overheat, thus adding to their operating life. A sub-miniature on-off switch might be useful also. In a case such as this, the resistor can also be used to reduce intensity of current reaching the headlight.

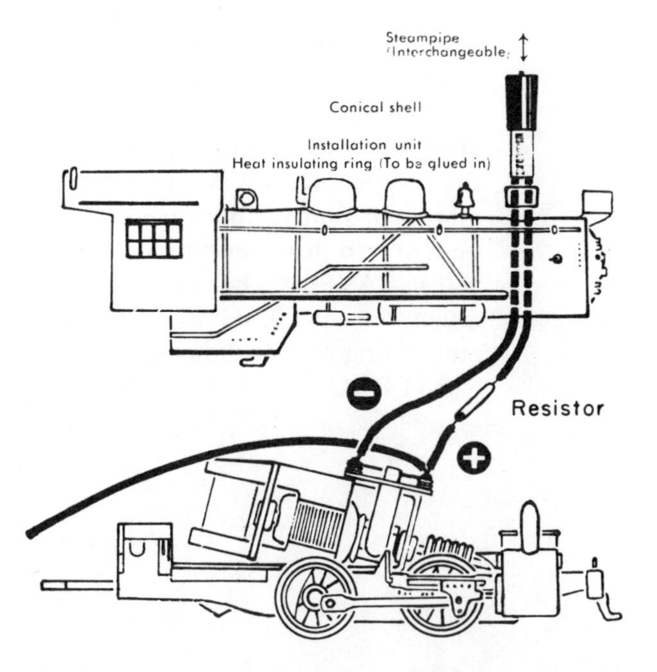

mediately graduated to cab control with a minimum of effort. On the other hand, if you were to use the five-channel K-5 unit, you wouldn't really be gaining anything, since you would still be limited to running one train at a time and you would have to install receivers in your locomotives to boot. But, you would have the decided advantage of not having to fumble around manipulating block toggles, which means you could devote all your time to operating your locomotives. So think about that while you are mulling over the possibilities of whether or not ASTRAC will or will not benefit you.

In the case of the more advanced modeler who already has some form of cab control, including a dual-throttle control panel with center-off block toggles, the conversion to or addition of ASTRAC presents no problem either. It is simply a matter of transferring the track power leads from the DC terminals of one of the power packs and connecting them to the AC terminals of the same pack. After that, you simply connect the ASTRAC unit or units with respect to the number of trains you want to be able to run simultaneously. As for the other power pack, just leave it as is, but with the power off. You can use it for DC operation whenever the need arises, either in juxtaposition with ASTRAC or independently. This operation will offer various advantages, since you will have the opportunity of providing AC or DC power and operation in any desired block or section of track. Last, but not least, flip all block and cab toggles to "on" position so that you have a continuous flow of current throughout your trackwork. Then operate without the frantic tripping of one switch after the other, with the exception of flipping the toggle switches connected to the switch motors of your various turnouts, which would be required in any event regardless of whether you use ASTRAC or conventional wiring. So much for ASTRAC where existing layouts and wiring are concerned.

ASTRAC should be perfect for the beginner, particularly one who is starting from scratch and hasn't even settled on a track plan, let alone the extent of wiring that will be necessary, depending on the type of plan he ends up with and the mode of operation he has in mind. For here is an opportunity for quickly achieving the refinements and prototype operating benefits of both block and cab control without having to become involved with miles of wiring. Thus, the opportunity of achieving the pleasures of multi-train control, without the special and often complicated wiring normally required for this type of operation, becomes an obvious advantage considering the fact that it can be easily accomplished by simply attaching comparatively few wires to the track. Therefore, auxiliary feeders, switch motors, and turnouts notwithstanding, the beginner, like anyone else who wants to get operating in a hurry (that's most of us), not only can do so without the need for complex wiring arrangements, but also has the bonus of multi-train operation in a more prototypical manner. And to further simplify things, through the use of current in the rails at all times within a continuous track system, the need for gaps or insulated plastic joiners can be completely eliminated simply by selecting the right track plan and track materials. This becomes especially evident where the use of sectional track is concerned, particularly if you are using Snap-Switch or Custom-Line turnouts which, as explained in the preceding chapter, are turnouts whose electrical characteristics permit the flow of current in all directions of track regardless of how the turnout is thrown.

Also in the last chapter you will recall that I spent considerable time extolling the virtues of "power routing" turnouts of the regular and Tru-Switch variety, which, to repeat briefly, *liven* or *deaden* sections of track depending on the position to which they are thrown.

Thus, "to power route or not to power route" again becomes the question, so let's review and consider it where ASTRAC is concerned. In the case of juice in the rails at all times, to deaden a siding will require gapping, an off-on toggle switch, auxiliary feeders—in short, special and additional wiring. However, with carrier control such requirements can be completely ignored, for an ASTRAC-equipped locomotive will add to the real flavor of prototype-engineer-operation. For now, after you enter a siding and your train has completely cleared the turnout behind you, by simply reducing the throttle (or to be more accurate, the frequency signal) you can come to a full stop. Then, after throwing the turnout back to mainline position, you can send another ASTRAC-equipped locomotive straight through, and the important thing to remember is that you were able to hold a locomotive in the siding without having to flip a toggle switch to deaden that particular section of track. Which only goes to point out and emphasize the beauty and flexibility of this form of carrier-control operation. Once the other locomotive has rolled past, you merely throw the turnout to the siding, throttle up the train that was standing by, and proceed back onto the mainline, independent of the other train's action or direction. Of course, as a matter of safety and prototype procedure, you must remember to realign the turnout from the siding back to the mainline or the next train coming through (depending on its direction) will be running against a switch, causing a derailment, short circuit, or both. Or it might highball into the siding involuntarily.

Now in the case of "power routing" turnouts, the situation where ASTRAC is concerned is slightly different, as follows: Once you have completely entered the siding and re-aligned the turnout to the mainline to permit another ASTRAC-equipped loco to barrel through, you cannot move out because the siding is now dead. By throwing the turnout back to the siding position, you restore power to that section of track, and you can now throttle things up and move back onto the mainline. This, in effect, becomes a sort of built-in safety feature, and prevents you from moving out of a siding against a turnout.

The purpose of the foregoing comparison is to stress the importance of observing the rules of the road. We will be getting to safe operating procedures in the next chapter. Suffice to say for the moment that you must watch what you are doing and where you are going with respect to the activities of one train in relation to the other. Because ASTRAC *will* permit locomotives to run hither and yon in similar or opposing directions, directly toward or behind each other, the necessity for observing the rules of the road and safe operating procedure becomes even more acute. It also increases the need for, or I might say forces you to operate in prototype fashion, unless you enjoy cornfield meets, derailments, and numerous other catastrophies. One thing is certain—the wide and varied flexibility in operating that a carrier-control system such as ASTRAC permits not only adds to your pleasures, but most certainly is a challenge to your skill and know-how as a model railroad engineer.

During the course of writing this chapter I tested a number of locomotives which I had equipped with receivers. By and large the response of each given locomotive to the ASTRAC powering was most gratifying. However, I must in all fairness admit that some locomotives responded better than others. But this is not due to any inconsistency on the part of ASTRAC, but rather due to the characteristics of the particular locomotives themselves. In short, a locomotive that is well broken in, is well-tuned and operates smoothly under conventional circumstances, will behave in the same manner when ASTRAC-equipped. A locomotive that is not a particularly good performer will not be any better through the use of ASTRAC. In other words: *smooth operation, performance, and response is only as good as the locomotive itself.* A rough locomotive will operate in that manner regardless of what type of power is applied. Therefore, don't expect miracles to

With power in the rails at all times, the track will serve as an outlet. By simply tapping current from the nearest section of track, you can electrify structures and other accessories without the need for wires running to the control panel or power packs.

ASTRAC receivers can also be used to control the operation of accessories, as well as locomotives. This close-up of Dick Seydell's realistic-looking scratch-built lumber mill includes a working table saw powered by a tiny motor and controlled by a simple on-off switch. By connecting a receiver to the motor you could not only control the on-off operation, but the speed of the motorized saw as well.

This close-up view of a refinery built by Dick Seydell includes a scratch-built operating oil well. An accessory such as this can easily be powered and controlled by an ASTRAC signal. The speed control on the ASTRAC transmitter will also act as a rheostat and, thus, govern the speed with which the oil well pumps oil.

To operate four different locomotives simultaneously or singly, and completely independent of each on a four-track railroad such as this would require dividing the trackwork into separate sections and powering these sections with individual cab controls. With ASTRAC no special gapping, separate sections and throttle controls are needed. Complicated and excessive wiring is completely eliminated, and flexible operation in a variety of ways becomes possible.

happen when you use ASTRAC. For this system is not to be construed as a cure-all for the erratic or rough operation of poor-performing locomotive equipment. You must administer the same loving care to ASTRAC-equipped locos that you do to others. Some locomotives have high-speed motors and different gear ratios than others. The result is that one locomotive will coast to a stop, whereas another will behave as if it hit a stone wall. Some locomotives will take off like an Olympic sprinter primed for a 60-yard dash, whereas others will take off more slowly—the latter of which is to be desired, of course, where realistic appearance in operation is concerned. How you handle your power-control dial also has a lot to do with whether you start off at a creep speed or lurch off like a jack rabbit, whether you gradually come to a stop or halt dead in your tracks. They say that beauty is in the eyes of the beholder, and by the same token, the beauty of smooth performance is in the hands of the operator, and, of course, the capability of the locomotive.

Therefore, in selecting a locomotive to be ASTRAC-equipped and -operated, be sure that it is properly broken in and that it runs smoothly to begin with. Assuming that it does, you can then expect the same type of performance and response when you give it the ASTRAC treatment. In fact, the following is a simple hook-up which will enable you to see for yourself without the necessity of having to actually install a receiver in the locomotive:

All you have to do is connect the AC power and ASTRAC control unit to the black and white wires of a receiver. Following this, connect test leads from the red and white wires of the same receiver to your track terminals. *Then place a normally wired locomotive on the track and run it.* The locomotive will behave in exactly the same manner as it would if you had connected the receiver directly to the motor. This relatively easy means of seeing how a given locomotive responds to ASTRAC can be applied to all the motive power on your railroad. And the way they respond will help you determine which ones you want to equip with receivers of a more permanent nature.

Since any number of questions are bound to arise concerning this new means of Automatic Simultaneous Train Control operation, a question and answer period might well be in order, so let's have at it.

One of the first things to come to mind will be the fact that once a given locomotive is equipped with a receiver, the model rail would only be able to operate it when powered by the low-voltage AC current we have talked about, and when an ASTRAC transmitter beams a signal to that particular receiver. Ordinarily, this would preclude the operation of such a locomotive on a normally wired layout, a case in point being the occasion when a modeler visits a fellow model rail to do a bit of operating on the latter's railroad. Therefore, unless the other fellow's layout was wired to handle ASTRAC locos, the visiting brass hat would not only have to lug along his receiver-equipped locos, but would also have to bring along the ASTRAC transmitter units as well. If not, the "togetherness" of operation would be limited to that of operating normally wired locos on the normally wired layout. However, there is a way to get around this form of restriction, and you can take care of it at the time you install the receiver in your locomotive. Simply connect a tiny sub-miniature off-on toggle switch between the red and black wires of the receiver, and, lo and behold, you will be able to operate on AC or DC at will. At "off" position, you operate in the ASTRAC manner. At "on" position, you are back to normal and can operate on DC. In short, a flip of a tiny switch and you can operate either way. Thus, you add additional flexibility to the operation of your equipment, and make it completely compatible with all other equipment and layouts regardless of how they are powered. There is another even simpler way

In spite of the fact that micro-receiver-equipped locomotives can go every which way on the same section of track without affecting one another's motion and without the need for blocks and accompanying cab control systems, there is still the question of the reverse loop. In other words, wiring and gapping for a reverse loop is essentially the same for ASTRAC as for conventional means. In addition, the same type of double-pole double-throw switch will be needed to match polarity. However actual operation is a bit different and, more important, the mainline polarity remains constant throughout the entire maneuver. Track power and ASTRAC signal is fed directly to the mainline at A and via the reversing switch at B for the "isolated loop section." The reversing switch has absolutely no effect on the ASTRAC signal, regardless of how it is thrown, and only controls the polarity of the current fed to that section of track. With this hook-up in mind the action is as follows: (1) Allow train to get completely within the loop; (2) Throw loop polarity switch; (3) At the same time, throw the forward-reverse switch on the ASTRAC unit; (4) After train has left the loop and re-entered the mainline, the loop polarity switch can be re-set to original position. The why's and wherefore's of the foregoing operation are worthy of additional discussion and will help you to better understand some of the mechanics of ASTRAC propulsion. Headed in an eastbound direction, the train enters the loop, and with polarity the same in the trackwork on both sides of the joint, the train continues around. When the train is completely within the loop and approaching the joints at the exit, the polarity will have to match that of the trackwork on the other side. Instead of reversing the polarity of the mainline track to match the loop, as in conventional means, we reverse the loop polarity to match the mainline instead. However, now the train will suddenly start to go backward. To counteract this we also throw the direction control switch on the ASTRAC unit so that the train will continue forward again. By flipping the loop polarity switch and the ASTRAC direction switch simultaneously we have a smooth transition, and there is no interruption of motion as the train continues around the loop and back onto the mainline. A flick of the loop polarity switch, and the loop is back to original polarity and receptive to the next train traveling in the counterclockwise direction. If the next train were to enter the loop and travel in a clockwise direction, the loop toggle would have to be flipped prior to entering (to match the mainline coming in) and once again in conjunction with the ASTRAC direction before leaving the loop. By way of summary, bear in mind that only one toggle switch is needed, and in addition it is important to remember that the polarity of the mainline remains the same at all times. This emphasizes the advantage of ASTRAC over conventional means where reverse loop operation is concerned, for you can operate in and out of a reverse loop without affecting the motion or direction of other trains operating on that same mainline—a feat that would be impossible in conventional operation unless you set up a system of blocks and separate cab controls for the other trains in question. Therefore, one can easily conclude that with ASTRAC, wiring for a reverse loop and all the operations adjacent to it is a much more simple proposition.

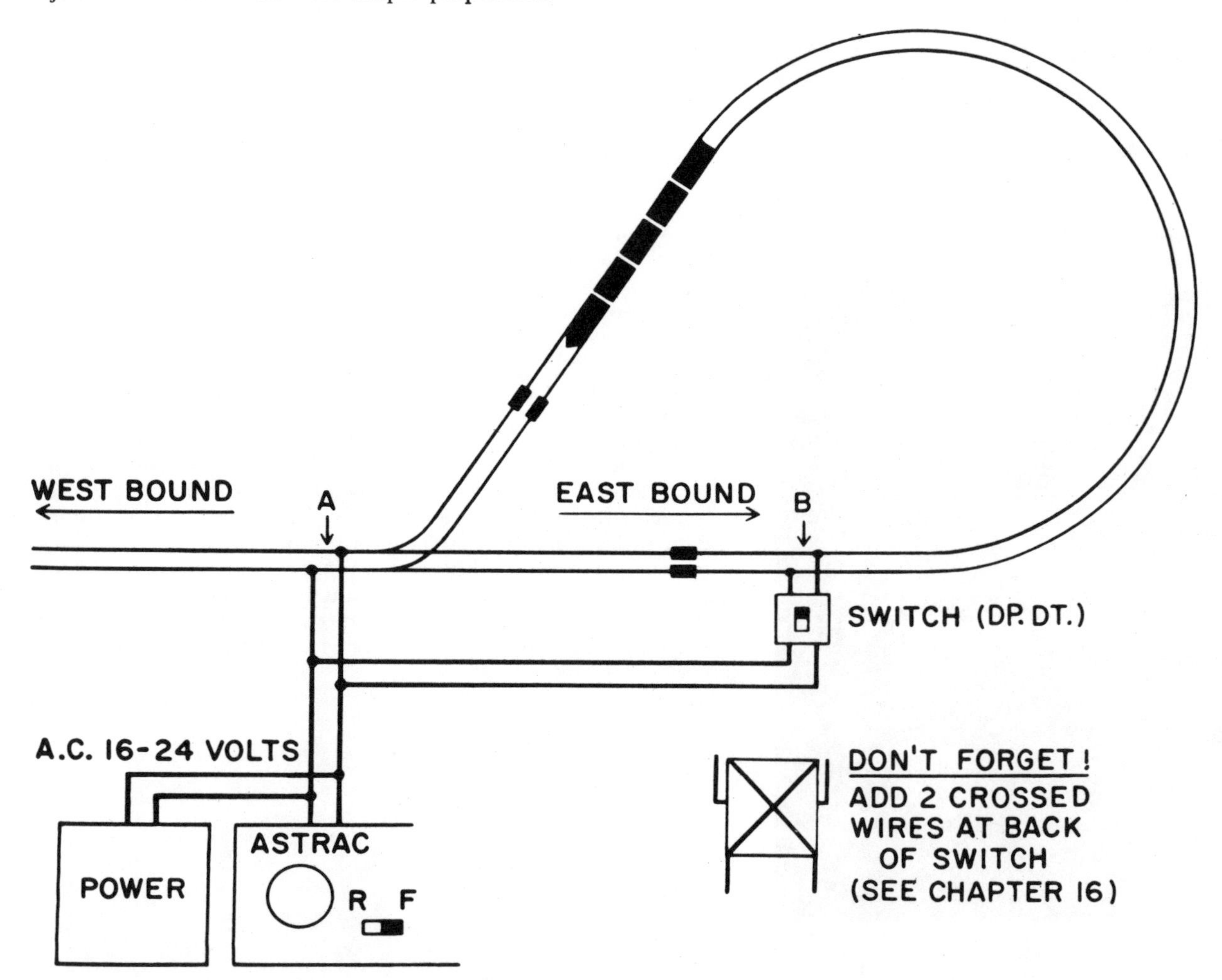

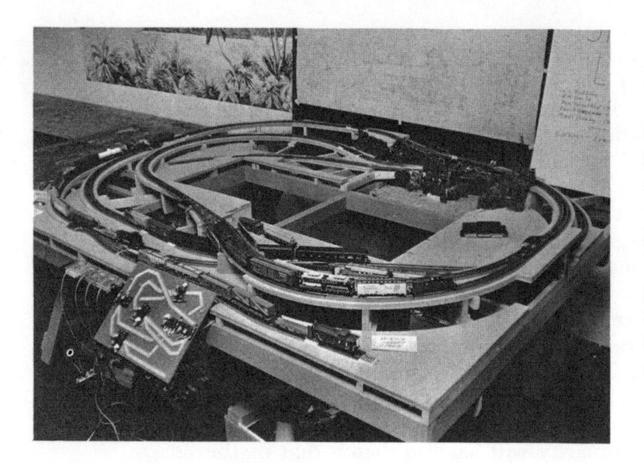

Radio-frequency control is not new to members of the Venice Model RR Club. Some years back, member Bob Smith devised a most unique form of radio control, and even before ASTRAC entered the scene the Venice Short Line was operating with such sophisticated refinements as electronic flywheel drive, transistorized throttle control and other advantages that embrace multi-train operation through the use of radio frequencies on a carrier control basis. Some of these locomotives are shown in operation on a layout designed and built by Lewis H. Creber and exhibited at a Pacific Coast Region NMRA meeting. Considering the fact that Bob Smith and his fellow members did not have the resources of General Electric at their disposal, their accomplishment where radio control is concerned is certainly worthy of praise and a fine indication of their own skill and ingenuity.

During the early stages of building a model railroad the desire for operating as quickly as possible becomes quite keen. After the last bit of trackwork has been laid, the next step is to divide the layout into various electrical blocks with an eye toward some form of cab control. Until your wiring is complete, your operation will be limited. However, with ASTRAC your operation is unlimited and, more important, offers you all the refinements of block and cab control operation from the start; without the complicated wiring that goes with it. No need for gapping and electrical divisions (blocks) other than a few to make it easy for you to check out various areas of your trackwork in the event of short circuits or other problems. In this scene a "Camelback" slowly makes its way along the open frame and trackwork at the Valley Railroad Club.

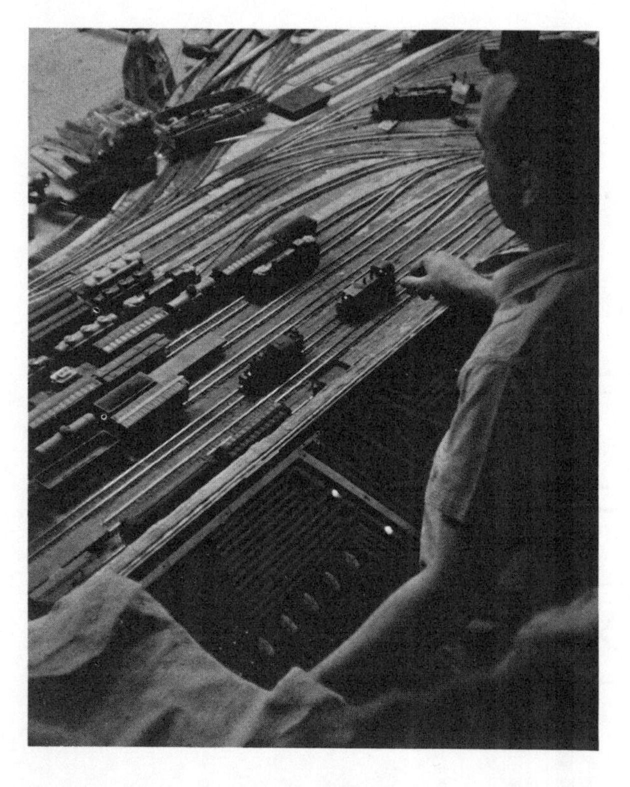

ASTRAC offers many advantages, the end result being an extremely versatile and long-sought-after form of flexible control during operation. However, do not misconstrue all this talk of multi-train operation to mean that we are encouraging the operation of more than one train at a time if yours is a one-man railroad. You can do it, but it will be hectic; you will be running trains, not operating them. In club operation it is another thing, for you can have as many operators as there are receiver-equipped locos to control. Therefore, bear in mind that the primary benefit of ASTRAC is *flexibility of control.* There isn't a section of your pike that won't benefit from such a hook-up, and a simple one at that. For example, it is particularly useful in yard areas, for you can now switch to your heart's content while using a variety of motive power. One yard hog brings in a string of cars, another loco sets them out. One switcher can operate on a section of track while another switcher occupying the same track remains motionless. No special gapping, blocks, toggles or individual cab controls to be wired in. The ASTRAC units take care of everything.

which will permit the operation of ASTRAC-equipped locos to run on DC, and we will get to that shortly. When you compare this mode against the other, I am sure you will agree that this is the best course to follow. And this should dispel any rumors or fears that once you are wired for ASTRAC, you are restricted to ASTRAC alone where operation is concerned.

As for the power supply, General Electric recommends the use of AC current in the 16-20-volt range. Therefore, you can take current from the AC terminals of a power pack you may already own. You may find, however, that one or more of your locomotives will not respond as well as they might have under more normal circumstances. But don't hit the panic button; this condition is easily remedied and we will get to it in a moment. Line voltage varies in various parts of the country. For example, rural areas may only be served with a 90-volt input, whereas the more populated metropolitan areas may have a higher line voltage input up to 130 volts. Therefore, what goes in and out of a power pack in one community may be different from the input and output of the same power pack in another community. To wit, the rated 16-volt AC terminals on a power pack may be slightly over or under depending on where one lives. In addition to this, the rectifiers in power packs sometimes have a tendency to short-circuit the ASTRAC control signals. Relax though, for there is a simple remedy for this also. Getting back to the fact that line voltage varies in different areas of the country, it is quite understandable that General Electric would take a broad approach to things in the initial introduction of ASTRAC to the model railroader, for this broad approach makes the application of ASTRAC more compatible wherever you live regardless of the high or low degree of voltage in the current that is supplied your community. In my own tests I have found that in some cases 16-20 volts have been more than sufficient, yet certain locomotives required in the neighborhood of 24 volts to aid them in overcoming their own inertia. One might conclude, therefore, that a 24-volt transformer would be more suitable and would cover a multitude of sins as it were. However, if you can get sufficient speed and response at the lower voltage, you will be better off because it won't require the use of as many dropping resistors where the lamps or other electrical accessories in the use of constant track power is concerned. For example, with each receiver a resistor is supplied. If the track voltage exceeds the rated lamp voltage of your headlight, you merely connect the dropping resistor to the bulb, as shown in the diagrams. Or, you can eliminate the necessity of using the dropping resistor by replacing the bulb with one that has a higher-rated capacity which will be more amenable to the higher-than-usual track voltage. Either procedure will increase the life span of the bulb. The same thing applies to other accessories, for you must bear in mind that the full transformer voltage is on the tracks at all times. Therefore, accessories that would normally have used 12 volts DC, such as a locomotive headlight, smoke units, and relays, may be damaged if used continually on the higher track voltage you will now be employing. Dropping resistors will solve the problem, so there is nothing to worry about in the final analysis. The same thing applies to accessories that would normally have been powered by 16 volts AC. Resistors will compensate for the pepped-up power that is now being fed to them. By the same token though, this precaution may not really be necessary, for many lamps and accessories that would normally operate off 16 volts AC have enough latitude to offset the increase of 4 or so more volts, so in actuality, you may not have to take any extensive corrective steps after all. Just check their ratings.

The reason I am going into such great detail is because I feel it behooves me to make as complete and comprehensive a report as possible. For, after all, we have before us a completely new and revolutionary means of power propulsion, and a careful scrutiny from A to Z will provide all of us with a better understanding of how it works and what to do when things appear to go wrong.

Fortunately, the men who head up the research department in the Educational Recreation Products Division of General Electric feel the same way about things, and they, too, are carefully scrutinizing the early units, those now in manufacture, and those that are forthcoming. In other words, like anything new, there are bound to be improvements in design, function, and performance, and it is apparent that G.E. is genuinely interested in the end result, for there are now a number of refinements which are almost as earth-shattering as ASTRAC itself.

By way of an example, newer units now contain a special speed-control adjustment that will enable the user to compensate for the high or low line voltage which powers his community. For, to repeat, these units were originally designed for use with the different line voltage ranging anywhere from 90 to 130 volts. This is quite a percentage variation, and the fact that a given ASTRAC unit can operate within such a wide range is a credit to General Electric to begin with, and certainly of great benefit to model railroaders wherever they may live. True, a model rail living in a large city might only need a slight turn of the speed control to get his locomotive started, whereas, in a rural area, the same set-up might require anywhere from a quarter to half throttle to get the same locomotive moving, but the refinement is now available not only in the newer units, but in the form of an easily attached accessory as well. So that takes care of that problem, and also goes a long way toward compensating and adjusting for the necessity of much higher than normal voltage in the tracks, which in turn, makes the use of your existing power packs more compatible with the ASTRAC system, and may preclude the use of dropping resistors as well.

I know this may start to sound like a round robin, for one moment I appear to suggest a problem or two and then, in the next breath, a solution. But when you consider the fact that if the refinements or improvements I mention did not come about, then the remedies to certain bugs here and there would be very important indeed. Therefore, all things must be given equal consideration not only for the benefit of those of you who are being introduced to ASTRAC for the first time, but also for those who might be using it with less success than can be employed, and lastly, to dispel any rumors or fallacies that might have existed concerning its use. And, needless to say, there have been a few. One of which is the suggestion that ASTRAC-equipped locos are subject to jack rabbit starts and cannot perform smoothly at creep speeds. To this, I can only say—nonsense. During tests with the earliest units, I have been able to have locos gradually crawl away from a standing still position, and by the same token have been able to have them slowly come to a stop without shaking up the freight or knocking passengers off their seats.

Nevertheless, there is another important refinement available in the form of a transistorized throttle. This accessory is easily plugged into the taped-over receptacle (s) at the rear of the transmitter unit (s). So, in case you were wondering what those doohickeys were for, now you know. It was for things to come and is now available. In line with the transistorized throttle is another device in the form of a brake lever, also easily attached. Precisely how these items work is quite exciting from a model railroader's standpoint, and they will be covered in greater detail in the following chapter on realistic operation. Suffice to say for the moment that they are an exciting innovation and will make even the most die-hard ultra-conservative veteran model rail give serious thought to switching over to ASTRAC. And to further whet your appetite and set your pulse throbbing is the fact that not only can you whittle down the size of the receivers, as indicated earlier, but the newer crops of receivers are smaller than the earlier models, some 30 per cent smaller at that. And these in turn can be cut down a bit further as your need to do so arises, particularly where tenderless switchers are concerned, not to overlook oldtimers. Furthermore, these micro-receivers will no doubt get smaller and smaller, and, in time, will probably be called micro-micro-receivers.

Pursuing the question of refinements a bit further, I might add that you also have the benefit of an "inertia control" device. This permits you to vary the inertia from instant response to a more gradual response, and ties in directly with the action of the transistorized throttle. These and other improvements not only add to the already established flexibility of ASTRAC operation, but also provide a tremendous amount of latitude where the illusion of prototype realism is concerned.

At this point, the excited murmurs might be, "Fine! But what happens if I get a sixth locomotive?" Ordinarily, you could only select a receiver for it with the same channel and frequency of one of your other locos. You would have to run them alternately since they would both respond to the same signal at the same time, or you could use them together in double-headed fashion. And there is another *or*—on a large layout you could divide it into two or more electrical systems so that locomotives tuned to the same signal could be operated independently of each other in different areas of your railroad on a simultaneous basis or otherwise. So, that should take care of any sour grapes concerning the fact that there are only five channels. And if that doesn't quiet the unbelievers, then the following blockbuster certainly will.

I'll preface the following glad tidings by saying, *club members take note!* Five more channels have been added to the ASTRAC scheme of things! It's the K-7 transmitter control unit, and, in essence, is the same as the K-5 model. The important difference, of course, is in the fact that the K-7 will handle five channels in the 50- to 100-kilocycle range. Thus, you could equip ten locomotives with ten different receivers and, by combining a K-7 with a K-5, operate any one of ten locomotives one at a time, or two locos simultaneously, etc. As to the operating possibilities and potentials available by combining the K-7 with any or all of the other models previously described and discussed, I'll leave it to your own imagination because I'm running out of ink.

I haven't run out of combinations, however, so by way of a breather, here is one which should be of particular interest to those of you whose existing layouts are wired along more conventional lines, and if you have block or cab control, then so much the better. In addition to the use of ASTRAC as outlined, and which we can call Phase 1 (for the sake of discussion), there is another mode of operation which we shall call Phase 2. In this phase you can operate ASTRAC-equipped locomotives on track powered by DC in the normal manner. The hook-up is the same except that the power comes from the DC terminals of your power pack rather than the AC supply. Now both ASTRAC locos and those normally wired can be operated on the same trackage. The motion, speed, and direction of the normally wired locomotives will be controlled by the power pack in the regular manner. ASTRAC locos will not move until you send their respective signals to them. After that, they will take off, but possibly at a lower running speed than the normally wired locomotives. This, of course, will depend on the particular locomotives themselves. The speed of the ASTRAC locos will depend on both the power pack and the ASTRAC transmitter control settings. Direction control of all locomotives will be determined by the power pack setting (DC polarity) and the direction control on the ASTRAC units will have no say in the matter. There is a possibility that you will have to insert a "choke coil" between one of the DC power leads and track terminal, for, as I mentioned before, the rectifiers in power packs have a tendency to short-circuit the ASTRAC signals. If so, the choke coil will greatly reduce such short-circuiting effects. You can make a choke coil by taking a spool of No. 18 or 20 wire and winding it around an empty spool of thread or a piece of wood dowel 1 inch by 2 inches long. Anywhere from 50 to 200 turns will be more than adequate—that's how you make a choke coil, at least a simple one such as the above needs may require. I didn't experience such a need in Phase 2, although in Phase 1 when I ran up to five trains simultaneously, the choke coil came in handy.

There are a few other phases which are a bit more complicated, whereby, with various modifications, the operation of ASTRAC and normal locomotives will become even more flexible. However, at this point I am sure you will agree that we have plenty of things we can do as it is. How these various phases can be put to particularly good use will be elaborated on in the next chapter.

I could go on and on extolling the virtues of ASTRAC, for this handsome and exciting breakthrough has opened innumerable avenues to pursue where the pleasures of prototype operation are concerned. For when you stop to consider that all of the foregoing can be accomplished with the simple addition of a few wires to your trackwork, the end result makes you feel like a millionaire. And remember that this is only a portent of things to come.

This much I can say: it is apparent, and happily so, that General Electric is in model railroading to stay, and from this point on, it will be offering one breakthrough after another. I am also happy to report that new equipment, accessories, devices, and other refinements that G.E. develops can be combined with presently used ASTRAC units at a minimum of cost. In other words, there is no fear of obsolescence where older equipment is concerned. The basic cash outlay will be in the purchase of the actual units themselves, and the cost of accessories, additions, and refinements will be substantially lower. Is that any way to run a business? Where the model rail is concerned, it sure is.

One final note. As far as actual cost is concerned, when you add up the savings you accrue through the elimination of miles of wiring, expensive toggle switches, and all the other ingredients that are required in conventional practice and normal wiring of a model railroad, you will discover that, dollar for dollar, you not only get more for your money if you use ASTRAC, but more realistic operation to boot. In fact, in the long run, ASTRAC will be less expensive, not only money-wise, but time-wise as well. For that time you would have normally spent engaged in the all-too-often complex wiring that any halfway decent track plan requires can instead be devoted to scenery, painting, weathering, and, finally, hooking up working signals that will serve a more prototype purpose rather than stand there as lifeless unfunctioning props. You won't have to spend most of your time manipulating block toggles and the like in rapid succession to get from one part of your road to the next.

You will rejoice at the fun of switching in the yard, signaling a Pacific to glide out of a roundhouse stall, and beam with pride as you highball down the main. But, most important of all, you will be able to experience the real and exciting flavor of being an engineer. For you will feel that you are right there in the cab of your locomotive, clanging the bell, tooting the whistle, and giving her the throttle as you head out for a run. For of such things are dreams made.

XVIII
Realistic Operation

Without a doubt the phrase "realistic operation" is not only the most dream-inspiring expression in the hobby, but also the most challenging. For we are embracing every conceivable facet of a pastime that has charmed the hearts of man and boy alike for many decades. There isn't one area of model railroading that can escape this all important connotation, unless you don't happen to care whether you are authentic or not. In fact, I could easily have prefaced my opening by saying that, "this chapter is for men only," since we have finally arrived at the point where we must separate the men from the boys. This all-embracing phrase not only denotes the manner in which you run and operate your trains, but how you build them, superdetail them, paint them, weather and age them, and a host of other things which in the end result will reflect a quality of workmanship and hobbyship in the most prototypical traditions. This also applies to how you build your railroad, the manner in which you lay your track, and, certainly, the logic of your track and operating plan. Then there is the question of cause and effect, and special effect, too. The backgrounds and scenic dimensions you create that present a believable and inspiring railroad environment will now offer something more tangible than the mental images you conjure up to hide flat perspectives, bare plywood, and uncovered skeleton-like benchwork. The authenticity of your operation goes further still to include a practical approach to the wiring scheme of things, for if you are not realistic about the track plan you employ, you may ultimately find that it will be virtually unfeasible or for that matter, quite impossible to complete your final hook-ups without the aid of a wizard standing by. And, more often than not, were you able finally to work out a system of wiring that was compatible with your railroad, you might find yourself with such a maze of overcomplication that you would spend more time maintaining than operating.

However, the purpose of this chapter is not to review all that has been discussed, but rather to emphasize the fact that the manner in which you have journeyed this far will afford you the greatest of model railroading pleasures that are still to come, providing your railroad serves a purpose and is not just a showcase to run trains hither and yon aimlessly.

Therefore, your railroad should be *purposeful* and *practical.* It should not be a financial liability by virtue of just running round and round. Instead, it should be operated on the profit side of the ledger, transporting passengers and freight from one destination to another, thereby avoiding the all-too-obvious round trip that comes from continuous laps about an oval. True, it is difficult to avoid one form of continuous operation or another because, regardless of how much space you can spare for your model empire, you will really never have enough. As a result, long mainline runs, while quite desirable, are often hard to come by, for on the average size layout no sooner do you open the throttle on the straightaway than, more often than not, a curve enters the scene and, before you know it, you are heading back in the direction from whence you came. While it is quite true that railroads *do not* and *should not* run in circles, but rather on a *point-to-point* basis of operation, the fact of the matter is that such an effect is not so easy to achieve within the realm of scale and prototype miniaturization. Especially when you consider that a space of, say, 15 feet (which is about as large as one can hope for in home operation) represents a distance in HO scale only 1/4-mile long, then you can easily understand the difficulties that are encountered when trying to reduce a prototype proportion and operation to the size and scale of an HO model railroad. Let's pursue this a bit further, for it is an important ingredient to the overall scheme.

We talk of prototype and we talk of scale, each in relation to one another. For in HO we have the most practical miniaturization of its counterpart where space, size, and many other factors are concerned. Yet, to be realistic about it, while a 50-foot box car measures just under 7 actual inches, the fact remains that these inches add up, become feet, and, before you know it, you run out of room. The reader who goes by a slide rule knows that 1 prototype foot is represented in HO by 9/64 inch. However, to make the discussion more palatable and less mathematical, we shall take the liberty of knocking off a fraction or two and pretend that 9/64 is 1/8 inch. Thus, 1/8 inch in HO scale will represent 1 actual foot of prototype measurement. One full inch on your model railroad will approximate 7 feet on a real railroad, 1 scale foot will be close to 90 actual feet, and so on. Which gets us back to where we started, to wit, a model railroad that can boast a stretch of trackwork 15 feet long is not only in theory alone a mere 1/4 mile long, but, from a practical standpoint, hardly enough for a real locomotive to get rolling, let alone develop a head of steam. So, you can see that it is going to take some highly imaginative and cleverly contrived illusions to make even a 15-foot layout look like more than just 2 or 3 acres, or a skimpy 500 yards of track on a real railroad. Conversely speaking, it is just the other way around on a model railroad, for in this case, while 15 feet is a pretty good-sized pike, the action can get pretty frantic if you have a heavy hand on the throttle. And the smaller the layout, the greater the need to adhere to respectable scale speeds, otherwise, you will have developed a head of steam and returned to your starting point before you have had a chance to ease up on the power controls. Therefore, a miniature railroad should not only serve a practical purpose, but should also be operated in observance of scale speeds and not in the manner that Count So-and-So races a high-powered sports car at the Grand Prix.

Since most model engines are quite capable of accelerating trains to full operating speed within a comparatively short distance of their starting position, the question of scale speed in prototype tradition becomes extremely important, particularly important to those who are genuinely interested in "realistic operation" to the point where they do it, not just talk about it. Therefore, consider the fact that on the prototype, acceleration is quite modest, for a heavy train may require several

A PFM Consol slowly makes its way along the steel truss bridge rising up from Giant Canyon, a canyon whose steep cliffsides actually extend up from the floor of John Allen's exciting Gorre & Dephetid Railroad. The eye-arresting outcrops of stone and clifflike strata were created through the use of rock, wood and plaster materials. Depth and height have been captured in outstanding dimensional form.

Depth, dimension, rugged looking terrain and the feeling that water is really flowing make situations such as these a blessing to any model railroad and a pleasure for the modeler who operates within a natural-looking atmosphere.

A fertile imagination is fine, and conjuring up visions to surround your operations is also okay, up to a point, that is. An operating coal chute such as this one built by Jim Foell gives a breath of live action and purpose to your operations. Up and down the line, from one point to another, you will be rolling in and out of spurs, sidings, mining and industrial areas, and providing a reason for the existence of your railroad, but, more important, a service as well.

The birth of a pike and a portent of things to come is quite evident in this scene at the California Central Model RR Club. Housed in an old freight depot, the club has set up a well-designed track plan which will serve them in good stead. It will also provide them with many days, weeks and years of pleasure-filled operation as they wire, scenick and otherwise pursue the many facets of model railroading that go into the making of a miniature empire such as this. All ties and track have been hand-laid and spiked down. They built their own turnouts and switch machines, and use Kadee Magne-Matic couplers exclusively.

There is nothing like a long stretch of track-work in a yard, for it provides you with countless hours of switching fun as you make up and break up trains. A switcher comes down the line at the Glendale Model RR Club to pluck off a string of cabooses, which are to be set out to tail-end trains that will be made up. A well-built and scenicked area, and an exciting source of realistic action and operation.

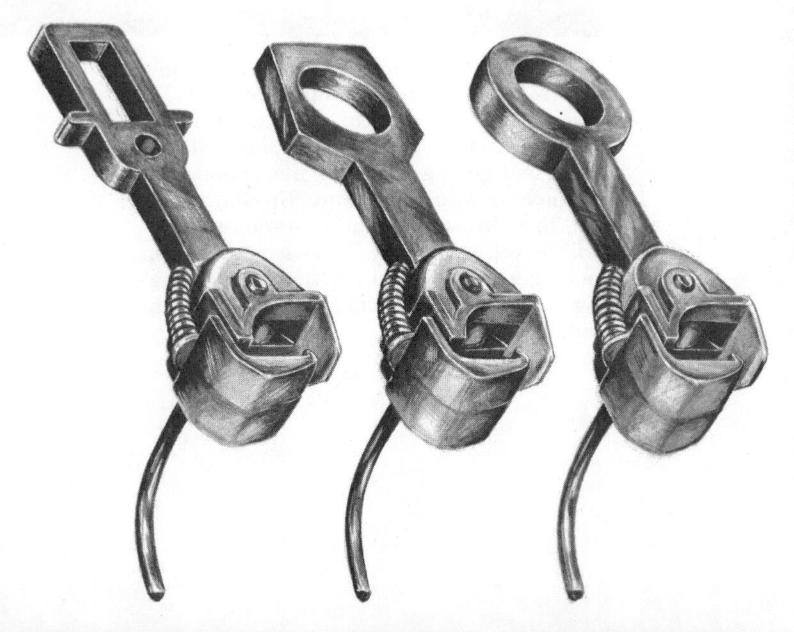

Realistic operation is not only in the doing, but also in the looking. These Kadee Magne-Matic couplers provide delayed action during operations offering not only realistic operation, but realistic-looking appearance as well. The couplers shown are just three of an assortment of Kadee couplers featuring various length shanks and designs which will fit and/or adapt to any and all locomotives and cars used in HO scale.

miles to reach a speed in the neighborhood of 70 miles per hour. The same thing applying where deceleration and braking are concerned. Of course, high drive ratios with which many models are endowed enable miniature locomotives to brake trains almost instantly from high speeds. However, instant stops such as these are toylike in appearance and certainly a far cry from the prototype system of braking, a system which needs time and distance in which to do its work safely. The start-run-stop cycle of a prototype train is a joy to watch and a realistic operation worthy of the greatest amount of imitation. It generally follows a particular pattern which we shall cover further along the line.

Thus, the ability to gauge model train speeds is another bit of pepper you can add to the pot. A quick, fairly accurate means of estimating the scale speed of a model train may be made by observation, using the following formula:

Train speed in scale miles-per-hour
equals actual inches traveled in:

5 seconds for HO scale	2.5 seconds for O scale
7 seconds for TT scale	3.5 seconds for S scale

On that basis, a model train moving 1 inch in five seconds will be creeping along at 1 mile per hour. Advance the throttle to move the train 10 inches in five seconds and you increase the speed to 10 miles per hour. And finally, using the "mile-a-minute" as the standard, by advancing the throttle further so that your train is covering 60 inches in five seconds, you will be rolling along at 60 miles per hour. In short, the scale speed works out so that when your train is moving from one point to the other at the rate of 1 foot per second, you will be doing 60 miles per hour.

Think this over very carefully and, for example, consider an average table-top pike laid out in a 5-by-9-foot area. A basic outer loop, passing siding, perhaps a crossover to an inner loop, etc. By way of a rough guess, let's say a plan such as this involves about 50 running feet, give or take a few. In view of the foregoing, if you traversed the trackage involved in fifty seconds flat, you would have been moving around possibly sharp curves, and through turnouts to boot, at the rate of 60 miles per hour. A more realistic span of time would probably be somewhere in the area of at least a minute and a half of running. A layout boasting no less than a 15-foot mainline is great and provides quite a bit of eye appeal as a fast passenger highballs on through at a legitimate speed in the range of 60 to 90 mph. Okay, so you open it up and shave a few seconds off the fifteen-seconds-for-15-feet-at-60-mph. But, start stealing any more seconds from Father Time and, before you know it, you will be hurtling along at double, even triple the speed, like 120 or 180 mph, or more. The grim reaper's pendulum-like scythe will swing so close that it will no doubt pluck the passengers right out of their seats. For that's no way to run a railroad. You will have much more fun operating at scale speeds, for you can determine the speed you are traveling at not only by the time it takes you to go from one measured point to another, but by the time it takes for the length (measured) of your train to pass a given point. Additional information in this respect is available in the April 1963, Issue 21, NMRA Data Sheet D8a .1, under the heading "Train Speeds."

Let us say that you are barreling along (at respectable speed, of course) and the freight station looms up before you. Don't slam on the brakes at the last moment for, if you do, the freight you are hauling is liable to resemble something like chop suey, or if you were on a passenger-run (heavens forbid) I doubt if your patrons would be back for a return trip. Visitors, especially fellow enthusiasts, might be inclined to snicker or sneer (silently or otherwise) while you, a veritable madman at the controls, put your railroad through a suicidal wringer. With a minimum of thought and effort you can operate your equipment in a more realistic and, to say the

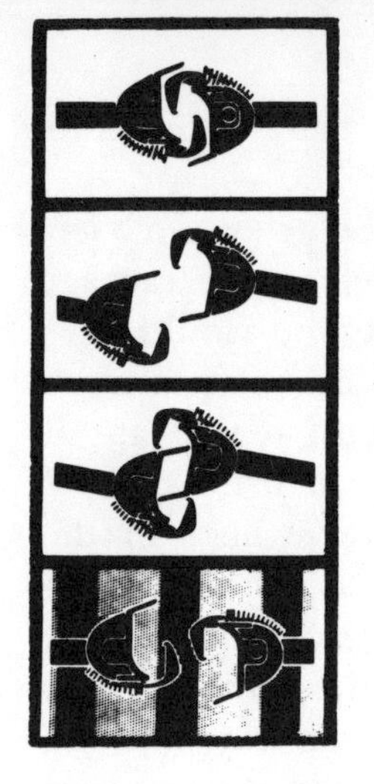

This is what delayed Magne-Matic uncoupling can do for you. Bear in mind that in past years all uncoupling was done by mechanical means, whereby uncoupling ramps caused the separating of cars (uncoupling); however, the car or cars would be left at the site of the uncoupling ramp. In other words, they could not be pushed and spotted elsewhere (shunting), otherwise they would re-engage again. Therefore, please note as follows: (1) Stopped over delayed magnetic uncoupler, knuckles have opened; (2) Withdraw slightly to disengage couplers; magnetic force draws couplers off center; (3) Then, enter again; couplers, now in delayed position; continue to push beyond uncoupler to desired location of any track elsewhere for spotting; (4) Withdraw, leaving car spotted; now the couplers will snap back to normal center position.

As for the uncoupler itself, this Kadee electro-magnetic uncoupler is the perfect mate for the Magne-Matic delayed action couplers. Purchase includes one uncoupler, a yard limit marker and whistle post, plus a quickie pushbutton, which can be installed on your control panel. When connected to the electro-magnetic uncoupler, you can energize (on a momentary basis) the uncoupler. In other words, a push of the button and couplers spotted over the uncoupler will spring apart, after which you follow through on the delayed action spotting previously described. The big advantage of the electro-magnetic uncoupler over the permanent bar magnet uncoupler is the fact that couplers coming to rest over the electro-magnetic uncoupler will remain in closed position unaffected. Therefore, during a stop period for storage, or whatever, when you roll on again you don't inadvertently uncouple and leave any cars behind—unless you want to, in which case you would activate the uncoupler by pushing the pushbutton switch in the control panel. On the other hand, where permanent bar magnet uncouplers are concerned, couplers on cars coming to rest over this type of uncoupler are subject to uncoupling automatically. Either uncoupler functions quite well indeed and both are quite popular. The major difference is in the actual operation. Uncoupling on the fly is probably a bit easier with the permanent magnet type of uncoupler, since you need only control the throttle and direction control; with the electro-magnetic uncoupler, you will also have to hit the pushbutton to energize it. In either event, the action provided adds to the fun in operation. Installation between the rails is a simple chore.

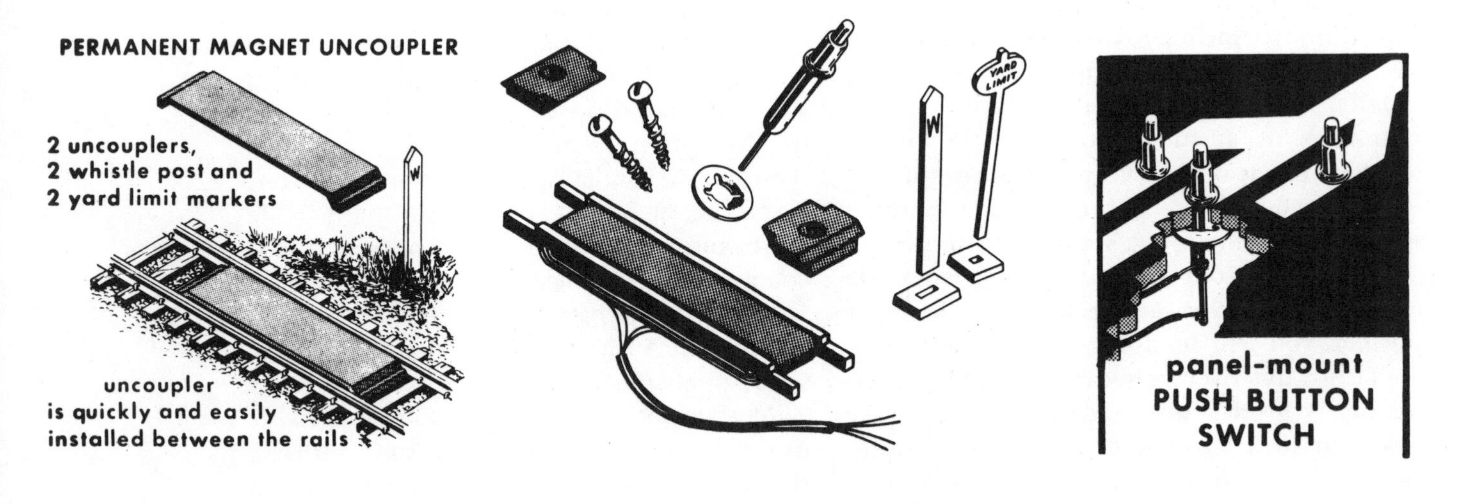

When you consider the fact that in past years spotting cars at points distant from uncoupling ramps was virtually impossible, you can appreciate what delayed-action uncoupling will mean where realistic and prototype operation is concerned. Furthermore, in years past the only way you could spot cars in various areas of your layout would have been by the installation of a number of uncoupling ramps located at the various spots you wished to drop cars off. In a yard, for example, you would have required an uncoupler ramp for every section of track, and even then you were limited. Now, thanks to Kadee, the entire picture has changed. The Edwards brothers, Keith and Dale, have seen to that in their latest innovation, as follows: Where yards are concerned, you need only install an uncoupler at a point between the rails of the yard lead. Once you have uncoupled a car, it can be pushed and spotted on any track ahead in the yard itself. After the cars have been spotted, another switcher can dart in and about the yard plucking a car here and there while making up a new train. By way of a summary, bear in mind that it is no longer necessary to install uncoupler ramps at permanent sites where you will be setting out cars. In other words, you are no longer forced to drop off cars only at uncoupler locations, a limited operation at best. Now you can have a more highly flexible means of switching and car spotting regardless of where the uncoupler is located. Last but not least, this type of uncoupling activity can be executed not only in yards, but on spurs, sidings and other sections of trackwork.

A siding or passing track has a turnout at both ends and enables you to keep a train on the siding while another train rolls through on the mainline. Also referred to as a "holding track."

A siding can also be used to "hide" a train as well as hold it. The siding can be located behind or under a range of hills or other scenic effects, and therefore will permit you to run a train onto the siding and out of view. The hidden train can be left there for a period of time to create the illusion of a longer running time from one point to another. Or it can be used on a hidden storage basis until such time as it is needed again. The hidden siding permits a variety of operations and purposes. Be sure to provide access to the hidden siding from behind the scenery.

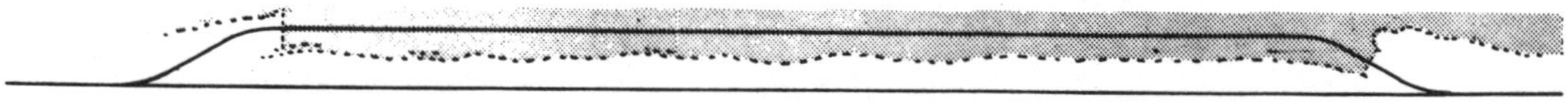

A spur has a turnout at one end, and the more you have the more you can add to the action of your operations. Spurs can turn out from the mainline, sidings or any other sections of trackwork. However, spurs should serve a particular purpose such as being a track feed to yards, storage areas, industrial sites, loading docks, etc.

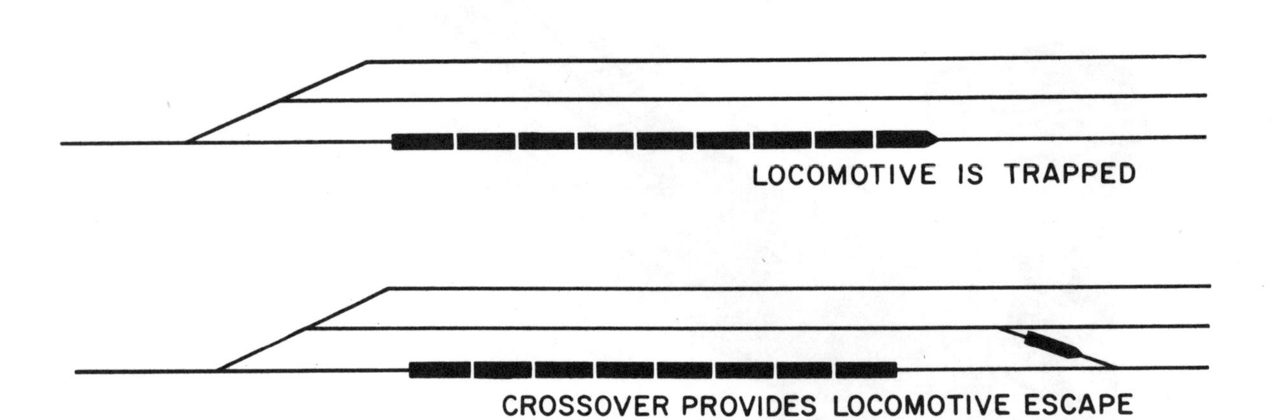

Another factor often overlooked is the need for a run-around track or "locomotive escape" which will permit a loco to bring a train into a section of the yard, dead-end spur, etc., without being trapped. A single crossover between the tracks, as shown in the diagram, will enable the locomotive to uncouple from the train, cross over to the adjoining track, back around and past the train it has left and continue elsewhere. Just be sure that you leave enough room on the track for the loco to move past the crossover, and be able to back into it and onto the other track.

Quite often during the initial stages of planning a layout, many a model rail has overlooked certain important operating possibilities, and by the same token has designed a plan that not only has built-in booby traps, but will limit operations on various points throughout the railroad. A case in point is shown in these diagrams from an NMRA Data Sheet concerning "Layout Planning For Realistic Operation." Figure 1 shows a typical yard adjacent to a mainline, a track arrangment employed by many a model rail, particularly the beginner. In this case, the yard is without a lead track, therefore the mainline is completely tied up when the yard is being worked. Figure 2 shows the same yard arrangement as in Figure 1 with one important difference: namely, the fact that a yard lead has been added. (It should be at least a train-length long.) Now yard activity cannot delay operations along the mainline.

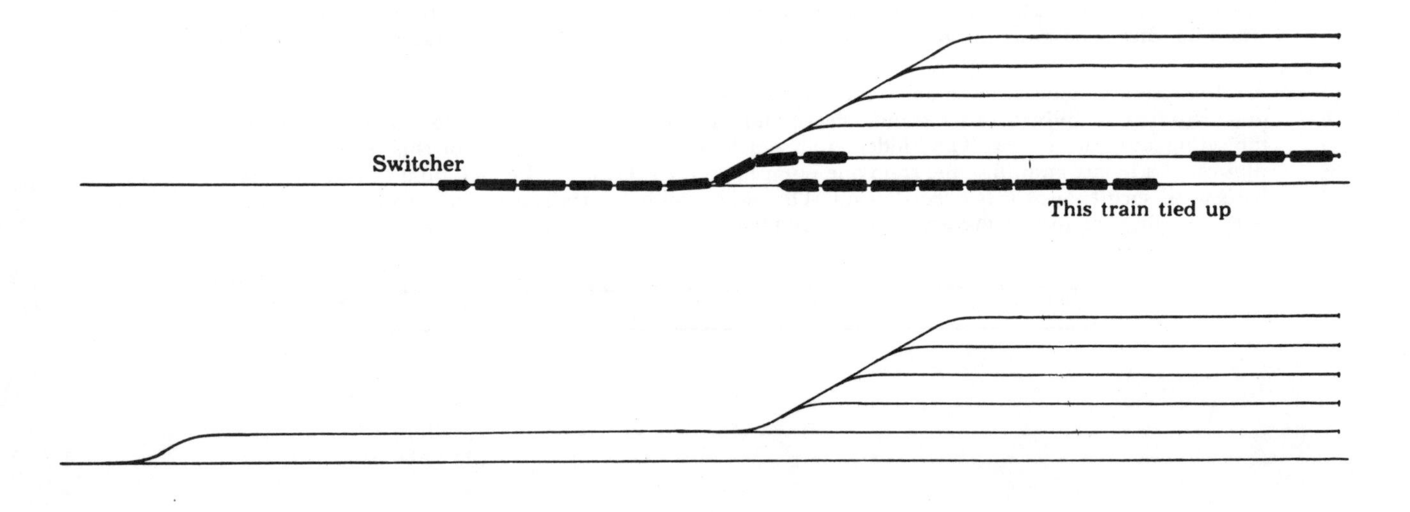

In addition to realistic operating procedure, a real life activity within a given scene gives an added boost to the overall scheme of things. This industrial area adjacent to the freight station on Jim Foell's pike illustrates the point nicely. It is loaded with creative detailing. A passenger freight has departed the whistle stop and a few passengers can be seen walking down the ramp. Local sightseers remain seated on the platform while a crew chief comes down the line to check the progress of his work gang. The combination of scratch-built, kit-built structures, coupled with the well-sculptured background and scenic effects, add to the dimension of a mighty realistic and believable-looking area.

Two different views of this highly rustic and imaginative saw mill and lumber camp area make realistic operation a pleasure. Just look at the details in the terrain. The water effect is great, as are all the other creative touches and adjacent activities. A Heisler chugs in to pick up a car, but he'll have to wait; it hasn't been unloaded yet. The more attractive you make a given setting, the more you will want to operate in a realistic manner. It will give you the incentive to operate along prototype lines.

least safer manner. For example, at a logical distance from the next stop or point of destination, start applying the brakes by reducing the throttle on your power pack, or, if you are an advocate of pulse power, switch over, if your pack is so equipped. In either event, you can now head on in, and at the point of arrival gently ease your locomotive and consist of rolling stock to a smooth stop. And you will have observed one of the basic fundamentals of railroading—safety in operation—for, to repeat, your freight won't end up like scrambled eggs and your passengers will be back for the balance of the round trip.

Many model rails, particularly newcomers, fail to observe this simple precaution and insist on racing through tunnels, around sharp curves, highballing over trestles, and the like, thus destroying the very illusion they are trying to create in the first place, a prototype-operated model railroad. This is generally more evident among the beginners who succumb to the ease of ready-to-run operation, for the kit assembler or the scratch builder who spends anywhere from four or five hours to a few months respectively in building up a locomotive knows better than to operate it as if it were a participant in the speed trials at Indianapolis. Naturally, the condition of one's equipment is certainly going to have a decided effect on how they will and are able to respond to the application of smooth starting and stopping. Yet, many modelers rely on the simplest form of power pack to control the operations of their locomotives. A paradox, indeed, when one considers the amount of refinements that have been added to power pack equipment in the form of transistorization and other means of smoothing out start and stop locomotion. It also seems strange that many modelers seem more than willing to pay for *scale and prototype appearance,* but blanche at the thought of spending an equal amount of money on power supplies where *scale and prototype performance* are concerned.

This brings us back to transistorized throttles and other devices which permit the very type of performance which is desirable. For, to repeat, if you have come this far and neglect to give your equipment and railroad the proper performance it is due, then no matter what the excuse, you are not only doing your railroad an injustice, but yourself as well. And in the long run, you will have deprived yourself of the final touch, the *pièce de résistance,* the basic concept of model railroading—realistic operation. You may be perfectly content with your present mode of operation, and the manner in which you move your trains in and about your model empire, for without a doubt you are having considerable fun in so doing, or you would have given up the ghost ages ago. However, I don't know anyone who isn't openminded enough to accept a chance to double or triple his enjoyment, so let's explore some of these possibilities in greater detail.

In the last two chapters we talked of power supplies, those used in conjunction with conventional wiring and those with respect to ASTRAC. Now would seem like a perfect time to pick up on the discussion, so by way of amplification, consider the following:

Along more conventional lines there are a number of power packs that incorporate so-called fly-wheel drive principles, pulse power, transistor throttles, and delayed action starting and stopping. Model Rectifier Corporation, for example, has a Controlmaster power supply in three different models to fit one's own pocketbook. These units, needless to say, embrace many of the refinements that permit the type of smooth and purposeful operation that we are discussing. However, there are also a number of power pack supplies which are of dubious repute, in that they lay claim to more than they are actually capable of performing. This is generally in the area of delayed starting and stopping, for I have observed that so-called delayed action is actually no more than a moment or two before maxi-

Hopper car ramp automatically dumps load in tripple hopper car in these action accessories from Ulrich Models. Other types available from Tyco, Revell, etc.

Dump car from Aristo-Craft operates by remote control and provides a definite touch of realistic action, as this before-and-after photo sequence shows. By activating a solenoid, the car will dump its load at a pre-designated point. This live action adds a real function to the car by highlighting the purpose it serves. You load the car with ore at one point and dump the ore at another point. The big point to consider is that your cars are doing something purposeful rather than running round and round.

Operating crossing gate by Revell is realistic in appearance and no wiring is necessary. Weight of train passing through lowers gate as red lights flash continuously. After passing, gate rises automatically. Track contact provides momentary charges of juice to signal lights as wheels roll over.

This crossing gate is available from Tower Engineering, Ideal Models, etc. Following an extremely simple hook-up, the gate is activated by approaching train which slows down at crossing. Flashing signals and other crossings equipment are also available.

Meanwhile, back at the crossing the flagman is getting a tongue lashing from the wagon master, who wants through. While crossing gates raise and lower whether there is through traffic or not, by adding a few figures, a horse-drawn cart, car, etc., you heighten the illusion of activity in and about the closed gate. This eye to details is particularly applicable in the case of crossing gates that do not operate and are simple props.

This authentic unit was built on a section of plywood away from the layout. When set in place with appropriate spurs leading to it, a host of operating possibilities will ensue. Those dump cars from Model Engineering look perfectly at home. Imagine a string of them being shuttled back and forth. Ease them in under the chute, move them along as each takes on a load, then take them out on a run to the next stop along the way in the operation of ore hauling. Keep a record of the cars involved and the points along the way at which they are to be dropped off. A card system is one of many ways to operate with a purpose in mind.

Reversing loop polarity signals will tell you when polarities within the loop and mainline match. As usual, green for go, red for stop. Do not cross gap on red signal, since it will indicate incorrect polarity. This is a good reminder and safety feature, since a quick glance will tell you whether polarities match before you enter or come out of a reverse loop. When the signal is red, all you have to do is flip the polarity switch, then proceed. This hook-up is applicable to either conventional or ASTRAC wiring systems. (Polarity switches, jumpers and gaps for regular turnouts have been omitted for clarity.)

The PhotoConductor Kit (PCK-10) from Sylvania includes three light-sensitive photoconductors, a mounting bracket, resistor, relay and a circuits booklet. Employing the electric-eye principle, you can use these units to automatically control turnouts and polarities in reverse-loop operation, gates and signals at crossings and a variety of applications where detection on automatic remote-control-triggered basis will help you eliminate some of the toggle switching involved in certain operations. You can hook things up so that you can go in and out of a reverse loop without having to do anything more than keep a steady hand on your throttle, and enjoy complete freedom of action without the interruption of toggling polarity switches and turnout positions, too, for that matter. The applications are numerous and I'm sure you come up with a number of your own. Strategic placement of these units will aid the cause of safety in operation and will also help reduce the hazards if you should run more than one train at a time.

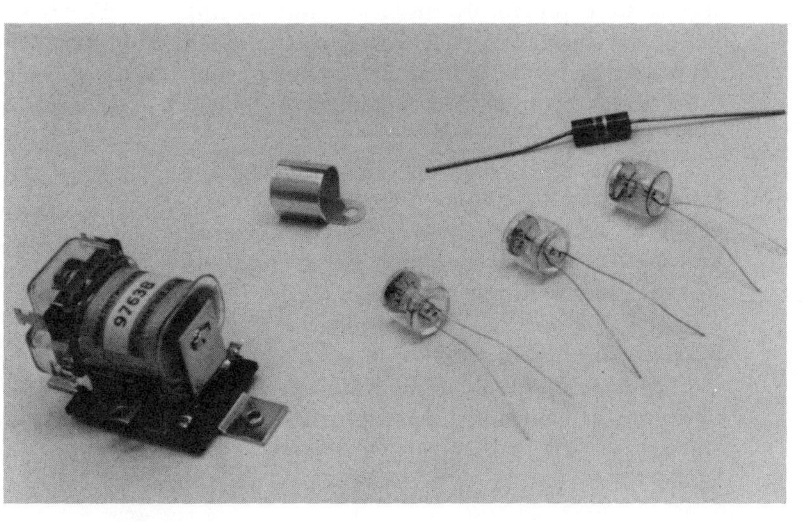

mum speed is obtained, and that the same thing applies to slowing down. Therefore, you are best advised to check a particular unit before purchasing it. Whether a given unit can or cannot perform in the manner it advertises is one thing; how it is able to do these things is another. We'll get to this in a few moments. This brings us back to the question of a start-run-stop cycle along prototype operating lines. A basic knowledge of train and throttle handling is important if you want to duplicate the action and movement of real railroad techniques, and generally follows this pattern so well described in another NMRA data sheet:

1. *Compress Slack.* Every prototype coupler-draft gear system embodies some fore-and-aft play, or slack, which may be used to reduce initial starting load. To compress slack, the engine backs slowly against the train. Electric-transmission engines may start trains without taking up slack, or heavy ones with the aid of the slack action of only ten to fifteen cars. Steam power usually compressed the slack of an entire freight train. Slack is minimized in passenger equipment by tight-lock couplers, buffers, and draft gear.
2. *Move Forward.* At a signal from the conductor, the engineer starts the train as gently as possible.
3. *Accelerate to Desired Speed.* As soon as all slack is taken and the entire train is in motion, power is increased and full acceleration begins.
4. *Operate at Authorized Speed.* Train speeds were previously discussed and should be observed, particularly on curves, grades (down as well as up), turnouts, crossings, and other areas of trackwork which require obvious reductions in speed.
5. *Coast Before Braking.* Nearing a stop, freight trains *drift* enough so that slack may again be compressed, while passenger trains may be stopped with enough power applied so that slack will not run in.
6. *Apply Brakes.* Air is applied and train brakes reduce train speed.
7. *Release Brakes.* As the train approaches the point at which it is to stop, the engineer reduces braking force so that the train rolls to a halt under light braking power.

The foregoing description is part and parcel of prototype operating technique, and any resemblance to same in miniature form should become part of your own *modus operandi.* Exactly how close you can simulate these conditions will again depend on the controlling features of your power supply and the ability of your locomotives to respond in kind.

In the preceding chapter I made reference to a transistorized throttle that works in conjunction with ASTRAC. The transistorized throttle consists of a braking device and an inertia control adjustment which will permit you to operate your motive power in precisely the same manner as the prototype start-run-stop cycle described above. To give you an example of how it works, consider an ASTRAC-equipped train at a terminal ready to move out. You turn the throttle full on, sending a signal along the rails to the receiver in the locomotive. The drivers want to move, then slowly do and the train starts to creep out of the terminal, gradually picking up speed till maximum speed has been achieved. You can, of course, turn the speed-control knob back a notch or two, depending on whatever speed you wish to level off at. The same thing happens in slowing down before arriving and stopping at your destination. You twirl the speed control to zero position, and gradually your train will roll to a stop. Now, when I say gradually, I mean just that, for your train will slowly start, pick up running speed, level off at the speed you desire, then, with reference to the destination ahead, your train will start slowing down and finally coast to a full stop. Gradually doesn't mean a few seconds in starting or stopping, for there is nothing realistic about that. You can accomplish that with dexterous handling of any speed control if your locomotive is of a mind to respond in that manner. What I do mean is that you can set your transistorized throttle so that it will take up to about fifteen

Here's a simple hook-up for turnout signals in connection with regular turnouts. (Jumpers omitted for clarity.) Can also be used with Tru-Switch turnouts.

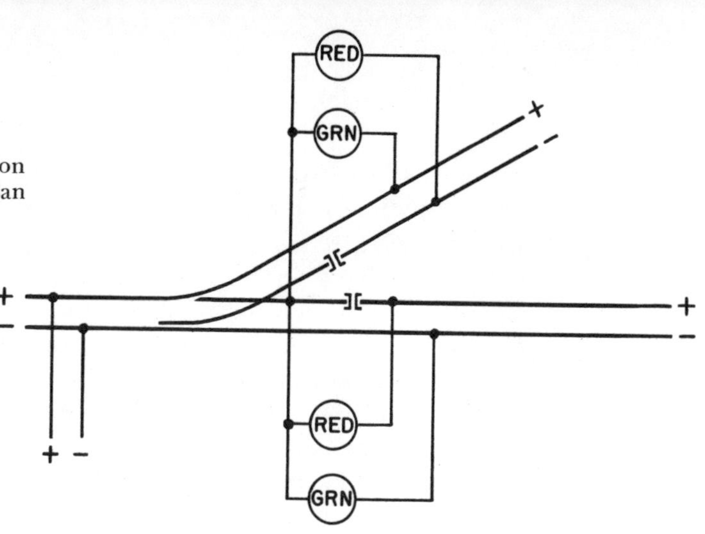

Floodlight and blinking relay towers are just some of the lighting accessories available from Aristo-Craft. Street lamps, clocks, traffic signals and a host of other illuminated devices, when set in place on your pike, will add to the excitement and pleasures of operating with the degree of realism your layout warrants. Just be certain that they fit the era. In other words, no blinking micro-wave radar towers or fluorescent street lamps for an 1890 setting.

seconds for your locomotive to develop a head of steam from starting position, and, by the same token, an equal amount of time for it to slow down and come to a stop. No instant jack-rabbit starts and no instant dead stops, for in the latter case, although the speed control knob has been returned to zero or off position, it will still slow down gradually as described.

It all has to do with the law of inertia, which in essence states, "a body at rest tends to remain at rest; a body in motion tends to remain in motion." This overcoming of inertia by gradual means is, therefore, accomplished through the use of a device within the transistorized throttle which is called an "inertia control." It will permit you to adjust the start-run and run-stop cycle to embrace up to an approximate fifteen-second period. In other words, you can vary the inertia from zero (instant response, as we normally have) to full inertia which, in effect, would be the fifteen-second delay we are talking about, or to whatever period of delay you wish to produce within that fifteen-second period. Bear in mind that the inertia control adjustment will not affect top speed, but rather the amount of time it takes to achieve top speed or whatever speed you have set the speed control for. Now in slowing down, as you coast into the station, or whatever the point of arrival, and see that you are going to overshoot, then you would use the brake as in normal operation. This "braking device," also part of the same transistorized throttle, is in the form of a *spring-loaded knob*, which, by way of a good built-in safety feature, will prevent you from leaving a train in a parked position with the brake fully on. It is features such as these that I am sure will endear ASTRAC to many a model railroader, for there is no denying that this system of operation, coupled with new refinements and those that will surely follow, make the application of prototype train handling not only a pleasure to behold, but a pleasure to be doing.

Ordinarily I would have left the details of the ASTRAC transistorized throttle in the preceding chapter but for the fact that it plays such an important part in the theme and concept of realistic operation. I'm sure you will agree. And to pursue it once more, without the interruptions and explanations which accompanied the foregoing commentary, let's take it from the top for the benefit of anyone who might have gotten sidetracked along the way.

In essence, the ASTRAC transistorized throttle will permit you to enjoy a type of operational control you may have never experienced before. Simply throw the throttle full on, and the locomotive drivers will slowly start to turn. Gradually, the train will start to move, picking up speed, little by little, until maximum speed has been achieved, which will be in the neighborhood of fifteen seconds or whatever period of zero-to-full-response you have set the inertia control adjustment for. Reducing speed is also a gradual process, after which the train will hold that speed. In similar fashion to the realistic period of time and response from start till maximum speed has been achieved, in throwing the throttle back to zero, it will take an equal amount of time for the train to slow down and coast to a stop. And should you appear to be overshooting your destination, a flip of the brake knob will bring you to a halt. Finally, the beauty of it all is that the transistorized throttle, which includes the inertia control and brake, simply plugs into the back of any given ASTRAC power transmission unit. With equipment such as this, it is easy to while away many hours dreaming up different types of realistic operation, but it is really more fun when you actually do it.

Since this description was with reference to ASTRAC transmission units and receiver-equipped locomotives, I'll add some food for thought concerning transistorized throttle control along more conventional lines for use in normally wired locomotives and model railroads. The Controlmaster I power pack made by Model Rectifier Corp. also provides transistorized throttle control, with an equal number of exciting features and refinements similar to that employed by ASTRAC. In short, whether you switch over to ASTRAC operation or stay with the previously established means of power propulsion, you have the opportunity of availing yourself of a means of smooth and realistic operating control which heretofore was limited to those who contrived and developed their own flywheel drive systems, or whatever their own ingenuity permitted them to not only dream up, but build as well. Unfortunately, not everyone is skilled or blessed enough to create or invent devices which aid the cause of realistic operation; therefore, many modelers have to rely on what the hobby manufacturers come out with. Fortunately, month in and month out, new products appear—some good, some bad—but the important thing to note is that the hobby is not standing still, and there are many refinements yet to come which will astound even the most dyed-in-the-wool veteran modeler. Before closing, we will look into the crystal ball and see what the future holds in store for our model railroading pleasures.

SIGNALS

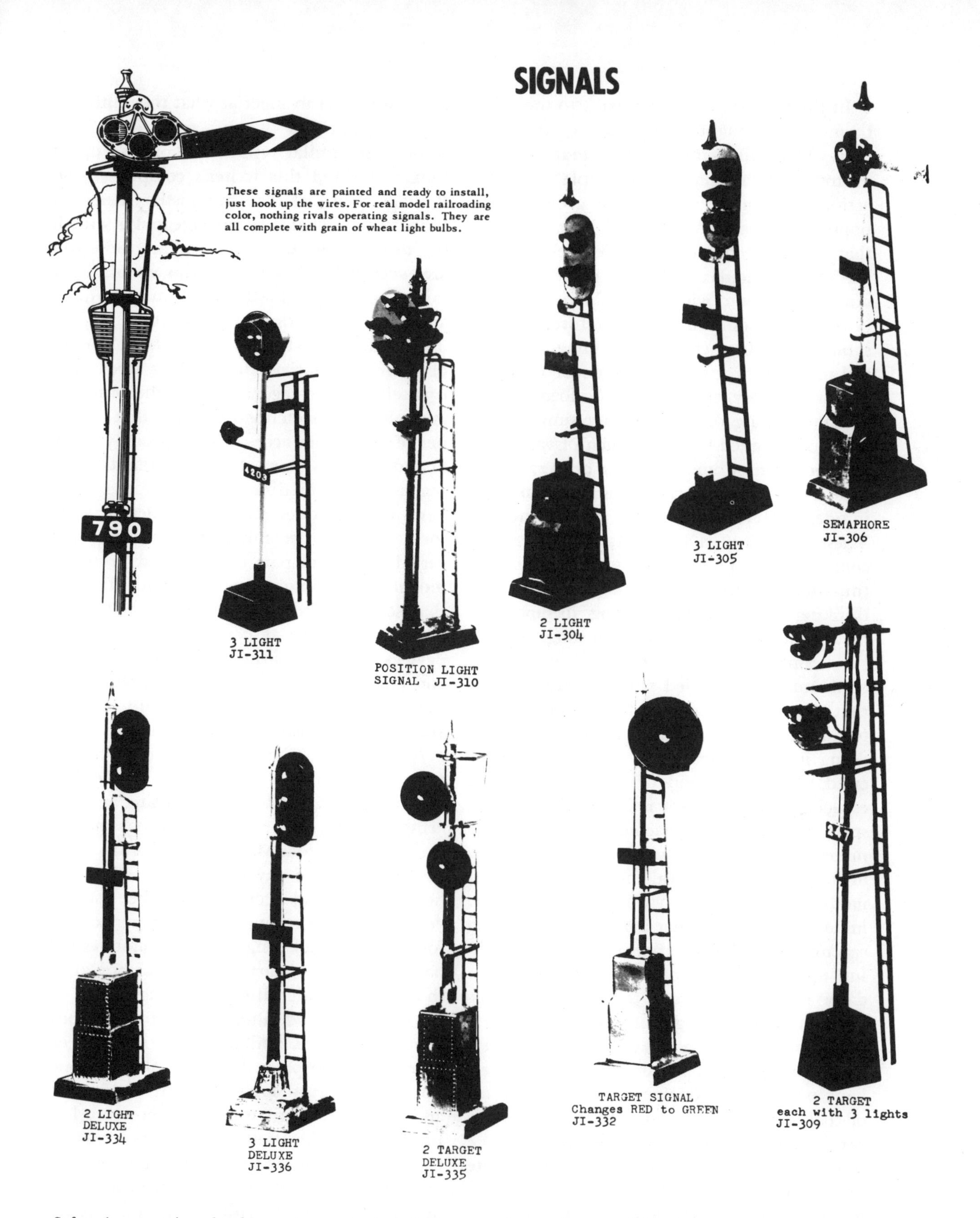

These signals are painted and ready to install, just hook up the wires. For real model railroading color, nothing rivals operating signals. They are all complete with grain of wheat light bulbs.

3 LIGHT
JI-311

POSITION LIGHT
SIGNAL JI-310

2 LIGHT
JI-304

3 LIGHT
JI-305

SEMAPHORE
JI-306

2 LIGHT
DELUXE
JI-334

3 LIGHT
DELUXE
JI-336

2 TARGET
DELUXE
JI-335

TARGET SIGNAL
Changes RED to GREEN
JI-332

2 TARGET
each with 3 lights
JI-309

Safety in operation should not be overlooked. Take a gander at these available Kemtron signals. Each serves a specific purpose and indication as to the road ahead, the block you are entering and the position of a given turnout—everything and anything to warn you whether you can proceed ahead. Not just props, but actual working authentic scale-sized signal lights, which after a simple hook-up will brighten things considerably. I have included individual order numbers to make it convenient for you when you visit the hobby shop to purchase them. Available from other sources as well.

In the meantime, let's get back to the main theme of this chapter, and pursue other avenues which will enable you to operate in truly prototypical fashion. For example, consider action accessories, which have grown quite popular in recent years. And bear in mind that when one model railroader belittles the use of a particular accessory, device, or system of operation, what he might really mean is that he doesn't use it—therefore, neither should you. In fact, the first time a model rail manufacturer offered a remote-controlled action accessory, such as a log-unloading car, a coal-dumping ore car, or any similar contrivance designed to add a touch of variety to the operation of one's pike, the cries rang out from coast to coast chorusing the same rejoinder, "Hey, what is this, a toy gauge?" These same stuffed brass hats who jeeringly commented, "This is Scale, ya know, not tinplate," continued on their merry way thinking unkindly of smoking locomotives, bell-ringing crossings, ore-dumping hopper cars, ramps, and any number of electrically or manually controlled working mechanisms that not only would give the operator more to do, but would give him more pleasure in doing it. Yet, these same chaps who have decried the introduction of action accessories, especially in the HO scale, think nothing of spending many hours assembling a Black Bart mine, and following this they do a neat job of fitting it into the wall of a well-scenicked mountainside, replete with newly laid spur, miners, and all the other ingredients that help capture an authentic appearance when picking up or dropping off ore cars during the daily run to and from the refining plant.

Then, they turn right around and rig up a tiny motor, or solenoid, to activate a lever, which in turn will open the hatch of the overhanging chute, depositing a few thimbles full of coal, or what have you, into the empty ore car directly below—and there you have a beauty of a paradox. For if there is a double set of standards in HO or any other scale, I haven't come across them as yet, and how these rail fans can sneer at what they unblushingly refer to as "trash" and "junk," yet accomplish similar types of action and operation, is beyond this writer's comprehension. Perhaps they feel they can justify their attitude because what they have created is scratch-built or close to it. Then, there are those who are even "holier" than that, who wouldn't permit even the slightest bit of movement or automatic operation within their layouts other than that which is created by the action of their locomotives and rolling stock. Fortunately, both categories are in the minority, and while I am inclined to agree that a number of the earlier accessories, especially in the O and S gauges, were about as authentic looking as a five-and-dime reprint of the Mona Lisa, the fact does remain that action accessories are fast becoming an established and eagerly accepted part of scale and prototype model railroading, notwithstanding the fact that some of the action accessories available today in HO are at best simply mechanical devices lacking charm, authentic operation, and appearance. But, like in everything else, there is the good and the bad, and no one's arm is being twisted. To each his own.

Nevertheless, the fact does remain that were it not for operating devices in the form of signals, clanging bells, and raising and lowering crossbars, the railroad crossings that dot the landscape from Maine to California would no doubt in one day make the traffic toll of holiday weekend accidents for the last fifty years look like a handful by comparison. As for the smoke-belching steam locomotives that have stirred the heart of man and boy alike, those sooty, cinder-filled billowing clouds rising into the wild blue yonder had to come from somewhere, and it wasn't from the engineer's puffing pipe. And what about hopper cars? Did a good fairy pop out of nowhere and, waving a magic wand, cause the ore load to dump out by itself? The hopper cars are backed into a tipple for automatic unloading. In fact, at some point of the operation, road men would stand by with sledge hammers and

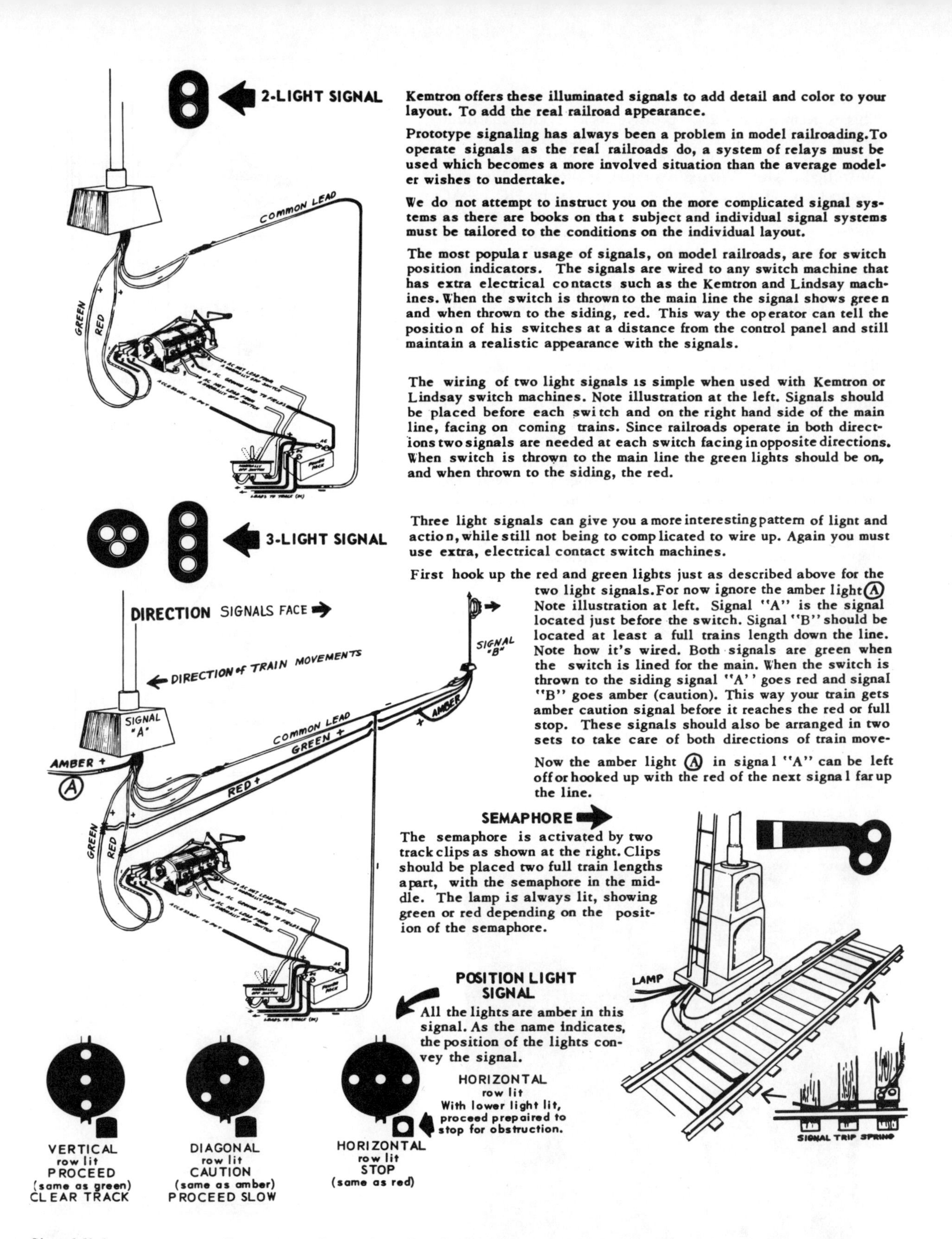

Kemtron offers these illuminated signals to add detail and color to your layout. To add the real railroad appearance.

Prototype signaling has always been a problem in model railroading. To operate signals as the real railroads do, a system of relays must be used which becomes a more involved situation than the average modeler wishes to undertake.

We do not attempt to instruct you on the more complicated signal systems as there are books on that subject and individual signal systems must be tailored to the conditions on the individual layout.

The most popular usage of signals, on model railroads, are for switch position indicators. The signals are wired to any switch machine that has extra electrical contacts such as the Kemtron and Lindsay machines. When the switch is thrown to the main line the signal shows green and when thrown to the siding, red. This way the operator can tell the position of his switches at a distance from the control panel and still maintain a realistic appearance with the signals.

The wiring of two light signals is simple when used with Kemtron or Lindsay switch machines. Note illustration at the left. Signals should be placed before each switch and on the right hand side of the main line, facing on coming trains. Since railroads operate in both directions two signals are needed at each switch facing in opposite directions. When switch is thrown to the main line the green lights should be on, and when thrown to the siding, the red.

Three light signals can give you a more interesting pattern of lignt and action, while still not being to complicated to wire up. Again you must use extra, electrical contact switch machines.

First hook up the red and green lights just as described above for the two light signals. For now ignore the amber light Ⓐ Note illustration at left. Signal "A" is the signal located just before the switch. Signal "B" should be located at least a full trains length down the line. Note how it's wired. Both signals are green when the switch is lined for the main. When the switch is thrown to the siding signal "A" goes red and signal "B" goes amber (caution). This way your train gets amber caution signal before it reaches the red or full stop. These signals should also be arranged in two sets to take care of both directions of train move-

Now the amber light Ⓐ in signal "A" can be left off or hooked up with the red of the next signal far up the line.

The semaphore is activated by two track clips as shown at the right. Clips should be placed two full train lengths apart, with the semaphore in the middle. The lamp is always lit, showing green or red depending on the position of the semaphore.

All the lights are amber in this signal. As the name indicates, the position of the lights convey the signal.

Signal lights are more easily connected to twin-coil switch machines which have additional contact points. Rotary relays, available at surplus stores, will do perfectly. Single-coil switch machines such as those Tru-Scale and Atlas offer for their respective turnouts will require a bit of electrical modification and the addition of contact points if they are used to actuate signals located at the site of the turnout, or they can be controlled from the control panel.

This is Kemtron's X-250 "positive lock" switch machine, and a beauty at that. It features a number of accessory circuits and contact points for signaling and other remote-controlled devices. Wiring is simple, as shown in Figure 1. Connect coil Taps 1, 2 and 3 to 10-15 volts DC or AC terminals of power pack through a two-way momentary contact switch to operate this switch machine. Feeding current to Taps 1 and 2 will actuate the machine and, in turn, the turnout one way, and when fed to Taps 1 and 3 will return it. A momentary impulse only, for, if contact is prolonged, the coil will burn out. The six blades and the numbered contacts shown in Figure 2 offer long trouble-free operation. They can be used for indicator lamps, signals and accessory circuits. The contacts are made and broken according to the throw of the switch, providing automatic response and operation from your control panel. These circuits are independent and may have AC or DC fed into the contacts at Points 8 and 9. Points 4 to 7 are the outputs. At other full-throw position the polarity Contacts 10 and 11 will feed the proper polarity of DC current to the frog through Outlet 12. This helps eliminate operating troubles due to poor contact at switch points. Under-layout mounting is easy, as shown in Figure 3. The important thing about the switch machine is the versatility it offers. Control panel indications are actuated by the position of the turnout, not by a toggle switch. The same thing goes for signal lights and other accessories. The result is proof positive and a tremendous aid in both the use of safety devices and the operations involved.

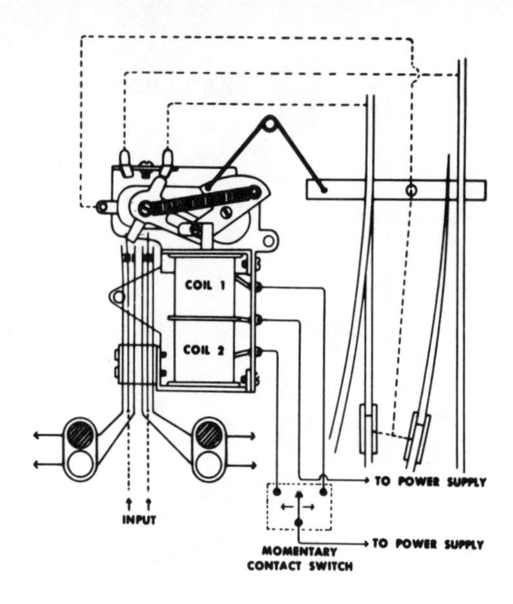

Control panels can be as detailed and fancy as you wish to make them. This partial view of a control panel at the Sierra Southern RR Club includes block toggles, turnout toggles, throttle, ammeter, etc.

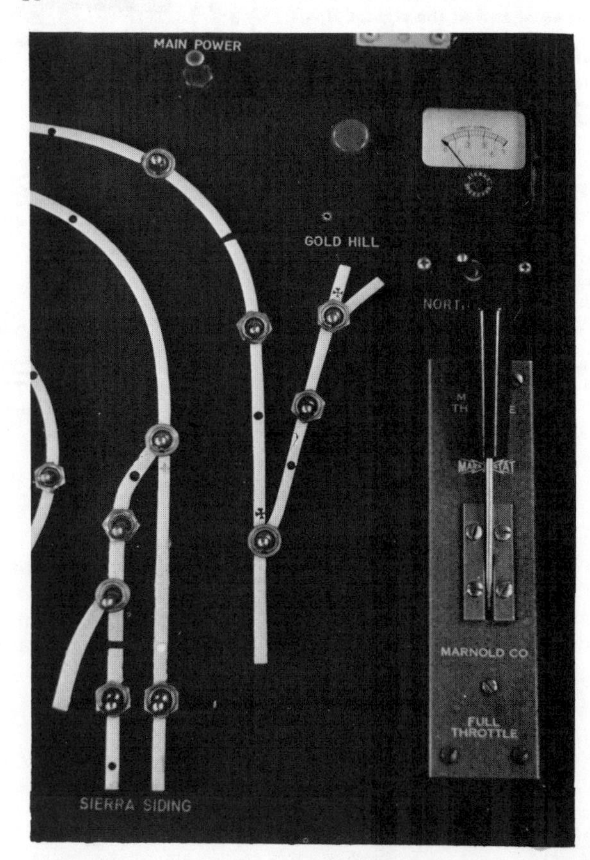

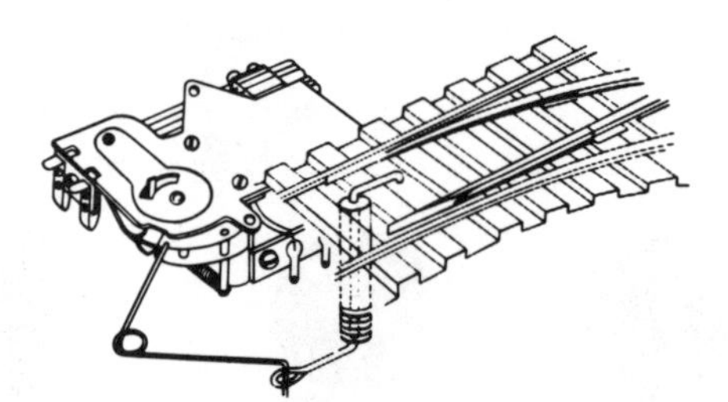

UNDER LAYOUT MOUNTING

To mount the switch machine under your layout, follow the plans as shown in these two drawings.

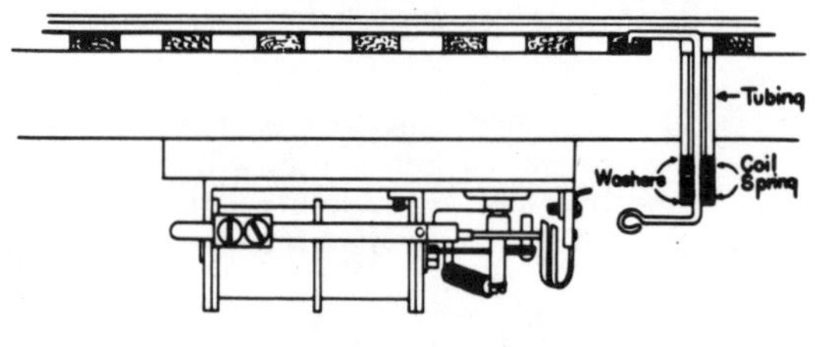

throw rod

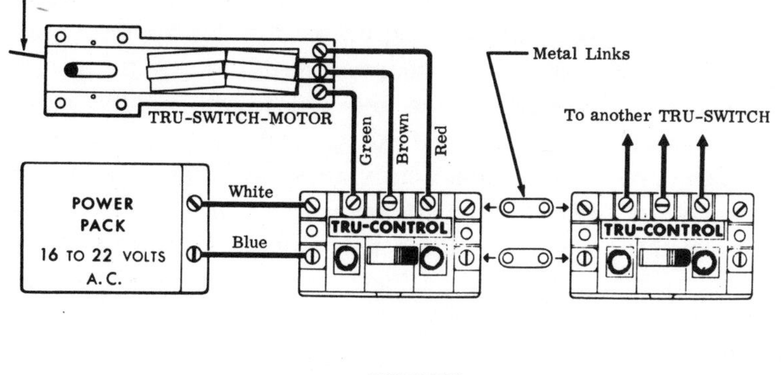

Tru-Control switches from Tru-Scale are perfect mates for their Tru-Switch motors. The switches feature indicator lights which tell you at a glance the position of the turnout. Hook-up is quite simple, and if the switch units are all in one area, they can be powered on a common-feed basis by connecting them together. If they are to be placed apart from each other on a control-panel design, they can tap power from the nearest feeders or terminals.

White
Blue
To
Tru-Switches

switch control
with indicator lights

Automatic Tru-Train (ATC) from Tru-Scale is a detection unit which provides various safety features during operation. Among other things, it will prevent one train from ploughing into the caboose of another train ahead. Instead, it will cause the train to stop until the front train is safely ahead. Will work with either conventional or ASTRAC operation.

pound the dickens out of the sides of the cars until every last piece of ore, ballast, coal, or whatever, fell out. That's what you call action from the working railroad standpoint.

The term "realistic operation" is as broad as it is long, since it embraces every facet of model railroading: building up models in keeping with prototype standards, constructing authentic-appearing railroad structures and, by the same token, the dwellings of the populace and industry. Scenic effects and logical track plans are but a few of the situations embraced under this heading. To paraphrase an earlier comment, assuming you had a 100 per cent authentic version of any given locomotive you care to name, if you are reckless in running it, if you are haphazard and negligent concerning its care and maintenance, and if you power it with a pack that couldn't get a rise out of a rubber band, then shame on you.

Though maintenance is not on the profit side of the railroad ledger, it is an operational must for obvious reasons, and the equipment used, such as water cars, work trains, derricks, etc., all come under the heading of "non-revenue" equipment, but they nonetheless play a vital part in the overall scheme of things. Without servicing and repairs, the railroads would be in a mess, schedules would be fouled up, and, to say the least, the safety factor would be akin to walking along the rails in a hump yard when things were in full swing. However, from the standpoint of repairs, servicing, inspection, *et al,* the railroads keep a round-the-clock vigil, so we can assume that they have such things well in hand. Therefore, maintenance is not only restricted to the chores you perform to keep your railroad and equipment in good condition, but for operational purposes as well.

This point of view will more than fit into the scheme of things within the framework of what you do on your railroad other than simply run trains endlessly, for it is important to note that there is a distinct difference between running trains and operating them. Therefore, when I speak of operation, I mean the moving of equipment in a purposeful and prototypical manner. Oddly enough, many modelers, new and old to the hobby, have never really tried operation along prototype lines, consequently, they have no way of knowing whether they will like it or not. The best way to find out if prototype operation is for you would be by actually trying it. It may or may not be your cup of tea, but you should at least give yourself the opportunity of having the experience on which your attitude is based. Regardless of how and where your interests lie, you are just as much a model railroader as the other fellow, though you may not be as prototype. Which is by no means a crime in itself, but rather a crime if you don't take at least one stab at it. By way of summarizing, we get back to my suggestion that the maintenance chores you perform to keep your railroad in top-flight condition can also be applied as an operation and function of and within the railroad itself. In that way, you can make up a work train and send it off on a day's run, servicing a signal here, repairing a stranded box car there, etc. Your own imagination will play an important part in this, for many pieces of equipment can be brought into action, such as water cars, track-cleaning cars, derricks, and other particular forms of maintenance equipment which not only aid you in keeping things running, but permit you to develop an actual schedule of maintenance operations. The end result will be threefold in that you will be keeping things in order, giving your railroad a specific purpose of operation, and, in the final analysis, broadening your horizons where realistic operation is concerned.

Now would be a perfect time to touch on a subject that is often misleading, and to say the least, confusing, especially to new converts to the fold. The subject is multi-train operation, simultaneous train operation, call it what you will. For this operation by any other name would be just as sweet. Sweet, that is, if you alone can successfully and safely handle the running of more than one train at a time. After all, we only have two hands to manipulate with and two eyes to see with. In short, I have interviewed a score or more fellow enthusiasts, and the consensus of opinion is that unless you are a magician or a two-headed engineer, it is almost impossible to operate two trains at the same time. Now remember I said operate—not run. Of course, it is obvious that your left hand can throttle one train while your right hand throttles another, and simultaneously at that. Nothing difficult about that; in fact, it is quite easy to do. However, try to move a switcher in and about a yard while making or breaking up a train at the time you also send another train out for a few or more laps about your railroad. You will find it quite difficult to control the actions of both of them at the same time without an element of danger entering the attempt at dual operation. If you are switching in the yard, you will be busy enough coupling and uncoupling cars, flipping toggles, and referring to the checklist which will instruct you as to the order in which particular cars are to be made or broken up. As for the other train, it is obviously on its own.

Therefore, to be technical about it, you are not performing a dual operation for, in effect, the only operation you are doing is in controlling the action of the switcher in the yard. As for the other train, it is running by itself—you haven't had any more to do with it then throw the throttle to get it rolling. And heaven help you if, while preoccupied with your switching chores, the other train, left untended, runs into some form of trouble or another, for you won't know it until a short occurs, a dozen speed regulations are violated, or something hits the deck. Perhaps I'm overdramatizing things a bit, but no matter how you look at it, when you set a train rolling and forget about it, you actually have what might be well considered a runaway train. There are, of course, many ways to get around this by means of automatic routing, signaling, and detection relay units, etc. However, the point I wish to stress is that you can only operate one train (in a purposeful manner) at one time if safety is to be considered, which it should be in prototype or model operation, whichever the case. Don't construe what I am saying to mean that I am against any form of cab control, which permits the operation of more than one train at a time. I'm not. I am simply suggesting that the basic purpose of multi-train control is not necessarily a means of permitting you to operate more than one train at a time, but rather to permit you to select and control the operation of a given train without setting another one into motion. Therefore, safety becomes an important part of realistic operation and, while the advantages of block, cab control, and ASTRAC have been expounded, a fair amount of prudence should be exercised concerning their use, especially in the case of ASTRAC, which will permit a heretofore unavailable flexibility of multi- and simultaneous train operation. In retrospect, and with direct reference to the preceding chapter, please note that while I went into great and happy detail explaining that ASTRAC permitted the simultaneous running of five trains, it would be ridiculous to assume that any one individual could possibly do so with even a fraction of credibility. And also take further note that when I mentioned the fact that this carrier-control system permitted a five-train operation, and then ten (following the introduction of five more channels), on a simultaneous basis, I always parenthesized the fact that club members should take note. So for the third time I repeat: multi- and simultaneous train operation is fine, on a selective basis if yours is a one-man railroad. For club operation, it is a different thing entirely. There can be as many operators and trains running as there are cab controls and space to accommodate. At the risk of sounding like the title of a lead story in *True Confessions,* I must confess that I ran five trains at once, but only to prove to myself that ASTRAC could live up to its claims, and also so I could

Operating time at the Burbank, Encino, and South Tarzana Model RR Club involves the use of a cab-control dispatch system. Members are assigned individual cabs and receive "work card orders" informing them of the operation they are to perform: a point-to-point passenger run with specific times of arrival at various points along the way; the dropping off of cars at different industrial sites during a freight haul; a yard assignment to make up a train for a road engine waiting nearby; or a similar assignment to break up a train after it has been brought in. As for the dispatcher, he sets up the various routes to conform to the respective operating assignments. Blocks are powered, turnouts are thrown, polarities in reverse loops are matched and, when things are clear, he will give the go-ahead sign to "take it out," after which the engineer will take over the throttle control. Things get a bit hectic when there are four or so cabs in operation at one time, and while the individual operators are only responsible for their particular train, the dispatcher must be constantly on his toes, keeping an alert eye on all the activity throughout the road.

Dispatcher Jack Guy gives the go-ahead to "take it out." Telephonic communications between dispatcher and cab operators add to the fun, and enable everyone to know what is going on and when. It helps you get the message straight, especially if there is a hub-bub of extraneous conversation going on among non-operating non-working featherbedders.

Bruce MacPherson gets the go-ahead to make up a train after drawing a yard assignment. When finished, he will haul it out to a siding off the mainline, where a road engine will take over.

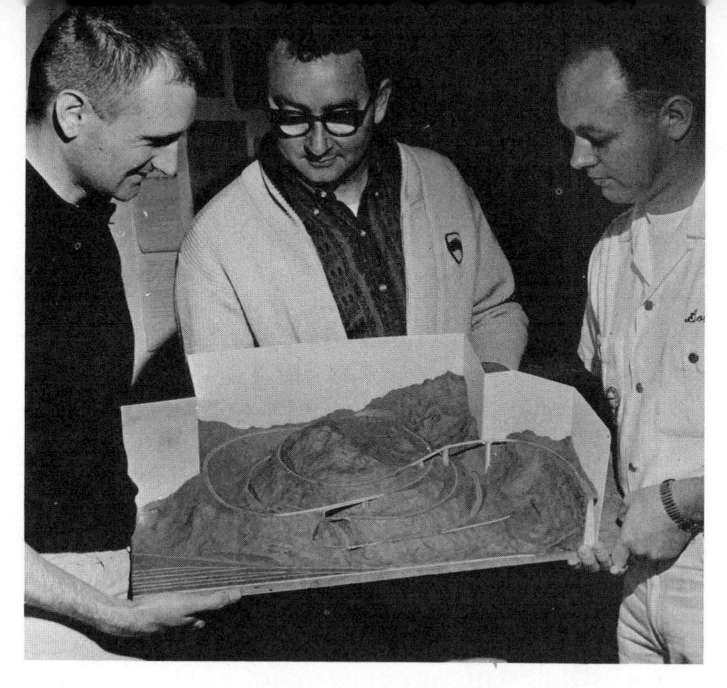

Long-range planning, that's the keynote toward successful completion of your model railroad. Eric Bracher, Jim Webb and Bob Semichy show the extent to which they and other members of their club went in working the bugs out of proposed scenic effects. A clay mock-up was shaped and re-shaped till the right type of topographical effect was achieved. Strips of bass wood serving as track were shifted about a number of times until everything was compatible, not only from a scenic standpoint, but an operating one as well.

Alan Stensvold checks and double checks during the planning of a new and bigger layout. Plan ahead for anything that might arise or be added to your original scheme of things: an extra building, a siding or a spur, and all the adjacent activity in the form of special effects that go with it. Be sure that you have room for everything that will be involved.

Photographing prized models is not too difficult a chore and you can obtain many special effects with simple lighting and close-up attachments. Low angles will add a "brute strength" appearance to a locomotive; a wide-angle lens will help. One light, or a main source of light behind the subject being photographed, will help achieve interesting silhouettes. These photographs were taken with 35-mm. cameras of the Nikon and Miranda variety. With proper lighting and angle of view, it will be difficult to tell a model from the prototype.

check performance and have a basis for the glowing description in the preceding chapter. To mention that I had my hands full would be superfluous. Fellow rail Alan Stensvold dropped by while I was giving things the acid test, and between the two of us we had our hands full trying to manage more than one train each at a time without having cornfield meets—and we did have a few of those, too. But then, this was a test and nothing more. The moral, if one is to be gained, is that regardless of whatever form of propulsion you are using which permits you to operate more than one train at the same time, you will have to be constantly on the alert. For if yours is a one-man railroad, you will find it difficult to watch more than one train at a given moment. Thus, you are best advised to operate on a single rather than a dual basis. At the very least, you as an engineer will be more prototype in your operation, and, with no other distractions, you will be able to put your train through the purpose for which it was designed and made up—to perform a logical service on your railroad.

There are a number of devices available which you can install within the network of your track to help you overcome certain problems which arise due to overcrowded operating conditions, expansion of your railroad from its original plan or concept, and other situations which not only provide the safety features needed to prevent or minimize accidents, but dress things up as well. Such things as signal lights for blocks and turnouts are fine. In the case of turnouts, a switch machine with sufficient contact points to activate the signal light to correspond with the position of the turnout is infinitely superior to a hookup which activates the signal light from the control panel. By the same token, it is better to power and activate turnout position light indicators in the control panel directly from the turnout switch machine also, rather than from the toggle switch in the panel. For in this way you will know for sure, in glancing at your board or given turnout signal, the actual position to which the turnout has been thrown. Of course, installing and wiring a complete set of signals is easier said than done. It isn't difficult. It just takes quite a bit of time, depending on the number of blocks, turnouts, and other areas of your railroad where such devices are warranted. Installation of signal lights is not done overnight. And while you will find that many well-scenicked pikes are liberally garnished with signals, almost 75 per cent of them are no more than props, and while they add to the railroad-like effect, they serve no other useful purpose. However, they are there and while only dressing things up for the time being, they will eventually be hooked up and working.

Signals, their proper application, and the messages and instructions they convey, are an extremely important and essential part of real railroading. The same thing applies in their miniature counterparts and while you may be weeks, months, or years in properly outfitting your railroad with these safety devices, you don't have to wait until everything else on your road is done. You can install a few here and there as you go along. For when you stop to think of it, most pikes are never really finished. There is always some new technique coming along, or a change of industry or community which will have you ripping up track or moving the location of a tunnel or turnout. That's why model railroading can offer a lifetime of pleasurable pursuit. For should the time come—and I doubt it will—that your railroad has everything that you could possibly desire, and you can devote all of your spare time to operation alone, then the sheer joy of operating in the most prototypical manner possible along the lines we have discussed will reflect itself in the best traditions of railroading. But you will still add an interurban line here or a narrow-gauge line there. That's the fun of it.

Getting back to action accessories, the only additional points I wish to add now are concerned not so much with their use as with

Meanwhile, back at the freight yards this late-model rail auto passed by, carrying a load of VIPs apparently out on a line check run. Quite common in railroading, rail autos such as these serve a variety of purposes, from ferrying visiting brass in and about the road to propelling crew chiefs up and down the line while supervising maintenance gangs. This one, of course, is quite sleek, with narrow white sidewalls yet. Compare this with the Thomas Flyer, circa 1907, built by Reu Richards from a Kemtron kit. All brass and loaded with details, this quaint and somewhat ancient auto car presents quite a contrast to its successor. Auto cars will add an interesting touch to your operations; just be sure that you keep the era in mind.

their application from a legitimate railroading standpoint. I'm not necessarily suggesting that you run out and buy a remote-controlled ore-dumping car because the action looks cute when you push the button. However, if within your schedule of operation you drop an ore car, hopper car, or whatever, along a spur under a coal chute, then return later to pick it up and haul it into town, where the coal trucks are waiting to load up and make their daily deliveries, why pretend that during the interim those imaginary little people who live and work in your layout have dropped a load of coal through the chute into the empty car below? Why pretend this has happened, or, for that matter, why reach across your layout and drop a few pinches into the empty bin, when for a modest investment you can build or buy an operating accessory which will behave in a realistic manner while you don't have to budge from your throttle or control panel?

As for the other end of the operation, the same thing applies, and instead of backing the heavily laden car into the coal yard where the trucks are waiting to load up (and letting it go at that), why not back it up onto an approach ramp, where a built-in tripping lever will actuate a door trip mechanism on your hopper, and you can dispense with the make-believe by dropping an honest-to-goodness scale load. In this way, you have not only added to the illusion from an action standpoint, but from one of prototype operation as well. For those who send their equipment rolling aimlessly and unrealistically throughout their setting, no matter how authentic in appearance it may be, are violating an important rule of railroading—operating with a purpose.

There is far more to realistic operation than observing scale speed, or not running a streamliner in a Civil War setting. You certainly wouldn't pick up a switcher by hand and drop it down at the other end of your freight yard because it might take ten minutes of switching to get it to its destination. Those ten minutes of switching are part of the operating fun, and for many model rails, the more complicated and frantic the switching, the better.

Tru-Scale has an interesting item on the market called Automatic Tru-Train Control or, in short, ATC operation. It is available for all scales using DC or AC, and while most of my commentary throughout this book bears a marked emphasis toward HO, I have talked in fairly general terms; therefore, the observations and ideas I previously covered are for the most part applicable to any and all of the scales and gauges in use today.

In capsule form, this is what Tru-Scale's ATC can do for you, whether you are starting with a simple oval or a well-laid-out track plan.

If the faster train, B, begins to overtake the slower train, A, then A will automatically activate a red signal light, causing B to stop until A has rolled on far enough ahead to avoid a rear-end collision. As soon as the danger of a mangled caboose and a twisted pilot has been eliminated, the red signal light will change to green, permitting B to proceed. It is all accomplished by relay control units, and once hooked up, you don't have to push any buttons or trip any levers, but just relax and watch a realistic operation unfold. The price is nominal, and you get not only the relay unit, but a two-color signal light. Instructions for hooking up are clear, concise, and specific; thus you can get to ATC application sooner than you think.

There are a number of other items available which will add to your railroading pleasures, and, while some of them are not quite prototype in appearance, they will nonetheless perform in a more than satisfactory manner.

The fun in using certain items will generally outweigh their shortcomings from the standpoint of appearance which, in the latter case, is not too serious a threat to one's railroading purity, since a dab or two of paint, a few pieces of lichen, and any other simple aging, weathering, or scenic effect will cover a multitude of sins. There are numerous other detection devices and relay-activated units on the market and available at your hobby shop, and, needless to say, they will continue to appear. The arguments concerning the use of various types of automatic train controls are evenly divided among the pros and the cons. Some feel that automatic controls remove the direction of the train's action from the hands of the operator, and that all he is accomplishing is a form of demonstration whereby he simply sits back and watches things run by themselves. On the other hand, there are those who maintain that devices—any devices which will remove the element of accident, danger, or hazardous operation—serve a definite purpose. In recent years there has been a rather widespread acceptance of such operating devices among model railroaders, and more will be forthcoming, accepted, and installed on layouts throughout the country as long as the appearance and action in the end result is no less than reasonable and logical. As for being absolutely and completely prototype, who is? You can go as far as you wish toward that end or you might even go somewhat in the other direction. It is up to you.

We have come a long way since climbing aboard, and during the course of writing this book, I have stressed and re-stressed many facts, techniques, and points of reference. I have tried to guide you toward higher plateaus in model railroading and the good fellowship that develops from meeting fellow enthusiasts. I sincerely feel that it is through talks and meetings of this nature that the information which is imparted from one model rail to another provides the very means by which new products and refinements in technique and application are fostered. I also feel that periodic visits to a local model railroad club in your area will not only enable you to see what other fellows are doing, but give you a much more practical insight into things, which in some cases will prove more beneficial from a practical standpoint than any number of books, articles, or literature may provide, comprehensive or otherwise. Most clubs generally have open house a few times a month and welcome visitors, especially fellow enthusiasts who might want to become members.

Most group activity, where model railroading is concerned, was born of necessity during the depression years of the early 1930s, when space was at a premium and finances at a low ebb. Modelers, frustrated in attempts to follow their love of scale and prototype railroading in what were generally cramped quarters, banded together in various groups, and, foregoing the personal pleasures of individual home layouts, pooled their equipment and resources into one collectively owned railroad. An empty store in a low-rent district, an unoccupied garage, some spare space in a factory or warehouse—anywhere they could congregate, do a bit of operating, and chew the fat was welcomed with eager and grateful hearts. Today, as in the past, rail fans join clubs for pretty much the same reasons:

1. They don't have any spare room at home to set up a decent-sized layout, or they don't have any space.
2. They had to tear down their layout to make room for the new baby, the mother-in-law, or new car.
3. They have gone off on an articulated kick and find that these long jobs look out of place on their minimum-radius trackage, and, for that matter, won't operate despite the statement in the advertisement that such and such a locomotive could negotiate an 18-inch radius.
4. They are interested in operating but are not inclined toward building the pike to do it in.
5. They want the experience of working with other fellow rails and holding off till the time they can indulge in the pleasures of individual ownership and operation.
6. They like to chew the fat and have a night out with the boys once a week, and still get in a bit of railroading.

Shoot pictures of prototype structures whenever you get the chance. It will help when you build and set the scene. I recorded these towers in their native surroundings. The view at the Sierra Southern RR Club more than speaks for itself.

Tunnel portals and bracings such as this are a snap to make and can be scratch-built in nothing flat. Bass wood, twigs, stones, pebbles, things you can easily find in your own backyard, will go a long way toward adding a realistic atmosphere to the area you operate in.

An improved and modified version of the track spiking gun shown in Chapter 8. While essentially the same in operation, there are a few notable refinements which are worthy of showing and describing. For example, an adjustable screw device permits you to adjust and vary the impact of the staple depending on the hardness of the ties and the baseboard they have been glued to. You can therefore adjust and compensate for plywood, Homosote, wood or cork roadbed, Tru-Scale slotted roadbed, etc. You can also adjust the impact penetration of the spike-type staple so that it grips the rail tightly but does not mash or bend the rail into the ties, causing kinks. The gun uses a "U" type staple, which is split as the driving blade carries it past the cutting bar, resulting in two spike-shaped staples being firmly positioned on each side of the rail against the rail base and centered through the ties. Staples come 2,000 to the box, which makes 4,000 when used with this gun. In addition, a gauge guide extending from the side keeps the track in line during spiking. Last but not least, additional gauge attachments permit its use for HOn3, S and TT gauges as well, in either Code 100 or Code 70.

These are but a few of the reasons why model railroad clubs are flourishing, and if you fit any of the above categories, then club operation and membership might well be the solution for you. Most clubs operate on a schedule; in other words, since they generally meet once a week, they devote one evening to building, maintenance, clean-up, or other chores required to keep things in tip-top shape. Another evening is devoted to affairs of state: business, the amount of money left in the treasury after they purchased a sorely needed trestle kit to span that new gorge one of the members carved out, and other functions pertaining to administration. The other evenings during the month are usually spent in both group and individual operation, where the members get a chance to show their engineering prowess at the control panels while indulging in some fancy and frantic switching operations, or running and testing some newly purchased or built-up equipment. Most clubs have a nominal initiation fee and an equally nominal monthly dues, both of which are based on the size of the membership, the age of the club, and the investment to date. Clubs are always looking for new members, but they want members who are interested in contributing more than their presence at the weekly meetings; in other words, members who will do their share of the work. This type of collective model railroadship is a great outlet for the rail fan who is a whiz at wiring but draws a blank when it comes to laying a piece of lichen at the foot of a trestle. It is also a good bet for the scenic wizard who doesn't know a hog from a crummy. In either case, within a short time both individuals will be well versed in the many other facets of model railroading.

Strangely enough, it is not unusual to find individuals within the ranks of club membership who also have their own big or small railroads at home. The explanation is simply based on the fact that getting together within the confines of a model railroading circle is not only informative and rewarding from the standpoint of gaining experience, but that during the interchange of ideas, opinions, and theories, new horizons in approach and operation are freely discussed and, for the most part, are both challenging and stimulating. I know that the first time I visited John Allen's "Gorre and Daphetid" RR empire, I was struck with the magnificance of his concept and creation. For what the maestro has accomplished is what dreams are really made of, and, in his case, it is virtually a dream come true. I have also had the pleasure of visiting Whit Towers (another name well known in model railroading circles) and watching the smooth, exciting, and prototype operation on his "Alturas and Lone Pine" RR. I came away with a lump in my throat and a desire to perhaps one day—well, you know. Being a lone wolf is fine, but information, ideas, and techniques rub off easily, and I don't know of any model rails who aren't willing to convey their thoughts to anyone interested and willing to listen. And since we are getting close to the end of the line, I'd like to get in a last few licks concerning the NMRA. In addition to all I have said about this society and the obvious benefits that accrue from becoming a member, I should also point out that while a United States-based national society, the NMRA also is divided into fourteen main chapters within the western, central, and eastern regions from coast to coast. And within these regions are a number of divisions, some of whose members might live right around the corner from you. The cost of regional membership is nominal: $1.50 a year, which includes the receipt of a monthly bulletin, and other newsletters and information in similar fashion that the national society provides. Thus, between NMRA and regional membership, you have a negligible yearly dues of $6.50, lower in cost than almost anything nowadays. And don't forget that the annual NMRA yearbook lists all members, their addresses, type of pike, plus model RR clubs who boast 100 per cent membership, and that is just about most of them.

This compilation of information is handy to have especially when you go out of town, on a trip, or abroad, too, for NMRA membership encircles the globe. It's like having a friend in almost every part of the country and in many parts of the world, too. One final word concerning the NMRA and regional membership. The $4 cost is a mere pittance to what you probably spend a week as a hobbyist. If you are not already a member, you couldn't make a wiser and sounder investment.

We have developed a full head of steam and with the end of the line only a few miles ahead, we had better start applying the brakes to reduce speed, for after all that has been said, we don't want to overshoot the ending and be typical; instead, let's make it a smooth stop, and be prototypical.

To put the cap on the theme of this chapter, remember that while it embraces virtually every facet of model railroading, as far as realistic operation is concerned, after you take up the slack and head out on a heavy freight drag or a high-speed passenger run, keep at the forefront the basic functions of your miniature empire: purpose, place to place servicing, prototype action and motion, scale speed, and safety in operation. A liberal mixture of these ingredients properly blended together will provide you with a true railroading flavor. I hope your cup runneth over.

We're coasting smoothly now and are coming 'round the bend, so let's see what the future holds in store. Transistorization will make more and more inroads within the hobby, and throttles will make locomotives run smooth as a baby's tender. Locomotives will be manufactured in even finer detail, with more varieties of prototype design. I even hear that before long many locomotives will come receiver-equipped and ready for ASTRAC operation. It may already be at your hobby shop, and you won't have to install it yourself. The long-awaited advent of radio-frequency control is now here, for General Electric has given us Automatic Simultaneous Train Control. Ten channels and various types of power control transmission units are now available, and we will no doubt have many more in the future. Transistorized throttle controls will offer additional fringe benefits—not only in the form of inertia control, variable response, and braking levers, which we now have—but in other refinements as well. The time will surely come when almost everyone will succumb to the desirability and flexibility of ASTRAC, either outright or in connection with their existing normally wired railroads.

In a deeper look into the crystal ball, I can see an exciting and bright view of operational things to come. Micro-receivers will become smaller and smaller, so that they will not only fit within the smallest of locomotive boilers, but will permit the modeler to change the channel or radio frequency by a flip of a tiny dial or by simply plugging in a different channel. You won't have to remove and reinstall a different receiver, for through this simple expedient of channel selection on the receiver itself you won't have to worry about controlling similarly tuned locos on an alternate basis. You will only have to change their respective signal response. And the day will surely come when you will be able to follow your train as it moves out of the terminal onto the mainline, walking along as it moves in and about your railroad. You won't be tied to the transmitter control panel or have to drag along an extension cable, for in your hand will be a tiny transmitter—and wireless at that. You will have a freedom you never dreamed could exist, for you will most certainly feel that you are sitting in the cab, on the inside looking out, not on the outside looking in. These things we now have give rebirth to a hobby which has charmed man and boy alike. We may not know it now, but one day it will be referred to as the Renaissance of model railroading. What else the future holds in store is anyone's guess, and I for one am willing to try anything, at least once.

Whether or not all of us at present and

Seven years of master building has resulted in this fine layout by Dick Seydell and this fine scene of a Southern Pacific "Daylight" passing alongside an oil refinery after leaving Summit Station. This scene captures all the feeling and realism I am talking about. A wig-wagging signal, a working pump oil well, trucks on the move—all are ingredients which breathe life, sound and view to the eyes and ears of the beholder, and the engineer as he operates in the most realistic of railroad traditions.

The first time I ever visited the famed Gorre & Dephetid RR I was struck by the magnificence of concept and planning that has resulted from the dedication, creative application and sheer wizardry of John Allen. Operation on the Gorre & Dephetid is the personification of prototype procedure and is surrounded by a truly lifelike atmosphere that will keep any visitor spellbound. When John says "How about a bit of operating?" you embark on an unforgettable experience. Like many a dedicated model railroader, John Allen sincerely believes that unless you plan carefully from the beginning for future traffic and operation, you may have a model when you are finished, but hardly a model railroad. Realism, rapport, research, romance, reconstruction, restoration, refinement and rewards are just some of the "Rs" that go into the making of a model railroad empire.

Another freight train realistically, and slowly, rolls around and along the side of Giant Canyon in this breathtaking view of John Allen's Gorre & Dephetid Railroad. In the center background, the depth and dimension of the "Akinbak Range" has been heightened by the careful and clever installation of a mirror. John had to exercise considerable skill in this installation so that at no time could he see himself from various vantage points and walk-in areas of the railroad. He confessed that he thought up the name for the mountain range because it cost him an "aching back" to create and produce the extended effect. The angle of view in this photograph is such that the scenery in the lower center of the photograph overlaps and, as a consequence, they appear to join. Actually, this is not the case, for there is a walk-in aisle with steep cliffs dropping down to the floor on both sides. This aisle permits easier operation both from a visual and accessibility standpoint. Through the use of removable sections, further access for additional construction and maintenance is possible. A striking scene, and an outstanding testimonial to the magic of model railroading.

those yet to join the ranks will avail themselves of these refinements in technique and operation does not hinge on any ironclad rule. For, there is no rule that says, "You can't use it, it's too revolutionary," and, fortunately, those who think in that vein are in the minority. Thus, progress will be served. I know that I will have a helping, and so will anyone else with an open mind. Devices, innovations, new products, accessories—they will come and they will go. Some will aid the cause of prototype procedure; some won't. A few die-hard purists may scoff at them. However, Dick Seydell's layout, which is shown in this chapter and other areas of the book, refutes any such puritanical thinking. And in operation, it is quite a kick when the Southern Pacific "Daylight" glides out of the terminal at Summit Station, and the wig-wagging signal at the crossing chimes a warning bell. The S.P. comes rolling down the mainline along the outskirts of a refinery, and out of the corner of your eye you catch the movement of the oil well pumping, you almost feel like a passenger looking out the window at the scenery flitting by—or, better yet, like the engineer in the cab, his hand on the throttle and his eyes scanning the track-work ahead. That's what you call realistic operation.

After all, bells clanged, hoppers dumped, locomotives belched, and while to some this may all add up to be slightly cacophonous, to the model rail it is "999" thundering down the stretch, the "Texas" chasing the "General," the "Best Friend of Charleston" blowing up, "Casey Jones" hurtling through the night, heading to Valhalla. It is the breath, the life, the very pulse of the railroads. It is the sound of angels.

Yes, the thrill is everywhere. In your backyard in the form of a pebble or twig or two for the mountainside, in research at the library, in the magazine ads which have company slogans perfect for billboards and sidecar advertising, at the hamlets from coast to coast where oldtimers once proudly rolled and now adorn the public squares. As your pike takes on the shape and appearance of a believable railroading atmosphere, your operating pleasures will increase a thousand-fold. Your locomotives and rolling stock will take on added significance against the scenic panorama you alone have created. All this, and the fun of operation, too. For in homes and clubs across the nation, tiny motors hum their song as their locomotives pull endless cars over river and dale, mountain and meadow.

So, a toast to that prancing, puffing "iron horse"; that bellowing, steaming behemoth; that powerful astounding articulated; that whining, speeding streamliner. A toast to the young in heart and the many fun-filled model railroading hours that await your pleasure. Have yourself a ball. Better yet, have a HIGHBALL!

For that is the Magic of Model Railroading.

Bibliography

For additional reading pleasure, information, research and reference, the following is a partial listing of books, periodicals, literature and other related works that are available in hobby shops, book stores and public libraries.

GENERAL

Guidebook to Model Railroading, by David Sutton, Trend Books, Petersen Pub.

Practical Guide to Model Railroading, Linn H. Westcott, ed., Kalmbach Pub.

LAYOUTS AND TRACK DESIGN

101 Track Plans, by Linn H. Westcott, Kalmbach Pub.

Custom Line Layouts, by John Armstrong, Atlas Tool Co.

Model Railroad Layout & Track Design, by David Sutton, Spotlite Books, Petersen Pub.

WIRING

Electrical Handbook for Model Railroaders, by Paul Mallery, Simmons-Boardman.

How To Wire Your Model Railroad, by Linn H. Westcott, Kalmbach Pub.

Wiring Your HO Layout, by Paul Mallery Associates, Atlas Tool Co.

SCENERY AND STRUCTURE

Railroad Structures Plan Book, by Alan B. Armitage, Kemtron Products Co.

Scenery for Model Railroads, by Bill McClanahan, Kalmbach Pub.

Styrene Fabrication, by Alan B. Armitage, Kemtron Products. Co.

LOCOMOTIVES AND ROLLING STOCK

Locomotive Cyclopedia, Simmons-Boardman.

Rolling Stock Manual, Harold H. Carstens, ed., Penn Pub.

Steam Locomotives Cyclopedia, Linn H. Westcott, ed., Kalmbach Pub.

Steam Locomotive Plan Manual, Harold H. Carstens, ed., Penn Pub.

Trains, by Robert Selph Henry, Bobbs-Merrill Pub.

PERIODICALS, PAMPHLETS AND ASSORTED LITERATURE

Model Railroader Magazine (monthly), Kalmbach Pub.

Railroad Model Craftsman Magazine (monthly), Penn Pub.

Trains Magazine (monthly), Kalmbach Pub.

National Model Railroad Association, Inc., Yearbook, Monthly Bulletin, Data Sheets and assorted literature.

Association of American Railroads, Washington, D.C., Wide and varied assortment of Literature available upon request.

Glossary of Railroad Modeling Terms

When railroads first entered the scene in the early part of the last century they not only gave rise to one of the greatest form of transportation known to man and the hobby of model railroading as well, but in addition gave birth to a language all its own. Down through the years many railroad terms, expressions and railroad slanguage, as it were, have been absorbed into the vocabulary and are now part and parcel of our daily speech. Within the following glossary you will no doubt find many a familiar sounding term of whose origin you may not actually have been aware. You will also find many an expression that has been begged, borrowed and/or stolen from prototype parlance and is commonly used within the framework of model railroading. From the rankest beginner to the most veteran brass hat there exists a colorful jargon the highlights of which are included herein from A to Z. For additional and comprehensive definitions and listings see back issues of *Railroad Model Craftsman Magazine* and NMRA Yearbooks, literature and Data Sheets.

A.A.R.–American Association of Railroads

Abutment–An anchoring foundation designed to support lateral pressure or thrust, such as an end pier of a bridge to hold back solid ground.

Alley–A clear track

Alternating Current (AC)–Standard household current. A current that reverses its direction of flow at regular intervals. Each move from zero to maximum strength and back to zero is known as a cycle.

Ammeter–Meter used to measure current strength; how many amperes are being used by a motor or other electrical device.

Ampere or Amp–Unit used to measure electrical strength.

Apron–Overlapping deck between cab and tender; hinged covering above locomotive and tender connection.

Arbor–wheel axle

Arc–Spark created by passage of current across a gap; also a curve.

Armature–The wire-wound rotating part of a motor.

Arrival Track–Track upon which passenger trains arrive at a terminal; or freight trains arrive in or near a yard.

Articulated Locomotive–Applies to any locomotive featuring two or more sets of wheels and cylinders mounted on separate or hinged frames. Permits loco to snake around curves more easily.

Automatic Block Signal–Signal activated by train entering a block.

Automatic Coupler–Couplers which will couple and uncouple automatically through the use of uncoupling ramps, permanent or electro-magnets; permits remote operation as opposed to manual or hand methods.

ASTRAC–Automatic Simultaneous Train Control (General Electric) (*see* Radio and Carrier Control)

ATC–Automatic Train Control (Tru-Scale, etc.)

Auxiliary Tender–A second tender; enables an engine to maintain longer runs by minimizing intermediate water stops.

Ballast–Usually gravel, cinder, crushed rock or similar material placed between ties and around track and roadbed to drain water, spread load, provide bearing for ties and track and help control weed growth.

Balloon Stack–Smokestack found on most old time wood burners. Many had large kite- or diamond-shaped housings.

Balloon Track, or Balloon–Technical term for a reverse loop.

Belpaire Firebox–Square-topped fireboxes typical of Pennsylvania and Great Northern Locomotives.

Belt Line–A short line used mainly as a connecting link between two larger lines.

Bend The Rails–Turn the switch in the track; change position of turnout.

Big Boy–Popular name for largest steam locomotive, the 4-8-8-4 Union Pacific.

Blind Drivers–Drivers without flanges which permit locomotives to take sharper curves than wheel arrangement would usually allow; widely used in narrow gauge.

Block–In prototype, the trackage between two signals; in model railroading, isolated electrical islands. Section of track under one control and accomodating only one train at a time.

Block Signal–Indicates whether block is occupied or not.

Bobber–A short four-wheeled caboose.

Bobtail Haul–An early slang expression indicative of the fact that a loco was only pulling a few cars and a bobber caboose; a few car haul; a short train.

Bogie–A swivel, four-wheel truck used on engines and tenders.

Boiler–Round cylinder-shaped section of locomotive in which steam is generated.

Booster–In prototype, a small secondary steam engine which assists and increases starting power. Some trailing trucks and tender wheels featured boosters which cut off automatically after a certain speed had been attained.

Box Cab–Electric or diesel loco with cab shaped like a box.

Branch–A track turning off the trunk line.

Brass Hat–President or boss of the line. A V.I.P.; in MR jargon a model railroader, usually advanced or in veteran status.

Brownies–Demerits issued at many model railroad clubs for infractions of rules or minor mistakes; a form of good natured punishment for goofing up.

Bumper or Bumping Post–Device that stops cars at end of a stub track.

Cab–Enclosure on locomotive to shelter engineer, fireman, etc.

Cab Control–Means of operating and controling one or more trains singly or simultaneously within model railroad (trains operating independent of one another's actions).

Cab-Forward–Articulated type steam engine, popular on Southern Pacific RR. Engines were reversed; cylinders toward the back, cab and smoke stack at front.

Caboose–Car for brakemen and other crew; office for conductor at rear of freight train; often used for temporary living quarters on long hauls.

Cab Signals–Lights on a control panel in front of operator which indicate condition of track ahead of his train.

Cab Unit–Streamlined Diesel Locomotive. The A Unit.

Camelback–A locomotive with cab located elsewhere than at an end—over-center or off-center; also referred to as a Mother Hubbard.

Car Barn–Storage house for trolley and interurban cars.

Catenery–A system of overhead wire construction used on electric lines from which power is drawn for propulsion.

Chassis–Framework or underbody of a locomotive, cars, etc.

Circuit–The path of an electrical current.

Circuit Breaker–A switch or fuse that automatically opens the circuit in the event of a current overload.

Classification Yard–An arrangement of tracks

where cars are sorted out with respect to destinations or routes.

Clerestory Roof–Typical of certain passenger cars featuring raised center sections and "clerestory windows" along the sides.

Coal Bunker–Storage bin directly behind cab or in tender.

Coaling Station–A point where locomotives stop to take on a load of coal. Tender is positioned under chute of coaling tower which supplies fuel by means of gravity feed.

Cornfield Meet–Slang for head-on collision—evolved from, "When they met, the wreckage was strewn all over the cornfield."

Coupler–The device used to connect and disconnect locomotives and cars.

Cowcatcher–Early term for pilot. A pointed device used on the front of the loco to shove lazy cows and buffalo off the track. In its present form the "pilot" is used to keep automobiles out from under the wheels.

Crankpin–Pin or screw attached to driving wheel holds side rods in place yet permits them to turn.

Crummy–Slang for caboose; also called a doghouse.

Cupola–Small cabin atop the caboose.

Diamond Stack–A tall smokestack with a spark arrestor on top, was widely used on old wood-burning locomotives; had diamond-shaped top.

DC–Direct Current. The type of electricity furnished by batteries and power packs to propel the small scale locomotives used in model railroading. Twelve Volts D.C. is NMRA Standard.

Double-Header–A train with two engines.

DPDT–Double pole double throw; a knife, slide or toggle switch featuring six terminals; used in model railroading for reversing polarity, etc.

Double Track–A two track railroad.

Drawbar–The bar that connects the locomotive and its tender.

Driving Gear–The group of rods and cranks which transfer the piston energy to the driving wheels.

Driving Wheels–On a steamer, the large wheels connected by rods; on electric or diesel locos, the motorized wheels.

Drovers' Caboose–A long eight-wheeled caboose containing a small passenger compartment for hauling and bedding down cattlemen who are aboard to care for their cattle enroute.

Dual Gauge–A mixed gauge, such as HO and HOn3.

Engine–Commonly referred to as the locomotive; is actually the cylinders and their drivers.

Feed Back–The result when separate circuits are so wired that some of the current from one circuit bleeds into the other circuit.

Feeder–Power connection from pack to track and elsewhere on model railroad; also a short branch road feeding traffic to a mainline.

Flange–The thin or projecting rim on a wheel which fits down below the rail and holds the wheel on the track.

Foreign Car–One that belongs to some other railroad other than the one it runs on.

Freezer–A refrigerator car; also referred to as a "reefer."

Freight Yard–A track arrangement used for the storage of freight cars.

Gauge–The distance between the rails

Goat–Slang expression for a loco, usually a switcher which operates in terminals and yards.

Grab Iron–The handhold on the sides of cars.

Gravity Yard (also called a Hump Yard)–A yard where gravity assists in the spotting and classifying of cars whereby they can roll along under their own momentum.

Herald–Trademark on locomotives and freight cars.

Highball–The go-ahead signal

High Iron–The main track.

Hog–Slang for a locomotive, yard switchers often called yard hogs.

Hot Box–A journal that has overheated due to lack of lubrication or introduction of some foreign matter.

Hot Shot–A fast through freight.

H_2O—A water train.

Interchange Point–The location where cars switch from one road to another.

Mainline—Track on which trains are operated by timetable, train orders and block signals.

Mallet–An articulated locomotive.

Mike–Abbreviated term for a Mikado type loco.

Milk Car–refrigerator car for milk.

Milk Train–A slow train.

Mother Hubbard–A locomotive with the cab straddling the boiler like a saddle (*see* Camelback).

Panorama–A picture that gives a wide sweeping view in all directions when seen from a central point. Often used on pikes to add dimension.

Pantograph–A device for making contact and drawing power from overhead trolley wires.

Pike–A model railroad.

Pilot–The framework at the front of a locomotive (*see* Cowcatcher).

Pilot Truck–The front or leading small trucks on a locomotive (depending on wheel arrangement); also referred to as a Pony Truck.

Plug–A small passenger train.

Prototype–A full-sized locomotive or car; the original unit from which the model has been scaled down and patterned.

Radio Control–A method of operating and controlling locomotives by means of radio signals beamed through the air or by means of a carrier control basis through the track (*See* Chapter 17 concerning ASTRAC).

Rail–In MR parlance—a model railroad fan; also referred to as a Model Rail.

Rat–Slang for a freight train.

Rectifier–A device which converts AC into DC

Red Ball–A fast freight train.

Reefer Block–A freight train consist of refrigerator cars.

Resistor–A device used to reduce the intensity of electricity.

Restricted Track–Trackage where trains must run at reduced speeds.

Retarder–Any device used for decreasing speed; brakes.

Right of way–The land on which a railroad is built.

Rip-Track–An area of the maintenance yard where equipment is stored pending repairs and servicing. In MR a few sections of track behind the roundhouse by the freight yard or even on a shelf above the workbench.

Road Bed–A prepared layer of earth or gravel which provides a foundation for ties and rail. In model railroading wood, cork, plywood, Homosote and other materials are used.

Road Engine–A locomotive used primarily for mainline service.

Roundhouse–A structure for the storage, service and repair of locomotives.

Shoo-fly Track–Temporary track used for a detour when the permanent line is being repaired or blocked.

Shuffle–To switch cars

Shunt–To switch to another path.

Side Bay Caboose–One with bay windows in the sides in place of a cupola.

Siding–An auxiliary track turning out from the mainline and rejoining at another point along the main; can be used as a holding track, passing siding or temporary storage area. Sidings can also be used in the form of a branch or short line to service a small town and rejoin the mainline at a distant point.

Single Track System–Consists of a single track between two terminals.

Smoke Box–Cylindrical section at head of boiler beneath the stack.

Spur–A track extending from the mainline for a short distance; can also turnout from sidings or other areas of trackage.

Station, Way–A small station with a passing track only.

Steam Chest–The compartment on top of the cylinders.

Stub Terminal–A dead end track with a bumping post; used in yards, industrial spurs, mining and logging areas etc.

Switch Machine–A mechanical device which will change the position of a turnout; can be used manually or by remote control from a control panel.

Terminal–The end of the line (or departure point); includes the station, switches, associated buildings, towers and other equipment.

Tin Hats–Prototype railroad V.I.P.'s

Tin Plate–Commonly associated with toy trains that do not conform to scale or gauge standards. The name "tin plate" originated during the last century when many an early model, crude or otherwise, was fashioned out of tin.

Toe Boards–Runningboards on the roof of a car.

Trailer Load–The cars a locomotive pulls. In MR parlance it is generally referred to as a "drag." For example: a freight drag.

Trailing Switch–One with the points facing in the opposite direction from the flow of traffic.

Trailer Truck–A rear locomotive truck with two or four small wheels.

Truck–The assembly that supports a car or locomotive and houses the wheels and axles.

Turbine Locomotive–One with power supplied by a steam turbine.

Turnout–A section of track that turns out from the mainline, often referred to as a switch.

Turntable–A rotating device that enables you to turn locomotives completely around, or to spot them for roundhouse stalls.

Underpass–A roadway going beneath an overpass, scenic effect, bridge, overhang, etc.

USRA–United States Railroad Administration. The USRA took over and operated American Railroading during World War I; was responsible for certain long lasting and "standard" locomotive designs.

Vanderbilt Tender–A cylindrical-shaped tender featuring a partially squared-off front; used for either coal or oil and especially popular among model rails.

Vestibule Cab–Closed cab on steam locos to protect engineer and fireman from inclement weather; includes doors and diaphragm connection to tender.

Volt–A unit of electrical pressure. Commonly, 12 volts of D.C. is used for scale model railroading.

Worm Gear–A gear with slightly slanted or dished teeth to mesh with the worm. In model railroading the worm gear is usually mounted on the driving axle.

Wye–A triangular shaped track arrangement used as a junction, and for turning trains and engines.

Yard–A group of tracks, generally within an enclosed area where switching chores are performed for storage, classification, making and breaking up of trains, etc.

Y Switch–A switch that turns off at both sides, but not straight ahead.

Zamac–Trade name for zinc-aluminum alloy die-casting metal used widely for pressure die-castings in model trains.

Zeal–The earnestness, devotion, dedication, passion, soul, spirit, ardor, fervor, verve, enthusiasm, eagerness, warmth and energy of a model railroader in pursuit of a most fascinating hobby.

Index